A People's History
of Poverty in America

The New Press People's History Series
Howard Zinn, Series Editor

A People's History of the United States:
The Wall Charts
Howard Zinn and George Kirschner

A People's History of the United States:
Abridged Teaching Edition
Howard Zinn

A People's History of the American Revolution:
How Common People Shaped the Fight for Independence
Ray Raphael

A People's History of the Vietnam War
Jonathan Neale

The Mexican Revolution
Adolfo Gilly

A People's History of the Civil War:
Struggles for the Meaning of Freedom
David Williams

The Darker Nations:
A People's History of the Third World
Vijay Prashad

A People's History of Poverty in America
Stephen Pimpare

A People's History of Sports in the United States:
250 Years of Politics, Protest, People, and Play
Dave Zirin

A People's History
of Poverty in America

STEPHEN PIMPARE

THE NEW PRESS

NEW YORK
LONDON

Requests for permission to reproduce selections from this book
should be mailed to: Permissions Department, The New Press,
38 Greene Street, New York, NY 10013.

Published in the United States by The New Press, New York, 2008
Distributed by W. W. Norton & Company, Inc., New York

LIBRARY OF CONGRESS CATALOGING-IN-PUBLICATION DATA
Pimpare, Stephen.
A people's history of poverty in America / Stephen Pimpare.
        p.   cm.
Includes bibliographical references and index.
ISBN 978-1-56584-934-1 (hc.)
1. Poverty—United States—History.   2. Poor—United States—History.
I. Title.
HC110.P6P56   2008
362.50973—dc22   2008016259

The New Press was established in 1990 as a not-for-profit alternative to the large,
commercial publishing houses currently dominating the book publishing industry.
The New Press operates in the public interest rather than for private gain, and
is committed to publishing, in innovative ways, works of educational, cultural,
and community value that are often deemed insufficiently profitable.

www.thenewpress.com

Composition by NK Graphics
This book was set in New Baskerville

Printed in the United States of America

2   4   6   8   10   9   7   5   3   1

for Kathleen Bergeron
and JoAnn McGravey

Stop a moment. I am going to be honest. This is what I want you to do. I want you to hide your disgust, take no heed of your clean clothes, and come right down with me—here, into the thickest of the fog and mud and foul effluvia. I want you to hear this story.
—Rebecca Harding Davis, 1861

We have come to know that every individual lives, from one generation to the next, in some society; that he lives out a biography, and that he lives it out within some historical sequence. By the fact of his living he contributes, however minutely, to the shaping of this society and to the course of its history, even as he is made by society and by its historical push and shove.
—C. Wright Mills, 1959

We tell ourselves our individual stories so as to become aware of our general story.
—Ralph Ellison, 1978

We are readers of history. Especially for leaders and organizers from the ranks of the poor, reading and interpreting history is a matter of survival. When discussions, explanations, and theories about us and our situation have been controlled by others—people who currently control the institutions of society—we must make our own, rooting them in our experience and interpretation of history.
—Willie Baptist and Mary Bricker-Jenkins, 2002

Many in our country do not know the pain of poverty, but we can listen to those who do.
—George W. Bush, 2001

Contents

Series Preface

Turning history on its head opens up whole new worlds of possibility. Once, historians looked only at society's upper crust: the leaders and others who made the headlines and whose words and deeds survived as historical truth. In our lifetimes, this has begun to change. Shifting history's lens from the upper rungs to the lower, we are learning more than ever about the masses of people who did the work that made society tick.

Not surprisingly, as the lens shifts the basic narratives change as well. The history of men and women of all classes, colors, and cultures reveals an astonishing degree of struggle and independent political action. Everyday people played complicated historical roles, and they developed highly sophisticated and often very different political ideas from the people who ruled them. Sometimes their accomplishments left tangible traces; other times, the traces are invisible but no less real. They left their mark on our institutions, our folkways and language, on our political habits and vocabulary. We are only now beginning to excavate this multifaceted history.

The New Press People's History Series roams far and wide through human history, revisiting old stories in new ways, and introducing altogether new accounts of the struggles of common people to make their own history. Taking the lives and viewpoints of common people as its point of departure, the series reexamines subjects as different as the American Revolution, the history of sports, the history of American art, the Mexican Revolution, and the rise of the Third World.

A people's history does more than add to the catalogue of what we already know. These books will shake up readers' understanding of the past—just as common people throughout history have shaken up their always changeable worlds.

Howard Zinn
Boston, 2000

A People's History
of Poverty in America

The Indignant Poor
and the Constants of Relief

I am reminded of the old lady who went from the interior to the sea. She had lived a life
of poverty. She had never had enough of anything. All the food that went upon her table,
all the clothing she wore, had to be carefully considered. One day, she was taken by some
kind relatives to the seaside. There she sat in silence, and not a word was to be had from
her at first; and, when they looked at her, the tears were rolling down her cheeks. "Why,
aunt," said her niece, "what is the matter? Are you sick?" "No," she cried, "I am not
sick; but, thank God, I have seen something there is enough of."

—Oscar McCulloch, 1889

One December early in the terrible depression of 1893, with Christmas approaching, a parade of finely attired ladies from the Children's Potted
Plant Society made their way down to the slums of New York's Lower East
Side on a charitable mission. Their plan was simple: they would give a small
plant to each of the neediest young cases, offering them a bit of life and
color for their grim, cramped abodes. They looked forward to the grateful,
smiling faces as they distributed their bounty, one little plant to each little
pauper. Perhaps that warm thought made up for the trepidation they must
have felt venturing into such foreign territory. Helen Gould (daughter of
Jay Gould, the ruthless robber baron) counted the society among her most
favorite charities.

Perhaps you can imagine their surprise, then, when instead of being met
by an orderly procession of humble suppliants, the children "rushed the

staging area, seized four or five plants apiece, and ran off to market them on the streets."[1] The women were beside themselves with fear, and perplexed. For some, it probably confirmed their belief that "the poor" were irredeemable: they were only trying to help, after all, and were met with incivility and ingratitude.

But the children were surely as perplexed as the women of the society: why would anyone bring them houseplants, which would inevitably die in their sunless, airless apartments, when they had so many urgent needs? And yet, useless plants could be turned into something useful. These children made their own judgments about what they needed and potted plants were not on the list, so they behaved as poor men, women, and children have behaved for centuries if they intended to survive—they took what little was made available to them and turned it to their own advantage. It might as well have been flour confiscated in an early American food riot, the milk and diapers taken by women during the supermarket raids of the New York blackouts, income illegally earned while receiving welfare benefits, or food and supplies looted from New Orleans store shelves in the awful aftermath of 2005's Hurricane Katrina.

On another occasion some years later, it was pots of geraniums that were given away by "some sympathetic and leisured ladies" to ten thousand children gathered from the New York tenements. Apparently no violence ensued this time, the flowers were successfully distributed, and the women must have felt well satisfied with having done such a good deed. One year after, they returned triumphantly, "in luxuriously equipped automobiles," to the scene of their benevolence, "to smile and be condescended to," and to award prizes to the worthy children who had best cared for their floral charges. It was to be a grand day. But few of the children were to be found, and even fewer of the flowers. Many were dead, of course, children and flowers alike. The women were shocked, and they probably returned to their homes a little unsettled, a little confused, just as their sisters had been in 1893.[2]

At around the same time, Alexander Irvine, who had risen to some success despite a boyhood in the poorhouse, brought a collection of poor children from the city to a friend's "lawn party" in Montclair, New Jersey, so that he might expose them to the salutary effects of fresh country air. The children, two-thirds of whom were Jewish, were suitably agape at such suburban wonders as elaborate flower gardens and towering trees, but, it would appear from Irvine's telling, insufficiently appreciative of the luncheon—milk and ham sandwiches.[3] By all accounts the children tried to be polite, and suitable food was found for them, but they too must have been a bit taken aback by the uselessness of the aid that was offered to them.

So it is with so many efforts to help, then and now: the good intentions of comfortable men and women, private charities, and governments is not enough, and they cannot provide meaningful assistance if they are blind to the reality of the lives they seek to improve. Novelist Edith Wharton, a sharp observer of class in America, said it well:

> Affluence, unless stimulated by a keen imagination, forms but the vaguest notion of the practical strain of poverty.[4]

Private charity and public relief have often lacked not just keen imagination but consistency, for plants and flowers have not always been deemed suitable comforts. Early in the 1900s, one social worker took a client to task because she had planted a few flowers in her yard. The poor woman was reminded that she should have devoted the space to growing something productive, something edible.[5] It is not known whether she dug them up to please her benefactors or kept for herself this corner of indulgence in her tiny garden. In other times, such as during the boisterous Lawrence "mill girls" strike of 1912, flowers even became a symbolic part of a claim that mere subsistence was not enough—dignity and beauty, too, were legitimate expectations, these working women insisted. As the song went:

> Our lives shall not be sweated from birth until life closes;
> Hearts starve as well as bodies; give us bread, but give us roses.
>
> As we go marching, marching, unnumbered women dead
> Go crying through our singing their ancient call for bread.
> Small art and love and beauty their drudging spirits knew.
> Yes, it is bread we fight for, but we fight for roses too.
>
> As we go marching, marching, we bring the greater days,
> The rising of the women means the rising of the race.
> No more the drudge and idler, ten that toil where one reposes,
> But a sharing of life's glories: Bread and roses, bread and roses.

Our lives shall not be sweated from birth until life closes;
Hearts starve as well as bodies; bread and roses, bread and roses.[6]

For this they received much scorn. But why shouldn't poor and working Americans expect more than mere subsistence? Why should it be ludicrous that they demand some measure of joy in their lives? And why should we accept the easy and arrogant presumption that philanthropists and relief agents should substitute their own judgment for that of their clients? As one homeless man recently said to me in response to new programs in New York City that pay welfare recipients and others for certain "responsible" behaviors, "I'm not stupid, I'm just poor. People don't seem to get the difference."[7] It is ironic, as historian Michael Katz has noted, that in the name of fostering independence among the welfare-reliant, public and private assistance alike often require their subservience and their supplication.[8] In 1789, those seeking aid from the Committee for Improving the Condition of Free Blacks were required to display "a becoming deference,"[9] just as New York City welfare administrator Jason Turner noted after 1996's welfare reform that a condition of aid should be that applicants exhibit "respectful behavior" toward caseworkers.[10] In 1967, one proud woman was held for "psychiatric evaluation" in Bellevue Hospital after having stubbornly refused to allow an agent of the welfare department to inspect her closets.[11] As some Alabama women told the U.S. Commission on Civil Rights in 1968, eligibility for relief has often been dependent upon other kinds of appropriate behavior, too:

They are not going to help you if they find out you are in the civil rights . . . they better not know you are participating in the civil rights movement.

When the commissioner asked what the consequences would be, a Mrs. Wage replied:

Well, if they have given you any money, they will try and cut your moneys off and just treat you cold and all; beat you to death, if necessary.[12]

There is something peculiarly counterproductive about the disapprobation that has been heaped upon poor, homeless, and welfare-reliant Americans, and the manner in which they have been infantilized, articulated here in 1973 by a Head Start parent, Mrs. Robert Manwarren:

> You see, the fact that most people who have never been poor can't understand is that it doesn't make any difference if you are poor white, poor black, or any of the combinations. You are forced to feel that you are not as good or as smart as other people. . . . How can we expect people who don't believe that they are worth anything, to get anywhere.[13]

Economist John Kenneth Galbraith has written that in an affluent society, "nothing requires it to be compassionate. But it has no high philosophical justification for callousness."[14] But Americans are callous, when not merely indifferent, and we have been throughout most of our history. Which brings me to one last flower story. In the late 1990s Walt, a homeless panhandler living in Washington, D.C., said this:

> There are people who are gonna be rude to you—that are gonna look at you like you're an animal. It's no different than looking at flowers. Some people look at flowers and they say, "That's a beautiful flower." And they stop and smell them. Others look at the thing and say, "That's just something growing in the yard."[15]

Today, as it has often been, poor men and women are thought of, when thought of at all, as just something growing in the yard. Perhaps social critic Dwight Macdonald had it right in 1963:

> There is a monotony about the injustices suffered by the poor that perhaps accounts for the lack of interest the rest of society shows in them. Everything seems to go wrong with them. They never win. It's just boring.[16]

These are almost random vignettes, but they highlight a few of the features that have been constants in American poverty and welfare history, and suggest the bottom-up manner in which I'll recast that history in the following pages.[17] There is a general ignorance about the lives led by poor Americans, an ignorance, whether real or feigned, that shapes public discourse about poverty and welfare, and policy itself. At the turn of the twentieth century, New York photographer and journalist Jacob Riis famously documented "how the other half lives."[18] But to learn *why* they lived as they did, or how they *survived*, we will have to turn elsewhere. One goal of this book is, with Edith Wharton's indictment in mind, to help form more than that "vaguest notion" of poverty—to more fully introduce readers to poor and working people, showing how thin the line has been and still is between just getting by and not getting by at all; to document the heroic efforts mere survival has often required; to celebrate the security that well-placed and reliable assistance can offer (while revealing its more oppressive face); and to demonstrate how a generous and fairly administered program of welfare can make responsibility and dignity possible by providing recipients with the ability to care for children or for frail parents, to attend college, to access health care for their children, to escape violence or abuse in the home, or to refuse degrading, dangerous, low-wage work. As we will see, welfare can make you more free.

More attention to those most affected by but often missing from our histories of poverty and welfare might also help unseat a cruel deceit at the heart of American political culture. A creed of individualism may well suit the better off, but it's a danger to the more fragile classes, who must share their resources and pool their need. Their interdependence is a necessity and a balm, and another constant throughout American history. One with ample funds, a bountiful table, and a stable, secure life can afford to be independent, alone even. The rest cannot, and must form communities of shared need. The complex webs of dependency that poor people have formed in order to survive have been too absent from our histories of poverty and welfare. Government is the largest of those communities, and the welfare state its most salutary ideal, a "compromise between capitalism and democracy," in the words of philosopher Eva Feder Kittay.[19] The independence that is hailed by so many (and they mean independence from government aid, not independence from grueling labor or loveless marriage or capricious charity) is a mirage and a trap. The wise man or woman will seek out those dependencies that will ease their struggle, enrich their lives, and comfort their neighbors and their children. An imposed independence can be antisocial, alienating, and dangerous; it should not be made a cultural, social, or political goal. There is no virtue in autonomy, necessarily. But there can be value in dependence, and public welfare is a requirement—the requisite dependency—for a moral and humane society. Thomas Paine, whose *Common Sense* helped rally public support for independence from Britain, saw this at our founding. He writes this in a tract called "Agrarian Justice":

> There are, in every country, some magnificent charities established by individuals. It is, however, but little that any individual can do, when the whole extent of the misery to be relieved is considered. He may satisfy his conscience, but not his heart. He may give all that he has, and that all will relieve but little. It is only by organizing civilization upon such principles as to act like a system of pulleys, that the whole weight of misery can be removed. . . . It ought not to be left to the choice of detached individuals whether they will do justice or not.[20]

Paine makes a deceptively simple argument for public relief: *It ought not to be left to the choice of detached individuals whether they will do justice or not.* But throughout American history it often has been, with predictable results. Among "advanced" nations, we have the highest or almost the highest rates of poverty (highest), childhood poverty (highest), elderly poverty (second highest), long-term poverty (highest), permanent poverty (highest), and income inequality (highest); we can boast of our rates of incarceration (highest), health-care costs (highest), CEO pay (highest), average hours worked (it's more only in Australia and New Zealand), and infant mortality (among the highest—it's lower in Taiwan, Belgium, Cuba, and the Czech Republic, among others). Seven advanced countries nonetheless have higher productivity than the United States, many with shorter work weeks. At the same time, the United States ranks among the very lowest for high school graduation, health-care coverage, mandated vacation and paid parental leave, voter participation, women in the national legislature, working-class wages, living standards among those at the bottom, and life expectancy.[21] A 2005 study by Save the Children found ten countries in which mothers and their children fare better than in the United States.[22] The infant mortality rate for African Americans in Washington, D.C., is higher than in the poor Indian state of Karala, and the overall infant death rate in the United States is the same as in Malaysia.[23] Men in Bangladesh stand a better chance of surviving to age sixty-five than black men in Harlem.[24] There is much that is exceptional about the United States, much that is extraordinary and worthy of celebration, but many Americans, perhaps most, would be better off elsewhere. As social-welfare analyst David Wagner has observed, it may be that our self-congratulatory rhetoric, what he calls our "virtue talk," obscures the less noble reality: Americans do less for the least among us than do other Western industrialized nations.[25]

American attitudes toward poverty and welfare have been fairly constant, too, with roots that run deep. In thirteenth-century Europe, one prominent theologian cited the "habitual idleness, debauchery and drunkenness" of poor people as their chief failing, much as the Hudson Institute's Joel Schwartz more recently argued that the remedy for modern urban poverty was to "remoralize" them to the "three cardinal virtues" of "diligence, sobriety and thrift."[26] As early as the fourteenth century the now-familiar manner in which we classify and judge poor people had appeared: the "poor with Peter," the voluntary *honest* poor of mendicant orders and the like, whose poverty was deemed an act of submission to God and a mark of humility; versus the "poor with Lazarus," those *dishonest* poor who suffered poverty not by choice but by circumstance and, perhaps, as punishment. They would become what we have called the "deserving" and the "undeserving," the "worthy" and the "unworthy," the working and the idle, the poor man and the pauper. The most recent brief against the welfare state by the American Enterprise Institute's Charles Murray brings us right back to these fourteenth-century conceptions, encouraging us to distinguish as a matter of policy between involuntary poverty ("when someone who plays by the rules is still poor") and voluntary poverty ("the product of one's own idleness, fecklessness, or vice").[27] Although the language has varied, we have, with rare exceptions, thought of poverty in just this way and classified those seeking aid accordingly. It is only slight exaggeration to say that those with political power have worried principally about the morals of poor Americans, while poor Americans have been concerned about their stomachs.

Some of our long-standing resistance to generous programs of public welfare can in part be traced to the pernicious myth of the lazy (black or immigrant) poor, who are supposedly glad to live off the dole and ready to exploit any effort by government (or private charity) to offer food, cash, or shelter.[28] As with any good myth, it persists despite the lack of evidence to support it. Even Josephine Shaw Lowell, one of the nineteenth century's fiercest opponents of poor relief (what we now call welfare), eventually came to realize it. Here she is writing to her sister-in-law Annie about the poor New Yorkers brought to the attention of her agency:

They all want work, work, work: many are widows with young children; many are men who have had accidents; so far we have not really found many "unworthy," or at least, those are not the ones that make an impression.

And later that same year, she wrote:

If it could only be drummed into the rich that what the poor want is fair wages and not little doles of food, we should not have all this suffering and misery and vice.[29]

No anomaly, this is also a constant, as we'll see. What poor Americans have usually demanded (when they have demanded anything at all) is not charity or welfare but a safe job at a decent wage. What they have had to settle for (when they could get anything) was paltry and demeaning aid or work with wages so low that they still remained poor. In either case, what has been available has often amounted to, in the words of songwriter Mike Millius, "Not enough to live on, but a little too much to die."[30] As a result, people in need have taken institutions and programs that sought to control them, or sought to aid them on the institutions' terms, and have turned them to their own purposes, like the children described above, sometimes much to the surprise of those who thought *they* were in control. Indeed, when poor people have behaved in this way, instead of being praised for their independence or ingenuity or for taking responsibility for their family's well-being, they have been castigated for their activism or offered gentle, condescending reminders that a more passive stance might be more appropriate to their station. In a January 1860 editorial, the *Chicago Weekly Democrat* railed against the poorhouse and its inhabitants and approvingly quoted a "sagacious old lady" who bridled at the insolence of those she called the "indignant poor."[31] Her scornful phrase captures the idea nicely—disbelief that poor people would be anything but grateful for the largesse that has been bestowed upon them. For them to make demands was beyond the pale, and still is.

That's another constant, the condescension that has governed American efforts at relief, rooted consciously or not in the belief that it must be moral failings that explain why people find themselves in need, and the attendant assumption that the reformer, the bureaucrat, the policymaker, and the social worker know best what poor people require and how they should behave. But just as it is with those who are not poor, poor people have varied histories and complex needs—bread we all need to survive, but to be fully human we need roses, too. We might allow recipients to rebut the pervasive presumption that they need to be taught the values of work, responsibility, and independence, especially given that evidence is rarely offered to support the claim that "pathologies" are widespread. *I'm not stupid, I'm just poor. People don't seem to get the difference.*

There is a danger even in writing of "the poor," for it suggests, at the very least, that poor people have more in common than not, that they share interests, beliefs, wants, complaints, or a common culture. In the past, the experience of need and of interacting with public and private relief agencies has been described by the objects of welfare policies in similar ways—so similarly, in fact, that contrary to conventional historical wisdom, the story of the American welfare state may not be the story of progress we've become familiar with, but a story of stasis, as I'll show.[32] But there is much variation in that experience, too, which we lose sight of if we treat poor and welfare-reliant Americans as an undifferentiated mass. I'll go so far as to argue that there has never been an American welfare state—instead, there have been many American welfare states, which vary depending upon who you are, when you live, and where you live. The welfare state has been a markedly different experience for women, for blacks in the South, for veterans, for middle-class whites in the North, for men, for children. And it has been different for different women, for different children, and so on.[33]

There has been yet another stubborn myth, another constant, that welfare, far from being a solution to poverty, is actually a cause of it. Charity reformer Frederic Almy made the claim this way in 1900:

> It is hardly too much to say that people do not beg because they are poor, but that they are poor because they beg, and that as long as they beg they will stay poor. For centuries the stream of charity has been steadily flowing, and the flood of poverty has been growing; and we have not stopped to consider that it might be merely cause and effect.[34]

The evidence for this, too, is negligible, but in words usually attributed to George Orwell, "We have now sunk to a depth where the restatement of the obvious is the first duty of intelligent men." So, to risk stating the obvious, welfare and the welfare state, for all their imperfections, do more good than harm. That public aid can reduce want is clear—there is a direct and well-documented connection between how much a nation spends on relief and the basic well-being of its citizens.[35] But it does more. Welfare removes older or other less productive workers from the labor market, and thereby increases the availability of jobs and wages for those who remain. It socializes the costs of caring for and educating the workforce, a burden that would otherwise be borne solely by businesses in need of healthy, educated laborers. It redistributes wealth and income, fostering equity, fairness, and even faith in democratic processes; it may, as a result, also reduce class conflict.[36] There is even a relationship between welfare and incarceration: if money is not spent on relief, pensions, jobs, job training, and education, it will, all else being equal, be spent on police, prisons, and repression.[37] And there is little evidence that the welfare state appreciably reduces productivity or economic growth—in fact, it may be quite the reverse.[38]

Even so, a defense of the welfare state must be undertaken with caution. We might keep in mind not only the manner in which programs and policies that purportedly help poor and working people have instead sought to control—and succeeded in controlling—their behavior regarding marriage, reproduction, and work or have degenerated into pools of political patronage. But we should also not ascribe virtue to poor people merely because they are in need—this would merely be a form of historical patronizing. Not all poor people are or have been heroic, and there is no nobility in poverty. There are those among the poor who are lazy, base, and corrupt, just as there are among the nonpoor, of course. Still, the scales have been so tilted toward one end of this spectrum that we might seek to reclaim some bit of truth from the sophists who insist, because it benefits them, that shared sacrifice and collective action is harmful, that poverty is natural, or that immorality is at the root of need. One welfare recipient in the early 1970s offers her perspective on why such myths endure:

> Myths are needed to justify the welfare system, a system that cheats the very people it is supposed to help. Myths are needed to discourage eligible, low-paid workers from applying for aid. Myths are needed to divert taxpayer frustrations away from the country's big welfare recipients—the rich and the military—and onto the defenseless, powerless poor. In short, myths are needed to hide the real welfare crisis.[39]

As *New Yorker* writer A.J. Liebling showed when he examined the sensational relief fraud case of the "Lady in Mink" in 1947, the mass media bear a portion of the blame. The politician and the ideologue seek to demonize recipients and delegitimize government assistance programs, while the press seek sensational stories to sell advertising. The truth of the individual case, much less the larger truth of who receives relief and why, is immaterial to both of these powerful players.[40] This is how the image of Ronald Reagan's "welfare queen" persists, despite the fact that she was a caricature crafted by a speechwriter.[41] Propaganda, stereotypes, and myth govern our thinking about poverty and poor relief much more than the facts do. By current, official measures, for example, more than one-third of poor Americans are children under eighteen years old, more than 10 percent are over age sixty-five, and nearly 40 percent of the adult poor are disabled—that is, most poor people are "deserving" or "involuntarily" poor due to old age, youth, or infirmity. Yet when we hear talk of welfare, it is still the welfare queen or the Lady in Mink whose image comes to mind, merely two more in a long line of demons that demagogues have used to whip up opposition to relief from the working and middle classes, obscuring the fact that the majority of Americans would benefit from dependable programs of health and welfare. It's an old story.

The different kind of story I'll tell here will not unfold chronologically. Because part of the goal is to reveal how similar the experience of poverty has been throughout American history, I move quickly back and forth across eras. This is not a complete history, either, and little effort has been made to make it one. It is instead thematic: an attempt to highlight the constants in our relief policy, to suggest how the traditional narrative that places the birth of the American welfare state in the Progressive and New Deal eras obscures more than it reveals about the much longer legacy of relief practice, and to answer a few ostensibly simple questions: What was it like to live in a poorhouse, and what brought people to choose to enter these awful refuges? Why did families surrender their children to an orphanage or an "orphan train"? What was it like to "tramp" the country and ride the rails in search of work in the age of industrialization? What is it like today to depend upon a food pantry to meet your family's needs or to wait in a two-hour line at a soup kitchen, in full view of a scornful public, and then be rushed through a meal so that the throng behind you can get their turn?

What is the experience of offering a cashier your food stamps and feeling the gaze of those behind you as they survey your purchases and judge the appropriateness of your choices? What tricks have poor people used to retain their dignity in the face of such disdain? Has that changed? What does it feel like to apply for welfare, and why do men and women choose to subject themselves to the process? And how much worse has it been for those ineligible for aid or unwilling to ask for help, and how have their experiences changed over time?

The pages that follow seek to describe poverty and welfare from the perspective of poor and welfare-reliant Americans, focusing on how they have created community (Chapter 1), secured shelter (Chapter 2), found food (Chapter 3), searched for work (Chapter 4), cared for children (Chapter 5), battled for dignity and respect (Chapter 6), experienced repression and control (Chapter 7), lost hope (Chapter 8), and fought back (Chapter 9). The epilogue offers a review of how we measure poverty; this may be where some readers would like to begin.

I've done my best to create spaces for the voices of those who have been subject to public and private programs of relief to come through, and have often allowed such speech to go on at length. In that way, this is an unusual kind of history, one filled to overflowing with extended quotation. One anonymous Eskimo girl said in 1973:

> My grandmother told me that the white man never listens to anyone, but he expects everyone to listen to him. So, we listen![42]

I take her complaint, and others like it, seriously. This is, in part, an exercise in listening, and, if I succeed, it's by acting as facilitator and tour guide—providing context and analysis when necessary and remaining silent when possible, allowing the men, women, and children here to take the microphone and speak for themselves, to tell their own stories, to sound out joys and sorrows and vent their rage and rightful, righteous indignation. Perhaps the least we can do, given the shelves fairly groaning under the weight of books about poverty by eminent Americans, is to make a small space for those seldom given voice. And to take them as seriously as we take the pronouncements of presidents, charity reformers, bureaucrats, think tank policy analysts, and scholars. This book, then, is built upon a simple conceit: we have told the history of welfare and poverty by focusing upon the activities of Great Men and Women (like Jane Addams, Franklin Roosevelt, and Lyndon Johnson) and upon key moments of policy innovation (the state-level reforms of the Progressive Era and the national-level interventions of the New Deal and the Great Society). As political scientist Jacob Hacker declared, "To write about social welfare policy is to write about why people support and design policies that have specific real-world effects."[43] But what if, instead of asking how and why has policy changed over time, as we have done for so long, we ask: how has the experience of being poor and in need of assistance changed (or not changed) over time? By doing that, and by allowing the objects of policy to evaluate it, by making room for them to describe their own experience and then taking that "life knowledge" seriously, we see a different story emerging, and a new kind of American welfare state history may be revealed.[44]

This can't help but be a distorted narrative. One distortion comes from the fact that only those voices that have survived in the historical record can be included. There can be no testimony here from those who never kept a diary, were never interviewed by a WPA worker or an anthropologist, never became part of a government agency or private charity's case file, who never wrote a song or a poem or a letter to the editor. More to the point, my decisions about what to include of the accounts I have gathered are, inescapably, biased, although they are intended to be not just revealing but representative. Perhaps this is best thought of not as the culmination of a project, but as the beginning of one, especially given that I have relied here mostly upon previously published letters, diaries, journals, and interviews. The narrative is also distorted, much like its inspiration, Howard Zinn's *A People's History of the United States*, by the nature of the project itself.[45] I set out consciously to offer a history of American poverty and welfare unlike the traditional ones. So, just as Zinn tells the story of Columbus's arrival in the Bahamas through the eyes of the Arawak Indians, showing us the communities destroyed and the families slaughtered by the Great Discoverer, I'll let the residents of Five Points, our most notorious slum, give us a glimpse into the dense, close-knit, and often joyous communities they formed there, or allow women on welfare to explain how their supposed "dependence" has made it possible for them to raise their children and behave, as they have seen it, responsibly. I highlight ways in which the familiar narrative can be upended or revealed more fully, but I do offer some of that narrative in order to set the stage or to argue against it. The reader should not need any prior knowledge of American welfare state history, although *A People's History of Poverty in America* might serve as both companion and counterpoint to any one of the fine traditional histories in print.[46]

To the extent that the book achieves any of its goals, it is in part due to those who have read and commented critically on it. My thanks to Mimi Abramovitz, Jocelyn Boryczka, Lauren Fitzgerald, Andy Hsiao, Joseph Luders, Furaha Norton, Sanford Schram, and the anonymous reviewers for The New Press. Thanks are due also to Hart Schwartz and Paul Adam for research and proofreading assistance; to Mary Ann Linahan and the Pollack Library for gracious assistance with voluminous interlibrary loan requests; to Mort Lowengrub for research funding and release time; and to Frances Fox Piven, Tim Cornell, and Joie Jacobsen, just because.

A last caveat: like so many of the histories that have come before, this one is filtered through the eyes and experience of a white, male academic from a middle-class background. That's important to acknowledge, since I pay so much attention throughout this book to the blindness of the affluent to the lived experience of poor and marginalized Americans, and take them to task for that lack of empathy. I'll assert that I'm better equipped than were the women of the Children's Potted Plant Society, but how much better will have to be for the reader to decide.

1

Survive:
My Brother's Keeper

On the one hundredth anniversary of the Emancipation Proclamation, novelist James Baldwin wrote this to his nephew:

> I know what the world has done to my brother and how narrowly he has survived it. And I know, which is much worse, and this is the crime of which I accuse my country and my countrymen, and for which neither I nor time nor history will ever forgive them, that they have destroyed and are destroying hundreds of thousands of lives and do not know it and do not want to know it . . . your countrymen, have caused you to be born under conditions not very far removed from those described for us by Charles Dickens in the London of more than a hundred years ago. . . . I know how black it looks today, for you. . . . This innocent country set you down in a ghetto in which, in fact, it intended that you should perish. . . . I hear them saying, "You exaggerate," . . . [but] they are, in effect, still trapped in a history which they do not understand.[1]

The modern ghetto is no longer walled off, with guards posted to keep the inhabitants contained, as were the ghettoes that once housed European Jews and other outcasts, but today poor and disreputable people are nonetheless often kept separate and apart, cut off from the rest of the world, restrained and confined.[2] Even though more poor Americans live outside the metropolis than within it, poverty is higher in the South than it is in the Northeast, and perhaps as few as one in ten welfare recipients actually lives in a "ghetto,"[3] when we think of poverty we typically think about the big cities of the North. Only during the Great Depression, and then for a brief time in the 1960s, thanks to Edward R. Murrow's documentary *Harvest of Shame* and Robert F. Kennedy's Appalachian "poverty tour," did rural poverty seem to catch the nation's attention.[4]

We often think of these urban ghettoes as a relatively recent development as well, due in part to Daniel Patrick Moynihan's infamous brief on "The Negro Family," the urban riots of the 1960s, and the Kerner Commission's report about those disruptions.[5] But areas of deep and concentrated poverty have been a constant feature of American life since at least the mid-1700s. Colonial-era historian Gary Nash reports:

> Wherever historians have studied individual cities carefully, they have found that those who lived in or on the edge of poverty probably "comprised at least one third and probably closer to one half of the residents of America's metropolitan centers."[6]

Another historian, John Alexander, writes this of late-eighteenth-century Philadelphia:

> The outskirts of the city, where the poor were most likely to live, also struck contemporary observers as the most offensive, unhealthy parts of the city. The air was impure and, in summer, filled with flies. Dead dogs, cats, and other putrefying bodies strewed the ground. Ponds of stagnated water admitted "noxious effluvia," making them, according to the conventional medical wisdom, not only "sinks of filth" but also "*hot beds* of disease."[7]

By the 1820s, the first ghettoes had already formed in New York City.[8] Its Five Points slum would become notorious the world over and the regular site of tours by foreign visitors and American notables—even Abraham Lincoln and Charles Dickens came to witness the spectacle for themselves. Here's one typical description of Five Points from a nineteenth-century observer:

> The streets are narrow and dirty, the dwellings are foul and gloomy, and the very air seems heavy with misery and crime. For many a block the scene is the same. This is the realm of Poverty. Here want and suffering, and vice hold

their courts. It is a strange land to you who have known nothing but the upper and better quarters of the great city. It is a very terrible place to those who are forced to dwell in it.[9]

The death rate at Mulberry Bend, a favorite spot of photographer, police-beat reporter, and tenement reformer Jacob Riis, was one and a half times as high as the rest of the city and three times higher for children under five.[10] Living in the tenements of the adjacent Lower East Side in the ensuing decades was little better, as Michael Gold makes clear in his memoir:

> Did God make bedbugs? One steaming hot night I couldn't sleep for the bed-bugs. They have a peculiar nauseating smell of their own; it is the smell of poverty. They crawl slowly and pompously, bloated with blood, and the touch and smell of these parasites wakens every nerve to disgust. (Bedbugs are what people mean when they say: Poverty. There are enough pleasant superficial liars writing in America. I will write a truthful book of Poverty; I will mention bedbugs.) It wasn't lack of cleanliness in our home. My mother was as clean as any German housewife; she slaved, she worked herself to the bone keeping us fresh and neat. The bedbugs were a torment to her. She doused the bed with kerosene, changed the sheets, sprayed the mattresses in an endless frantic war with the bedbugs. What was the use; nothing could help; it was Poverty; it was the Tenement. The bedbugs lived and bred in the rotten walls of the tene-ment, with the rats, fleas, roaches; the whole rotten structure needed to be torn down; a kerosene bottle would not help.[11]

The modern ghetto, and the public housing projects that often form its core, here described by Baldwin, can likewise be an oppressive, ugly place:

> The projects are hideous, of course, there being a law, apparently respected throughout the world, that popular housing shall be as cheerless as a prison. They are lumped all over Harlem, colorless, bleak, high, and revolting. The wide windows look out on Harlem's invincible and indescribable squalor: The Park Avenue railroad tracks . . . the unrehabilitated houses . . . the ominous schoolhouses . . . and the churches, churches, block upon block of churches.[12]

Here's how another American novelist, Ralph Ellison, put it:

To live in Harlem is to dwell in the very bowels of the city; it is to pass a labyrinthine existence among streets that explode monotonously skyward with the spires and crosses of churches and clutter under foot with garbage and decay. Harlem is a ruin—many of its ordinary aspects (its crimes, its casual violence, its crumbling buildings with littered areaways, ill-smelling halls and vermin infested rooms) are indistinguishable from the distorted images that appear in dreams, and which, like muggers in a lonely hall, quiver in the waking mind with hidden and threatening significance. Yet this is no dream but the reality of well over four hundred thousand Americans; a reality which for many defines and colors the world. Overcrowded and exploited politically and economically, Harlem is the scene and symbol of the Negro's perpetual alienation in the land of their birth. . . . This is a world in which the major energy of the imagination goes not into creating works of art, but to overcome the frustrations of social discrimination. Not quite citizens and yet Americans, full of the tensions of modern man but regarded as primitives, Negro Americans are in desperate search of an identity. Rejecting the second-class status assigned to them, they feel alienated and search for answers to the questions: Who am I, Where am I, and Why? Significantly, in Harlem the reply to the greeting "How are you?" is very often, "Oh man, I'm *nowhere.*"[13]

And here's thirteen-year-old LeAlan Jones in the 1990s talking about his Chicago neighborhood:

If you act like a little kid in this neighborhood, you're not gonna last too long. 'Cause if you play childish games in the ghetto, you're gonna find a childish bullet in your childish brain. If you live in the ghetto, when you're ten you know everything you're not supposed to know. When I was ten I knew where drugs came from. I knew about every different kind of gun. I knew about sex. I was a kid in age but my mind had the reality of a grown-up, 'cause I seen these things every day! . . . In Vietnam, them people came back crazy. I live in Vietnam, so what you think I'm gonna be if I live in it and they just went and visited?[14]

According to the United Nations, slum dwellers were 30 percent of the world's urban population in 2005.[15] By a slum we tend to mean deeply poor and often squalid cityscapes, and while we may overestimate how many poor Americans live in the city, in 2000 there were nonetheless 2,510 neighborhoods in the United States in which 40 percent or more of the population was poor; 8 million lived in modern ghettoes. Since the 1970s, the number of Americans in areas of concentrated urban poverty had doubled.[16]

The consequences are serious. Growing up in a poor neighborhood has negative effects on the behavior, development, and ultimate success of poor children, beyond those that result just from having poor parents. Asthma, diabetes, depression, and heart disease are more common, as are smoking and drinking. A poor child is three times as likely to drop out of school, twice as likely to give birth while a teenager, twice as likely to be sick, one and a half times as likely to have a learning disability, twice as likely to repeat a grade or be expelled, and less likely to get that chance, since she is twice as likely to die in infancy. Areas of concentrated and persistent poverty are seen by business as unattractive, which reduces competition (and thus raises prices for goods and services, or requires poor people to travel outside the neighborhood for them) and reduces employment opportunities; that, in turn, reduces the networking opportunities that are so important to successful job seeking. Schools, for a variety of reasons, tend to be inferior, further reducing opportunities for upward mobility, given the close correlation between education and income.[17] Crime tends to be higher, and residents are much more likely to be the victims of violence.[18] Finally, physically isolating poor people results in fewer encounters between people who are not poor and people who are: poverty is therefore an abstraction, easily dismissed or understood only through the propaganda of the privileged, contributing again to so many forming "but the vaguest notion" of poverty.[19]

The causes of concentrated poverty today are less clear, although sociologist William Julius Wilson's explanation, despite challenges and refinements, still predominates: middle-class "white flight" from the central cities to the suburbs sapped cities of tax revenue from higher earners and left behind a poorer population that contributed less in taxes and needed more in public services. Exacerbating the problem, with deindustrialization the jobs available to less-skilled and less-educated urbanites moved away, creating a "spatial mismatch."[20] Even before, from at least 1864 to 1923, there was an American "ethnic cleansing," in which entire counties were forcibly emptied of blacks.[21] Government itself has fostered segregation: with the complicity of the Federal Housing Administration, banks and mortgage companies for many years engaged in redlining, a policy of refusing to extend loans to African Americans for homes in predominantly white neighborhoods, or at all. Deeds were written with restrictive covenants that forbade their sale to blacks or Jews. Perhaps just as important are practices, historical and ongoing, of insurance companies refusing to write policies in black neighborhoods in the inner city.[22] Those who remain in poor urban areas, disproportionately African American and Hispanic, may be rightfully cynical about their prospects for advancement and have little belief that positive collective change is possible.[23]

The Pathology of the Ghetto

The slum is not a recent invention, not an anomaly or an aberration; it has been a constant feature of American life. These poor neighborhoods have been so identified with crime, disorder, immorality, and danger to the "better" classes that we have often chosen to isolate or destroy them rather than engage in the more complicated work of improving them. As James McCabe declared in 1872:

> The greatest mortality is in these over-crowded districts, which the severest police measures cannot keep clean and free from filth.[24]

No doubt. But what measures beyond those involving the *police* might more reasonably be expected to keep "clean" the slums? As early as 1829, a group of concerned New York citizens pressured the Common Council to level some Five Points tenements to make way for a new road, citing their occupation "by the lowest description and most degraded and abandoned of the human Species."[25] Even the famed Trinity Church was a slumlord until publicity outed it; its response was to raze the dilapidated tenements it owned, putting up office buildings in their place, thus destroying more housing, however bad it may have been.[26] Owing to the efforts of Riis and others, Mulberry Bend (where we could find the Bandits' Roost and Thieves' Alley made infamous by his iconic photographs) was finally destroyed late in the nineteenth century, leaving many uprooted and homeless.[27] Boston leveled an entire Irish neighborhood, "squalid Fort Hill," in the late 1860s,[28] just as more recent slum clearance and urban renewal projects ("negro removal," some called it during the 1960s) also destroyed intact, if fragile, communities, ones that may not seem to be communities in the minds of well-to-do reformers.[29] While it is undertaken in the guise of a progressive-minded reform, one wonders what happens to the denizens of these poorest of areas, for whatever the rhetoric, urban renewal has been a project of the white middle and business classes. In post–World War II New York, it was black and Puerto Rican neighborhoods that were displaced for new housing or commercial ventures, but few blacks and Puerto Ricans were to be found after the "improvements" were made. By 1960, Stuyvesant Town, a massive new housing complex just above the Lower East Side that had replaced a poor, ethnically and racially mixed neighborhood, had only 47 black and 16 Puerto Rican residents out of a total of 22,405.[30] Vinnie Caslan discussed similar events in his neighborhood after the war:

> After we got back [from the navy], some of the guys came home lookin' for their mothers, and they couldn't find 'em. It was all tore down. There was an editorial in the *Times*: "Do away with the ghetto." There was no ghetto. There was poor people, but they were all white-collar workers, blue-collar workers, no ghetto.

But then he suggests that maybe it was just as well, for if the neighborhood hadn't been torn down, "you know what would be livin' there now—San Juan right on each corner."[31]

Today, we can look to the HOPE VI program of the 1990s, which funded the destruction of (often badly designed and poorly funded) public housing units built in the postwar period to make room for mixed-income units. In a play by Anu Yadav, drawn from three years of interviews with many of the four hundred families who inhabited the Arthur Capper–Carrollsburg project in Washington, D.C., Miss Rhonda says this about their impending "relocation":

> I went down to relocation and they didn't even have a picture of what the new community is going to look like. And I just wanted to tell that woman, you are getting paid to help me move, and part of your mandate, is to make sure I can come back to this community if I want to. And you don't even give a shit what it looks like. You don't give a shit whether I come back or not because guess

what? You GOT a house in Maryland or Virginia! You GOT a place to live. You GOT a good job. You only got shit to worry about. I'm not a heartfelt cause to you. I'm a piece of paper that you shift on your desk. And oh, I got thrown out and so what because you did your job that day, you get your paycheck, and you get to get in your motherfucking car and drive home. . . . It might seem to be a small thing. But it's still people's lives.[32]

The director of the Housing Authority, as recounted by Yadav, said that Capper–Carrollsburg was being torn down "to transform this neighborhood into a viable place." This reveals another pattern: it seems not to register with the creators of such experiments that public housing residents exist in complex networks of friends, neighbors, families, churches, social service agencies, and more; these networks can be essential to their survival, and are disrupted when their housing is destroyed and they are scattered. For all the promise that attended HOPE VI, across the nation fewer than half of all displaced residents returned once redevelopment was completed, and while most were living in areas with lower poverty rates (it would be hard for them not to be), almost all were still in segregated neighborhoods, more than half had higher expenses, and most had difficulty paying the rent or keeping up with their utility bills.[33]

This is neither a defense of our neglected public housing system nor a condemnation of efforts to improve it, but a reminder that policies are usually created and implemented with little knowledge of the practical strain of poverty, and with a dim understanding of the richness even of "dysfunctional" and "distressed" communities. Home is more than mere dwelling.[34] Too often when governments and business look at poor communities, they see pathology, disorganization, and the potential for development and profit. Residents, however, see homes, neighbors and neighborhoods, the support networks of friends and local businesses, and a large extended family—a community, in short. And if crime and other forms of disorganization are more apparent in these neighborhoods, we might wonder why. As Ramsey Clark, Lyndon Johnson's attorney general, observed:

Mark the part of your city where crime flourishes. Now look at the map of your city. You have marked the areas where there are slums, poor schools, high unemployment, widespread poverty; where sickness and mental illness are common, housing is decrepit and nearly every site is ugly—and you have marked the areas where crime flourishes. . . . Poverty, illness, injustice, idleness, ignorance, human misery, and crime go together. That is the truth. We have known it all along. We cultivate crime, breed it, nourish it. Little wonder we have so much. What is to be said of the character of people who, having the power to end all this, permit it to continue?[35]

Clark offers a much-needed corrective: instead of placing blame for the ghetto upon the character of its residents, we might better blame those with the political and economic power to do something about it.

Despite our association of poor neighborhoods with danger, vice, and failure (or perhaps because of it), we have had a peculiar fascination with them. Riis himself turned his photographs of the slum into a theatrical slide show, setting them to music and touring the nation with this "entertainment."[36] This is part of what writer Luc Sante calls "a sort of pornography of race," from the paid walking tours in which the well-to-do would view the exotic "incomprehensibility" of the Chinese, the "slumming tours" that paraded through Harlem in the 1920s, right on through to the gospel brunch tours that bring tourists to the Harlem of today: as one advertised their excursion, "Join a local congregation for the Sunday worship service and experience the soul stirring power of gospel music. Afterwards, enjoy a delicious soul food gospel brunch."[37] Historian Tyler Anbinder suggests that "slumming"—middle- and upper-class men and women venturing to poor neighborhoods as if they were on safari—was invented in Five Points.[38]

Another Side of the Slum

Our conception of poor neighborhoods has been one-dimensional, fixing lewdly upon the "pathologies" we identify there, highlighting its otherness, as if to distance ourselves from it and absolve ourselves of it. But humans are adaptive and resilient creatures, and life in the ghetto is complex; more than violence, poverty, welfare, and dysfunction, it is also the site of tight-knit families and communities, of hope and resistance, of people like Baldwin's young nephew struggling to escape the constraints they face there. Here's LeAlan Jones again, now seventeen years old:

I'm five foot seven and 147 pounds. I live in the ghetto. I'm supposed to be a loser. I'm supposed to be on the six o'clock news shooting people's heads off. I'm supposed to be the one that you grab for your purse when I walk by. I'm the person that doesn't vote. I'm the person that is supposed to drink. I'm the person that is supposed to smoke weed. I'm the motherfucker that is supposed to fill your jails. I'm the person that you make examples to your kid of what not to be like. I'm supposed to be a basketball player. I'm supposed to make it only because of affirmative action. I'm not supposed to be positive. I'm not supposed to be educated. I'm not supposed to know what I know. But I do.[39]

When we home in only on the dark side of areas of concentrated poverty, we fail to appreciate what a life lived there is really like. Most descriptions of our early slums and of poor neighborhoods since then have been through the eyes of the middle-class observers who have focused on the worst in them. But poverty and privation are not the only experiences of people who live in ghettoes—life in a slum is varied and rich, as it is elsewhere. Riis concluded that "life there does not seem worth the living,"[40] yet people did, somehow, manage to endure. They did go on living, as people do. As Ace Backwords, who lived on the streets in San Francisco for the better part of two decades, wrote in 2001:

Everybody knows that money, fame, and success don't necessarily bring happiness. But the other side of that equation is also true: poverty, obscurity, and failure don't necessarily bring *un*happiness.[41]

Here's another view of the Lower East Side from Michael Gold, one that portrays a different world:

I can never forget the East Side street where I lived as a boy. It was a block from the notorious Bowery, a tenement canyon hung with fire-escapes, bedclothing, and faces. Always these faces at the tenement windows. The street never failed them. It was an immense excitement. It never slept. It roared like the sea. It exploded like fireworks. People pushed and wrangled in the street. There were armies of howling pushcart peddlers. Women screamed, dogs barked and copulated. Babies cried. A parrot cursed. Ragged kids played under truck-horses. Fat housewives fought from stoop to stoop. A beggar sang. At the livery stable coach drivers lounged on a bench. They hee-hawed with laughter, they guzzled cans of beer. Pimps, gamblers and red-nosed bums; peanut politicians, pugilists in sweaters; tinhorn sports and tall longshoremen in overalls. An endless pageant of East Side life passed through the wicker doors of Jake Wolf's saloon. The saloon goat lay on the sidewalk, and dreamily consumed a *Police Gazette*. East Side mothers with heroic bosoms pushed their baby carriages, gossiping. Horse cars jingled by. A tinker hammered at brass. Junkbells clanged. Whirlwinds of dust and newspaper. The prostitutes laughed shrilly. A prophet passed, an old-clothes Jew with a white beard. Kids were dancing around the hurdy-gurdy. Two bums slugged each other. Excitement, dirt, fighting, chaos! The sound of my street lifted like the blast of a great carnival or catastrophe. The noise was always in my ears. Even in sleep I could hear it; I can hear it now.[42]

Davey Crockett—soldier, frontiersman, and congressman—offered this almost quaint vision of Five Points some two years before he would be killed at the Alamo:

The buildings are little, old, frame houses, and looked like some little country village. . . . It appeared as if the cellars was jam full of people; and such fiddling and dancing nobody ever saw before in this world. . . . Black and white, white and black . . . happy as lords and ladies.[43]

As Anbinder emphasizes:

Five Points had more fighting, drinking, and vice than almost anywhere else; but also more dancing and nightlife, more dense networks of clubs and charities.[44]

This is some of the Five Points that English novelist (and no stranger to slums) Charles Dickens captured in his *American Notes*—the joyous celebrations and the easy integration of the races.[45] In fact, there's a case to be made that Five Points was the first racially integrated neighborhood in the United States, although that's not to say that it wasn't also the site of racial tensions. This "race mixing," unusual for the time, troubled many American observers and surely accounts for some of their disdainful view of ghetto culture.

Kin and Kinship

It has been the mutual dependence of poor neighbors that has eased their struggle and made survival possible, something evident from the comment of a Five Points charity worker that, "the kindness of these poor people to each other . . . is frequently astonishing."[46] Or from sociologist Katherine Newman, who put it this way at the end of the twentieth century:

> What we fail to recognize is that many inner-city families, especially the majority who work to support themselves, maintain these close links with one another, preserving a form of social capital that has all but disappeared in many an American suburb.[47]

Settlement House leader Jane Addams made a similar observation in 1899:

> A very little familiarity with the poor districts of any city is sufficient to show how primitive and frontier-like are the neighborly relations.[48]

She contended that many were always ready to borrow and to lend to one another, and that they came to expect the same of the charity worker or the relief official (the "friendly visitor" in Addams's day). Thus, the bureaucratic routine, the delays, and the investigations seemed "the cold and calculating actions of a selfish man" who has the ability to give but would not. This, thought Addams, was one of the many ways in which relief failed to comprehend those it would assist, and why it was often seen as an enemy, not a friend. These kinds of relations have been ignored by those who find only disorder in poor families and their communities. Since our founding and before, virtual strangers brought themselves together in common cause, pooled their meager resources, and helped those in need with the knowledge that, more than likely, they would someday need help too.

Let's turn once more to Gold and the early 1900s:

> That winter even pennies were scarce. There was a panic on Wall Street. Multitudes were without work; there were strikes, suicides, and food riots. The prostitutes roamed our street like wolves; never was there so much competi-

tion among them. Life froze. The sun vanished from the deathly gray sky. The streets reeked with snow and slush. There were hundreds of evictions. I walked down a street between dripping tenement walls. The rotten slush ate through my shoes. The wind beat on my face. I saw a stack of furniture before a tenement: tables, chairs, a washtub packed with crockery and bed-clothes, a broom, a dresser, a lamp. The snow covered them. The snow fell, too, on a little Jew and his wife and three children. They huddled in a mournful group by their possessions. They had placed a saucer on one of the tables. An old woman with a market bag mumbled a prayer in passing. She dropped a penny in the saucer. Other people did the same. Each time the evicted family lowered its eyes in shame. They were not beggars, but "respectable" people. But if enough pennies fell in the saucer, they might have rent for their new home. This was the one hope left them.[49]

Before there were regular programs of government assistance, urban Americans had little choice but to find ways of caring for themselves, and for one another. So in big cities like New York, ethnic mutual aid societies were established early by the Scots (1756), Irish (1784), English (1786), Germans (1787), Welsh (1803), and French (1809). Boston, Baltimore, and other cities followed a similar pattern, although Boston had already formed its first society by 1657.[50] Occupation-based charities were established early on too, many of them created by and for seafaring men and their widows. From the Marine Society (1769) to the African Marine Society (1811), widow's pensions were an early feature of the American welfare landscape, though for our first century and a half it was left to private citizens and groups of fellow workers to provide them. Other trades would soon follow—"carpenters, cartmen, butchers, tailors, teachers, shipwrights, shoemakers, printers, accountants, firemen, clergymen, and even tavern keepers." Such associations formed programs of sickness, disability, and unemployment insurance, programs we too often think of as having been invented by elite reformers during the Progressive and New Deal eras.[51] Not so.

Because they housed so many poor people, cities were the first sites of American welfare state programs. Missionary Lewis Pease established the Five Points House of Industry in 1853, which soon grew into a large homeless shelter and something of a residential job training program, employing poor New Yorkers at wages that could reach $2 to $2.50 a day, better than many could earn in the free market. In the winter of 1854 and 1855 he set up a large soup kitchen, which would serve some 40,000 meals in four months; from May 1865 to May 1866, that number would be over 422,000, over 1,100 meals per day.[52] When viewed together with its broad array of other programs, Anbinder suggests, "virtually all the hallmarks of the modern welfare system—food, shelter, job training and placement, substance abuse counseling, and foster care—were offered by the Five Points charities."[53] The welfare state was not an innovation of the national government during the Great Depression but a creation of the first large American cities, much of it crafted by poor people themselves.[54]

Other forms of relief have also been neighborhood- or community-based, with the less poor caring for the very poor. Since the 1600s, paupers were "boarded out"—the city would contract with a family to provide for them for a fixed fee. Many of those who took in boarders did so because they needed the money (and the labor); and many women who hosted boarders later appeared on the relief rolls themselves and were, in turn, taken in by others.[55] More than one in four families in Five Points may have depended upon boarders to help ends meet.[56] Other locales "bound out" their paupers, releasing them to an employer for no fee; in return for room and board, he received the pauper's labor. Children often served as such indentured servants.[57] In many locales poor inhabitants could be auctioned off—turned over to the lowest bidder or whomever agreed to care for them for the least amount of money. Here's one fairly typical notice:

Articles to vendue the Poor belonging to the Town of Sandown and supported by the Town agreeable to a vote passed in town Meeting March 19th 1832 to the lowest bidder for one year from the first day of April AD. 1832 viz.: Anna Harvey, Ruth Collins, Molly Blough.

Article 1st   The purchaser shall move the person or persons he bids off to the place where he intends to support them.

Article 2nd   The purchaser shall provide the person or persons he bids off with suitable Meats, and Drinks, Bedding mending, Nursing, & Tobacco if needed, the Bedding belonging to the poor is to go with them.

Article 3rd   If the purchaser shall refuse to take the person or persons struck off to him, he shall pay all damages that shall arise to the town by such refusal.

Article 4th   The Town will provide Clothing & pay Doctor's Bill for the poor.

Article 5th   No person's bid shall be taken that in the opinion of the Select-men have not competent means of supporting them.[58]

Or there's this revealing case. Around 1790 or so, sometime after it became apparent that one John Baker was no longer able to provide for his wife and children (apparently due to some form of mental illness that, at least later in life, would include delusions and hallucinations), the town of Thetford, Vermont, took it upon themselves to provide for the family. The four youngest children were each boarded out to separate homes. The town's richest man, Captain William Heaton, took in twelve-year-old Zechariah and received no compensation for it (other than what labor he could glean from the boy); for Simon, the Judd family received a cow; and the Way family received ten pounds, nineteen shillings for Abigail, an infant who was years away from being able to make a productive contribution to the household. Mrs. Baker was boarded out to numerous homes throughout the town, including on some occasions relatives, in between periods in which she apparently was able to live on her own: it was a common practice of the period for city residents to take turns taking in the boarded-out poor. They were variously compensated for her food, washing, gin, tobacco, sewing equipment, and for tending her cow.[59]

Only when all other resources have been exhausted—from family, from neighbors, from credit provided by local merchants, from the opportunists in the pawn shops—do many seek help from private or public agencies. Perhaps because privation was so widespread in the 1930s Depression (or perhaps simply because we have such good records from this period), accounts of mutual support are abundant. Dan Carpenter:

> The safety net at the time was the big families. Even though you were unemployed, there was always somebody working, and the families somehow managed to hold together.[60]

Selma Hannish:

> Oh, things were so bad. You borrowed from everybody. When you didn't borrow, you didn't have, but you didn't go on charity. One winter it was so bad my mother had to cut up the dining-room furniture piece by piece and feed it to the stove. They talk about poor today![61]

Hannah Vance:

Everybody was poor, but I remember every time the insurance man would come—it was a nickel policy—my mother would have him sit down, and she'd give him a cup of tea. . . . And we had nothin'. Whoever came into the house, if it was a bum who knocked on the door to beg for bread, she would think nothin' of makin' him a sandwich.[62]

Henry Fiering, unemployed, then a volunteer organizer for the Textile Workers Union, put it this way:

The essential thing that people learned out of the Depression was that rugged individualism was a hoax. They knew that because they were one-on-one during the Depression and they starved for it. The biggest lesson they learned out of the Depression was that if they were going to survive they had to pool their strength. It was the only way to compete with their employers. Now they were determined they were going to protect themselves, so organizing during the war was relatively easy.[63]

Cuban American José Yglesias:

Aunt Lila and her husband were the first in our family, and the last, to go on WPA. This was considered a terrible tragedy, because it was charity. You did not mention it to them. That didn't mean you didn't accept another thing. . . . [It's just that] you yourself didn't ask. . . . Neighbors have always helped one another. The community has always been that way. There was a solidarity. There was just something very nice.[64]

Rube Kadish:

I really don't know how it is that so many people survived, but I do know if you were flush, and somewhere along the line you had two or three dollars in your pocket, you certainly shared it.[65]

Jack Kirkland, author of the stage version of the then-scandalous novel of Southern poverty, *Tobacco Road,* said this to oral historian Studs Terkel:

It was a more generous time then. There wasn't this miasmic fear of unnamed things out there. Then it was specific: hunger. We had a more specific enemy to overcome. We were all in such a mess. When you're in trouble, you never go to rich friends to help you, you go to poor friends.[66]

By February of 1930, there were more than eighty New York breadlines that served over 82,000 meals daily. But as settlement house leader Lillian Wald reported, it was not just the city or even private charities that did the yeoman's work here, but the Lower East Side community itself:

> If all the relief that has been given the poor by the poor in small amounts of food, clothing and cash relief could be totaled, I do not doubt that it would surpass many times the amount raised for organized charity relief.

The ad hoc nature of such relief provision—and their lack of control over it—frustrated many charity workers.[67] Curiously, the Great Depression may actually have been a boon to the poorest Americans, for only when distress was both deep and widespread was relief distributed broadly enough to reach those whose poverty usually drew no attention and inspired no efforts to relieve it. Lillian Brandt wrote in 1932 that she thought that everyone was worse off except for those in the poorest neighborhoods, where "people were rather better-off than usual because of the many new sources of assistance."[68]

Alice Tibbetts remembers:

> In some ways it was a good time. Everybody had lots of time. That was another thing, there wasn't tension about getting a job like there is now, because nobody had jobs, and there was lots of time to sit around and talk. Day after day. I read, this one came to my room, and that one came, and we sat around and talked.[69]

Because there were no longer enough jobs for them, many children remained in school when otherwise they would not have, which may have been advantageous to their long-term value in the labor market. College enrollments rose too.[70]

Peggy also had fond memories of the Depression:

> I remember it was fun. It was fun going to the soup line. 'Cause we all went down the road, and we laughed and we played. The only thing we felt is that

we were hungry and we were going to get food. Nobody made us feel ashamed. There just wasn't any of that. Today you're made to feel that it's your own fault. If you're poor, it's only because you're lazy and you're ignorant, and you don't try to help yourself. You're made to feel that if you get a check from Welfare that the bank at Fort Knox is gonna go broke.[71]

The Political Economy of the Ghetto

One of the things that makes communities of concentrated poverty distinct and the necessity of mutual support so great is their isolation. Ghettoes are often physically isolated, to be sure. But it is more than this: the resources that are taken for granted in other neighborhoods—banks, grocery stores, and the shops that might provide for daily needs—are harder to find or simply not present. In a 1963 book entitled, appropriately enough, *The Poor Pay More*, David Caplovitz documented a range of exploitative practices in East Harlem and the Lower East Side, practices that were (and are) common to most poor neighborhoods—from bait-and-switch advertising and wildly expensive rent-to-own schemes, to the higher prices charged overall (especially for food) and the ubiquity of usurious loan sharks ("credit merchants," he calls them, more politely).[72] This too is not new: for centuries poor people have been prey to profit-seeking opportunists. Mrs. William E. Gallagher, president of St. Mary's Settlement and Day Nursery in Chicago, described the situation as follows in 1912:

> The expenditures of the poor in the main are for daily table and living expenses. Consider the meagre labor wage and against it place rent, groceries, meats, milk, light, heat, fire and life insurance (the latter, too often, the ten cent a head, weekly variety, paid for awhile, then dropped, and insurance company thereby benefited) then the foolish Sunday treats for the children in bags of cheap candy, popcorn, ice cream cones, bottles of pop; the pernicious 5 and 10 cent theatres; and to all this may frequently be added, the weekly call from the book, rug, picture, clothing or furniture collector for goods bought on time, and often worn out, before calls cease, or a realization had of the interest tacked on at the tail end, which of course the dealer never emphasized, so as to be understood, when contract was made. No, the poor constitute the lawful

SURVIVE: MY BROTHER'S KEEPER

prey of the powers farther up the scale of civilization and craft. Food purchases of the poor are generally made at the corner grocery, where the book account carries a balance due, year in and out, and what about the goods furnished? Highest prices too often, for seconds in many food products; second, third and fourth grades if possible, to say nothing of short weights and measures.[73]

In 1967 Janie Boyd said the following to a House subcommittee examining price gouging by supermarkets in poor neighborhoods:

A very dear friend of mine and I were talking about work and she remarked to me that her husband was angry when she got home at 12 midnight the day before from work. I asked why she worked so late and she said to me, "Janie, don't you know that just before the first of the month we work late upping the prices. . . . this is the time business is good, when the welfare checks come out and food stamps are most used."[74]

The economy of low-income neighborhoods is characterized by what John Caskey calls "fringe banking." There are the pawnshops, as there have been for many years. Gold again:

I went with my mother to Mr. Zunzer's pawnshop. . . . It was a grim, crowded little store smelling of camphor. There were some gloomy East Side people standing around. The walls were covered with strange objects: guitars, shovels, blankets, clocks; with lace curtains, underwear and crutches; all these miserable trophies of the defeat of the poor.[75]

While by 2003 there were still some 11,600 pawnshops in the United States, Caskey suspects that payday loan brokers are replacing them as the emergency resource of choice. Perhaps as many as 15 percent of all Americans had used these high-cost (but easily obtained) loans by 2004, paying annualized rates of 350 to 1,000 percent. There were ten thousand institutions in this lucrative business by 2001, increasingly owned by large corporations with multiple storefronts throughout the country. Those who use check cashers instead of bank accounts are charged as much as 3.5 percent for each check they cash, and pay $1.50 (and more) per money order; they are more likely to be younger, less educated, poorer, black, and Hispanic. There were over sixteen thousand of these by 2003. And by 2001 there were also some three thousand rent-to-own stores, serving about 3 million customers and charging up to three times retail prices.[76] A 2006 analysis by the Brookings Institution confirmed that poorer households paid higher interest rates on mortgages and car loans than did others, and paid more for cars, insurance, groceries, furniture, and appliances. Perhaps we should think of this as a poverty tax. It totaled some $6.5 billion in twelve metropolitan areas alone. And this is before calculating the impact of the subprime mortgage crisis of 2007–2008, which has had its largest effects in poor neighborhoods.[77]

Because of such exploitation, and the dearth of institutions that others take for granted, poor neighborhoods have had to develop communal solutions to the problem of survival. As anthropologist Carol Stack writes of "the Flats," a predominantly black neighborhood on the south side of Chicago where she conducted interviews in the mid-1960s, residents there were profoundly interdependent and had created their own local economy, in which they would "trade food stamps, rent money, a TV, hats, dice, a car, a nickel here, a cigarette there, food, milk, grits, and children."[78] Said Ruby Banks:

I don't believe in putting myself on nobody, but I know I need help every day. You can't get help just by sitting at home, laying around, house-nasty and everything. You got to get up and go out and meet people, because the very day you go out, that first person you meet may be the person that can help you get the things you want. I don't believe in begging, but I believe that people should help one another. I used to wish for lots of things like a living room suite, clothes, nice clothes, stylish clothes—I'm sick of wearing the same pieces. But I can't, I can't help myself because I have my children and I love them and I have my mother and all our kin. Sometimes I don't have a damn dime in my pocket, not a crying penny to get a box of paper diapers, milk, a loaf of bread. But you have to have help from everybody and anybody, so don't turn no one down when they come round for help.[79]

Philippe Bourgois observed in his examination of crack dealers in East Harlem in the 1980s that, "according to official economic measures, well over half the population of El Barrio should not be able to meet their subsistence needs."[80] Yet they were able, thanks in part to their underground economy. In many big-city high-rises there are apartments to go to for gambling, prostitution, and drugs (a crack house was the business featured in Bourgois' tale), but one can also find entrepreneurs who make and sell clothes, prepare hot meals or lunches for children to take to school, babysitters, hairdressers, handymen, and car mechanics. Not only do these local businesses offer goods and services more cheaply, but they may also be part of informal credit systems, key to the survival strategies of cash-strapped women, as Judy reports:

> When money was tight . . . it really helped that you could pay folks with prom-ises or maybe by giving them something you made, or something you stole, in-stead of having to give money.[81]

In neighborhoods with few jobs and poor access to transportation, these enterprises might not only constitute the best employment available, but also offer the control over their daily lives that the self-employed among the "middle class" enjoy. These kinds of self-sufficiency are part of the story of ghetto life, too, as is prostitution, another trade disproportionately concentrated among poor women, especially among those with histories of physical and sexual abuse. In the nineteenth century, as today, prostitution was a means to escape abusive or unwelcoming homes, an option for young women who had few, "neither a tragic fate, as moralists viewed it (and con-tinue to view it), nor an act of defiance, but a way of getting by, of making the best of bad luck." In 1855, prostitution was a greater portion of the New York economy than shipbuilding, furnace making, hatmaking, boot-and shoemaking, butcher shops, bakeries, printing, or breweries. As many as 10 percent of all women under thirty years old in turn-of-the-century New York prostituted at some point, historian Timothy Gilfoyle estimates:

> Like peddling, scavenging, and ragpicking, prostitution turned something with little value into something with cash value. When work was slow or money slack, milliners, servants and peddlers alike reported to prostitution.

In the early decades of the twentieth century, prostitution declined as employment opportunities, wages, and working conditions improved for women. Today, as Jody Raphael writes, "the prostitution industry has con-tinued to entice the same kinds of low-income girls for the same complex reasons it did at the turn of the twentieth century."[82] One need not be naïve about the dangers and depredations prostitutes may face to resist disparaging women for turning to the profession; similarly, one must take in the real (not imagined) opportunities available to low-skilled, poorly educated black urban men in the late twentieth century before offering a reflexive condemnation of those who sell illegal drugs. The point is not to celebrate drug dealing and prostitution, but rather to examine those choices in context and separate out middle-class moralizing from the conditions that constrain choice and limit opportunity among poor men and women.

Communities of Support

By Stack's account, in the Flats almost 20 percent of children were being raised by family other than their mothers, a common part of how this web of extended families functioned.[83] A generation later, sociologist Karen Seccombe reported of another poor community:

> Few women acknowledged how much they rely on family members for help. Although they acknowledged how indispensable this exchange is to them for sheer survival, many women did not view it as "assistance" or "help" *per se*, because of the strong norms associated with sharing among members of the extended family. . . . I was told in numerous interviews that they received little or no "help" from family members, but on further elaboration, women would reveal receiving either cars, free rent, baby-sitting, clothes for their children, or numerous Christmas presents.[84]

Around the same time, rural Wisconsin resident Colleen Bennett told sociologist Mark Rank about her family:

> We're all very close. We take care of each other if anybody has a problem. My husband and I have had financial problems on and off for years. And my brother recently lost his job. So when we have something where we can help them, we go ahead and give them a couple of dollars for gas in their car so they can find a job. 'Cause we know what it feels like when you don't have it. And when we're low, they'll give to us. And nobody asks anybody to pay it back. It's like a running loan company.[85]

As historian Ruth Herndon shows, even in early New England poor women formed common households, "communities of support," as she puts it, "bound together in some measure by their vulnerability to official interference."[86] Atypical and female-headed families are not an innovation of the twentieth century. Another more recent study found, likewise, that poor young mothers survived only because of the income support and child care supplied by nearby family.[87] The strategies women used in the first decades of the twentieth century follow familiar patterns, as we see in Beverly Stadum's examination of three hundred women who were aided by the Minneapolis Charity Organization Society; the kinship networks that made survival possible—grandmothers, aunts, and sisters sharing food, money, fuel, care giving, and housing—differ little from those described by Stack. Most women worked, just as they do today (from 1900 to 1930, some one-third of all widowed and divorced women were in the formal labor force), and a common complaint among them was the difficulty in finding satisfactory child care; over one-fourth cited it as an impediment to employment. As a result, children were often left alone while their mothers were at work.[88] So-called latch-key children are a constant, too.

The networks that Stack and so many others have identified among poor people, black and white, is not a phenomenon unique to them, obviously. But the interdependence of middle-class families takes on a different character for the simple reason that they have more resources. Here's Mrs. Hastings in the early 1950s speaking to Yale researcher Marvin Sussman:

> We have "launched" our children. We gave them cash, furniture, and helped them in buying their homes . . . and now they will have to carry on by themselves. We enjoy giving them gifts, especially something they can't afford.[89]

Some of the fathers in Sussman's study were able to offer their sons or sons-in-law something no poor family could likely offer one of its members: a good job with prospects for advancement. When considering "independence," we should not overstate the extent to which people achieve mobility solely through their own labor: witness those who, in a quip usually attributed to Texas columnist Jim Hightower, were "born on third base and think they hit a triple." Sociologist Loïc Wacquant rightly suggests that the ghetto "does not suffer from 'social disorganization'" but "is organized according to different principles, in response to a unique set of structural and strategic constraints that bear on the racialized enclaves of the city as no other segment of America's territory."[90]

Poor people have had to depend upon one another because too few outside their communities have cared. In fact, when data about charitable giving are examined, the poorer one is, the more of one's income has historically been given away.[91] *New York Tribune* editor Horace Greeley noted a century ago something we see throughout our history—the shared responsibility of poor and unemployed people for one another:

> I saw men who each, somehow, supported his family on an income of $5 per week or less, yet who cheerfully gave something to mitigate the suffering of those who were really poor.[92]

Even Benjamin Franklin had taken note:

> A man being sometimes more generous when he has but a little money than when he has plenty, perhaps thro' fear of being thought to have but little.[93]

Perhaps this, from Helen Howard, might shed more light on why this is:

> Am I my brother's keeper? I have to be. The poor people, who live just above the welfare and relief, have to live by that old saying, "I can see farther over the mountain than the man who is standing atop it." We know and see the problems, because we *have* to live so close to them. We know that we have a sense of responsibility, and we (some of us) have tried to instill some of the ambitions we could not realize into our children. . . . Am I my brother's keeper? I have to be. . . . We (the poor) know what the "nitty-gritty" poor is like. The "nitty-gritty" poor is the hopeless and bleakness we have to face night and day. You, the so-called middle class, and the rich, cannot begin to know how much harder we have to work, and still not accomplish a thing. . . . Am I my brother's keeper? I have to be. When we apply for aid from the relief or the welfare, we get turned down. Why? Because we make *too much money*, so they say, or our husbands haven't been gone three months, or we haven't starved to death or been put outdoors yet. . . . We try to make it, honestly we do; it's not a case of being "lazy" or not wanting things for ourselves, no matter what you have heard or what you may think. We do have dreams. We do have ambitions. . . . Am I my brother's keeper? I have to be. I see all these things going

on around me, things like selling liquor, writing numbers, boys gambling on the street corners, and transient houses. No . . . I don't and I won't call the po-lice to these people, because the people who are doing these things are the people with ambitions, the people who are making a better life for them-selves, and their family. . . . These are the people who want to and will get a lit-tle respect. This is why I am, why I have to be my brother's keeper.[94]

2

Sleep:
A Place to Call Home

I thought I knew what it was like to be homeless, but actually, I never really knew. To me, it was those people with the shopping carts, maybe an old man with a bottle. Homelessness was nothing that could ever happen to me. I had too much going. . . . Now when people hear that I am homeless, they don't see who I am. First, they see in their heads that old bag lady, then they think of me, and somehow try to figure out how we are alike. Damn them!

—Anonymous, 1996

See, the first thing they think—that we're all bums. Next they think we're criminals. Am I right? Or we're drug addicts. Or we're chronic alcoholics and don't mean no good to ourselves or anybody. Since we're homeless they think there's got to be something wrong with us, you know.

—T., late 1980s

People in the shelters feel that they are choking. The physical sense of being trapped, compacted, and concealed—but, even more, the vivid recognition that they are the objects of society's avoidance or contempt—creates a panic that they can't get air enough into their lives, into their lungs. This panic is endemic. The choking sensation is described repeatedly by many adults and their children. Physicians often hear these words, "I can't breathe," in interviews with homeless patients. I hear this statement again and again. Sometimes it is literally the case.

—Jonathan Kozol, 1988

I'm not homeless. I'm familyless.

—Abigail, 1993

They have slept under bridges, in parks or abandoned buildings, under-ground in subway tunnels, on the streets, or in poorhouses, workhouses, welfare hotels, orphanages, and shelters. Some have taken to the road, moving from town to town in search of work. These men, women, and chil-dren have gone by many names—tramps and hobos, lodgers and bums, va-grants and vagabonds. Today, we lump them together under the generic category of "the homeless," although this term is a relatively new one: not until 1983 does the category of "homeless persons" appear in the index for the *New York Times*, for instance.[1] Cities often have done badly by their poorest residents, in part by design: if the "treatment" for poverty is suffi-ciently unattractive, after all, fewer will seek it. They will instead take what-ever work they can find at whatever wage, increasing the pool of cheap laborers and saving public dollars at the same time.[2] It is during periods of growing inequality when the most punitive approaches to direst poverty seem especially visible in the historical record; perhaps regressive redistri-bution and repression go hand in hand.[3]

Life in the colonial poorhouse was closely regulated, as it was in the nine-teenth century, just as it is in the shelter today. Residents were summoned to wake and eat with the bells, assigned work (often with production quo-tas), and punished for failing to comply. Among many poorhouse regula-tions were those that governed the demeanor of inmates. In 1784 new laws for the poorhouse and workhouse in Manhattan decreed:

> None shall ever swear, abuse, or give ill-language to one another or be clam-orous but all shall behave themselves soberly, decently, and courteously to each other and submissive to their superiors and Governors.[4]

Although present since the early seventeenth century, it was in the nine-teenth century that the poorhouse was most widespread. Over most of our history, they housed a diverse range of persons who had little in common but their poverty. They were home to infants and children as well as the el-derly; in one poorhouse there might be men and women, the sick and the able-bodied, the sane and those deemed insane, the epileptic, "idiots," the deaf, and the blind.[5] Also likely present were criminals and alcoholics, who were sometimes sentenced to labor in the workhouse as punishment for their offenses. Although there were exceptions, they were dark, dirty, dilapidated, overcrowded, and ill-funded. Residents were likely to be poorly fed, cheaply clothed (often in uniforms), and treated with brutality or indifference by badly trained and underpaid staff. Sickness and disease, rats and mice, and lack of heat were common. Overseers and superintendents of the poor—the city or county officials usually responsible for the care of those in need—earned low wages and were little supervised. Some almshouses were paid a flat fee for each inmate, creating an incentive for them to keep their spending low. To punish inmates, leg irons and chains were sometimes used, along with beatings, solitary confinement, and diets of bread and water. Work was often required for food and shelter, whether the institution was called a workhouse or not. Although some engaged their residents in "productive" work (operating laundries, small-goods manufacturing, chopping wood, or agricultural production), others created make-work projects (moving stones from one side of the yard to the other then back again, or forcing inmates to run on treadmills) in the belief that the reform of the inmate would proceed more effectively if the values and habits of work were inculcated in them. Indeed, many such institutions saw as part of their mission the rehabilitation of their charges, whose moral lassitude was believed to have brought them to poverty. Some required inmates to attend educational or motivational lectures; others imposed religious observance.[6]

Early in our history, the sick poor depended upon private religious and ethnic charities for housing and care, like the Scots Charitable Society or the German Gesellschaft in Philadelphia. Albert Deutsch places the date of the first recorded public hospital—guesthouses, as they were sometimes called—at Jamestown in 1621; Boston followed in 1658. Other towns erected "pesthouses," isolated cabins, often in the woods, to house those thought to have communicable diseases. Many of these were small shacks, like the ones for the supposed insane, designed to isolate and house a lone inhabitant. Some paupers, like James Turner, who sought help in 1744 from St. Peter's parish in Virginia, had become poor only after having already exhausted their resources on doctors and medicines; then, as now, sickness was often a cause of poverty and bankruptcy.[7] Another constant. Not until 1751 in Philadelphia do we see the establishment of what we might today recognize as a hospital—a large, congregate-care facility specifically for the ill, with physicians and other medical personnel on staff.[8]

The first asylum followed in Virginia in 1769. Only then could a mentally ill colonist have a chance of receiving appropriate treatment and decent care. But it was only a chance, for asylums also have a dark history. Confined in airless, windowless, dark, and dirty rooms, inmates were sometimes bound together by the neck or legs, or to iron weights or tree trunks, and fed a thin diet of stale bread and gruel; they were described in reports as "wallowing" in their own excrement and rarely bathed. "The air [was] so fetid," noted one state report, "as to produce nausea, and almost vomiting." One seventy-year-old man, the state of New Jersey reported, had been held for twenty-five years and had been unchained only once. To be in such places as Bellevue Hospital was to live among disease and death, foul smells, and dirty drinking water; to work long, hard hours at a range of occupations; and to be used as practice for medical students or as subjects for medical research. Even children and the "infirm" were required to labor for their keep.[9] Remedies for those incarcerated included "fetters, whips, confinement, starvation, and suffocation in water almost to drowning." Much of what many institutions sought to cure was intemperance, what we would today call alcoholism, although the disease was then seen as needing moral reform rather than medical intervention.[10] It was easier to fixate upon drink as the cause of misfortune, perhaps, than to see it as merely a symptom of more complicated problems. Lars Eighner makes the point while recounting his experience of contemporary homeless shelters:

> It would have been greatly to my advantage if I could have admitted to being an alcoholic or a drug addict. The social workers have no way of assisting someone who is sane and sober. My interview with the social worker made it clear that only three explanations of homelessness could be considered: drug addiction, alcoholism, and psychiatric disorder. The more successful I was in ruling out one of these explanations, the more certain the others would become. Professional people like to believe this. They like to believe that no misfortune could cause them to lose their own privileged places. They like to believe that homelessness is the fault of the homeless—that the homeless have special flaws not common to the human condition, or at least the homeless have flaws that professional people are immune to.[11]

Intrepid reporter Nellie Bly (she is invariably described as intrepid) contrived to get herself admitted to the Women's Lunatic Asylum on Blackwell's Island in 1888. The place she found was cold, with lousy food (rancid butter, bread with a spider baked into it, spoiled meat) and not enough of it. Towels and linen were dirty; the inmates' clothes were washed seldom and none too well:

> I watched crazy patients who had the most dangerous eruptions all over their faces dry on the towels and then saw women with clean skins turn to use them.

The doctors had little apparent interest in their patients. The nurses were cruel or indifferent, their behavior ranging from mere neglect to violence, with a seemingly constant effort at degradation and humiliation, demanding blind obedience and docility of their wards, as overseers and jailers do everywhere. Said one nurse to Bly:

> People on charity should not expect anything and should not complain.

Said another, upon refusing Bly a nightgown:

> You are in a public institution now, and you can't expect to get anything. This is charity, and you should be thankful for what you get . . . you don't need to expect any kindness here, for you won't get it.[12]

The uses made of the asylum could have little or nothing to do with curing the ill and much to do with confining or punishing the rebellious; as with other institutions of the welfare state, it was a means of regulation and control and a site in which citizens fought one another for power and for property. Elizabeth Packard, to take one example, was involuntarily committed to an asylum in 1860—"kidnapped," as she characterizes it— solely upon the oath of her minister husband, who was troubled by her unorthodox religious teachings. Mr. Packard, she insists in a long, angry, and thoughtful memoir of her ordeal, was also seeking to seize property that she would not give to him. "It is for your own good that I am doing this," he told her upon her incarceration. "I want to save your soul!" The law readily permitted a husband such power over both his wife's property and her freedom, and she was confined for three awful years to her "asylum prison." There she encountered many similarly situated married women, who, she observed, were released only after having demonstrated themselves willing to be subservient to their husband's will.[13]

Children have found themselves incarcerated, too. While America was not the penal colony that Australia was for the British Empire, after 1733 over eighteen hundred young paupers were sent to Georgia in its first decade, a practice evident elsewhere in the colonies since at least the early 1600s, when thousands of London children were sent to work in Virginia (anticipating the orphan trains of the Children's Aid Society many years later). Children were committed to workhouses and poorhouses, just as adults were, and were expected to labor for their keep, just like their elders. Reformers, until the first decades of the twentieth century, were content to break up families, even to put an entire ocean between poor parents and their children, in the belief that degraded parents would only spread the disease of pauperism to their offspring. Poor parents, often barely able (if able at all) to afford to care for their children, had little power to intercede when their children were taken from them.[14]

Life Inside

For all their dark affect, their cruelty, and their control, the poorhouse and its sister institutions have also served as the closest thing many had to community, to home. Poor people have consistently used them as part of their survival strategies, much to the chagrin of the overseers.[15] Men, women, and even entire families would enter the poorhouse, staying until they could get back on their feet. Women would give up their children during periods of scarcity (often sacrificing the youngest, whose care created the greatest burden and who was unable to work and contribute to the family economy), and reclaim them when they could again afford them. Some women, too poor to afford medical care, would enter the poorhouse during the late stages of pregnancy and remain there for childbirth and a time afterward, to receive a doctor's attention and have more regular access to food for themselves and their newest, and most fragile, family member. Some of the more enterprising residents smuggled out some of the house's possessions when they left.[16] Some women applied for admittance to the poorhouse not actually seeking admission, but to bring state power to bear on their husbands, knowing the overseers would try to force him to support her in order to spare the public the expense.[17] But it was the use of poorhouses by able-bodied men that most drew the scorn and outrage of reformers and politicians, who characterized some as "winter resorts" for tramps: given the seasonal nature of so much employment, many men would admit themselves for the winter and check themselves out once spring arrived and work again might be found. To evaluate the poorhouse or the shelter, therefore, we need to examine not only how the poorhouse used its inhabitants, but how its inhabitants used the poorhouse.

This is how Mary Smith characterized the poor female inhabitants of one San Francisco almshouse in the early 1890s:

> The character of these women presents special difficulties. The majority are more or less feeble-minded, deficient, or erratic in memory; all are prolix in thought and speech; many lie with facility.[18]

They were, she proclaimed, "the dregs of society." Nearly 70 percent of the adult women there were widows, three times the number in the female population at large. As many as three-quarters came from poor families. More than a third had been admitted (or had admitted themselves) two or more times. Smith was particularly disapproving of that practice, and frustrated by her inability to distinguish between the "decent and the indecent, the capable and the incapable." Of the old, she reported that they were:

> often resigned to their fate because they are led to believe that the almshouse is a State institution, and that it is the business of the State to take care of them. Often it hurts their pride less to be dependent on that abstract thing, "the State," than upon children and relatives who are ashamed of them.

Her case notes reveal some of the diversity among inmates, the manner in which they were prone to be classified, and the easy judgment she made of their character:

> Difficult temper
> Respectable, industrious, cries incessantly for her children
> Filthy; prostitute
> Spy in Civil War, camp-follower; says she saved Grant's life and he gave her a

watch; married twice, once to a gambler, second time to an embezzler; one daughter an actress, good-looking and disreputable woman, who puts mother in almshouse when she goes on tour

Speaks gently; is now growing childish

Was found wandering in the park

Stares vacantly; seldom speaks

Very neat and docile

Belligerent, venomous tongue

Untruthful, vulgar

Has to be bathed

Magpie instinct; stows all sorts of stuff under her bed

Six years ago fell from a horse while herding cattle

Behaves precisely like a horse, and has to be cared for like a baby; ought to be in an institution for the feeble-minded, although uneducable

Speechless; cries all the time

Exceedingly timid; lacks initiative; does very well when directed. Feminine dependence has become pauper instinct

Very slovenly; thinks her husband will return

Has several times tried to commit suicide

Husband a jeweler, who sent her to city hospital because "times were hard"; hospital sent her to almshouse. Husband says he will take her out as soon as "times are better." One well-dressed daughter and one son in city who come to see her and say "times are hard"

Probably makes a convenience of almshouse

Has concluded that this is cheapest place to spend her latter years

Stupid, quarrelsome, shiftless

Thinks herself Queen of Ireland

Was seduced in her youth, which is said to have made her insane; has been twice in an asylum; relatives do not want to keep her there because it costs something

This is Boxcar Bertha's description of the women's wing of New York's Municipal Lodging House in the mid-1930s:

When all had deposited their purses and possessions, the whole line started for the bathroom, as baths were compulsory. Our clothes were placed on hangars and fumigated. We were given nightgowns. In the bathroom I had a chance to see my fellow guests. The most startling thing was that the bulk of them seemed old women. All about me were sagging, misshapen bodies, stringing grey hair, faces with experience written deeply into them, tired lusterless eyes. The average age, I found out later, was between forty and fifty, but most of the women looked much older. Together they appeared all middle-aged, hard-working housewives. Certainly none of them looked like criminals. The majority were Irish and Irish-American. About ten percent were Negro, and there was a sprinkling of Polish, Lithuanian and English. A few showed signs of drink. A number appeared to be sisters of the road. All bore the marks of poverty. Most of them were talkative and friendly. Half of them told me they were widows. At least one in four told the same story. "Our home was broken up . . . my husband lost his job . . . we couldn't pay the rent. My old man's in the men's side, next door." Some had been there only a few days, others for months. Most of them came periodically. When they got a job they would leave, and when it failed they came back. Between jobs they looked upon the Municipal Lodging House as a home. I heard no dramatic, tragic stories. They accepted without resentment the fact that they were the product of "the system," a society that hires and fires, of a society in which landlords must have their rent. There were only a few like me who didn't need the place, just tramps on a little excursion. We slept in double-decked cots with comfortable mattresses, clean sheets, blankets and pillows. I didn't sleep much. Many of the women were hacking and coughing, many of them groaning and talking in their sleep.[19]

Some poor women and their children have lived in what we have recently called "welfare hotels," longer-term residences for those with no access to public housing and no better options. Although known best as a literary critic, Edmund Wilson produced some powerful reporting during the Depression. Here's his 1932 description of what was once the Ozark Hotel in Chicago:

There is darkness in the hundred cells: the tenants cannot pay for light; and cold: the heating system no longer works. It is a firetrap which has burned several times—the last time several people were burned to death. And, now, since it is not good for anything else, its owner has turned it over to the Negroes, who flock into the tight-packed apartments and get along there as best they can on such money as they collect from the charities. There are former do-

mestic servants and porters, former mill-hands and stockyard workers; there
are prostitutes and hoodlums next door to respectable former laundresses
and Baptist preachers. . . . For light, they burn kerosene lamps, and for
warmth, small coal-stoves and charcoal buckets. The water closets do not
flush, and the water stands in the bathtubs. The children go to play in the
dark halls or along the narrow iron galleries of an abysmal central shaft,
which, lighted faintly through glass at the top, is foggy and stifling with coal-
smoke like a nightmare of jail or Hell. . . . The two top floors have been
stripped by fire and by the tenants' tearing things out to burn or sell: apartments have lost their doors and plumbing pipes lie uncovered. These two
floors have been condemned and deserted. Relief workers who have visited
the Angelus Building have come away so overwhelmed with horror that they
have made efforts to have the whole place condemned—to the piteous distress of the occupants, who consider it an all-right-enough place when you've
got nowhere else to go. And where to send these sixty-seven Negro families?
Brought to America in the holds of slave-ships and afterwards released from
their slavery with the chance of improving their lot, they are now being driven
back into the black cavern of the Angelus Building, where differing standards
of living, won sometimes by the hard work of generations, are all being reduced to zero.[20]

Notice that the relief workers want to solve the problem simply by tearing it down. Writer, schoolteacher, and activist Jonathan Kozol offered this
description more than fifty years later of another residence for homeless
families, the Martinique Hotel in New York City:

The Martinique is not the worst of the hotels for homeless families in New
York. . . . In visiting the Martinique, one tries to keep this point in mind; but it
is, at first, not easy to imagine something worse. Members of the New York City
Council who visited the building in July of 1986 were clearly shaken: "People
passing by the hotel have no sense of the tragic dimensions of life inside. Upon
entering the hotel, one is greeted by a rush of noise, made in large part by the
many small children living there. These children share accommodations with
a considerable cockroach and rodent population." . . . It is difficult to do full
justice to the sense of hopelessness one feels on entering the building. . . .
Even the light seems dimmer here, the details harder to make out, the mere
geography of twisting corridors and winding stairs and circular passageways a

maze that I found indecipherable at first and still find difficult to figure out. . . . Above and beyond are all those rooms, some as small as ten feet square, in which the residents do what they can to make it through the hours and the years. . . . I find the Martinique Hotel the saddest place that I have been in my entire life.[21]

Hell is the name of a twenty-eight-year-old Puerto Rican woman in late 1980s Philadelphia; here's her experience with a family shelter:

I was in a couple of shelters and any shelter I was in, it was dirty. We had cock-roaches the size of mice. . . . And the food . . . and violence. . . . If the shelters were any better a lot of people would go to them. But they're not any good. You know, you don't get any respect. It's like you're under martial law. And it's hard.[22]

Grace said this, a few years later:

When you live in a shelter, other people control your life. They tell you when you may come in and when you must go out. They tell you when you can take your shower and when you can wash your clothing. Control, control.[23]

Gwendolyn Dordick found this control very much in evidence in the small, private shelter she studied; it saw as its mission to "change" the residents, and even described their volunteers' role as "visiting." The friendly visitor (the intrusive, haughty social worker of the nineteenth century) is still with us and little changed, it sometimes seems. As one volunteer noted with surprise:

I expected "dirty people." They're all so clean; you would never know they are homeless.[24]

As Dordick puts it in writing about a men's shelter:

The men live in a fishbowl, their progress monitored constantly in the log-book by well-meaning volunteers who want their clients to be more like them.[25]

There are exceptions. At the Refuge, a shelter that ethnographer Elliot Liebow spent time in, the director, Rachel, maintained:

We are not here to change the women. We are here to offer them a safe, warm place to sleep at night.[26]

However, even here, Liebow could find the friendly visitor:

One of the women came back to the kitchen and said she didn't really like tonight's tuna casserole, and could she have something else? The pantry was uncharacteristically bare that evening and I gave her some peanut butter, jelly, and crackers. The volunteer shook her head in disapproval and spoke with great earnestness. "Those seven people who were killed last week [the *Challenger* astronauts]—they gave so much to the world, and they died giving more. But these people, they give nothing. All they do is take and take and ask for more."

As Liebow comments:

That a serving of peanut butter and jelly could tap this much resentment is a measure of its depth.[27]

As bad as women's and family shelters have been and continue to be, the conditions in men's shelters have often been worse. This is from a 1933 account of life in a New York flophouse,[28] and initially it sounds much like Bertha's description:

Now everybody makes ready to go to bed: though it may be only six, there is literally nothing else to do. One may not smoke or read during the evening; all clothing, all belongings are handed in to a checkman in the large dressing room adjoining the cafeteria. Our new man, along with scores of others, disrobes completely, and wears only a brass check given as a receipt for his clothing, which is rushed down on a sort of hand-car to the fumigating chamber below, to be baked at a temperature of 220 [degrees] Fahrenheit. Then he is given a swift doctor's examination; sent in a crowd through the hot shower room, and so, de-loused, washed, ticketed and clad in a rough fumigated nightshirt which hangs down to the knees and open at the sides—so, in a long shuffling nightshirt parade, to bed. The beds, two-story army cots set close together in endless rows, have numbers which correspond with one's brass check.

Yet, he continues:

It is like nothing else, save perhaps a scene from Dante. One reposes in the "world's biggest bedroom," made of a covered pier-shed which extends 800 feet over the East River and houses 1,724 idle citizens. Truly a man need no longer feel himself alone or "forgotten." Here he is in the bosom of an immense family of his fellows who will be coughing and snoring at him all night; hundreds upon hundreds of them in their rumpled nightshirts, now sitting up in bed, or climbing out or getting in, or leaning down to talk to a neighbor in the lower bunk, or simply sitting still and staring at their feet. Here are Negroes and whites, Jews and Gentiles of all kinds, their faces haggard and wild under the ghastly light that falls from big lamps overhead, which are turned low not long after seven.

As it is today, it's often the smell that most distinguishes American refuges for homeless men. From the same account:

The place is warm enough, almost too warm, and filled with a mighty human stench. This stench will become the most familiar thing in the world to the guest of the city's lodging-house system; it is made up in part of the inevitable disinfectants, in part of the odor from the hundreds of human bodies, less sweet than cows'. Less fragrant than horses'. It will be fixed for good in his rumpled clothing handed back early in the morning, at six a.m., when he is waked for his only other meal of the day: watery oatmeal and black coffee. Then he will be marched out into the street, still grey at seven o'clock—for no loitering is allowed here during the day—in a long line of robots with baggy trousers and disheveled coats, robots without work and a day of leisure before them.[29]

Alexander Irvine described a men's lodging house in 1909:

The strips of canvas arranged in double tiers were full of lodgers. The floor was strewn with bodies—naked, half naked and fully clothed. We had to step over them to get to the other end. There was a stove in the middle of the room, and beside it, a dirty old lamp shed its yellow rays around, but by no means lighted the dormitory. The plumbing was open, and the odours coming therefrom and from the dirty, sweaty bodies of the lodgers and from the hot air of the stove—windows and doors beings tightly closed—made the atmosphere stifling and suffocating.[30]

Edmund Wilson again, describing a 1932 Chicago shelter:

On the floors befouled with spittle, in the peppery-sweetish stink of food cooking, sulphur fumigations, bug exterminators, rank urinals doctored with creosote—ingredients of the general fetor that more or less prominently figure as one goes from floor to floor, from room to room, but all fuse in the predominant odor of stagnant and huddled humanity . . . they flop at last on the army cots or in the bunks in double tiers, where the windows which are shut to keep out the cold keep in the sour smell.[31]

One resident of a Chicago lodging house focuses on sound, rather than smell:

The symphony began. It started pianissimo with the winds—belches, groans, farts, incipient snores. It rose in a crescendo of tubercular coughing, bibulous slurping, snorting and snoring, a vomit, and many-stringed cot-creaking. After a climax of nightmare yells, partitions-pounding, and cries of protest, a brief intermission called by the night clerk. Then on again, till dawn's early light brought the quiet of windless exhaustion.[32]

And, finally, note this, from a 2004 study of men in a New York shelter:

The cavernous corridors and drill floor amplified and echoed the sounds: mainly shouts, radios, conversations, laughs, orders and curses. The smell of industrial disinfectant and warehoused bodies so characteristic of the shelter added to the alienating institutional atmosphere. At times one could see bloodstains on the floor of the hallways. They were reminders of the violence latent just beneath the surface of shelter life. In these corridors assaults and revenge often took place. Everyone walked through them with cautious attention and seldom alone.[33]

There is, as we've now seen, a dreary sameness to descriptions of the shelter, the lodging house, the poorhouse, and the welfare hotel, and most descriptions in one era could apply to any other. The noise. The stench. The surveillance and control. The danger. The hopelessness. Indeed, to conclude his examination of six nineteenth- and early-twentieth-century New England poorhouses, David Wagner compared them with our contemporary homeless shelters. The results do not bode well for those who argue that however bad things may be today for homeless people, they are clearly an improvement over the past. Among other things, Wagner notes that contemporary shelters, because most of them are designed to provide temporary housing, cannot create the kind of community that was sometimes found in the almshouses and poorhouses of the past; and contemporary shelters are "less humane," he maintains, because they tend to offer refuge only at night, leaving their residents still homeless during the day. Almshouses provided more of a home, in this sense.[34]

In fact, because of this daily expulsion, in many cities "public libraries have become de facto daytime shelters for the nation's street people; while librarians are increasingly our unofficial social workers for the homeless," a Utah librarian reported in 2007:

In bad weather—hot, cold, or wet—most of the homeless have nowhere to go but public places. The local shelters push them out onto the streets at six in the morning and, even when the weather is good, they are already lining up by nine, when the library opens, because they want to sit down and recover from the chilly dawn or use the restrooms. Fast-food restaurants, hotel lobbies, office foyers, shopping malls, and other privately owned businesses and properties do not tolerate their presence for long. Public libraries, on the other hand, are open and accessible, tolerant, even inviting and entertaining places for them to seek refuge from a world that will not abide their often disheveled and odorous presentation, their odd and sometimes obnoxious behaviors, and the awkward challenges they present to those who encounter them. Although the public may not have caught on, ask any urban library administrator in the nation where the chronically homeless go during the day and he or she will tell you about the struggles of America's public librarians to cope with their unwanted and unappreciated role as the daytime guardians of the down and out. In our public libraries, the outcasts are inside.[35]

In respect to "sleeping areas, waiting lines, food, and so on," Wagner concludes that living conditions in the poorhouses of the past were "probably better" than in a modern shelter, and though there is much variation in the quality of shelter provided, then and now, this is a claim with much to recommend it. Moreover, the formal rules and mechanisms of control over inmates are as stringent today, or more so, than they were in the past century. Finally, Wagner writes that:

> While workers faced massive barriers to stability that were in some ways harsher than today—lack of Social Security and unemployment insurance, lack of health care and other benefits at work—they also faced in other ways a more flexible pattern of daily survival compared to the twenty-first century. Housing costs were not astronomical as in our current day; strangers as well as family took in lodgers and boarders; lack of enforced inspection and building codes meant far more units, albeit decrepit, of housing; and sharing of wood, food, clothes, and other provisions may have been more common among extended families and nonfamilies of the same ethnic group.[36]

Between 1987 and 1995, one in twenty New Yorkers used a homeless shelter at least once; between 1987 and 1992, it was one in ten for African American children.[37] One 2007 poll found that more than one-third of New Yorkers were "very" or "somewhat worried" that they, too, could become homeless.[38] Some have more reason to worry than others, of course: 70 percent of all New York City shelter residents from late 2004 to mid-2005 came from just 30 percent of the city's fifty-nine community districts, districts with the highest rates of child poverty, domestic violence, foster-care placements, single female–headed families, and building code violations.[39] And by 2007, in some big cities as many as one in five homeless youths were gay, and there were some twenty-five shelters nationwide set up especially for their care and protection.[40]

On the Streets

To be utterly homeless makes for a hard life. It's often access to a bathroom and to showers that presents the greatest challenge to someone without a traditional home or admittance to the poorhouse—ironic, notes Steven VanderStaay, given that it's hygiene that is among the most prominent complaints about homeless people.[41] Jackie Spinks, writing in 1996, describes the challenge:

> For seven months, my home has been my 1973 Dodge van. Life in a car is similar to life in a garbage can: trash filled, cramped, and with a smell to die from. Before that, I lived in a shed. I live here because I was kicked out of the shed. . . . I eat at the mission. . . . Often the food at the mission is spoiled, but nobody reports it, as it's better to be sick than risk closure. The bathroom, which is next to the kitchen, has been without toilet paper or paper towels for months. Four of the six toilets don't flush and nobody mops or uses cleanser, so you can figure it's a shopping mall of microbes, but nobody expects Trump Towers. Often I puke. Once, I did it for two days, but as one guy said, "How do you know it was the food at the mission. It could have been the flu." . . . How do I live? Well, I use a can for my bowels and dump my loo near some pole beans and tomatoes in a garden nearby. I expected big beans and red, ripe tomatoes in that spot, but to my surprise they're limping along. One of my fellow car-dwelling aficionados said, "Living on the streets, you probably got toxic crap." I do my "miss congeniality" smile, but don't think it's funny. I don't think he meant it to be funny. I use recycled newspaper for toilet paper. . . . Apart from begging, the thing about poor people that riles rich people the most is our grime. Cleanliness is identified with goodness in America. It's next to Godliness. Dirt is evil. I think we're supposed to clean up and pretend we're real. I don't oppose cleanliness. It's that cleanliness for someone living in a car is a labyrinthine ordeal. First, to wash and dry two loads of clothes—it costs about $5.00 total. Plus, you need a way to get to the laundry; plus, you need soap; plus, you need something to wear while you're washing the clothes. But now and then a car-dwelling paisano does spiff up. Once cleaned up, he isn't too bad. I wonder why I've been going on ad nauseam about cleanliness and appearance? I must have some insecurity there.[42]

Similarly, note this entry from the diary of Timothy Donohue:

> *Thursday, January 30*: I slowly came to realize that the previous years of homelessness had formed in me the idea that the simple efforts required to live a clean, healthy life—things like shaving, taking a shower, getting dressed,

shopping for and preparing food, cleaning one's room, and the like—were supposed to be such arduous activities that no time should be left for anything else. Protracted homelessness had inculcated in me the notion that the minimum activities necessary to survive were enough. And if they didn't seem quite difficult enough, once I was living inside, to eclipse all other activity, then I made them that way by drinking to the point where I could hardly move without thinking that I had just dumbfounded the world with accomplishment.[43]

And lest we think it some sort of modern novelty to see men asleep in homes made of refrigerator boxes, note this report from Morris Shloss, arriving in San Francisco from Poland in 1828:

I brought with me a wagon packed in a large box and, at the landing, a man asked me what was in the box. I told him, a wagon, and he asked the price of it. I answered $125, and he offered me $100, which rather surprised me, as the man had not seen the contents of the box. I accepted his offer, and he paid me in gold dust. I had only paid $15 for this wagon in New York, so I thought this was rather a good beginning for me. The man was very careful in opening the box not to break the lid, and then, taking out the wagon, he said to me: "Stranger, you may keep the wagon, for I only want the box" (for which I had paid $3). "That case is what I want," he said. "I am a cobbler, and in the day-time it will be my shop, and at night, my residence." That box measured seven feet by four feet.[44]

As a woman told Studs Terkel a century later:

One family with a whole lot of kids were living in a piano box.[45]

It's a hard life, often made harder still by harassment at the hands of police. Here's Lars Eighner:

I did not then know that there was an ordinance against sleeping at any time in any public place. I did not know it because, of course, the ordinance is never enforced against picnickers or sunbathers, but only against those who have no better place to sleep. I often heard from attorney friends that the law in its majesty forbids the rich as well as the poor from sleeping under bridges.

In truth I saw that the rich—or at least the middle class—slept in public places, unmolested by the law.[46]

Joe, from Philadelphia, in the late 1980s:

You see, you a human being, but you not treated like one. You go in the train station and the cops chase you out. It's rainin', it's cold, you gotta go someplace. You can't stay in the street. That changes the rules. 'Cause the streets are survival, total survival. And only a few actually survive and get out of 'em. People don't know this. The mayors, the governors, the people in power, most of the time they come from middle-class, upper middle-class, and wealthy families. They can't relate to a person who never had no money. Most of 'em can't. They've been taught, "Anything you want to be in America you can be." But that's not necessarily the case, not for everyone. This is especially true of the single male. People have no sympathy for the male, he the one society really hate and reject. 'Cause they've always had a stigma in this country that any man that's not out liftin' 200 pounds per load is a bum. So they treat you that way. And if you treated that way for long enough you start to act like one.[47]

Rounding up the visibly homeless during conventions and sporting events (to hide them from view) has become a regular feature of contemporary policing, but it too is a long-standing practice: when Philadelphia was preparing for the nation's centennial, "every sleeper on every park bench" was rounded up and hidden.[48] Of late, homeless men are apparently even more dangerous than we have been led to believe—according to the Associated Press in 2005, a U.S. Attorney's Office circulated an e-mail warning federal employees that terrorists might disguise themselves as homeless people, in part because they "easily blend into urban landscapes."[49]

But Ace Backwords offers this caution:

It's important for people on both sides of this conflict—the street person AND the citizen—to realize that, on the issue of homelessness, the cops are neither the problem NOR the solution. At best, the cop is a social garbage man, called in to clean up the mess that society has created. In truth, society has no clue, no general consensus, about what to do about the homeless problem, even as they keep screaming at the cops to do *something* about it.[50]

It's a hard life, and difficult to know how many live it. One 2005 list of "homeless counts" in fifty-six cities and counties reveals an average "visible" homeless population of about one-half of 1 percent of the population.[51] Recent national estimates of the total population vary, from 500,000 to 600,000 in 1988; about 700,000 per night and 2 million over the year according to one 1999 analysis; and one estimate of a total of 7 million homeless Americans between 1985 and 1990.[52] One analysis in the early 1990s sought to know not how many people are homeless at any one point in time, but how many are ever homeless over the course of their lives; they estimated that 14 percent of all Americans are homeless at least once, including living doubled-up with friends or relatives, although more than half were absolutely homeless, sleeping outdoors or in a shelter. Almost half of all homeless "spells" were from between one month and one year, and 13 percent were for more than a year.[53] There are even some five thousand people living underground in the New York City subway system; most have significant histories of previous employment, and most continue to work, if not consistently; perhaps 40 percent are women.[54]

Backwords describes the streets where he lived in San Francisco as being "like one big, brawling, dysfunctional family. But a family nonetheless." He thought those family members fell generally into the following categories: hippies and punks; the classic bum (a "parasitic leech"); the con man; the perpetually helpless (genuinely, but constantly, in need); lost souls ("crippled in all sorts of ways that aren't visible"); flaming assholes; trust-fund babies (Beat writer and heroin addict William Burroughs is his example); teenage runaways; hermits; Vietnam vets; blacks; the sexually damaged; in-and-out-of-the-joint; the secret homeless (these are the majority, he says; you would never identify them as homeless by merely looking at them); skid row types; bohemians; spiritual seekers; the martyrs (who take comfort in their own degradation); acid casualties; natural leaders; and those who just can't pay the fucking rent.[55]

Each city or neighborhood could add or subtract from this to categorize those on its own streets, but his list helps emphasize the fact that there is no simple explanation to the question of why people end up "sleeping rough," as they say in Britain—it's a diverse community. According to a homelessness survey by the U.S. Conference of Mayors, 41 percent of homeless Americans were single men; 40 percent were families with children; two-thirds were single-parent families; over one in five were mentally disabled; 10 percent were veterans (other studies show 25 percent or more); and almost one-third were drug- or alcohol-dependent. Fully half were African American.[56] One meta-analysis of sixty surveys conducted during the 1980s found that, on average, between one-fourth and one-third of all homeless people had been in a psychiatric hospital, undergone detox, had a current mental illness or alcohol addiction, or described themselves as having no friends. Over 40 percent had been in jail, prison, or both. They were more likely to have been raised in foster homes.[57] And according to a study in Los Angeles, 42 to 77 percent of homeless people do not receive benefits they are eligible for.[58]

It's a hard life, and a dangerous one. From 1999 to 2004, the National Coalition for the Homeless recorded 386 hate crimes against homeless people, including 156 deaths. The victims were overwhelmingly male. In 2004, the greatest number of incidents occurred in Texas and Colorado. In NCH's month-by-month summary for one year, we see an appalling diversity in the manner of attacks in which homeless men were beaten and killed. Some were kicked, and one was "stomped to death"; others were assaulted with fists, bats, garbage cans, a pipe, bricks, a golf club, a belt buckle, scraps of lumber, a log, or a shovel handle; a few were stabbed; a few shot. A sixty-three-year-old Chicago man had fireworks exploded in his mouth. One man in Nashville was sent to the hospital after another drove a pickup truck into his shopping cart because he was "lollygagging in the road being a safety hazard." Men were set on fire with surprising and gruesome frequency. When Daniel Fetty was beaten with boards and bricks, stripped naked, and left in a Dumpster, it took twelve hours for him to die. Fetty had lost his home to fire and was living in his car, working and saving for a new place to live.[59]

While police were occasionally the perpetrators (and in one case, a park ranger), it is civilians, and often teenagers, who committed these crimes. They seemed prone to describe it as either just something to do or as sport: "bum hunting," some New Jersey teens called it. There even developed something of a cottage industry in which homeless men and women were offered food, alcohol, drugs, or money to fight one another or to perform stunts on camera—like the man at BumShow.com who was encouraged to drink a bottle of Windex for a dollar. NCH observes that the first video of their series, *Bum Fights*, grossed $6 million in one month alone. The Associated Press reported in 2005 that Los Angeles teens who had just seen a

Bum Fights DVD and wanted to try it for themselves beat two homeless men with baseball bats. One Florida teenager paid a homeless man $5.00 to drink what turned out to be cleaning chemicals; as the man's sister told a Florida news station:

> It was acid. It ate through his esophagus and they don't know how much more damage. It ate his gums, his tongue. He's on a ventilator now.[60]

Perhaps all too predictably, one analysis shows that media attention to homelessness rises prior to Thanksgiving and peaks for the year in December; charitable donations, in that analysis, followed the same holiday pattern. Interestingly, but also not surprisingly, even international famine coverage has followed the cycle. Once a year we concern ourselves with the poorest and most vulnerable people in the United States and throughout the world, excusing us from having to care too much, or pretend to care, throughout the rest of the year.[61] Such is the extent to which we've made homeless Americans a distinct, subaltern class of citizens.

Homelessness and Veterans

According to the U.S. Department of Veterans Affairs, a quarter of a million or more American veterans are homeless on any given night, and one-third of all homeless men are vets. By mid-2005, soldiers returning from the invasions and occupations of Iraq and Afghanistan were already to be found homeless in significant numbers: two hundred at that point, it would be three hundred by mid-2007; by early 2008, it may have been as many as 1,500.[62] As wounded petty officer Luis Arellano expressed it upon his release:

> They put us in a warehouse for a while. They treated us like cattle. . . . It's all about the numbers. Instead of getting quality care, they were trying to get everybody demobilized during a certain time frame. If you had a problem, they said let the [Department of Veterans Affairs] take care of it.

But the VA was full, he told a reporter, and his depression got the better of him. He ended up on the streets. One in five Iraq vets who sought care from the VA was diagnosed with a mental disorder; by mid-2007 it was one in three or higher; and fully half of all returning National Guard members reported psychological problems.[63] This is, alas, another old story: part of why so many nineteenth-century "tramps" formed hierarchical, military-style organizations (they sometimes called their moving camps "industrial armies") is that many of them were veterans of the Civil War.[64] Even gazing back into British history we can identify increases in homeless populations coincident with the demobilization of armies.[65]

While veterans have reliably been a significant portion of the American homeless population, they have also been the recipients of our earliest national efforts at providing relief. As law professor William Quigley notes, in 1779 the Continental Congress voted to pay a lifetime disability pension to Margaret Corbin, who had helped her husband defend Fort Washington; and they increased it in 1880.[66] These "private members' bills" have been a constant of national lawmaking, and while they were not broad national programs, they are clear federal efforts to relieve the needs of (select) groups or individuals. But our first truly national cash relief program came early, with the Pension Act of 1818. It entitled Revolutionary War veterans to assistance of $8 per month for soldiers or $20 per month for officers if they could demonstrate need and would forfeit any claim to a disability pension (disabled veterans had had access to "invalid pensions" of half-pay for life since at least 1776; and certain categories of veterans of the Revolutionary War and the War of 1812 had been entitled to free land parcels in exchange for military service). By 1832, most veterans no longer needed to prove poverty to be eligible, and by 1836 we had the first national widow's pension program. This last was seen as long overdue by many, like this woman:

> I have Don as much to Carrey on the Warr as maney that Sett now at ye healm of government. . . . ye poor Sogers has got Sum Crumbs That fall from their masters tabel . . . Why Not Rachel Wells have a Little intrust?[67]

As many as eighteen thousand veterans and sixty thousand of their family members benefited from the Pension Act, at a total cost of $22 million or more. Most were very poor indeed.[68] As would be the case with Civil War pensions, the Revolutionary War program quickly became a focal point of partisan politics and a source for spoils, and because of the unanticipated demand, the program's exploding costs, and stories of corruption, fraud, and maladministration, Congress set about almost immediately to try to scale back the act. So, the enactment of our first national cash entitlement program, even though it targeted its benefits to the most "worthy" of those in need, led almost immediately to a backlash and to cutbacks; this is another recurring pattern. By about 1835, veteran's pensions comprised some 20 percent of all federal spending. By 1855, every man who had served in any war since 1775 was eligible for one hundred and sixty acres of land; Mexican War vets could choose a $100 interest-bearing bond instead. As political scientist Laura Jensen points out, when President Pierce famously vetoed a bill that would have set aside land for federal insane asylums, his fear that it would set a precedent was unfounded—the precedent had been set long before.[69]

Civil War pension programs comprised as much as 25 percent of all federal expenditures between 1880 and 1910, reaching perhaps eight hundred thousand veterans, widows, orphans, and others by 1910. But just as with Revolutionary War pensions, it became a vast political patronage fund, extending its reach well beyond veterans and their dependents.[70] Then, from 1917 to 1921, 2.1 million souls received $570 million in World War I benefits, with payments as high as $65 per month (about one-third the average for Civil War pensions), about half a soldier's wartime pay.[71] The most comprehensive moment of the veterans' welfare state was the Serviceman's Readjustment Act of 1944, the so-called GI Bill. World War II vets, as long as they were not dishonorably discharged and had served for at least ninety days, received an array of supports—relatively lavish unemployment benefits; low-interest home and small business loans; and free vocational or college education, which came with a cash stipend for up to four years. Its provisions were more generous than any veterans' program that came before, or any since.[72] By 2003, the U.S. Department of Defense provided cash and benefits to almost eight hundred thousand military families, including housing, health care, child-care subsidies, and death benefits, along with pensions as high as 75 percent of their previous salary. In 2005, there were some 3.5 million veterans on the benefit rolls,[73] including perhaps 250,000 who were homeless. They remain some one-third of the homeless population.

On the Road

Tramps were men who traveled from town to town, often by rail, in search of work, food, and shelter. They've also been known as beggars, vagrants, vagabonds, hobos, and bums. Though in evidence by the 1820s, the tramp didn't emerge in significant numbers until the late 1870s, and didn't become a prominent feature of the social, cultural, political, and economic landscape until the 1920s. In the late nineteenth century the tramp was typically a source of pity, fear, scorn, and disgust; he was treated as a criminal, a problem for the police rather than charity or public relief. In 1877 alone there were more than 1 million vagrancy arrests in the United States. There followed nearly three decades in which cities and towns throughout the nation enacted laws that made begging illegal, criminalized appearing in public without a "visible" means of support, and demanded work in exchange for any form of public assistance. In numerous states, tramping could be punished with imprisonment (often at hard labor) for up to three years, or with fines as high as $50. Those who couldn't pay such fines were put to work, as were those who could not pay the costs of their arrest, conviction, and transportation to public prison or private labor camp.

Most tramps were just men in search of work in the chaotic new industrial economy, and tramp populations changed with the seasons and with labor market conditions. Contrary to widespread assumptions that the average tramp was a lazy, ignorant immigrant, one typical late-century survey showed that 57 percent of tramps interviewed had a skilled trade or a profession, and half had jobs (like sailors or railroad brakemen) that required them to travel. Fifty-six percent were born in the United States and 90 percent were literate. Most worked, off and on, throughout the year. Most were men and single (then, single men were laid off before married men were).[74]

Whether it has been described as wanderlust or the more obscure "dromomania," there has been a pathology associated with the transient—he is danger and disease.[75] Perhaps, as historian Erik Monkkonen wrote, "We do not know how to think about tramps."[76] Indeed, tramps did not really agree upon how to think about themselves. The taxonomy of the tramp can be complex. One account by "The Famous Tramp" distinguishes between pillingers, moochers, floppers, stiffys, timbers, mush fakers, stickers, pegs, blinkys, wingys, pokey stiffs, phoney stiffs, proper stiffs, gandy stiffs, alkee stiffs, stew bums, fuzzy tails, gay cats, dynamiters, yeggs, Jockers, preshuns, punks, gonsils, and more. Nels Anderson adds peggys, hop heads, sniffers, guns, jack rollers, mission stiffs, grafters, bad actors, jungle buzzards, and fairies.[77] Ben Reitman suggested instead:

> There are three types of the genus vagrant: the hobo, the tramp, and the bum. The hobo works and wanders, the tramp dreams and wanders and the bum drinks and wanders.[78]

Tramp accounts, the autobiographical and the biographical, are filled with attempts to categorize. Most common, and perhaps most simple, is the declension from hobo to tramp to bum, like Reitman's. Jeff Davies, the "King of the Hobos" in 1908 (there are many who laid claim to the title, just as many would claim to be their queen), said this on the distinction between tramps and hobos:

> It is the tramp who steals the farmer's chickens—the hobo gets the blame. It is the hobo who prevents the railroad wreck—yet newspapers, unthinkingly will give credit to the tramps. But credit or no credit—facts are facts. Hoboes are hoboes—tramps are tramps—and bums are bums.[79]

Novelist Jack London, himself a tramp for a time, wrote:

> While all tramps are vagrants, all vagrants are not tramps: Many are worse, a thousand times worse than the tramp.

London described what he calls "the sharp lines of caste" in Trampland. There's the "profesh," the professional tramp who has "reduced begging to a fine art" and who "lives better and more easily than the average workingman." These, he warns, are "the class most to be feared." By contrast, reported eighteen-year-old London, was the "working tramp," the greatest in number—the men who carried their beds with them (or their bindles, hence "bindle stiffs") and tramped the land season-to-season in search of employment. The "stew bum," passive and hopeless, was neither dangerous nor diligent. The alcoholics, or "alki stiffs," were more likely to live in small communities (perhaps then as today). The "transients" were in transition, farm boys leaving the city in despair and returning to the land, "broken down actors," some running from the law, and more. The "fakirs" were the quacks and medicine men, traveling in search of innocents to fleece. London's final caste were the "road-kids":

> [They] abound in our land. They are children, embryonic souls—the most plastic of fabrics. Flung into existence, ready to tear aside the veil of the future; with the mighty pulse of dawning twentieth century throbbing about him; with the culminated forces of the thousand dead and the one living civilization effervescing in the huge world-cauldron, they are cast out, by the cruel society which gave them birth, into the nether world of outlawry and darkness.

In a 1902 article entitled "Rods and Gunnels," London would write:

> He who knows but one class of tramps can no more understand that class of tramps than he who knows but one language can understand that language.[80]

Jim Tully, in his 1924 autobiography, carries this taxonomy further, applying tramp categories to the population at large:

> A famous writer of tramp life said that the poor always give to the poor. Writers should not make definite rules about humanity. They are always wrong. Some of the poor give to hoboes, others do not. . . . All of the philosophical stuff written about tramps should be taken lightly. The non-producers of the nation are tramps in one sense or another. The prattling parasitic club woman, the obese gambler in bonds, the minister in a fashionable church, all are tramps who happen to have beds and bath, and the economic security that men go mad to obtain. In fact, the tramp is merely a parasite who has not been admitted to society.[81]

Anderson suggested, provocatively and plausibly:

> The hobo was American in the same sense that the cowboy was. The cowboy emerged in frontier history for the same reason that the hobo did; there was a labor market need for him. The cowboy was a hobo type.[82]

Or is it that the hobo was a cowboy type—wives and children left behind to fend for themselves while they roam the open country, moving from job to job, traveling in a virtually all-male world, one in which the homophobic and the homoerotic mix and mingle? Anderson estimates that in the early 1920s homeless men constituted from 1 to 2.5 percent of Chicago's population. Then, as now, these men tended to be concentrated and segregated in one section of the city, but within those communities, and especially in the "hobo jungles," Anderson finds integrated enclaves of whites, blacks, and Hispanics. A majority—perhaps as many as 90 percent—were native-born.[83] There were nonetheless relatively few blacks among the tramps, perhaps because the tramp's survival depended on kindnesses from strangers for lodging (whether from the police for a bench in the station shelter or from a farmer with a dry barn), food (from charities or gleaned from knocking on an unknown door), and transportation (from railroad workers willing to look the other way).[84] Still, like other post–Civil War tramps, former slaves found themselves moving from job to job, from place to place, in an effort to eke out a living. Others lived in shantytowns established in the Union-occupied South.[85] Those blacks (and Mexicans) who did ride the rails could find a life even harder than it was for others, since some of the white trainmen ("bulls"), when they allowed anyone to ride, would allow only whites to do so (often after having extorted a fee), "viciously throwing off only the blacks," reports Robert Bruns.[86] Some of the especially cruel bulls, like Denver Bob or Jeff Carr, developed nationwide reputations among tramps, stories of their ferocity undoubtedly growing with each telling. Many would studiously avoid their jurisdictions.[87]

For some tramps, the journey was an adventure. One man describes riding the rails:

When I was pulled through the door of the boxcar, I was pulled into another world, a world of adventure and hardship. . . . I felt that my past life had been shut out. I was no longer a plodding farmhand. I had stepped outside the law, into the realm where men lived by their wits. If we were caught it meant prison, but the idea filled me with an elation hard to describe.[88]

In some trades it became part of professional culture. Some traveled because they felt it gave them more control over their personal lives and their work routines—if they did not like their treatment from a particular employer, they could simply pack up and seek work elsewhere, like Andrew Hanson in the early 1900s, who, along with sixteen of his brethren, quit his job in solidarity after two other workers were fired.[89] It was, for some, a particular kind of freedom and power.[90] Hank Sims said:

> No one ever got fired in them days. All you had to do was criticize a man and he quit. There was none of this sucking around like you have now, and a man didn't hang onto his job like a priest to a parish. Every once in a while we just drug down our pay on principle, and went down the road to a new job. They'd call us hoboes now, I guess. But in them days we was known as Overland Johns.[91]

Riding the rails, this man discusses the secret language of the nineteenth-century American tramp fraternity:

> The men moved back and forth in a restless manner. Some read old newspapers over and over again. Four men played poker with a dirty deck of cards, with matches and toothpicks for stakes. Another amused himself by cutting his moniker on the window sill. When he had finished, he stood up and admired it like an artist. An arrow was cut through the letters of his name. It pointed west, and denoted the direction in which he was traveling. The month and the year of the trip were cut beneath the name. These monikers are cut, written, or painted on water tanks and other places where hoboes gather. They form a crude directory for other tramps who might be interested in the itinerary of their comrades. Once in a while a tramp sees such a moniker of a friend and starts in the direction of the owner.[92]

Newspapers catering to particular trades (carpenters, cigar makers, etc.) were filled with notices from women in search of their husbands, who had gone out tramping for work and had become lost to them.[93] Still, James McCabe would insist in the 1880s:

> The more fortunate tramps patronize the cheap lodging-houses of the Bowery, where a bed can be had for ten cents a night. An old church for colored people, at Prince and Marion streets, has been turned into a tramps' lodging-

house. Each occupant is provided with food, lodging, and a bath, in return for which he must assist in sawing, splitting, and bundling kindling-wood, the sale of which provides a part of the revenue of the house. The place is not popular, however, as the tramp disdains to work.[94]

Nowhere does there seem to be evidence in his writing that McCabe has interviewed the tramp, yet he is certain that the tramp avoids work. Complaints about transient workers take on a familiar character. Here's one example from the early twentieth century:

> A man becomes a casual [worker] when he acquires the casual state of mind. . . . He lacks the desire, the will-power, self-control, ambition, and habits of industry which are essential to [restore himself to steady employment].[95]

What he really lacks is the willingness to subject himself to other people's notions of proper work, to relinquish control over his own life, or the ability to find work. One 1877 letter to the *National Labor Tribune*:

> I am a vagrant and a vagabond. One year ago I was an industrious, respectable head of a family. My family are now a thousand miles away, scattered and broken up. They and I hardly hope to meet again. The world is a desert to us. I have no friend. I have no roof to live under, no table to eat at, no clothes to distinguish me from thieves. Yet I am not a thief. I have nothing. I am welcomed by no human being; and I am at the mercy of the lowest; yet I do not feel as if I could honestly take a pair of shoes or a coat without the owner's consent. What has brought me to this?

Two years earlier, a letter in the same paper offers another typical demand for dignity and a plea for work:

> I have faced starvation; been months at a time without a bed; the thermometer was 30 below zero last winter [when] I slept in the woods, and while honestly seeking employment I have been two and three days without food. When in God's name, I asked for something to keep soul and body together, I have been repulsed as a "tramp and vagabond" by those who thanked God for his Mercies and Praised charities.[96]

One late-century unemployed carpenter chronicles the search for employment:

> The plundered victim of greed bade adieu to friends and kindred, took a last look at boyhood's home and started on his weary march to the Occident. From Ohio to Missouri, tramping over the plains, scaling the snow-clad Rockies, a pitiless fate follows in his footsteps. Now he takes a spin into the Black Hills, now he turns to Carbonate Camp and again he is in Mexico. He follows the wide valleys, he is on the line of every railroad, but somehow or other, there is always a surplus crop of his tribe. . . . With his face toward the setting sun he renews his toilsome march and finally reaches the Pacific shore. . . . Here he finds a population enacting the same scene he has witnessed everywhere. . . . Alas, the promised land is a myth.[97]

Women on the Road

Too little noted, perhaps, has been the female tramp, the "sisters of the road." Among those of legend were Boston Mary, Boxcar Bertha, Peg-Leg Annie, and Creole Helen. Boxcar Bertha, who we've already heard from, may be the most famous, although she was actually a composite character based upon women Ben Reitman knew. Reitman was himself a hobo (and more than once crowned King of the Hobos), an anarchist (and a lover of Emma Goldman), and the founder of Chicago's Hobo College.[98] It's even harder to gauge the number of female hobos than it is males. First, many women dressed as men and sought to disguise their identity, in part to protect themselves from rape; second, as Tim Cresswell observes, in the public imagination the tramp was a threat not only to moral order generally, but to women in particular, to supposedly helpless wives and daughters.[99] This made it hard to even conceive of a female tramp. One investigation found ten thousand female tramps in 1933; by the end of the Depression, they seem to have largely disappeared, or disappeared from sight, anyway.[100] Journalist (and children's book author) Meridel Le Sueur wrote in the *New Masses* in January 1932:

> It's one of the great mysteries of the city where women go when they are out of work and hungry. There are not as many women in the bread line. There

are no flop houses for women as there are for men. . . . You don't see women
lying on the floor at the mission in the free flops. They obviously don't sleep
in the jungle or under newspapers in the park. There is no law I suppose
against their being in these places but the fact is they rarely are. Yet there must
be as many women out of jobs in cities and suffering extreme poverty as there
are men. What happens to them? Where do they go? . . . I've lived in cities for
many months broke, without help, too timid to get in breadlines. I've known
many women to live like this until they simply faint on the street from priva-
tions, without saying a word to anyone. A woman will shut herself up in a room
until it is taken away from her, and eat a cracker a day and be as quiet as a
mouse so there are no social statistics concerning her. I don't know why it is,
but a woman will do this unless she has dependents.[101]

By contrast, in his autobiographical novel of one man's struggle to get by
in the early years of the Great Depression, Tom Kromer does find women
among the visibly poor:

In a soup-line like this you will always see plenty of women. Their kids are too
young to come after this slop, so they have to come themselves. I look at them.
I look at their eyes. The eyes of these women you will see in a soup-line are
something to look at. They are deep eyes. They are sunk in deep hollows. The
hollows are rimmed with black. Their brows are wrinkled and lined with
worry. They are stoop-shouldered and flat-chested. They have a look on their
face. I have seen that look on the face of dogs when they have been whipped
with a stick. They hold babies in their arms, and the babies are crying. They
are always crying. There are no pins sticking them. They cry because they are
hungry. They clench their tiny fists. They pound them against their mothers'
breasts. They are wasting their time. There is no supper here. Their mothers
have no breasts. They are flat-chested. There is only a hollow sound as they
pound. A woman cannot make milk out of slop. How much milk is there in a
stale loaf of bread? They shift their babies from hip to hip. They do not say
anything. They do not talk. They do not even think. They only stand in line
and wait. It does not matter how long. At first it matters, but after a while it
does not matter. They are not going anywhere. When they have taken this
stuff home and eaten it, they will be just as hungry as before. They know that.
These babies will keep pounding their fists against their mothers' breasts. Tomorrow they will have the same hollow sound. They are all old, these women

in the soup-lines. There are no young ones here. You do not stay young in a soup-line. You get crow's feet under your eyes. The gnawing pain in the pit of your belly dries you up. There are no smart ones in this line. The smart ones are not in any soup-line. A good-looking girl can make herself a feed and a flop if she works on the streets and knows how to play the coppers right. She don't mind sleeping with a copper once in a while for nothing if he will leave her alone the rest of the time.[102]

There were often separate aid programs just for poor women, which may explain why some accounts by men note their absence from the ranks of the tramp.[103] The Salvation Army opened a women's "free food station" so that they might not have "the harrowing experience of having to eat the bread of charity in public," and there was the Women's Canteen and Rest Room, and an Emergency Home for Women and Children.[104] Bertha thought that perhaps half of all women tramps came from "broken homes," either from divorce or the death of one or both parents. Many of the rest, she surmised, were drawn from orphan asylums and jails. Bertha explains:

> I have thought a lot about why women leave home and go on the road. I've de-cided that the most frequent reason they leave is economic and that they usu-ally come from broken or from poverty-stricken homes. They want to escape from reality, to get away from misery and unpleasant surroundings. Others are driven out by inability to find expression at home, or maybe because of parental discipline. Some hobo their way about to far away relatives, or go to seek romance. The dullness of a small town or farm, made worse by long spells of the same kind of weather, may start them off. Or some want better clothes. But others are just seized by wanderlust. The rich can become globe-trotters, but those who have no money become hoboes.[105]

The female tramp persists, of course, although in somewhat different form. One 2005 study of homeless women living in Los Angeles's skid row found that 17 percent had been arrested within the previous year, and a total of 40 percent had had some interaction—arrest, incarceration, or citation—with law enforcement within the year, almost all for minor so-called quality-of-life offenses, like jaywalking, which accounted for 40 per-cent of all citations. About 18 percent reported drug or alcohol abuse in the previous year, and about as many reported being in recovery. More than one-third reported mental illness or a mental health problem within the previous year, and slightly more noted a physical illness during the same period. More than one in three said she was often lonely, and one in five said she had no one to confide in. More than half reported domestic violence in their past, over one-third within the past year; of those, almost 60 percent attributed their homelessness to fleeing violence. More than one-third reported having been victims of physical or sexual assault as children, and one-third reported sexual assault both as children and as adults.[106]

The Anomaly of National Aid

From 1933 to 1935, there was a federal program for those who were homeless, the short lived Federal Transient Aid Program, which ultimately provided aid to more than three hundred thousand people (including over five thousand single women), spending over $100 million—$5 million a month at its peak. Federally funded, it was a reimbursement program that gave states and localities wide discretion to provide for transients as they saw fit, as long as they offered adequate and appropriate care, imposed no time limits, and emphasized work programs. New York offered food, shelter, clothing and shoes, laundry, barbers, outpatient medical care (the program did not reimburse for hospitalization), and case work. Some men found themselves in state-run reference bureaus, which referred applicants to a night of shelter and then sent them to transient centers or transient camps. Once at a transient center, typically an urban phenomenon, a man might get a broad array of long-term assistance—meals, shelter, and modest job training or work programs (often make-work or maintaining the facility) for a dollar a week or, for more elaborate works projects, as much as a dollar a day. Such jobs were fiercely fought over, highly prized, and far too few for all who wanted them. The rest of the men would play cards, listen to the radio, or sit quietly, waiting, wondering what to do and what was to come next. By contrast, men who found themselves in one of the almost two hundred transient camps that had been established by 1934 could expect to be sent out of the city and engaged in more productive labor—building the camp facilities themselves, maintaining them and the farms that grew food for the camp, or providing services to the other residents as barbers, cooks, waiters, launderers, and tailors. Some camps published their own newspapers; others offered college-equivalent educational programs. Some took on civic improvement programs in the neighboring communities, building or renovating parks and playgrounds, roads and paths. Still, nearby residents often fought to have the camps closed or moved. In addition to the common fear of the tramp lay an economic concern: since the Federal Transient Program did not fund hospitalization, towns worried that they would have to bear the expense of caring for so many destitute, and often sick, men. And some wondered what would happen when the federal funds dried up and they were left with hundreds of men with nowhere to live and nothing to do. The fear was not unfounded, for when the program, along with other emergency relief measures of the early New Deal, ended in 1935 (while the Depression raged on), few men from the camps were able to secure coveted Works Progress Administration jobs (less than half the men in New York camps could), and were back to where they had begun, older, but no better prepared to provide for themselves and their families. Some towns loaded up their transients into trucks and brought them to the next state or county. And on they marched.[107]

The Kindness of Strangers

We have seen how those with little have nonetheless shared what they had with their poor friends and neighbors. So, too, did tramps. For many, the life of the tramp was not the solitary one of myth, for their survival was often made possible only by banding together to secure and share food and information about jobs or where the fiercest bulls were; and it was the generosity of strangers, upon whose doors they'd knock, seeking a meal or a bed for the night, that made it possible to get by and go on to the next town, where they might finally find work.

Lora Albright remembers:

Yes, Yes, Oh, yes, We had what we called bums. We were living in a half-finished house here, and the bums were riding the railroads, and they would be in the jungles at Arrow, you see, because there was the railroads that come down both ways. And I never refused to feed anybody that came to my door and asked. And Raleigh sometimes felt that if they were young and healthy that they should do something to help earn it. And there was always things on the ranch from chopping wood to hoeing that they could do. . . . I don't think that you have a right to deny any human being—I'm saying this and thinking about some people that might chisel you, and take advantage of you. And I have had to settle to my own mind—Should I resent or should I judge, or should I just be an easy mark and let 'em get by with it? And this again, is situation ethics. I play it by ear, and if I think that they'd been too demanding because, I am sure in the old days that some of those bums made—left some kind of mark out here, that we were easy marks. Because we had so many and they never passed us up, they all stopped. They always did. But I never turned them down either, because we had—the Lord was good to us, and we always had milk and we always had bread and we always had vegetables.[108]

Dawn McCulloch to Studs Terkel:

I remember that our apartment was marked. They had a mark, an actual chalk mark or something. You could see these marks on the bricks near the back porch. One mark signified: You could get something at this apartment, buddy, but you can't get anything up there. We'd be out in the alley playing, and we'd hear comments from people: "Here's one." They wouldn't go to the neighbors upstairs, 'cause they didn't give them anything. But ours was marked. They'd come out from Chicago and they'd hit our apartment, and they knew they'd get something. Whatever the mark meant, some of them were like an X. They'd say, "You can't get money out of this place, but there's food here anyway." My mother was hospitable to people, it didn't matter who they were.[109]

Jack London observed this in 1894:

The very poor constitute the last resource of the hungry tramp. The very poor can always be depended upon. They never turn away the hungry. Time and again all over the United States have I been refused food on the big house on the hill; and always have I received food from the little shack on the creek or marsh, with its broken windows stuffed with rags and its tired-faced mother, broken with labor.[110]

Historian Alexander Keyssar notes that town officials in Massachusetts in the 1890s "observed that tramps were more likely to be fed 'on the factory ground' than 'up on Main street,'" while others said that "the most successful begging is among the poorest classes in the poorest streets."[111] From one "list of helpful hints for beggars" we get the advice to "pick laborers or shabby looking men; the less wealthy prefer to believe that they belong to a class that gives rather than a class that receives" and to "avoid Protestant clergymen; they will raise your hopes, waste your time, and send you along with nothing more than pompous commandments."[112] Emma Tiller, a cook in Texas, suggested that blacks might be more generous, too, and that "Negroes would always feed these tramps."[113] Harry Hopkins, who administered American relief programs during the Depression, wrote:

> The poorest have in large numbers been kept alive by the slightly less poor. Besides his wife and family, the American worker, more often than not, has had various invisible dependents in the offing with whom he has shared what he had.[114]

The message is clear: if you are in need, do not depend upon the rich, but those closer to your own station, those, ironically, with less to spare. Another constant of relief.

In another effort to pool scarce resources, the Depression saw the creation of what came to be called Hoovervilles, what in the past were merely encampments of tramps. Bullets Bressan describes one:

> They had shantytowns up around 75th near the river. Oh, there was a lot of them. The veterans had them up there. Some of them had some pretty good things there, fixed it nice, pots and pans, clean, neat. Some were tin, cardboard. There were 200 or 300 up there. We used to go up there all the time. There were two fellas in the neighborhood who were in the war. They had a shanty. It was like the Bonus March in Washington. They were like showin' their solidarity. Then they got their checks. Some guys got $2,000. When they got them, there were more drunks around. Two thousand dollars was a lot of money in them days. During the Depression, three-quarters of the neighborhood was on relief, on welfare.[115]

There are our modern Hoovervilles, too. Most are illegal and, as a result, precarious. One of the exceptions is Dignity Village, a community of otherwise homeless men and women in Portland that, for most of its life, has negotiated legal settlement with the city. As one of their number writes:

> On December 16th of the year 2000, a group of eight homeless men and women pitched five tents on public land and Camp Dignity, later to become Dignity Village, was born. We came out of the doorways of Portland's streets, out from under the bridges, from under the bushes of public parks, we came openly with nothing and no longer a need to hide as Portland's inhumane and Draconian camping ban had just been overturned on two constitutional grounds. We came armed with a vision of a better future for ourselves and for all of Portland, a vision of a green, sustainable urban village where we can live in peace and improve not only the condition of our own lives but the quality of life in Portland in general. We came in from the cold of a December day and we refuse to go back to the way things were. . . . Our purpose is to create a safe, sanitary, self-governed place to live as an alternative for Portland's poor, an alternative to the over-burdened shelter system where there are about 600 shelter beds for about 3500 homeless people, an alternative to sleeping alone in the doorways, under the bridges, or in the jails where we are occasionally housed for urinating in public, jaywalking, camping, whatever.[116]

It's yet another form of independence they seek, to build a community on their own terms, to solve their homelessness problem in their own manner, without the patronage or the patronizing of the established public and private relief agencies.

3

Eat:

Dumpster Diving

People ask me: Why do you write about food, and eating and drinking? Why don't you write about the struggle for power and security, and about love, the way others do? They ask it accusingly, as if I were somehow gross, unfaithful to the honor of my craft. The easiest answer is to say that, like most other humans, I am hungry. But there is more than that. It seems to me that our three basic needs, for food and security and love, are so mixed and mingled and entwined that we cannot straightly think of one without the others. So it happens that when I write of hunger, I am really writing about love and the hunger for it, and warmth and the love of it and the hunger for it . . . and then the warmth and richness and fine reality of hunger satisfied . . . and it is all one.

—M.F.K. Fisher, *The Gastronomical Me*, 1943

To understand what Wharton called the "practical strain" of poverty, official rates are insufficient, and we would do well to explore the means by which Americans living on the edge meet their most basic human needs—for food, security, and love, as Fisher puts it. How apt that many researchers now refer not to hunger, but to "food insecurity," defined by the Census Bureau as "not always having access to enough food to meet basic needs." It is widespread. The USDA estimates that more than 35 million Americans lived in food-insecure households in 2005, which were insecure on average for six months during the year. According to Second Harvest, a national network of emergency food providers, in 2005 over 25 million Americans used soup kitchens (which provide prepared meals to eat on site), food pantries (which provide bags of groceries to take home), or ate in shelters supplied by their food distributors over the course of the year. That's about 4 million separate people in any given week, 9 percent of the population who couldn't afford food annually. It's almost 15 percent in big cities. About one-third were children, and 11 percent were elderly. One-third of the nonelderly adults in need were employed at the time of the survey, and about half of all food recipients had income above 130 percent of the poverty line, making them poor enough to need help but probably not poor enough to qualify for food stamps. About one-third did receive food stamps (although nationwide only about half of all those who are eligible actually receive them; in some cities it's as low as one in four), but they reported that their monthly supply lasted only about 2.5 weeks.[1] As the sardonic saying goes, "Sometimes there's a lot of month left at the end of the money." Barbara, in the "boom years" of the 1990s, said this:

> We don't get many food stamps to feed us. They say we get what we are entitled to, but when it comes time to feed us all, its cannot be done. The social worker told me that I had to divide up the food better. She told me to give [my] kids ¾ a hard boiled egg, or a half a peanut butter sandwich for lunch, because that officially meets their nutritional requirements. What do they think I'm going to do—feed hungry kids just a dab to please government recommendation? They are crazy. I end up giving [the kids] my share, because I will not stand for my kids to go so hungry.[2]

Other families ration in different ways. As Franklin Folsom recounts:

> In *Nation in Torment*, Edward Robb Ellis tells the story of a teacher in a coal mining town who asked a little girl in her class if she was ill. The child replied, "No, I'm all right. I'm just hungry." The teacher urged her to go home and eat something. "I can't," the child said. "This is my sister's day to eat."[3]

Nationwide, 20 percent of requests for emergency food went unmet in 2004: one in five times an American sought emergency food, he or she was denied because there wasn't enough. Even when available, food relief has rarely been sufficient. In 1911, once each month Denver distributed bags with enough flour, sugar, potatoes, rice, cornmeal, lard, and tea to sustain two people—for two weeks.[4] Those who do receive food from food pantries typically have little or no choice in what they get, face limits on the number

of times they can visit over the course of a year (this is one way food programs ration scarce resources), and rarely receive fresh fruits, vegetables,
milk, or eggs. In many locales, kitchens and pantries are closed on the
weekends, making securing food an even more difficult task.[5]

This is not a problem confined to some small minority. Over the course
of their lives, almost half of all American children will receive food stamps
(for two-thirds it will be more than once); the same is true for adults (although three-fourths of them will depend upon food stamps more than
once, one in ten for five consecutive years).[6] Half of all infants participate in
the Special Supplemental Nutrition Program for Women, Infants and Children (WIC).[7] Even our military personnel are "dependent" upon welfare to
eat: according to the Department of Defense itself, "about 11,900 junior enlisted service members and their families receive[d] food stamps" in 2005."[8]

There Is No Hunger Here

Many resist acknowledging this, perhaps because it so contradicts our best
notions of our national self. Recently, in response to the release of reports
on homelessness and hunger by the U.S. Conference of Mayors, Robert
Rector of the Heritage Foundation has produced articles dismissing their
claims of "hunger" (his quotes) in America as exaggerated.[9] It's an intel-
lectually dishonest exercise: in one instance, Rector compares the rates of
hunger in the Conference of Mayors report with Census Bureau and Second Harvest figures, which are lower, and suggests that the Mayors report
therefore can't be right. But the report collects data on only twenty-seven
cities, many of which have very high rates of poverty and need. Also, many
city residents have to spend more to obtain adequate food than their rural
and suburban counterparts do; since the other surveys are national aver-
ages, it is no surprise that they report lower numbers. Rector is astute
enough to know this.

Douglas Besharov of the American Enterprise Institute offers another
variant of this "there is no real hunger in America" theme. In a December
2002 piece entitled "We're Feeding the Poor As If They're Starving," he
lays the blame for higher rates of obesity among poor people on food
stamps, WIC, and school meals programs, since food coupons, redeemable
only for food, cause people to buy food they otherwise would not, he

posits, and regulations for school lunch and breakfast programs focus on caloric content, not nutritional value. As with so many anti–welfare state tracts disguised as social science, Besharov offers no evidence to support his claim. He's right about the quality of many school meals programs, and his suggestion that food stamps should be distributed as cash instead of vouchers has merit.[10] But the point of the article seems to be to delegitimize government efforts to reduce hunger and food insecurity, and to further minimize the extent of need throughout the nation. In fact, as an analysis of the (albeit fairly limited) extant literature confirms, there is no evidence of a causal relationship between food assistance and obesity.[11]

Besharov's argument was nonetheless widely disseminated. On January 9, Fox News ran a story entitled "Research Links Food Stamps and Obesity" and reported, unchallenged, a claim by Besharov that "today most poor have no problem getting enough to eat." United Press International reported it as "U.S. Food Programs Make the Poor Obese." On January 21 in Townhall.com (then a project of the Heritage Foundation), it was reported as "America's Overweight Poor," by *National Review* editor Rich Lowry. In a January 22 Mona Charen column in the *Washington Times*, the headline was "Government-Sponsored Obesity." On February 27, Kate O'Beirne wrote "Poor and Fat" for the *National Review*. On February 23, the *New York Times* even asked, "Are the Poor Suffering from Hunger Anymore?"

Perhaps the best response is from John Anderson, reacting to the Fox News article:[12]

Neither Professor Douglas Besharov nor Roberto Salazar, administrator of the federal Food and Nutrition Services has any idea of how we poor folk live. I would like to suggest that they each have a friend hold $125 for them,[13] keep $5 in quarters in their pockets, and then spend a month with nothing but the ability to get some of the money from the friend.

Besharov [wrote]: "In a time of mass obesity, encouraging the poor to consume more food makes no sense at all." OK, but how much are you going to eat at $4/day when bologna is $3.78/pound? A box of cereal is $3.27? Oh, and eat that cereal dry, the way Kellogg intended, because milk is $3/gallon and you have no access to refrigeration. And be careful with that $5, it costs $2.50 to get to the store and back and you can't use the money your friend is holding for anything but food: no soap, toothpaste, toilet paper, alcohol (except vanilla extract, yuk), tobacco.

Salazar [wrote]: "I have not seen any evidence that our programs cause or contribute to obesity." Then you haven't looked. A package of cupcakes you can carry around with you costs less than a pound of salami you must eat before it goes bad, ie today. And if you can ration yourself, you can make it last three or even four days, so your very limited travel money lasts longer. Fruit may be inexpensive, but does not last long being carried around on the street. You can't cook or store food at the shelter, and don't have things like mixing bowls either. If you are lucky, you may have a fork and spoon in your pocket—but not a knife, even a butter knife, unless you stay on very good terms with local cops. Tip: if a cop does harass you, do not kick him—that is assault-with-a-deadly-weapon and since it is a felony the shelter won't let you in. . . .

OK, this is the extreme end. But the extreme does exist, I was there for six months. I am a bit better off now, I have my own room at the Y and can store non-refrigerated food. I even have access to the microwave in the common area, though only 12 hours/day and queued with the other 116 people here. Were I able to work, I'd get all this for only one-third of my pay, which is not a bad deal compared to anywhere else. I do miss things like toast, but at least I can heat water for coffee in the microwave. . . .

No guys, you are both reminding me of the people who want to know why I find it difficult to get around on the public transportation system which covers about 5% of the city and costs money I don't have, then climb into their cars in the garage of the downtown hotel to go home from the meeting where they have been complaining I don't use the bus which they want to cut subsidies for.

Mrs. Harris, in the mid-1960s, put it this way:

People don't understand what it means to go hungry and to skimp and save to eat and have clothes. Even people who grew up poor forget. They want to forget. . . . The hardest thing is to make things stretch. How to feed a family on a dollar—and then worrying about tomorrow. . . . It is *not* easy to get on welfare. Welfare says you've got to go to relatives when the unemployment checks run out, even if you have kids. And sometimes the relatives just can't support you. . . . When you go to welfare, they have pictures on the wall, "Each child must have three glasses of milk a day!" and signs like that about vitamins and fruits. But what they give you wouldn't *allow* you to give each child that in a day—or even in a week![14]

As Anderson suggests, although there is no clear relationship between food stamps and obesity, there is a relationship between poverty and obesity. High-calorie, high-fat, and high-sugar foods are typically cheaper than more nutritionally rich fresh foods, and often more attractive because they are more satisfying (this is true for nonpoor Americans too, of course). In a world of scarcity, poor families often choose quantity over quality when buying food, obtaining the maximum number of calories for the minimum number of dollars. Fresh fruits and vegetables and other healthier alternatives (whole-wheat breads, low-fat cheeses, etc.) are more expensive and less available in poor neighborhoods. Poor women may cut back on their own food intake in order to ensure their children are well-fed, which can result in weight gain over the long term if their response to scarcity is then to binge when money comes into the household. For many, it is. Here's Meridel Le Sueur, in a piece entitled "Women on the Breadlines," in which she describes a conversation in a Depression-era Free Employment Bureau:

> No one saves their money, she says, a little money and these foolish young things buy a hat, a dollar for breakfast, a bright scarf. And they do. If you've ever been without money, or food, something very strange happens when you get a bit of money, a kind of madness. You don't care. You can't remember that you had no money before, that the money will be gone. You can remember nothing but that there is the money for which you have been suffering. Now there it is. A lust takes hold of you. You see food in the windows. In imagination you eat hugely; you taste a thousand meals. You look in windows. Colours are brighter; you buy something to dress up in. An excitement takes hold of you. You know it is suicide but you can't help it. You must have food, dainty, splendid food and a bright hat so once again you feel blithe, rid of that ratty gnawing shame.[15]

Further contributing to obesity, poor neighborhoods often have fewer spaces for safe outside play, which may reduce physical exercise among poor children; and poorly funded schools may be more likely to cut back on physical education programs. If poor Americans are more depressed than their nonpoor counterparts (and evidence suggests that they are), that too might serve as part of the explanation given the relationship between depression and obesity. And, finally, if it periodically does not have enough food, the body adjusts and becomes more efficient at storing fat.

All that said, in recent years the greatest increases in obesity rates have not been among poor populations, and evidence is mixed as to how much greater incidences of obesity were among poorer Americans to begin with (although rates do seem to differ by gender—with poor men less likely to be overweight than poor women).[16]

But Besharov's claim also has a longer history. Here's a 1967 letter to the Senate Finance Committee in response to testimony by members of the National Welfare Rights Organization (see Chapter 9 for more on the NWRO):

> Dear Senator Long, I was outraged by the conduct of the people who appeared before your Committee on September 19. How dare they be permitted to act in this manner before a Senate Committee? What kind of rot is getting into this country when these people continue to receive welfare aid and refuse attempts to find them jobs? They were all fatties—so they must be getting enough to eat. The riots in our cities are caused by these lazy loafers with too much time on their hands. I hope Congress will take positive action against those who abuse our welfare rolls. There is no need to reply to this letter.[17]

One former welfare recipient here speaks to the manner in which such public scorn is inscribed upon those who are poor:

> Poverty becomes a vicious cycle that is written on our bodies and intimately connected with our value in the world. Our children need healthy food so that we can continue working; yet working at minimum-wage jobs we have no money for wholesome food and very little time to care for our families. So our children get sick; we lose our jobs to take care of them; we fall more and more deeply into debt before our next unbearable job; and then we really cannot afford medical care. Starting that next minimum-wage job with unpaid bills and ill children puts us farther and farther behind, so that we are even less able to afford good food, adequate child care and health care, or emotional healing. The food banks we gratefully drag our exhausted children to on the weekend hand out bags of rancid candy bars, past-pull-dated hot dogs, stale and broken pasta, and occasionally a bag of wrinkled apples. We are either fat or skinny, and we seem always irreparably ill. Our emaciated or bloated bodies are then read as a sign of lack of discipline and as proof that we have failed to care as

we should. . . . Ultimately, we come to recognize that our bodies are not our own; that they are, rather, public property. State-mandated blood tests, interrogation about the most private aspects of our lives, the public humiliation of having to beg officials for food and medicine, and the loss of all right to privacy teach us that our bodies are useful only as lessons, warnings, and signs of degradation that everyone loves to hate.[18]

Faith and Food

Humiliation and control can take more subtle forms, too, especially given that so many emergency food providers are private, church-run programs. In many, food is offered only to those who will attend a service. The Rev. Ezra Stiles Ely, in 1812, made the point clearly:

To the poor old creatures [in the almshouse] I gave neither silver nor gold; but what may be of more use to them, a sermon, and some sacred songs.[19]

Ace Backwords, from 2001:

Since the recent cuts in government welfare programs, it's been the churches who have pretty much taken up the slack. Among them, the Catholics have a pretty good reputation for serving up the grub with a minimum of proselytizing. The Gospel Soup Kitchens, on the other hand, are generally loathed. They usually force a captive audience of hungry bums to sit through an hourlong sermon/harangue, screaming at us for being a bunch of sinners, assholes, drunks, and sodomites, before they give us our soup.[20]

Backwords's is an old complaint, one that was set to the tune of "In the Sweet By and By" by labor activist Joe Hill in 1911 as "The Preacher and the Slave":

> Long-haired preachers come out every night,
> Try to tell you what's wrong and what's right;
> But when asked how 'bout something to eat
> They will answer with voices so sweet:

You will eat, bye and bye,
In that glorious land above the sky;
Work and pray, live on hay,
You'll get pie in the sky when you die.
(That's a lie).

And the starvation army they play,
And they sing and they clap and they pray,
Till they get all your coin on the drum,
Then they'll tell you when you're on the bum:

Holy Rollers and Jumpers come out,
And they holler, they jump and they shout
"Give your money to Jesus," they say,
"He will cure all diseases today."

If you fight hard for children and wife—
Try to get something good in this life—
You're a sinner and bad man, they tell,
When you die you will sure go to hell.

But the song envisions a day of reckoning:

Workingmen of all countries, unite,
Side by side we for freedom will fight;
When the world and its wealth we have gained
To the grafters we'll sing this refrain:

You will eat, bye and bye,
When you've learned how to cook and to fry.
Chop some wood, 'twill do you good,
And you'll eat in the sweet bye and bye.
(That's no lie).[21]

The result of such faith-for-food trades is that, as Nels Anderson observed, "the missions attract men who are religious primarily for profit."[22] Boxcar Bertha agreed:

Some of the girls made a specialty of all the words and attitudes that went with "being saved," and used them all successfully to get the watery soups and the coffee and bread that were put out by rescue missions in the name of the Lord. Some of them made up circumstantial stories of the Jewish ancestry (being Irish) and got emergency help from Jewish agencies. Or they manufactured Roman Catholic backgrounds (being Jewish) and got help from Catholic missions. Others had acquired the language of various lodges and fraternal organizations and in the name of fathers and brothers and uncles who were Masons, Moose, Woodmen, Kiwanians, they were given food or clothes or money for transportation.[23]

Complains another, much more recently:

I went from agency to agency, and from church to church, asking for help. These places all want to know about your work history, your money, troubles you got into when you were twelve, your sex life—anything to find dirt on you. When I got mad about the questions and the waiting list to get emergency help, they told me that if I didn't want to cooperate, I could just leave and get nothing. The churches all expect me to love Jesus and become regular churchgoers at their church if they gave me clothes or food. They would give help once, but if you don't show your face on Sunday morning, there won't be no more help. Guaranteed. Nobody gives something for nothing; everybody wants something in return.[24]

Americans in need realized long ago that private charity—precisely because it is private—might be even more controlling and coercive than public assistance, imposing what can seem like arbitrary rules and regulations, enforcing their own mercurial moral codes. Nor are private charities free from the same corrupting influences of patronage that can hinder public agencies. From a New York missionary, no less:

The churches and synagogues are of little vital importance there [in the tenements], because they ignore social conditions, or largely ignore them. And there is a reason for this also, and the reason is that they are supported by the people—the very people who perpetuate the evils against which prophet, priest and pastor ought to cry out continually. The protest against such conditions is a negligible quantity.[25]

In the past, more than a few churches charged "pew rents," and as in the theater today, the most generous donors received the seats closest to the front. Slaves were typically given the balcony, and poor whites were offered, sometimes quite grudgingly, seats at the very back, until some enterprising philanthropists began fundraising for "free chapels," segregated houses of worship expressly for the poorer classes, to be erected, if at all possible, next to the poorhouse. As historian Barbara Bellows acerbically observed:

> Many were quite happy to support efforts to bring the church closer to the poor as long as the church did not bring the poor closer to them.[26]

Economist Robert Solow makes the case succinctly, responding here to those who have argued that we would do well to leave efforts at relieving poverty to private charity:

> I cannot see that taking alms from the well-off is any less damaging to "independence" than is a wage supplement from the state, or even the dole. If anything, I would guess that the psychological-sociological balance favors the state. Servility and gratitude toward one's "betters" is not my idea of propriety in a democracy. A citizen's right, even if sometimes abused, is better. A claim on private charity can also be abused, by both parties.[27]

It is no easy task, even when faced with no other options, to "eat the bread of charity." This is from a 1903 account by a fifty-year-old man who lost everything when his business failed:

> During the first week of my enforced sojourn [of sleeping] in the parks my mental and physical sufferings were greater than in subsequent weeks. My mind was in a complex state. I was not hopeless, nor did I become so at any stage of the game. I keenly felt the humiliation of my position and the sense of disbarment from all sweetness of life was overwhelming. I dreaded to meet any one that I knew, lest he should apprehend my outcast state. Physically I was demoralized. From want of regular sleep my brain became wearied and sluggish. The pangs of hunger tormented me and sapped my energy. As yet I had not eaten of the bread of charity, but at the end of the week of starvation the boast of a lifetime that I would steal before I would beg seemed trivial. At

midnight on Sunday I fell into the long line of men waiting for the portion of stale bread that a philanthropic baker nightly doles out to the homeless. The line is always formed ahead of time, for the first two that arrive are given a double portion, for which they sweep the sidewalk of crumbs, while those at the end of the line go away empty handed when it happens that the supply of bread is short.

While I awaited my turn my thoughts were busy. On one side of the array of hungry men loomed the great building erected by a merchant prince, who added to his tens of millions by driving small dealers out of business and by cutting the wages of labor. On the other side rose the marble walls of Grace Church, the worshipping place of the rich and powerful. The tall and ornate spire pointing heavenward recalled the words of the Galilean: "He that cometh to me shall never hunger; and he that believeth in me shall never thirst." But on that Sunday night of which I write the hungry were fed by the baker and not by the church. As the men received their allotted portion they slunk away, not in groups or pairs, but solitary and alone, munching the bread as they went. The status of the men of the parks was easily determined by the way they ate their bread. The newcomers ate ravenously; those of longer experience more slowly but with evident relish, while the old-timers ate with an effort, forcing the bread down as a necessity to life. A continuous diet of bread alone does not satisfy the inner man, and in this connection one of the bread eaters unintentionally said a good thing. He voiced the cry of his stomach and described his emaciated condition by the single remark that the skin was cracking on his bones for the lack of meat. As for myself, I ate the bread of charity for the first time in my life, and it did not choke me; on the contrary, it appeased my fierce hunger. Swelling it up with water from the fountain at the park, I settled into a seat on a bench and slept until an officer on his morning round aroused me with a rough shake and the command to "Wake up and take a walk."[28]

Eating Trash

During the Great Depression food was so scarce that one administration official received a plea to ask the dining public not to put their cigarettes out in their plates so that the unfinished food might be passed on "for the deserving poor."[29] One Chicago area newspaper reported that "lines form every day at the garbage dump from eight in the morning to five in the afternoon."[30] As Edmund Wilson wrote:

> There is not a garbage-dump in Chicago which is not diligently haunted by the hungry. Last summer in the hot weather, when the smell was sickening and the flies were thick, there were a hundred people a day coming to one of the dumps, falling on the heap of refuse as soon as the truck had pulled out and digging in it with sticks and hands. They would devour all the pulp that was left on the old slices of watermelon and cantaloupe till the rinds were as thin as paper; and they would take away and wash and cook discarded turnips, onions and potatoes. Meat is a more difficult matter, but they salvage a good deal of that, too. The best is the butcher's meat which has been frozen and has not spoiled. If they can find only meat that is spoiled, they can sometimes cut out the worst parts, or they scald it and sprinkle it with soda to neutralize the taste and the smell. Fish spoils too quickly, so it is likely to be impossible— though some people have made fish-head soup. Soup has also been made out of chicken claws. . . . [One widow] fed herself and her fourteen-year-old son on garbage. Before she picked up the meat, she would always take off her glasses so that she would not be able to see the maggots; but it sometimes made the boy so sick to look at this offal and smell it that he could not bring himself to eat. He weighed only eighty-two pounds.[31]

Eating from the trash remains part of the lives of many Americans, especially homeless men. Ace Backwords takes some pride in his talent for it:

> I could be dropped, blindfolded, into almost any city in America, with nothing but the shirt on my back, and . . . I would be able to survive, *comfortably*, totally on my own. Don't underestimate the psychological value of this realization, or the sense of independence that it can give. . . . Of course, on the other hand, I'm a bum eating out of the garbage, so what do I know?[32]

He continues, in his guidebook on how to survive on the streets:

> There are many street people who don't get welfare checks or sue the charity agencies, and yet manage to survive almost exclusively from scrounging. As the ever-resourceful and supremely self-sufficient Hate Man put it: "I prefer

just digging in the trash to find what I need. I feel a lot of the social agencies are a parent/child set-up. I prefer the trash. It's floating down the river. I don't owe anybody anything."[33]

Restaurant Dumpsters can be good targets—wait until just after closing time, and you may be rewarded with a sizable bag of discarded food. Lars Eighner described the first moment of Dumpster diving:

At first the new scavenger is filled with disgust and self-loathing. He is ashamed of being seen and may lurk around, trying to duck behind things, or he may try to dive at night. . . . Every grain of rice seems to be a maggot. Everything seems to stink. He can wipe the egg yolk off the found can, but he cannot erase from his mind the stigma of eating garbage. That stage passes with experience. The scavenger finds a pair of running shoes that fit and look and smell brand-new. He finds a pocket calculator in perfect working order. He finds pristine ice cream, still frozen, more than he can eat or keep. He begins to understand: People throw away perfectly good stuff, a lot of perfectly good stuff. At this stage, the Dumpster shyness begins to dissipate. The diver, after all, has the last laugh. He is finding all manner of good things that are his for the taking. Those who disparage his profession are the fools, not he.[34]

Such strategies do not come without risks, however. Says Eighner:

When you live out of Dumpsters, dysentery is an occasional fact of life. . . . In the middle of nowhere, the result was inconvenient. In the city, as I had yet to discover, intestinal distress and the dearth of truly public rest rooms provide a number of unpretty options.[35]

Not all risks are so benign. During the Great Depression, one man told another, named Cass, that he always was able to eat because he "kin get garbage out o' any old can." But:

Cass knew better than that. He knew that once a week, on Saturday, all open garbage was sprayed by the city. (In order to keep paupers from poisoning themselves on Sunday, which was the Sabbath.) So to the sullen shoulders in front of him, to a flat-backed head on a hairy neck he said, "They're puttin' stink-oil on the grab-cans now. That guy won't find even crap left clean. Ah seen 'em sprayin' it on last summer, back o' Commerce Street in Dallas. It was green kind o', looked like to me."

Another man told them that it was coal-oil.[36] In 1884, the *Chicago Tribune* advised:

When a tramp asks you for bread, put strychnine or arsenic in it, and he will not trouble you any more, and others will keep out of the neighborhood.[37]

Even now some restaurants pour ammonia over the food they discard in order to keep homeless people away from their trash, a practice reinaugurated in full measure in the 1980s.[38]

Scrounging through the trash for food is not confined to homeless men living on the streets of big cities. This is Jeanette Walls, who would grow up to become an MSNBC.com gossip columnist:

When I started sixth grade, the other kids made fun of [my brother] Brian and me because we were so skinny. They called me spider legs, skeleton girl, pipe cleaner, two-by-four, bony butt, stick woman, bean pole, and giraffe, and they said I could stay dry in the rain by standing under a telephone wire. At lunchtime, when the other kids unwrapped their sandwiches or bought their hot meals, Brian and I would get out books and read. Brian told everyone he had to keep his weight down because he wanted to join the wrestling team when he got to high school. I told people that I had forgotten to bring my lunch. No one believed me, so I started hiding in the bathroom during lunch hour. I'd stay in one of the stalls with the door locked and my feet propped up so that no one would recognize my shoes. When other girls came in and threw away their lunch bags in the garbage pails, I'd go retrieve them. I couldn't get over the way kids tossed out all this perfectly good food: apples, hard-boiled eggs, packages of peanut-butter crackers, sliced pickles, half-pint cartons of milk, cheese sandwiches with just one bite taken out of them because the kid didn't like the pimentos in the cheese. I'd return to the stall and polish off my tasty finds. There was, at times, more food in the wastebasket than I could eat. The first time I found extra food—a bologna-and-cheese sandwich—I stuffed it into my purse to take home for Brian. Back in the classroom, I started worrying about how I'd explain to Brian where it came from. I was pretty sure he was rooting through the trash, too, but we never talked about it. As I sat there trying to come up with ways to justify it to Brian, I began smelling the bologna. It seemed to fill the whole room. I became terrified that the other kids could smell it, too, and that they'd turn and see my overstuffed purse, and since they all knew I never ate lunch, they'd figure out that I had pinched it from the trash. As soon as class was over I ran to the bathroom and shoved the sandwich back in the garbage can.[39]

The enterprising can find more than just food. David Zuccino relays this story:

Odessa prided herself on the quality of her trash picking. She had a discerning eye. She did not bring home junk. And for her there was no stigma attached to the base origins of these objects. Each item she dragged home represented to her a form of independence. She might be on welfare, but she wasn't dependent, and she certainly wasn't helpless. She did not expect anyone to give her anything, but she saw no reason not to take advantage of what was available. Just as she qualified for welfare, she was also entitled to root through people's trash cans and seize for herself those things that others lacked the common sense or initiative to put to good use.[40]

How much of Odessa's pride was genuine, and how much merely a means by which to obscure what could have been shame, is impossible for us to know. But her tale, and those of many others, cautions us against assuming that getting by by picking through other people's trash must be degrading and humiliating: "independence" can be found in awkward places. Timothy Donohue:

Wednesday, September 26, 1990: . . . I have become much more adept at dealing with poverty. I was in a state approaching terror back then at the possibility of running completely out of money. It is not like that now, of course. Now I can say that I am capable of going broke anywhere in the world without considering it even worthy of a passing conversation. . . . Part of this equanimity must be due to my having learned how to use resources like missions and meal programs. But a lot of the sangfroid is derived from an indifference to the kind of pain that comes with an utter depletion of financial resources. I think repetition must inure the human animal to certain kinds of agony.[41]

Walls again, recounting an exchange years later with her now-homeless mother:

> "You want to help me change my life?" Mom asked. "I'm fine. You're the one who needs help. Your values are all confused."
>
> "Mom, I saw you picking through trash in the East Village a few days ago."
>
> "Well, people in this country are too wasteful. It's my way of recycling." She took a bite of her Seafood Delight. "Why didn't you say hello?"
>
> "I was too ashamed, Mom. I hid."
>
> Mom pointed her chopsticks ate me. "You see?" she said. "Right there. That's exactly what I'm saying. You're way too easily embarrassed. Your father and I are who we are. Accept it."[42]

There are now entire poor-relief industries based upon the notion of food reclamation—not-for-profits which "rescue" (that's their language) food that would otherwise be thrown out from restaurants, grocery stores, and private and corporate parties, and then distribute it to soup kitchens, homeless shelters, old-age homes, and community centers. It's food that makes it easier for threadbare organizations to provide for their clientele or allows them to spend scarce funds on other necessaries; and much of it is fresh and expertly prepared. That's all to the good. But it is still distributing garbage to poor people. These practices also have their antecedents: among black female household employees, the "service pan" was often an essential part of their survival strategy. One Southern nursemaid describes it as:

> The general term applied to "left-over" food, which in many a Southern home is freely placed at the disposal of the cook. . . . if it were not for the service pan, I don't know what the majority of our Southern colored families would do. The service pan is the mainstay in many a home. . . . And, I tell you, with all of us poor people the service pan is a great institution; it is a great help to us, as we wag along the weary way of life.

She admits that many take more than just leftover food, such as small portions of flour, or scraps of used soap:

But I indignantly deny that we are thieves. We don't steal; we just "take" things—they are a part of the oral contract, exprest or implied. We understand it, and most of the white folks understand it.[43]

Indeed they did, for the service pan could also be taken away to exert control or exact punishment, as Harriet Jacobs reported in her autobiography of life as a slave:

If dinner was not served at the exact time . . . [the mistress of the house] would station herself in the kitchen, and wait until it was dished, and then spit in all the kettles and pans that had been used for cooking. She did this to prevent the cook and her children from eking out their meagre fare with the remains of the gravy and other scrapings.[44]

As M.F.K. Fisher suggested, this is why it is hard to separate discussion about food and hunger from questions about power and security; and just as the Lawrence strikers demanded bread as well as roses, we must attend not only to our rank physical needs but also to "our wilder, more insistent hungers," as Fisher put it: our hunger for dignity, for self-determination, for independence, and for love.

4

Work:
(In)Dependence

When a man is compelled to eat the bread of idleness because social conditions over which he has no control deny him the right of access to work, he is as much a victim of injustice as though he were sandbagged on his way home and robbed by the highwayman or assassin of the fruit of his daily toil. It is this social injustice, I say, that breeds and perpetuates vice, poverty, and crime.

—S.M. Jones, Mayor of Toledo, 1897

In November 2006, a new Times Square store advertised that it would be hiring for about two hundred positions, one-third of them only part-time. Unexpectedly, not hundreds but thousands of people showed up to apply. Crowd control became impossible, mounted police were dispatched to keep order, and the job seekers were sent away and told to mail in their applications. As one man from the Bronx told the *New York Times*, "I was very disappointed. It burns the spirit." A Brooklyn woman lamented, "This is what unemployment looks like in New York City. I wanted to cry." And a local businessman said, "All those people applying for that many jobs. It's so sad that it's funny."[1] Franklin Folsom shows us that this is an old pattern. From 1837:

One hot day in August, 500 men in New York applied for work in response to an advertisement for twenty men to wield a spade in the country at four dollars a month plus board. Men posted notices in City Hall that they would do any kind of work for three dollars a week.[2]

According to Jack London, in 1894 one reporter:

Made a casual reference, in a newspaper column she conducts, to the difficulty two business men found in obtaining good employees. The first morning mail brought her seventy-five applications for the position and at the end of two weeks over two hundred people had applied.[3]

In 1896, recounted Mrs. L.P. Roland:

A man working in a gun factory was killed. Eighty men applied for the vacant place. Within three weeks the accepted applicant was killed, and promptly forty men stepped forward to fill his place. What remained for the thirty-nine?[4]

And in 1914, we learn from Leah Feder:

The Labor Exchange asked all unemployed people who were willing to work at anything for any price to register with them; and within a week 11,000 persons had enrolled.[5]

A few years earlier, an ice company announced a few available jobs and five hundred men showed up, with one observer suggesting that there were another twenty thousand who could have joined in.[6] Nels Anderson tells us that in 1920 one Chicago public employment agency catering to skilled laborers found as many as three hundred homeless men at its doors each day; only those who met stringent notions of worthiness were even considered.[7] In one Minnesota county during the Depression, three thousand men registered for three hundred relief jobs.[8] At around the same time in Sioux City, Iowa, too many men showed up for a work relief assignment and they literally fought one another for shovels.[9] In a study of homeless New Hampshire families in the 1990s, Mary Newton says this of herself and her husband, Bruce:

We have tried and tried to find jobs. There simply aren't any. We must apply for a dozen jobs every day. We read want ads every night. We walk around looking for "help wanted" signs in windows. We are applying for jobs that we would never have considered before. And we can't even get them. We have to eat. We have to take care of our children. People look at us like, "what kind of losers are you?" It is so upsetting the way they look at us. We didn't do anything wrong. We just lost our jobs, and now everything is awful. How dare they look at us like that! It could happen to them—but I guess they don't know that.[10]

In what has become a seminal examination of unemployment in New York, Katherine Newman discovered:

Among central Harlem's fast food establishments, the ratio of applicants to available jobs is 14:1. For every fortunate person who lands one of these minimum wage jobs, there are thirteen others who walk away empty-handed.[11]

The examples could be multiplied many thousand times over, although to some extent they reveal little more than the fact that we have always had unemployment. Rates have varied enormously, from highs of as much as 40 percent in some places during the worst of the 1893 depression and Great Depression to around 5 to 9 percent over the past few decades. Official data systematically undercount unemployment, however, and if we add in those who have been unemployed for so long that they have given up looking and those working part-time because they can't find full-time jobs, the numbers typically double today. In July 2005, for example, according to the National Jobs for All Coalition's calculations, the official rate of 5 percent was more likely to be 10.9 percent.[12] And even the official data show substantially higher rates in poor urban neighborhoods. The vignettes above and these data matter because so much of the critique of welfare and the welfare state is rooted in complaints about the supposed laziness of those who are poor. To rebut this presumption, we should attend to how consistently throughout our history poor men and women have competed against one another for scarce jobs, and just how desperate many have been for work, in times of crisis and in "normal" times, too.

Work *and* Welfare

The plea for work, not welfare, is a constant. But not just any work. A report from the late 1700s:

It is said that our poor are indolent, and will not work. . . . [But] give the poor a sufficient compensation for their work; let the demand for their exertions be constant and steady . . . and it will soon be found that the charge of indolence, is a calumny on the most destitute part of our fellow citizens. . . . As far as our experience extends, we have always found the people anxious for employment, and to perform it with fidelity.[13]

Lorena Hickok, writing to update Harry Hopkins during the Depression:

"Those fellows don't want to work," they say and cite instances where a man on the relief rolls was offered a job for a day or two and turned it down. What they don't understand is that the unemployed have learned that accepting one of these temporary jobs takes them off the relief rolls, and that the clerical work involved is apt to keep them off long after the money they earned on the job may have run out. . . . Therefore, you can hardly blame a man for not wanting to run the risk of being cut off the relief rolls for a job that may last a day or so and pay him two or three dollars.[14]

John Dawson, 1965:

I don't think a man should stay on welfare if there's any way possible he can get off it, we're not in favor of ridin the relief rolls till you're dead, but I don't believe he should be put out in the street on a job that he couldn't make a living on. I think he should have a job, but a decent job where he could take and make a living for his family, and give him enough money that he could lay some money aside for sickness or something like that.[15]

One New York woman noted a similar kind of problem after the welfare reform of 1996 and its new work requirements:

The job developers try to give you a temporary job that only pays $5 an hour. . . . I don't want a three-week job that only pays $5 an hour. As soon as you have one of these terrible, temporary jobs, your benefits get cut and then you have to start the process all over again once the three weeks is up. I have a family to support—I need a real job.[16]

One former welfare recipient, a Native American woman, said it this way:

> I want to give my kids someone to look up to. People should work if they can. I
> was embarrassed being on welfare. People think you're lazy. I wanted to better
> my future. I don't want to depend on my family. I'm an independent woman.[17]

But the desire for work does not necessarily translate into the ability to
work: poor Americans often have less education and fewer skills, which
limits their options to jobs with low pay, few benefits, and little security.[18]
Such jobs seldom pay enough to cover child care. Poor women are twice as
likely as those with incomes above 200 percent of the poverty line to have
health problems, and about half of all women on welfare report having
poor physical or mental health (other studies suggest that about one in
four women with experience of welfare had problems with their mental
health). Some 10 to 15 percent of recipients, perhaps more, have a disabled child.[19] Women on welfare are more likely to have been victims of
domestic violence, and it is common in such relationships for men to sabotage women's efforts at work, training, or education, as we'll see.[20] Numerous studies have shown how difficult it can be for black men to find
work: white men with prison records are more likely to get jobs than iden-
tically qualified black men without prison records.[21] The point is that
obstacles to employment are significant and belie facile complaints that recipients are irresponsible, lack a work ethic, or don't try hard enough.[22]
Take it from LaVerne, around 1995:

> I don't know why life should be so hard. Life seems like I get on a boat and I
> get going and something happens and then I fall back again. Then I have to
> start all over again. Then I get back in the boat and work hard and then some-
> thing happens and I have to start all over again. It seems I never get anywhere
> but I work real hard. The big question for me would be to figure out how I
> could get somewhere and stay there and keep going. But I don't know how to
> do that.[23]

When they do work, less-educated women receive less in the bargain.
One working mother told sociologist Kathryn Edin and anthropologist
Laura Lein:

> There were many days when I got my paycheck and I just looked at it and
> cried. It was not enough to pay my rent, and I had to work almost the full

month to pay the rent. It was never enough that I could go buy groceries. And I had the two kids and they had to watch one another and I didn't want welfare. And it is just one up and down after another. . . . Somehow, you can even feel like you're not even a part of society because you're standing there looking at the American Dream and you feel like it's passing you over.[24]

This is the reality of women, work, and welfare. The majority use relief (and usually do so reluctantly) for brief periods of time, often between jobs. They move on and off the rolls over their lives because the jobs they are able to get do not provide them with enough in wages and health insurance to care adequately for themselves and their families. The nation's largest employer, Wal-Mart, knows this: it has encouraged its employees to apply for food stamps, Medicaid, and other public benefits because it knows that few people can live on what Wal-Mart pays.[25]

In a particularly cruel irony, while we have castigated women on welfare for not working, throughout the history of the AFDC program they were forbidden to work while on the rolls if they wanted to retain their full benefits. This was not lost on recipients. Rebecca:

> You know, that's what I think is really stupid about welfare, because one of the reasons there are so many stereotypes about people on welfare is because they won't let you work. Most people, well, a lot of people that are on welfare, work. And I mean, you want to say that people on welfare are lazy, but most people do work. It's just that we can't tell you that we work![26]

In recent decades, a majority of women on welfare have worked officially, about one-third at any given time, and many more, like Rebecca, worked without reporting it.[27] It's another old pattern. In one study of nearly a thousand widows who sought assistance in 1910, 84 percent worked while on relief, and perhaps as many as half worked for thirty hours or more each week.[28] Women on welfare work because they want to, and because benefits have been so low that they have to. As a result, they have been obliged by the government to lie and deceive. One woman described working as nothing less than "civil disobedience." Another added:

> You're breaking the law by making sure you and your kids don't starve on the street—well, that's not *my* law.[29]

Some receive the assistance of sympathetic caseworkers who help them game the system, like Anne, who told researcher Lisa Dodson:

> I tell them when to say "I don't know," what to ask for, and how to get the most out of it. I use my body language. Like when they answer something wrong—*maybe honestly*, but wrong to get the service—I kind of wince or make a face, and they get it. I mean they're not dumb, you know, they're poor.

Dodson continues:

> And what does that make you? I ask Anne. She looks me in the eye when she answers, "A social worker." Anne believes that, if you do social work, you eventually have to make a choice. You can learn to see the worst in people, and then to identify deeply with the institutional mandates which express social stigma. Or you begin to see the world standing in another woman's shoes. If you do, you start to think differently about what is right. You start to think, if I was there and that was my baby, what *wouldn't I do* to get over the blockades.[30]

Jo Lynn said this about her unreported income:

> The system makes us fraudulent. It makes us fraudulent. I can tell you right now it makes everyone that is on the system fraudulent. They might as well tell you. They might as well tell you the truth. I'm fraudulent, and everybody else that I know is. Because to get by, you have to do things that they're not going to allow.[31]

When asked how they felt about not reporting income, most of the Ohio women political scientist John Gilliom talked with responded similarly. Said Shawana:

> It makes you feel . . . like you are ripping them off. Like you are a thief.

Marilyn concurred:

> It makes you feel like a dog. To lie in order to make it month to month. It makes you feel like a low life.[32]

Their complaints were made decades earlier by a resident of the Lower East Side:

The investigators [caseworkers] were always nice to me. They were never mean. The one I had when they found out I was working said he knew I couldn't make it on welfare money, but there was nothing he could do. That's the worst thing about welfare. The way it is now, they're making people cheat so they can live right. The way I grew up, that was the only way we could stay alive. There ought to be a way for people on welfare to improve themselves without having to cheat.[33]

As one of his correspondents reported to Hopkins:

Relief clients are often tempted not to report these temporary, poorly paid jobs. That is called "chiseling," and people have been arrested for it. But again—heads of families, ashamed and defiant, have led investigators into their homes and have pointed out to them where those few, pathetic dollars went. Dishes, towels, clothing, badly needed bits of furniture, drugstore supplies, "things you can't get on relief."[34]

Rose Halpern agrees:

The Depression hit us very badly. My mother lost her job. Finally, our neighbors started to plead with her to go on welfare. Grandma thought, how could she do that to me? To us it was a terrible thing. Finally, they were about to put us out, and she agreed. We applied for it, and they asked us a million questions. I had to go for my mother, to be the interpreter. They asked you if you worked, how much money you had. You had to be poor all the time. They paid your rent and a little more, but you couldn't exist on that little money, so my mother finally got herself a part-time job. She didn't report it.[35]

Such women have been in a triple bind: the wages available to them in the labor market have been insufficient, they have care-giving responsibilities pressing in upon them, and when they do choose relief over work, the benefits have never been enough, forcing them to supplement them with unreported income. Katherine Newman makes this observation in her late-twentieth-century study of low-wage workers in New York:

Rather than paint welfare and work as different worlds, it makes far more sense to describe them as two halves of a single coin, as an integrated economic system at the very bottom of our social structure. Kyesha's family is a clear example of this fusion. Her mother needs the income her working child brings into the house [from her job in a fast food restaurant]; Kyesha needs the subsidies (housing, medical care, etc.) that state aid provides to her mother. Only because the two domains are linked can this family manage to make ends meet, and then just barely.[36]

The insulting, though common, claim that poor people must be forced to work is no modern innovation. As early as 1619 the Virginia Assembly required compulsory labor from the "slothful," and there were workhouses later erected throughout the colonies. Alexander Hamilton, in his *Report on Manufactures*, urged this approach, and in 1789 he helped begin the New York Manufacturing Society, designed to reduce beggary and provide work for the "honest poor." Such organizations became a regular part of New York's charity landscape.[37]

Relief workers of the nineteenth century were willing to remove children, the elderly, the infirm, and other dependents from the home and place them in institutions so that the female caregiver could go to work, and thereby end her reliance upon public or private aid. In written reports charity agents castigated their charges for undue sentimentality when they resisted having their home broken up, resistance they often attributed to inferior cultural backgrounds. Sometimes it took months of persuasion to get women to surrender their children to institutions, many of which were so far away that mothers would not be able to visit for years. If women ultimately refused to cooperate, aid was sometimes simply cut off. Mothers resisted these efforts and fought for relief so that they could keep their family together. Further, some children were needed at home to work and supplement the family income or to supervise other children or the sick while adult women were out at work. These were nested dependencies and complex networks of support, seldom appreciated by the welfare agents.[38]

Other Dependencies

African American women have always worked, and for much of our history they have done so without compensation. As former slave Angelina Grimke Weld revealed, it is whites who have been dependent, and dependent upon blacks. She writes:

> [One mistress] told a friend of mine, that she was entirely dependent upon her for *all* her comforts; she dressed and undressed her, gave her all her food, and was so *necessary* to her that she could not do without her.[39]

Black women have historically been responsible for maintaining white households (cooking, cleaning, washing clothes, shopping), raising white children, tending to whites' animals and gardens, and serving as the unwilling sexual partners for white men.[40] It was true in mill villages, too:

> Without the services that the southern black woman provided, that system would not have worked for most mill families. She was cook, housekeeper, and surrogate mother in a home where the real mother spent most of her time in the mill. It was her job to raise and maintain a family of potential mill workers even as she was not allowed to work in the mill herself. . . . It was not uncommon for white women to be jealous of the amount of time black women spent with their children in their homes. Meanwhile, the black woman would have to struggle with the fact that she had left her own children to fend for themselves while she went off to take care of white children.[41]

Other poor women have also always worked: women's entry into the labor market is not some late-twentieth-century phenomenon, as we've seen, not merely the fruits of second-wave feminism. Poor women's work, and the work of their children, has been an essential part of family survival strategies. One native-born Brooklyn woman in the early 1900s, who took in sewing at home, described her condition:

> It's awful, but I must work else we shall get nothing to eat and be turned into the street besides. I have no time for anything but work. I must work, work, work, and work. Often we go to our beds as we left them when I haven't time

or strength to shake them up, and Joe, my husband, is too tired or sick to do it. Cooking? Oh, I cook nothing, for I haven't time; I must work. I send the little girl out to the store across the way and she gets what she can—crackers, cake, cheese, anything she can get—and I'm thankful if I can only make some fresh tea.[42]

As journalist John Spargo observed when recounting this woman's story:

Under better conditions she might have been a model housewife and mother, but it is not within the possibilities of her toil-worn, hunger-wasted body to be these and at the same time a wage-earner.[43]

This is precisely the point that Eva Feder Kittay makes when she discusses "derived dependency." It's not the dependence of children that exorcises the critics of welfare, but the dependency of their mothers: few today insist that a five-year-old should stop being so lazy and get a job, after all. Yet the mother and child are inexplicably linked, in what Kittay calls "dependency relations." This derived dependency is structural, not "characterological," she observes, because one cannot both provide the fiscal means for care and the caring itself.[44] That is, we accept the dependence of children, and this means that they need care; but the caregiver cannot both work and provide care, so the caregiver will, of necessity, be dependent as well. Kittay's insight is important, building upon what's now a fairly robust literature in what political theorists call "the ethic of care."[45] Yet New York's Edward Devine anticipated Kittay and others by nearly a century when he made this observation in 1904:

It is neither natural nor possible for a widowed mother to carry the double burden of earning an income and making a home for herself and her children; and under a social regimen in which the male head of the family is universally the normal wage-earner, it can scarcely be pauperizing to substitute for his earnings, when he is removed by death, a regular income from some suitable charitable source.[46]

Indeed, because of the vital caregiving and housekeeping role women played (and play still), Devine estimated that the death of a mother, even if she was not otherwise employed, could reduce family income by half.[47] Jane Addams understood this as well:

> I could but wonder in which particular we are most stupid—to judge a man's worth so solely by his wage-earning capacity that a good wife feels justified in leaving him, or in holding fast to that wretched delusion that a woman can both support and nurture her children.[48]

Even American charity reformer Stephen Humphreys Gurteen, as dedicated an opponent of public relief as any in the nineteenth century, identified the dilemma in this observation about the London poor, even if he did not understand the implications:

> In the large majority of such cases, the man is not the only bread-winner. The wife also has to work so as to shut out starvation and beggary. What then in the past (and not so very long ago), was a woman to do with her children during the day, while she was busy at work adding to the scant, daily income?[49]

Kwazee, while living in a shelter not too long ago, articulated it more concisely:

> Sometimes my mother couldn't get everything she needed, because she was getting us everything we needed.[50]

Cora on President Clinton, welfare reform, and time limits:

> How can he do that? Like my younger kids, he gonna put me on welfare for two years, so otherwise what you sayin' when my baby get five years old I can't get welfare no more? So what am I supposed to do? He got jobs lined up or something? 'Cause if he got some jobs lined up, and it ain't makin' like two dollars or three somethin' an hour, that'll work. But my baby require my attention. Unless they're gonna pay somebody to take care of him, you know, with the problems we have. And why not pay me? I'm his mother. They're gonna pay somebody else? They're gonna be doin' the same thing I'm doin' you know. I can do it. It seem like they're gonna pay someone else to do the same thing that I been doin'.[51]

In the wake of relief cutbacks in late-nineteenth-century Philadelphia, women were pushed off the rolls and into the labor market, just as they have been more recently. Many took jobs as live-in servants, just as others now get work as child-care providers. And so, in caring for others' homes they were rendered unable to care for their own; as a result, in the former period fully one-fourth of all charities serving women were for child care.[52] As Simon Newman tells us:

> Jane Ridley made money in one of the only ways she could, by hiring herself out as a wet nurse, while entrusting her son Alexander to another, cheaper wet nurse.[53]

Then as now, it does not count as "work" unless it enters the market.[54] But the results are clear: in American cities today, almost 50 percent of unemployed parents don't work because they choose instead to care for their families, while another quarter are unemployed due to disability or illness— in turn creating the need for others to care for them.[55] Responsibility takes many forms.[56]

As historian Jay Kleinberg contends in her history of poor women with children in the late nineteenth and early twentieth centuries:

> Constrained by their dependents' needs, women with young children had a different perspective on economic activity than single or childless women did. They considered remuneration, of course, but also evaluated a job's child-friendliness. . . . Mary Brewer, a white widow in North Carolina, wrote to the Children's Bureau for advice on avoiding the prospect outlined by her state's superintendant of public welfare. He wanted to place her two older children in a home and board the baby with relatives so she could live in as a domestic servant. The thought of putting her children in an orphanage and possibly losing all contact with them drove her to despair.[57]

Was Brewer's reluctance to work a mark of laziness and dependence? How odd it seems that such women should be castigated for their unwillingness to give over their children to the care of strangers. As Nancy Fraser and Linda Gordon have shown, dependence was not always an epithet, nor was women's failure to work always a mark of failure.[58] Note this curious entry in Amy Morris Bradley's diary, written while she was a hospital volunteer during the Civil War, after having been mistaken for paid labor:

> To think that I, *poor Amy Bradley*, would come out here to work for *money* and that, the paltry sum of twelve dollars per month and Rations! He got my opinion of him and a good many other things in very plain terms, I can assure you. He apologized wonderfully—had he known I was a volunteer, he certainly would have left me at Fortress Monroe, etc. etc. So then for twelve dollars a month a person could be sold and driven around just where the "Staff" chose—Thank God I had a higher motive than a high living & big salary.[59]

She holds her dependence as a badge of honor, and "independence" attained through wage labor as demeaning and a mark of inferiority.

Finally, we should note the ways in which adults have been dependent upon children, and the longstanding importance of child labor for poor families. Child labor has been an essential part of the household economy; up until the twentieth century it could constitute as much as one-third of all household income. In 1900, industries as diverse as cotton, mining, glassworks, cigar manufacturing, soap-powder factories, canning, and more owed no small part of their growth and profitability to the very low wages of their youngest laborers, some as young as four and five years old.[60] "What can four-year-old babies do?" asks Spargo. Here's one woman's answer:

> They are pulling basting threads so that you and I may wear cheap garments; they are arranging the petals of artificial flowers; they are sorting beads; they are pasting boxes. They do more than that. I know of a room where a dozen or more little children are seated on the floor, surrounded by barrels, and in those barrels is found human hair, matted, tangled, and blood-stained—you can imagine the condition, for it is not my hair or yours that is cut off in the hour of death.[61]

From the death of one pauper, another creates wigs for people who will meet such indignity neither in life nor in death. Most history books tell the story of the introduction of child labor laws as a humane and long-overdue intervention by government to prevent exploitation. But some households, poor and barely managing to get by, were thrown deeper into poverty, thanks to child labor and mandatory education laws, which deprived them of the income that was brought into the house by their children. In many instances, overworked women worked yet more hours just to break even.[62] Attesting once again to the blindness relief providers could display, the Society for the Prevention of Cruelty to Children would, in many cities, even remove children from the home if they were found to be begging for alms—thereby depriving an already desperate household of one of its members and the income they contributed toward the family's survival.[63] Little wonder, then, that the organization was often referred to as simply "The Cruelty."

We think of child labor as a remnant of the past, ended in the United States with the Progressives. But it continued to be a vital part of family income on into the midtwentieth century, especially in the rural South. Orphan Ruby Phillips Duncan, who eventually escaped to Las Vegas and became a leader of the local welfare rights movement in the 1960s and 1970s (see Chapter 9), could pick as much as one hundred pounds of cotton in a single day by the time she reached her early teens, but that was not enough to make her feel that she wasn't a burden to the sharecropping family members who took turns taking her in. As she tells Annelise Orleck:

I was always getting a beating because I couldn't pick enough cotton.[64]

Even today, children in some poor families provide as much as sixteen to twenty hours of household labor—labor seldom recognized as such but often vital to the survival of the family. From caring for their siblings to cooking, cleaning, shopping, and more, this work consumes much of their time and energy. And many, of course, work outside the home as well.[65] The willingness to work is not the problem, nor has it been.

5

Love:
Women and Children First

See, the people I've seen killed or hurt, it's because the other people are hurting. Inside.
It's not because you need money, or food—you got enough places to eat down here. It's
more the hurting. People downtown don't need to be fed, they need to be loved.

—Lana, 1980s

Men are the source of all happiness and all despair.

—Mary Childers, 2005

Being on welfare is not an aberrant behavior confined to the idle and undeserving poor, as myth would have it. Over the course of their lives, 65 percent of all Americans use some form of means-tested aid, which you must
be poor enough to qualify for—food stamps, Medicaid, disability income,
or cash relief.[1] Most of us will be on welfare. This makes sense, given how
widespread poverty is in the United Sates (see Epilogue). But still, of that
majority who will need public assistance, only 16 percent will receive it for
five or more consecutive years: welfare is used, as most people seem to
think it should be, as an interim measure that allows recipients to find another job, care for a sick child or parent, escape an abusive relationship, or
even care for themselves. The welfare queen remains a creature of myth.

Rethinking Responsibility

There are three potential locations for our dependence: the labor market, the family, and the state. That is, we are all dependent, to varying degrees, upon our jobs, upon our kin and community, and upon our government. Most of us can sustain failure in one of these, and sometimes even in two, but when all fail, that is when we find ourselves in profound crisis— homeless, hungry, desperate. We shouldn't, therefore, underestimate the security and reliability of a welfare check. However inadequate, its presence can be counted upon, creating security not possible if a woman depends solely upon the support of marginally employed men, or upon her own low-wage and often precarious employment. We will examine the oppressive side of relief, in which women trade "a man for the man," in welfare activist Johnnie Tillmon's apt phrase, but the point for now is a simple one, although one rarely uttered in policy debate. Welfare can make women free: free from want, if only for a time; free to raise their children; free to get a college degree; free from abusive men. Sugar Turner:

> Welfare means that there ain't no man buyin' your groceries for you. Welfare means you don't get to be married. You don't get to have successful relationships. The most successful relationship you can have is with welfare. Welfare loves you. Welfare gives your kids Christmas presents when your man won't. Welfare makes sure you eat every month. . . . Welfare doesn't cuss you out. It doesn't call you "bitch." It doesn't screw other women on the side.[2]

Women on relief are castigated for refusing to work, but as we have seen, most do work; yet for those who do not, welfare may be a means toward being a responsible parent. A caseworker in Minneapolis in the 1920s scribbled this in her report about one of her clients:

> Talked to Mrs. R about getting work. She said she is afraid to leave the children alone. The older ones all went wrong so young that she [feels she] ought to stay home with them now.[3]

Here's Darlene, speaking to the same issue many decades later:

I feel like I rationalize a lot about being on aid. Because I don't feel like I'm not a productive person. I do feel that because of this I have been a better person, and I've had more time. I think when I was not on aid, I know clearly that all I was doing was working, sleeping, and I was not giving [my son] James any attention at all. I really wasn't. . . . People who know I'm on aid will say, "Welfare's the worst thing that could have happened to black people. . . ." It's a very humiliating experience. And the shame is really inside. I don't tell people I'm on aid now. You feel like you're living down to people's expectations and you're a statistic. My father doesn't like it, being on aid. Most people just feel that you're not carrying your load in society. You know, that you're getting away with something. That everybody's taking care of you.

But, she continues:

I think I lead a really good life. I think I lead a better life than a lot of people. And I think I lead a better life than most people who are working forty hours a week because I have chosen to live with less money so that I can have more time with my kid. . . . [It] would be nice not to be looked down upon. . . . I think it would be nice if people recognized that everybody here is contributing. That I couldn't be here and not contribute.[4]

Laurel, another caseworker:

If you're flipping burgers at McDonald's and you have no money to feed your children at the end of the month, then going on welfare is a *responsible* decision.[5]

For some women, welfare is a rational, prudent choice, especially given the lack of safe, affordable child care. Kara said this in 1996:

The welfare people, you know, they look down upon you. . . . They say, "She just sitting at home having those kids and getting that welfare check. She can get a job." They don't think of it as that's the choice you made. Even though I am poor, if I did have the money and I didn't have to be on welfare, I still would choose to be at home with my kids. They wouldn't think of it as that. They would think of it as she just sitting at home. You don't have a choice really.[6]

Laura, in Florida, the year prior:

I think it's more beneficial for my family that I be home than to compromise our lives in other ways, in sending them out to be cared for by somebody else. I would rather have a system that helped people take care of their kids and take care of their kids well.[7]

Ingrid Rivera, who became a successful consultant and performance artist:

I am a lesbian, I am a mother and I was a welfare recipient for about eight years. Because I was on welfare, I was able to give birth to my daughter in a hospital. I was able to obtain an apartment. I was able to feed my daughter more than just breast milk. I was able to clothe my family, get childcare, and an education. I was able to lift myself out of poverty.[8]

Diane Dujon:

Although I am no longer dependent on a welfare check and the whims of politicians, I am now dependent on a paycheck and the whims of bosses. . . . I feel fortunate to have been on welfare because . . . I also got to know my daughter in a way that would have been impossible if I had worked full-time while she was younger.[9]

Rosemary Bray, examining the present through her own past:

I was treated to the spectacle of William Jefferson Clinton throwing a party on the White House lawn as he signed a welfare reform bill that, had it existed thirty years ago, would have guaranteed my family's dissolution. By the time I was ten years old, my mother's eligibility for welfare—as well as her children's—would have been at an end. She would have had to withdraw from us to focus on her race against time; she would have had to choose between saving us physically by earning money through workfare, and saving us psychologically, by being present and attentive in the midst of our difficult lives.[10]

Sugar Turner makes the point in a way that might even appeal to the self-interest of the middle classes:

The money I was making wasn't important enough for me to miss my kids' formative years. Those are the years that you bond. Those are the years that you instill in them the values that's hopefully gonna keep them from bein' some horrible person. Society should value that work, 'cause the son that I don't raise right is the boy that's gonna hit you in your head, steal your stereo, break in your house. You should be glad that I want to stay home, if that's what I'm doin'. There's a lot of parents that are not doin' that. And maybe they are just simply welfare leechin', but I was tryin' to raise my kids. So, no, I didn't think it [working] was a fair trade. . . . When I stopped working and got a check, I felt better not having to get my ass out in the cold, catch four buses. I felt better stayin' at home, scrubbin' my kids, makin' sure their hair was combed neatly, sending them out, being there if the school called, going to all the school programs, being able to applaud my children as they played whatever vegetable in the school play, going to be a room mother. I feel better doin' those things. I've seen it from both sides.[11]

Such decisions do not come easily for most, given the disapproval they will inevitably receive. But let's not assume too much, for there are also women like Rosa Lee, a junkie for most of her children's upbringing, who taught many of them to use drugs and who lured her daughter into prostitution. She too collected a welfare check.[12] And Sugar herself used her welfare check for drugs, when, for a time, she was a crack cocaine addict. It's complicated. One young Philadelphia man to Elijah Anderson:

I done see where four girls grow up under their mama. The mama turn around and she got a job between 3 p.m. and 11 p.m. These little kids, now they grow up like this. Mama working three to eleven o'clock at night. They kinda raise theyself. What they know? By the time they get thirteen or fourteen, they trying everything under the sun. And they ain't nobody to stop 'em. Mama gone. Can't nobody else tell 'em what to do. Hey, all of 'em pregnant by age sixteen. And they do it 'cause they wanta get out on they own. They can get they own baby, they get they own [welfare] check, they get they own apartment. They wanta get away from Mama.[13]

Sandy was on welfare for about two and a half years after she left her job to raise her first child. She reports being happier working, despite the fear and insecurity that comes with being a paycheck or two away from dire straits. She, like so many, is ambivalent about relief:

> I don't like the idea of being on welfare. It's not fun to report to the state every month. I made a mistake and got pregnant, but I wouldn't change being on welfare. It was an accident. I didn't plan it. If you're gonna give me a year [of welfare] then I'm going to be grateful for a year. But it was a mistake. I know it's not the taxpayer's fault, but should my daughter have to suffer? It's not something I really regret, and sure I think about what my life would have been like if I hadn't gotten pregnant, but I couldn't not [have Kim] [she pauses]. How could you look at her and trade her for anything?[14]

Karla from St. Louis, in the late 1980s, highlights what we know from studies of welfare: women are less likely to apply for relief if they have health care.[15]

> I do have qualifications for a lot of jobs, but they're all $3.35. And it's not worth getting a job where you have no medical or dental insurance, not if you have kids. It's not worth giving up welfare. I would work for $3.35 if they let me keep Medicaid and the food stamps, but they don't. They'll cut you off.[16]

Yet women on welfare can be a boon to their buildings and neighborhoods, making it possible for other women to work. As welfare-reliant Lynn reported to political scientist Joe Soss:

> I'm a stay-at-home mom who drives. That's a rare find. I'm on every kid I know's emergency contact for school. If I were in the workforce, too, a lot of these moms would end up losing their jobs. . . . There have to be some mothers in the neighborhood who are going to do this, or none of the mothers, even the ones who want to work, are going to be able to work.[17]

As Katherine Newman attests:

> It takes time to monitor public space. Mothers on welfare often shoulder the burden for working mothers who simply cannot be around enough to exercise vigilance. They provide an adult presence in the parks and on the side-

walks where it is most needed. Without these stay-at-home moms in the neighborhood, many a working-poor parent would have no choice but to force the kids to stay at home all day.[18]

This is the point that urbanist Jane Jacobs has made about the importance of a watchful eyes and mutual policing for a healthy, safe neighborhood.[19] And there's this interesting observation by one journalist writing about recipients in Washington, D.C.:

> Although neither mother not daughter talked about it directly, there was another difference between wages and a welfare check. Michelle spent her wages, and Mrs. Manley didn't feel she could lay down the law and claim a share of them. But in the Manleys' world, a welfare check—no matter whose name the government puts on it—is socially obligated to the household. A paycheck belongs to the person who earns it.[20]

The determination of poor women to ensure that their children are not just well taken care of, but appear so to the public, is another constant.[21] Miss M.A. Parker, in the April 1869 *American Freedman,* reported from North Carolina:

> There is one woman who supports three children and keeps them at school; she says, "I don't care how hard I has to work, if I can only sen[d] Sallie and the boys to school looking respectable."[22]

The sacrifice was not insignificant, given low wages and the high cost of clothes and books. Sonia, more recently:

> Even though I was on welfare—I ain't gonna lie—I always like my baby to wear name brand things, you know? So they could never say that they ever seen my son dirty, in bad clothes or shit, that I wasn't taking care of him.[23]

So mothers on welfare will find ways to dress their children in name-brand clothing, or spend $100 or more on a pair of sneakers. Such "indulgences" can be more than merely a struggle not to appear poor. Newman again:

[Patty] has gone without things she needs for herself so she could afford air-conditioning and a Nintendo machine, items that sound like luxuries but turn out to be the key—or at least one key—to keeping her kids indoors and safe through the hot summer months.[24]

The behavior of mothers like these is condemned by welfare critics as the wasting of scarce resources. But Sonia and Patty, in their own eyes, were behaving responsibly—one working to present her child to the world with the markings of middle-class status and responsible parenthood, the other making a rational cost-benefit analysis in which "extravagance" could purchase her children's safety and security. This is part of what makes claims that because many poor people today have televisions and air-conditioning they are not truly poor seem callous and uninformed by knowledge of the practical strain of poverty.[25]

Motherhood

Women who are branded irresponsible for being on welfare are also branded irresponsible for having children without the benefit of a husband. Welfare itself can assume some of the responsibility for poor female-headed households, given that throughout most of the life of AFDC only unmarried women were eligible; through "man in the house" and "suitable home" rules, they were forbidden to have men in their lives. As Rosemary Bray said, "On welfare, my mother joined the ranks of the unskilled women who found the state more reliable than their husbands." She explains:

Mama found an autonomy denied her by my father. It was she who could decide, at last, some part of her own fate and ours. A.F.D.C. relegated marginally productive men like my father to the ranks of failed patriarchs who no longer controlled the destiny of their families. Like so many of his peers, he could no longer afford the luxury of a woman who did as she was told because her economic life depended on it. Daddy became one of the shadow men who walked out back doors as caseworkers came in through the front. Why did he acquiesce? For all his anger, for all his frightening brutality, he loved us, so much that he swallowed his pride and periodically ceased to exist so that we might survive.[26]

When we take a closer look at poor women's beliefs about the importance of having children, and the potential harm that can come to them at the hands of men, it is difficult once again to dismiss their behavior as irresponsible or irrational. As one young woman told Robert Coles in the early 1960s:

> To me, having a baby inside me is the only time I'm really alive. I know I can make something, do something, no matter what color my skin is, and what names people call me. When the baby gets born I see him, and he's full of life, or she is; and I think to myself that it doesn't make any difference what happens later, at least now we've got a chance, or the baby does. You can see the little one grow and get larger and start doing things, and you feel there must be some hope, some chance that things will get better. . . . They tell you we are "neglectful"; we don't take proper care of the children. But that's a lie, because we do, until we can't any longer, because the time has come for the street to claim them. To take them away and teach them what a poor nigger's life is like.[27]

Sociologists Kathryn Edin and Maria Kefalas's interviews with 162 poor Philadelphia women reveal that they "judged children to be a necessity," while marriage was a "luxury," something they hoped for but did not believe they could or should rely upon. The delay of marriage has many causes, but these women, having (accurately) concluded that most marriages will not be permanent, wanted to achieve some economic independence for themselves and their children before marrying. Contrary to the conventional wisdom, it is not lack of respect for the institution of marriage that accounts for lower marriage rates among poor women, but instead a near reverence for it and a concomitant disdain for divorce.[28] This may help to explain why so many are particularly disapproving of marriages entered into solely as the result of a pregnancy. And to suggest that marriage alone could serve as a solution to the poverty of poor women is illogical. As Barbara Ehrenreich wryly observed in 1986, if we are to eliminate poverty in African American families, one husband—given the likely earnings power of a black male—will be grossly insufficient. But four husbands might be enough, by her calculations.[29] This is the reality that poor women understand—marriage is not necessarily a solution, and for too many it merely creates new problems.

Again and again, poor women identify their children as the best part of their lives, not, as many others would have it, as a mistake and burden that limits their opportunities or their ability to be "independent."[30] For many, the birth of their first child, the new demands made of them, and the profound obligation they felt had the effect of "bring[ing] order out of chaos." The emotional need that children fill was also a common refrain. Aliya reported to Edin and Kefalas:

The way I was raised, [with] so much violence and confusion going on around me, I just wanted to love somebody.[31]

As they write:

This does not mean we accept at face value that these mothers are right when they say they are better off having had their children when they did. Some could probably have benefited from waiting. . . . [But] before we dismiss their claims about the redemptive value of children, however, we should contrast their lives to those of their male counterparts, who do not usually bear the primary responsibility for their children. By any measure, the behaviors of men who populate these neighborhoods are considerably worse than those of the women. We simply do not know what these mothers' lives would be like without the responsibility for children, and the sense of identity, purpose, connection, or demand for order that it brings. . . . These women put motherhood before marriage not primarily out of welfare opportunism, a lack of discipline, or sheer resignation. Rather, the choice to mother in the context of personal difficulty is an affirmation of their strength, determination, and desire to care for another. In the end, establishing the primordial bonds of love and connection is the ultimate goal of mothering.[32]

Among those they spoke with, adoption was dismissed virtually out of hand, which is not surprising given the centrality of motherhood to their conception of a full life. These women consistently reported disapproving of abortion unless circumstances were truly dire—and, indeed, more affluent teens are more likely to terminate an unplanned pregnancy than poor ones are, although this may not reflect their desires, but rather their relative ability to get access to or afford abortions.[33] But the reluctance to resort to abortion is surely not an unmitigated good. In a memoir about

being raised poor and white in the Bronx with six siblings in the 1960s by
her alcoholic mother, Mary Childers recounts this event:

> After ceremoniously turning off the television, Mom tells us in a hushed,
> trembling voice that she's not sick with the flu. She's pregnant. Concerned
> about her poor health, the doctor hinted he could grant a medical abortion
> to protect her life. But no, she couldn't kill a baby. Joan and Alice hug and kiss
> her as if this is glorious news; I tighten my fists. "Abortion, abortion!" I urge
> them all. "We can't have another baby. There's no room. I can tell you now,
> I'm not helping with another baby." I break down and plead, but they ignore
> me. "You're the meanest eleven-year-old alive," Lacey chides me later. "Mom
> is having a baby and that's that." That's that. Mom is sick all the time and yells
> at me that I care more about those retarded girls [I tutor for pay] than my own
> family. I taunt back: "I care about providing for myself instead of asking wel-
> fare or drunken men for money." I will never forgive my mother for balling yet
> another hit and run father. For the first time in my life, Lacey slaps me in the
> face; she doesn't approve of me saying Mom is like a fire hydrant male dogs
> piss all over before completing their business and trotting off. Furious, during
> class I scribble curses and doodle images of devils and demons in my school
> notebooks. Keening with shame, I no longer wonder why people hiss the word
> *welfare* and landlords deny us apartments. We are an infestation.[34]

The birth of an unwanted child into a poor and fragile family can seem
an unmanageable crisis. Each instance of a newborn found in a Dumpster
works its way into the headlines of our local newspapers and television
broadcasts. Too often, such ugly instances serve as jumping-off points for
tirades about the decay of our modern culture or the social disorganization and moral rot of our cities. But these awful acts are not innovations of
the modern world. Women in seventeenth-century Massachusetts were in-
dicted for infanticide at twice the rate of Londoners, at least three women
in Philadelphia alone were hanged for the offense in the mideighteenth
century, and during the Victorian era it was not uncommon for there to be
significant expression of sympathy for the accused, given the trials and rig-
ors of childbirth and child-rearing. Infanticide rose during periods of economic crisis.[35] Eliza Rafferty strangled her newborn alive in 1849, as the
Herald breathlessly reported,[36] while others were abandoned, although
never in numbers so great as they were in the public imagination or mer-

ited by the attention of the press. Then, as now, the desperately poor could think of an unwanted pregnancy as a danger to the household, whose budgets would break with another mouth to feed. This is not to suggest that infanticide constitutes just another decision about managing scarce resources. But we might wonder just how dire a life in the United States must be to be driven to such deeds, ones we would prefer to consign to Greek tragedy. We might also note, as anthropologist Thomas Crist reports, that "by the 1920s, indictments for infanticide had all but disappeared, the result of better living standards, increased wages, and greater access to health care for women of all economic levels."[37]

As to the charge that being on welfare encourages out-of-wedlock childbearing, the social science evidence on the subject is clear—there is no relationship between the two.[38] We can note that nonmarital childbearing has increased for all women, not just those on welfare; that nations with more generous welfare benefits have lower rates of teen pregnancy and out-of-wedlock childbirth; that during the late twentieth century, when nonmarital births were rising, the value of welfare benefits was declining; and that welfare recipients have no more children, on average, than other women do.[39] Poor women treat the very notion with disdain. Here is Tara speaking to Cheri, both of the Kensington Welfare Rights Union:

[Former Speaker of the House] Newt Gingrich has the nerve to say a young girl is going to deliberately get pregnant so she can get a bigger welfare check. . . . Puhleeze. He thinks I'm gonna have a kid just for the lousy extra hundred dollars every two weeks, or whatever it is? I hate to burst Newt's bubble, but people don't think that way. Does he really think a young girl is going to say: I'm gonna have a baby and put myself deeper into poverty for the next eighteen years? And Congress—it doesn't want to pay for welfare, but it won't pay for abortions either. So what they're saying is: If you get pregnant, you better have that baby—and raise it in poverty because we won't pay to help it.[40]

There are exceptions, as there always are. Here's Sugar Turner again:

Goin' on welfare is what you do. It's like, there's money for you, go get it. You lay down with the man, you done got pregnant, you goin' to have a baby, you might as well get a check. It's almost like a bonus. . . . There's no shame.

You just go get welfare. Nobody would look down on you for going to get welfare. You'd be more ashamed not to!

But even she dismisses the idea that women get pregnant in order to receive a check:

White people think you're having more kids to get more welfare. You don't do that. You just have babies 'cause you like 'em. They're fresh, they're pretty. They give you something to do all day. Give you something to show off. I mean, if you got one baby and you're on welfare and your house is clean, people just say that she keeps a nice house. It's not that hard to take care of one kid. But the girl with five! Hey, if you've got five, you're doin' somethin'! You are a helluva woman! You are a helluva girl! So that's somethin'.[41]

But it's not easy. Tonya Mitchell:

My first recognition of the stigma that poor single mothers face came with my initial visit to the welfare office in my third month of pregnancy when I applied to receive medical benefits. Racism was rampant in the county office: As I approached the reception desk, a clerk looked at my small, brown, and still not showing body and bitterly remarked, "Pregnant, I suppose!" From there, it went downhill. During my screening, the caseworker sarcastically stated, "I suppose you don't know who the daddy is"; stifled a laugh when I said I planned to finish my GED and go on to college; and glared at me when I told him that I refused to have my teachers—who did not yet know I was pregnant—sign notes for the welfare office stating that I was still in school and in good standing. To be frank, I was shocked. I had always known and hated racism when I saw and experienced it, but this was something more. It was racism mixed with the sense that someone had the right to hate me, to laugh at me, to disrespect me openly and blatantly because I was black and poor, because I was pregnant, and because I was alone.[42]

There is a habit among certain social critics to argue in abstractions about the moral and immoral behavior of others, and to ignore the actual conditions poor and marginalized Americans have faced and continue to face. Many condemn poor women (and especially poor black women) for

bearing children out of wedlock. But too often these are the same comfortable observers who, in the guise of a war on crime, have worked to fill
our federal prisons with poor black men, the majority of whom are serving
time for nonviolent drug offenses.[43] If they truly sought to create opportunities for poor women to raise children in two-parent households, they
might seek an end to policies that systematically strip our poorest neighborhood of men.

Fathers

When we turn to the men in this complicated equation, we can see even
more clearly that the motivation of poor parents is not welfare, but forces
more powerful, and more deeply human. As David Simon and Edward
Burns wrote in *The Corner*:

> As for baby-making—that would be almost welcome as the final proof of man-
> hood. A fatalistic streak in [sixteen-year-old] DeAndre and the rest of his crew
> holds that they'll soon enough be dead or in prison. Against that notion, the
> production of a child, a male child in particular, would guarantee some tan-
> gible evidence of a brief existence. . . . It's not the lure of check-day that pro-
> vokes these children to make children; something stronger than a couple
> hundred dollars is at issue, something that goes to the heart of the matter.
> Check or no check, the babies will come.[44]

They add:

> For the girls—but never for the boys—life actually changes when the child
> arrives.[45]

And it's freedom from men that is a central feature of relief made available to women with children. Monica:

> What does he do for me? He's in jail, I have two kids, I'm raising them, I'm
> working, I'm doing this, I'm doing that. What was his *purpose*? I started think-
> ing, "I don't need him." He was just like an extra burden. It was actually easier
> without him.[46]

In listening to poor women's accounts of their lives before, during, and after welfare, a pattern emerges: almost all of them report abuse by men—some as children, subject to physical and sexual violence from fathers, brothers, uncles, family friends, and neighbors; almost all as adults, from husbands and boyfriends.[47] We know that "abused women [are] five times more likely to attempt suicide, fifteen times more likely to abuse alcohol, nine times more likely to abuse drugs, and three times more likely to be diagnosed as depressed or psychotic."[48] While about 6 percent of households nationwide are sites of domestic violence, the number is likely between 20 and 30 percent for households containing women receiving welfare. As many as two-thirds of all recipients are current or former victims of domestic violence. Women on welfare experience violence in the home at rates three times that of women not on the rolls; as a result, many pregnancies of poor and welfare-reliant women may not be by choice, but because of rape.[49] One estimate by the New York Coalition for the Homeless suggests that as many as half of all homeless mothers have histories of abuse.[50]

Women are more likely to leave an abusive relationship if they have a source of income.[51] Carol, who was beaten by her husband, told psychologist and researcher Virginia Schein a fairly typical tale:

> I just dealt with it until I decided I wasn't going to deal with it anymore. When my son was about seven months old I came back here. I got an apartment, went on welfare, and took care of my kid. I was seventeen years old. When I got married I intended it to be forever, but it didn't work out that way.[52]

Ehrenreich described a friend and welfare recipient:

> Lori is no more demoralized by welfare than I am by an unexpected royalty check. True, she resents the days spent in the welfare office, the long waits, the interrogations about her limited inventory of household possessions. But she feels that she and her daughter have rights in the matter, like the right to a standard of living on some level exceeding vagrancy. She was not always, she will tell you, so assertive—certainly not in the two years when she was married to a man who routinely beat her and had once chased her around the house with a gun. Only welfare made it possible to leave him, a move she says was like being born again, "as a human being this time."[53]

Yet Bernice comes to the conclusion that welfare exacerbated her abuse:

> As a welfare recipient, I knew that society didn't accept me. I was in a different total class. An untouchable class. Women on welfare know that they are an untouchable class, that is how they are seen. Because they are already suppressed by being on welfare, these women are already there. All the abusers have to do is maintain the situation. We have nothing, and we don't know how to stand up for ourselves. That is why abusers encourage welfare usage. With welfare, you are being given something, but that something really stigmatizes you in society. That stigma lowers your self-esteem and keeps you in line.[54]

Jody Raphael suggests that fostering addictive behavior, sabotaging employment, and even keeping a woman pregnant all constitute ways used by men "to imprison her at home,"[55] One client, discussing her boyfriend to her caseworker:

> You know, I think he likes the fact that I use drugs because he knows I won't go anywhere. He has even supplied me to keep me from leaving.[56]

Bernice on Billy:

> Whenever I opened a door in my life, he wanted to close it.[57]

As one man told a Florida reporter in 1997:

> I didn't want her to succeed. I didn't want her to see a better life. If she sees a better life, she'll know she doesn't need me.[58]

And indeed, some studies have shown that poor women who live with their boyfriends were more likely to drop out of school. Moreover, "to keep them in line their abusers often threaten to call the welfare department to report their own illegal presence and financial support in the women's lives."[59] As Raphael also asks, is it not more likely that these factors explain the choices made by poor women better than so-called culture-of-poverty notions?[60]

The households in Beverly Stadum's study of relief applicants from 1900 to 1930 are also ones in which addicted, philandering, and abusive men are common, men whose presence, as often as not, is deemed by women to be more harmful than beneficial; sometimes even by caseworkers who usually sought to enforce a "traditional" family structure—even they could see that a two-parent home was not always the best solution.[61] Finally, as Raphael writes:

> The presence of abusers in the lives of large percentages of women on welfare means that we need to seriously rethink conventional wisdom about the large numbers of single mothers supposedly raising their children without the presence of a male.[62]

Sex, Power, Poverty

Throughout American history, relief policy has been obsessed with the sexual and reproductive behavior of poor women, if not always in a consistent or coherent fashion. Some of this might be traced back to English Parson Thomas Malthus and his fear that the unchecked reproduction of the lower classes would lead to scarcity in the food supply. Malthus had a profound influence on the English Poor Law of 1834 (which sought to end cash relief and provide aid only in the workhouse) and, by extension, on ours.[63] Much of his line of argument was adopted by the morality-minded reformers of the Gilded Age, like Josephine Shaw Lowell:

> While the acknowledgment is made that every person born into a civilized community has a right to live, yet the community has the right to say that incompetent and dangerous persons shall not, so far as can be helped, be born to acquire this right to live upon others. To prevent a constant and alarming increase of these two classes of persons, the only way is for the community to refuse to support any except those whom it can control—that is, except those who will submit themselves to discipline and coercion.[64]

It became common again with late-twentieth-century welfare opponents such as George Gilder and Newt Gingrich, among others, taking eugenicist and racist form with Charles Murray and Richard Herrnstein's *The Bell Curve*.[65] Here's how Robert Rector expressed the need to control poor women:

True charity begins by requiring responsible behavior from the beneficiary as a condition of receiving aid. True charity seeks to generate in the recipient the virtues, commitment, and self-discipline necessary for success in society, rather than passively subsidizing ever-escalating levels of social pathology.[66]

These too are old ideas. In colonial cities, relief applicants often had to prove their moral fitness by presenting a reference from a freeholder, just as one Delta woman noted at the end of the 1960s:

In November when they start qualifying you for commodities, they say you got to find out how many people you worked for and get them to sign for you as being poor. If they don't feel like signing . . . you don't get commodities.[67]

When Quakers opened an almshouse in 1713, many years before the first public one, it was available only to their own members who could pass a character test.[68] Under ADC and later AFDC, similar standards of "moral fitness" were required of applicants. Between 1949 and 1960, twenty-two American states imposed "employable mother," "suitable home," "man in the house," and other policies to restrict access to benefits.[69] The Supreme Court struck down such laws in the 1960s, but caseworkers continued to choose among those applicants who comported to their idea of moral rectitude, as they still do.[70] Many states, in the pre-TANF period of welfare experimentation, sought to pass legislation requiring that welfare recipients agree to subcutaneous birth control implants, like Norplant or Depo-Provera. None ultimately succeeded. But welfare reform did, once again, attend to issues of reproduction: the 1996 Personal Responsibility and Work Opportunity Reconciliation Act allows states to refuse to increase aid if new babies were born while their mother was already receiving benefits; allows reductions of as much as 25 percent if a recipient will not identify the biological father of her children to relief authorities; set aside some $500 million for abstinence education programs; and made cash bonuses available to states that most reduced out-of-wedlock births without increasing their abortion rates.

Some practices have been worse. In November 1934, Martha Bruere reported to Harry Hopkins what the welfare commissioner of Jamestown, New York, had to say on the subject of relief recipients and motherhood:

That families on relief should continue to bring children into the world, particularly irks him. He thinks the doctors should do something about this. It is rumored that he gave orders to have such maternity cases as came to the hospital on relief, sterilized to prevent further additions to the relief load.[71]

Reports of forced sterilization are not unusual. In California in 1966, Nancy Hernandez, mother of two and a welfare recipient, pled guilty to "being in a room where marijuana was present." She was given the following choice by Judge Frank Kearney: be sterilized or serve a six-month jail term. "It seemed to me," said the judge, "she should not have more children because of her propensity to live an immoral life." Even in overruling Judge Kearney, the appeals court expressed sympathy with his position and the frustrations of "law-abiding taxpayers." While it was unusual for the courts to be involved in such matters, it was not unusual for women on welfare to be encouraged—subtly or with direct threats—to undergo sterilization. Hernandez initially agreed to the judge's recommendation for sterilization because, as she put it, "I didn't want to go to jail and leave my children."[72]

In the 1970s the General Accounting Office revealed that large numbers of Native American women had been sterilized against their will at the hands of the Indian Health Service and other governmental agencies.[73] In the 1960s and 1970s, as many as 25 percent or more of Native women between the ages of 15 and 44 were sterilized; it was possibly as many as 50 percent between 1970 and 1976. Many gave their "consent" while under anesthesia, during labor, or under threat of losing their children or their welfare benefits.[74] At about the same time such practices came to light, writes David Sink, Senate hearings showed "that the removal of Indian children from their natural families to non-Indian foster or adoptive homes was pervasive and systematic."[75]

This is from testimony in 1973 before a Senate committee by the general counsel of the Southern Poverty Law Center. He represented Mary Alice and Minnie Relf, two Montgomery, Alabama, girls, ages twelve and fourteen, respectively, who lived with their parents in public housing and were sterilized without the informed consent of the girls or their parents:

In order to begin to understand why it happened to these children, I think one must examine the social services system under which they and their families exist. They receive $156 per month from the Alabama Department of Pensions and Security [welfare]; they receive food stamps; they receive subsidized medical assistance; and, I suppose, there are other forms of aid unknown to me at this time. In other words, each member of this family lives his or her existence under a microscope. They are visited on an almost weekly basis by some social service person. . . . They are surrounded by a welfare state upon which they depend for their very existence, and they are easily "coerced" into doing what the welfare people recommend to them. It is a very sophisticated, probably unintentional, form of coercion, but it is extremely effective.

As Niel Ruth Cox told that subcommittee:

When the welfare caseworker found out I was pregnant, she told my mother that if we wanted to keep getting welfare, I'd have to have my tubes tied—temporarily.

She eventually realized—after the operation—that it was, of course, not temporary:

I know now that I was sterilized because I was from a welfare family.[76]

In 1964, Mississippi passed what the Student Nonviolent Coordinating Committee (SNCC) called the "genocide bill," which made it a felony to bear a second illegitimate child, carrying a penalty of up to three years in prison. An original provision, stripped out before passage, offered sterilization in lieu of incarceration.[77]

But as another reminder that we should not expect public policies to be either consistent or rational, in other locales in the South during the same period, black women had difficulty finding doctors who would perform tubal ligations (and those who would required a husband's permission) or prescribe birth control (even after *Griswold v. Connecticut* made contraception legal for married women). Some white doctors, perhaps sympathetic to plantation owners' desire for abundant, cheap labor, encouraged black women to bear many children, and others even prescribed sexual activity to preteen girls "as a way of keeping fit."[78] As Orleck reports, in the early 1960s:

In Chicago, single women who had babies while on AFDC were threatened with jail time, but caseworkers were prohibited from sending them to Planned Parenthood clinics that dispensed free contraceptives.[79]

Shirley Chisholm, the first black woman to be a member of the U.S. Congress, called it "compulsory pregnancy" for poor women.[80] And yet, by the early 1930s the forced sterilization of the "unfit" and the "feeble-minded" had been expressly permitted in thirty states, and twenty-two states still had such laws on the books in 1973.[81] Perhaps this reveals a national cognitive dissonance regarding black women: their fertility is, on the one hand, a perceived threat to the public purse and to white domination, yet their ample reproduction can help the continued production of a cheap, docile labor force.

As with so much, debates about birth control take many forms. A 1968 statement by the Black Unity Party of Peekskill, New York:

The Brothers are calling on the Sisters not to take the pill. It is this system's method of exterminating black people here and abroad. To take the pill means that we are contributing to our own GENOCIDE. However, in not taking the pill, we must have a new sense of value. When we produce children, we are aiding the REVOLUTION in the form of NATION building. Our children must have pride in their history, in their heritage, in their beauty. Our children must not be brainwashed as we were. PROCREATION is beautiful, especially if we are devoted to the Revolution which means that our value system be altered to include the Revolution as responsibility. A good deal of the Supremacist (White) efforts to sterilize the world's (Non-whites) out of existence is turning toward the black people of America. New trends in Race Control have led the architects of GENOCIDE to believe that Sterilization projects aimed at the black man in the United States can cure American internal troubles. Under the cover of an alleged campaign to "alleviate poverty," white supremacist Americans and their dupes are pushing an all-out drive to put rigid birth control measures into every black home. No such drive exists within the White American world. In some cities, Peekskill, Harlem, Mississippi and Alabama, welfare boards are doing their best to force black women receiving aid to submit to Sterilization. This disguised attack on black future generations is rapidly picking up popularity among determined genocidal engineers. This country is prepared to exterminate people by the pill or by the bomb; therefore, we must draw strength from ourselves. You see why there is a Family Planning Office in the Black Community of Peekskill.

Here is the reply, from Patricia Harden (welfare recipient), Rita Van Lew (welfare recipient), Sue Rudolph (housewife), Catherine Hoyt (grandmother), Joyce Hoyt (domestic), and Patricia Robinson (housewife and psychotherapist):

Dear Brothers: Poor black sisters decide for themselves whether to have a baby or not to have a baby. If we take the pills or practice birth control in other ways, it [is] because of poor black men. Now, here's how it is. Poor black men won't support their families, won't stick by their women—all they think about is the street, dope and liquor, women, a piece of ass, and their cars. That's all that counts. Poor black women would be fools to sit up in the house with a whole lot of children and eventually go crazy, sick, heartbroken, no place to go, no sign of affection—nothing. Middle-class white men have always done this to their women—only more sophisticated-like. So when whitey put out the pill and poor black sisters spread the word, we saw how simple it was not to be a fool for men any more (politically we would say that men could no longer exploit us sexually or for money and leave the babies with us to bring up). That was the first step in our waking up! Black women have always been told by black men that we were black, ugly, evil, bitches and whores—in other words, we were the real niggers in this society—oppressed by whites, male and female, and the black man, too. Now a lot of the black brothers are into a new bag. Black women are being asked by militant black brothers not to practice birth control because it is a form of whitey committing genocide on black people. Well, true enough, but it takes two to practice genocide and black women are able to decide for themselves, just like poor people all over the world, whether they will submit to genocide. For us, birth control is freedom to fight genocide of black women and children. Like the Vietnamese have decided to fight genocide, the South American poor are beginning to fight back, and the African poor will fight back, too. Poor black women in the U.S. have to fight back out of our own experience of oppression. Having too many babies stops us from supporting our children, teaching them the truth or stopping the brainwashing as you say, and fighting black men who still want to use and exploit us. But we don't think you are going to understand us because you are a bunch of little middle class people and we are poor black women. The middle class never understands the poor because they always need to use them as you want to use poor black women's children to gain power for yourself. You'll run the black community with your kind of black power—you on top![82]

Children

Just as some have used the poorhouse to their own advantage, so have others used foster care, adoption, and the orphanage, surrendering their children, if only for short periods of time, because it was the best of the bad options. The reasons for giving up a child were varied, but most boiled down to the inability to afford them, especially young ones who could not themselves contribute to the household income. A note to accompany a baby abandoned around 1862 to the Charleston Foundling Hospital read, simply:

Alice
not christened
Poverty the Cause.[83]

As Mary Van Allen wrote to an orphan asylum in early 1884:

i have got a little boy . . . and i want to no if you will take him there for a while for me. it takes every cent i can earn to board him and i cant keep him half clothed let alone my self and not a soul to help me to one pennys worth and i think it is pretty tough. if you will keep him for a few years till i could get something ahead and could i get him back again all right. if so i should like very much to send him.[84]

Barbara de Nike, who spent much of the World War II searching for an affordable place to live with her son and daughter, notes that one winter:

My little girl got pneumonia and I had to put her in the hospital. I left her in as long as I could so she'd have a warm place, but finally they just said I had to take her home.

Later, determined to be with her husband during his short leave in Portland, Oregon, and without the means to take her children and no other place to leave them:

> A friend of mine said he could arrange to have them kept in a Catholic orphanage in Syracuse. So I put them in the orphanage and took the train to Portland.

Upon returning:

> I left the children in the orphanage while I looked for a place to stay. Finally, the sister at the orphanage said, "Don't come again to visit them until you can take them." It was just too confusing.

She did reclaim them not long after, to bring them to meet her husband's ship, this time in Charleston, South Carolina. At a stop on the way:

> In the middle of dinner all of a sudden my son burst into tears. "What's the matter," I asked. "I want to go home," he said, but he didn't know where he meant and I didn't know where he meant. . . . He didn't know where he belonged anymore.[85]

But the option of using the orphanage in this way could be limited, since in some locales a male signature was required if a child was to be admitted.[86] Some orphanages tried to discourage such practices by requiring that parents permanently abdicate their legal right to their children, which also eased the way toward the children's indenture.[87] Some parents paid fees to the orphanage for the care of their children; the rest were supported by public funds. This is an 1885 exchange between widower William Cowan and asylum director Albert Fuller. Cowan:

> i am a man that has lost my wife and I have a little boy that is six years old. he is smart and lurns well at school. i would like to get a good home for him a year or to. i am willing to pay for him for it. . . . i can not keep him and tend to my work to. So can you take him for i want him ware he can go to school and have good care. if you can take him, in your ancear state the price a week that you will charge and if you cant take him pleese inform mee of a home,

but I would like to get him in albany for it is not far a way to come see him. So pleese oblige.

Fuller responds:

Dear Sir: Your favor of this date is just in hand and contents noted. If your child is healthy we will take it if you desire to send it to us. You can bring him any Thursday. Our regular charges are $1.75 per week but will give you the benefit of our special rate which is $1.50 per week or an average of $6.50 per month payments to be made monthly in advance. Our institution is very full just now (over three hundred and twenty children) and if you decide to send your child please let us know at once so that we can retain a place for him. Our location is pleasant and also very healthy as is shown by the fact that notwithstanding our large family we have had but one death in over two years. I enclose a print of one of our dormitories which will give you a little idea of the rooms.

The records Judith Dulberger uncovered from the Albany Orphan Asylum in the 1880s and 1890s are filled with letters from parents explaining why they sent so little, or nothing, or why payments were late, detailing their struggles to help support their children. There seems no evidence that Fuller returned children to parents who were unable to pay; instead he sought support from his town overseers, and asked parents to approach their local poor officials and ask for money to be sent for their children.[88] This was a public-private venture in ways that are common to American relief practice. Not so typical, the letters reproduced in Dulberger's account reveal an unusually benign and benevolent institution—much of that likely because of Fuller himself; indeed, shortly after his death, the orphanage began its decline.

As with many "orphan" asylums, nearly half of the children there had two parents, and almost half again had one surviving parent. Few residents were true orphans. Most were American-born, Protestant, and white, although a spattering of Catholics and blacks could be found. A study in 1889 showed that as many as one in one hundred children in New York State and one in thirty-five in New York City could expect to spend a portion of his or her life in an institution.[89] While by 1883 there were over 350 orphanages in the United States, 276 of them would not accept African

American children (and nine were exclusively for black girls and boys); by 1933, there were more orphanages overall, but fewer of them accepted children of color, although well into the first decades of the twentieth century poor African American children were "placed out" in white homes, often living not as members of the family but as unpaid servants, denied access to education and medical care, and sleeping in a shed or on the kitchen floor. S.J. Kleinberg called it "state-sponsored neglect." It would not be until the 1960s that black children and families had access to children's institutions in significant numbers.[90]

Many parents feared that their institutionalized children would be indentured and sent far away to work. Here a letter to the Albany asylum from Mrs. Hal Rowley:

> I hope you will pardon me for writing you a few words in ragard to my lettle gril that I have sand to you by Mr Cook our poor master. I hard last week that you was going to give her away to some boday. of [course] I give you my garil to breng her houp as a good gril for I could [not] see to her my self for I had to work but if you are going to give her to [someone] else I wish you would not for I would rather Pay you some thing and have you ceps her for me ontell nex Spring for now I am laft a lone. my husband [he is] crazey and gone to the crazey house and I have [two] bebys with me, one I give [to] his [folks] and the beby I have with me and I am vary poor and I am not in vary good halth but I have to work and if you will [keep] my gril for me ontell nex spring then she be old anough to takir of the beby and let me work by the day. you know it is hard for a mother to part with her chardren but god sand me the bad lock and I [must find no fault] for he is our master. he [knows] what he doset for.

Her daughter hadn't been indentured, but the superintendent did not rule out the possibility, merely promising that she would be placed in a good home.[91] Not all indentures—we might call them adoptions, today—were to the adoptive parents' liking. Here's a letter of complaint sent to one orphanage:

> We all [a]long were greatly in hope that [Ella Brown] would be just the child which we would want, and therefore have reported the bright side of her life here, but am now a little afraid she will not answer our purposes. 1st her eyes seem to be quite weak; 2nd She is very selfish; 3rd Procrastination seems to

predominate; 4th She has no taste for learning and prefering to sit idle with her hands in her lap rather than taking a book to study; 5th is gifted with a peculiar temper which is not loveable and which she for the last week or more has liked to show.[92]

While the stay for many was for a few years, there were exceptions, as Dulberger reports:

> Katy Bertha spent nearly fifteen years at the Albany Orphan Asylum. Six days before her eighteenth birthday the asylum discharged her to the care of the same poorhouse in which she had been born.

Rose Schneiderman, writing in 1905 of the heavy load she bore while her mother worked her eleven-hour day, remembers:

> I was finally released by my little sister being taken by an aunt, and the two boys going to the Hebrew Orphan Asylum, which is a splendid institution, and turns out good men. One of these brothers is now a student in the City College, and the other is a page in the Stock Exchange.

Notice that Rose talks of the orphanage as if it were a boarding school.[93] Similarly, New York's juvenile hall—the House of Refuge—was used by residents perhaps as much as it was used to control them: historian Christine Stansell posits that as many as half the children confined in the first decades of the nineteenth century were there not for a public crime, but a private one—sent by their parents as a means of discipline or as a way to relieve the family, if only for a time, of the cost of their care.[94] The length of their incarceration varied, though many were invited to return home only when old enough to work or care for their younger siblings.

There were options for poor families other than the poorhouse or the orphanage. In 1854 Charles Loring Brace began his "orphan trains," which sent city children away to live in less urban climes. The practice continued until 1929, with about 250,000 children and teens placed by Brace and other agencies. As with those in orphanages, fewer than half were full orphans, and one in four had two living parents. Most went to the West or Midwest, yet New York received more of Brace's wards than any other state. Some were sent south, replacing the labor of newly emancipated slaves. "In the early days," reports Stephen O'Connor, "the society's agents tended to be very casual in both the acquisition and dispersal of their charges" to their new "parents" or "employers" (it was no secret that many families agreed to take in an "orphan" out of need for cheap labor on the farm). On the very first trip of Brace's Children's Aid Society, one agent simply "gave one of the little boys to a woman from Rochester who thought her sister would like to take him in." Writes O'Connor:

> For the farmers, it was just another way of getting needed labor; for poor parents, it was just another place to park children during hard times; and for the older teenagers at least, it was just another employment service.[95]

Brace described the process in 1876:

> Public notice is given, some weeks beforehand, that a company of orphans and homeless children from New York will come there on a given day. The farmers gather from the country for miles around. The little company of unfortunates, under charge of an experienced agent, are billeted around among the families of the village, fed and washed, and then appear in the town hall or whatever place has been selected for the meeting. Here the agent, advised by some of the citizens, forms a committee of some of the leading men present. This committee decides upon the applications, on consultation of the agent. After a few hours' labor, each child is placed in a home, and it usually happens that these homes are the best in the country 'round. The employers agree to send the children to school in the winter, and of course to treat them kindly. Beyond that, there is no agreement and no indentures are made out. The relation is left much to the good feeling of both parties.[96]

One sample by Clay Gish of 432 case records from 1853 to 1890 showed that 55 percent were young men seeking work and using the society to help them. Most of the young men left their placements within a year to take better-paying work, to move to better living conditions, or to return home.[97]

As so many have before and after, they proved that to be poor does not mean that one is passive or powerless.

6

Respect:
The Price of Relief

When government . . . hands out something of value . . . government's power grows forthwith; it automatically gains such power as is necessary and proper to supervise its largesse.

—Charles Reich, 1964

When you are on welfare, you know you are a parasite, living on the taxes of reluctant people who wish you didn't exist. Having made so many bad choices, having done things that her early upbringing in a Catholic orphanage and in foster homes branded her for in her own mind, my mother recognized herself in the disparaging characterizations of welfare mothers; she looked in the mirror and saw an image that deserved public disdain. In that completely understandable act of capitulation, she further diminished the notion of herself as an active citizen. The very public discourse that could address the problems of the welfare system today tells women and children that they are the problem. This identity, when it is shamefully internalized by people already weakened by want and danger, this acceptance of one's own worthlessness, is much more responsible for the cycle of dependency than the causes so often cited by the Right.

—Mary Childers, 1997

To be poor is to be subject utterly to the agents of the law. . . . Middle-class people have rights and they like to think that everyone does. The rich, of course, know that rights are bought and sold, and the poor know it too. Those between them live in an illusion.

—Lars Eighner, 1993

The claim that government efforts to alleviate poverty inevitably fail, or even make it worse, are as unfounded now as they always have been. That's not to say that all relief programs are efficient or effective, but the suggestion that government itself is the problem is political propaganda, not policy analysis. For example, one 2005 study examined the effects of the American safety net programs such as food stamps, Medicaid and Medicare, the Earned Income Tax Credit (EITC), Social Security, and unemployment insurance; it found that together these programs lifted some 27 million Americans above the official poverty line, cutting the rate in half. The EITC, which is available only to those who work, now raises more children out of poverty than any other program (and consumes more of our relief budget than Temporary Assistance to Needy Families, our traditional welfare program, which succeeded AFDC). Social Security and other programs reduce the poverty of the elderly by 80 percent, not eliminating it, but coming closer than for any other group. Medicare, Medicaid, and state-level children's health insurance programs reach some 40 million Americans each month and have had measurable effects on reducing infant and child mortality and increasing poor women's access to screenings for cervical and breast cancer, among other things. These government-run health programs provide care at a lower per-person cost, with lower administrative expenses, than private insurance. A report by the GAO estimated that for every dollar spent on the WIC program, which ensures that new mothers have nutritionally appropriate food for their babies, $3.50 is saved in health-care costs over the child's first eighteen years, and one USDA report estimated that 113,000 children would be dead without the intervention of WIC.[1]

In fact, American poverty could easily be reduced by more generous and universal welfare state programs, just as it is elsewhere. By the mid-1980s, for example, France, West Germany, the Netherlands, Sweden, and the UK each had a pre-transfer poverty rate (poverty as measured before counting the effects of welfare programs) that was higher than the United States; yet the highest post-transfer poverty rate (poverty rates that take account of government aid) among those nations was 5.2 percent (in the UK), while the United States', by contrast, was 13.3 percent.[2] If Canada's welfare system were extended to U.S. families, we would reduce poverty by 30 percent.[3] Gøsta Esping-Andersen estimated that the cost of eliminating childhood poverty in the United States would be less than one-half of 1 percent of our gross domestic product.[4] It may be true that in other "advanced" nations there is some drag on the economy that relates to the generosity of social programs, whether because of the simple costs of transfer payments or because of the more complicated effects of programs that may serve to discourage work, reduce the labor supply, and drive up wages.[5] But as one labor economist puts it:

> Whether social programs are judged as successful or unsuccessful should depend on how effectively they deal with the problems they are designed to address, not on their seemingly modest effects on the labor market's flexibility and long-term unemployment.[6]

The more nations spend, and the better they target that spending to their poorest citizens, the lower their poverty rates.[7]

Despite the effectiveness of relief programs, access to them has always been limited in the United States. From 1630 to 1645 in Plymouth Colony, while some 13 percent of inhabitants were on the relief rolls, many more than that were poor and received no aid.[8] Throughout the eighteenth and nineteenth centuries, cities periodically purged their rolls and, in order to conserve public funds, regularly sought to exclude those in need from the poorhouse or from cash relief. Robert Hunter estimated in 1904 that although 10 million were poor, only 4 million were "public paupers."[9] Perhaps one-third of those eligible actually received the Progressive Era mother's pension, and only 3 percent of that total were received by African American women.[10] In 1933, running what was described as the best system of relief in the United States at the time, New York provided help to only about one-fourth of those in need.[11] By September 1962, at best one in six poor children received AFDC.[12] In the early 1980s, only 45 percent of the unemployed received unemployment insurance benefits; by 2004, not even four in ten workers qualified, and the value of those benefits had declined from about 54 percent of wages to 43 percent.[13] One review of sixty separate studies of homelessness done in the 1980s found that, on average, only 20 percent of people who lived on the street or in a shelter received general assistance, 10 percent received Supplemental Security Income, and 8 percent received AFDC.[14] In 1999, about one in eight of those eligible received child care, three in five received food stamps, and eight in ten got the EITC.[15] Between 1981 and 1996, somewhere between 77 and 86 percent of all those who were eligible for cash welfare received it; by 2002, in the wake of welfare reform, the rate was down to 48 percent; food stamp participation rates declined as well, also reaching 48 percent by 2002 (it had been 70 percent in 1994).[16] And so on. Even in "normal" times, significant portions of the population might depend upon aid, but never did all those who were poor and in need actually receive assistance. Rarely was that assistance enough to get by on, and never enough to live well: since at least the 1820s, the value of welfare benefits has changed little, offering only between 25 and 30 percent of the wage of a "common" laborer.[17] This is another constant of relief.

More Than It's Worth

Nonetheless, many have claimed that aid programs, instead of helping those in need, do them harm: welfare, this argument goes, saps initiative, undermines the work ethic, and leads to dependence, thereby exacerbating poverty rather than relieving it. The social Darwinist William Graham Sumner stated it this way in 1885:

> We have seen that if we should try by any measures of arbitrary interference and assistance to relieve the victims of social pressure from the calamity of their position we should only offer premiums to folly and vice and extend them further. . . . In truth, the human race has never done anything else but struggle with the problems of social welfare. That struggle constitutes history, or the life of the human race on earth. . . . It would be hard to find a single instance of direct assault by positive effort upon poverty, vice, and misery which has not either failed or, if it has not failed directly and entirely, has not entailed other evils greater than the one which it removed.[18]

This 1937 letter to Eleanor Roosevelt from Minnie Hardin, of Columbus, Indiana, offers a powerful example of the manner in which such ideas became widespread and the contempt many antiwelfare ideologues have had for poor Americans:

> Mrs. Roosevelt: I suppose from your point of view the work relief, old age pensions, slum clearance and all the rest seems like a perfect remedy for all the ills of this country, but I would like for you to see the results, as the other half see them.

Presumably, no irony was intended in referring to herself as among "the other half" and the reference to Riis's *How the Other Half Lives* was unintentional. She continues:

We have always had a shiftless, never-do-well class of people whose one and only aim in life is to live without work. I have been rubbing elbows with this class for nearly sixty years and have tried to help some of the most promising and have seen others try to help them, but it can't be done. We cannot help those who will not try to help themselves and if they do try, a square deal is all they need, and by the way that is all this country needs or ever has needed; a square deal for all and then, let each paddle their own canoe, or sink. There has never been any necessity for any one who is able to work, being on relief in this locality, but there have been many eating the bread of charity and they have lived better than ever before. I have had taxpayers tell me that their children came from school and asked why they couldn't have nice lunches like the children on relief. . . . As for the clearance of the real slums, it can't be done as long as their inhabitants are allowed to reproduce their kind. I would like for you to see what a family of that class can do to a decent house in a short time. Such a family moved into an almost new, neat, four room house near here last winter. They even cut down some of the shade trees for fuel, after they had burned everything they could pry loose. . . . They are just a fair sample of the class of people on whom so much of our hard earned tax money is being squandered and on whom so much sympathy is being wasted.

Note that in this worldview the desperation that drives a family to burn portions of their own home to keep warm is derided as a moral failure and a mark of being "lower class." Not even the elderly, usually counted among the "deserving" poor, escape this woman's disdain:

As for the old people on beggars' allowances: the taxpayers have provided homes for all the old people who never liked to work, where they will be neither cold nor hungry: much better homes than most of them have ever tried to provide for themselves. They have lived many years through the most prosperous times of our country and had an opportunity to prepare for old age, but they spent their lives in idleness or worse and now expect those who have worked like slaves, to provide a living for them and all their worthless descendants. Some of them are asking for from thirty to sixty dollars a month when I have known them to live on a dollar a week rather than go to work. There is many a little child doing without butter on its bread, so that some old sot can have his booze and tobacco: some old sot who spent his working years loafing around pool rooms and saloons, boasting that the world owed him a living.

Yet she turns her attention briefly from the poor to the powerful:

You people who have plenty of this worlds goods and whose money comes easy, have no idea of the heart breaking toil and self denial which is the lot of the working people who are trying to make an honest living, and then to have to shoulder all these unjust burdens seems like the last straw. . . . The crooked-ness, selfishness, greed, and graft of the crooked politicians is making one gigantic racket out of the new deal, and it is making this a nation of dead beats and beggars and if it continues the people who will work will soon be nothing but slaves for the pampered poverty rats and I am afraid these human parasites are going to become a menace to the country unless they are disenfranchised. No one should have the right to vote theirself a living at the expense of the taxpayers. They learned their strength at the last election and also learned that they can get just about what they want by "voting right." They have had a taste of their coveted life of idleness, and at the rate they are increasing, they will soon control the country.[19]

The perception that relief is fraudulently obtained, overly generous, and a mark of sloth or incompetence endures even today, of course (it was especially evident during the debate over welfare reform in the 1990s), and it has always had consequences.[20] In her memoirs of growing up poor in Alabama in the 1960s, Barbara Robinette Moss tells us that her father was a proud man—not too proud to abuse his wife and children, not too proud to cash his meager paycheck at a bar and spend most of it there in one night, not too proud to disappear and leave his family with no food and no money for weeks on end, but he was, as she reports, "too proud to accept any government help, even when he was out of work, and he had a low opinion of those who did."[21] Her mother was just as reluctant to apply for welfare, because she was afraid that if she let the government into their lives, "Social Services would take her children away, divide them up and put them into foster homes. Maybe that's why," Moss suggests, "we were all so careful to hide our situation—fear we'd be taken away. *Anything* was better than living without Mother."[22]

This is the practical upshot of a political culture that vilifies public assistance and degrades, shames, and instills fear in those who would accept it—children go hungry, families get evicted, women are trapped, and threadbare lives are that much coarser and crueler.

As an adult, having escaped an abusive husband and barely able to support herself and her son, Moss faced the choice of seeking aid or dropping out of college. She made what she judged to be the most responsible decision. She swallowed her pride, "put on my best dress and heels, smoothed my curly hair and tied it back with a ribbon, put on makeup," and applied for food stamps. And suffered for it:

> We were the only family in our neighborhood that had ever received food stamps—and the postman made certain everyone knew about it. On food stamp delivery day, the man next door would shout at me, "That comes out of *my* pocket." How could I explain to my neighbors that I was doing the best I could? I imagined sitting down with them and explaining that I planned to contribute to society as soon as I got out of school. I wanted desperately to be accepted, to be part of the community. My mind ran in circles, confused by who I'd been in the past, whom I was now, and who I planned to be in the future; three distinctly different people. And the person in the middle—the present me—needed financial help. As embarrassing as government assistance was for me, it was truly a blessing. Overnight, we had enough food. And we had medical care. . . . I don't know how we would have survived without this program. It still scares me to think about it. As a mother, I'm supposed to protect my child; and when I did not have the resources to do that, our government provided assistance. With all the criticism Social Service has received through the years, it's hard to think of them as heroic. But every day they help mothers feed and protect their children. . . . To spend the food stamps, I'd disguise myself—wear my mother's old glasses and tuck my hair under a baseball cap—and drive to a faraway grocery store. I always got out of the store as quickly as possible and never looked at anyone, including the cashier, for fear I'd be recognized.

To hide the dread fact of public aid from her son, she lied and told him that his frequent visits to the doctor were paid for by the university where she studied, and was always at home when the food stamps arrived so that he wouldn't see the telltale manila envelope. One day, as the mail was delivered:

> I reached for the envelope and [the postman] pulled it back as if to keep it, and thrust it toward me and said, "Here is your mail—much to my great grief and sorrow." As he stepped off the porch, he muttered, "Scamming off of society." It took a second for me to grasp the full meaning of what he'd said. Tears spilled down my cheeks as I watched him deliver mail to the next house. When he headed back, I met him at the sidewalk. . . . "Do you think I'm deaf? Do you think I like being on food stamps?" The postman turned into another house. When he came back to the sidewalk, I was still waiting. "Much to my great grief and sorrow. That's what you said." I shook the envelope in his face. "This is all the food we'll have for the next three weeks. Do you think we should starve? We don't deserve to eat?"

But it got worse:

> That evening someone left a handwritten note on my door that read, *Food stamps come out of the taxpayer's pocket! Why should I have to raise your child?* I was furious and horribly embarrassed at the same time. Once again I thought about dropping out of school and getting a job. . . . The anger burned away, but the embarrassment remained. The next day there was another note: *Your trash must be off the street before sundown.* How was I supposed to get the trashcan off the street before sundown if I didn't get home until after dark? This time it was the anger that remained.

So, in bold, bright colors, Moss painted two Biblical injunctions on her trashcans: "Do unto others as you would have them do unto you" and "Thou shalt love thy neighbor as thyself." For good measure, she added, on the large snow shovel, "Judge not that ye not be judged." As she reports, "I never found another note on my door."[23]

Moss's story is no anomaly. The testimony of relief recipients from throughout our history suggests that they do in fact pay for their benefits, and the price is extracted in shame and degradation. By 1707, the New York Common Council commanded that churches:

Put a badge upon the clothes of such poor as cloathed by the City with the
word: N. Y. in blue or red cloth at their discretion.

By 1718, the law required any public relief recipient and their entire
family to wear a *P* along with the first letter of their county or city.[24] When
it does not merely stigmatize, relief demands deference and greets independence, displays of pride, and resistance to its terms as ingratitude, an
indication of unworthiness.[25] Charles Dickens understood this phenomenon well: see only Mmes. Jellyby or Pardiggle in *Bleak House* for portraits of
women who get far more than they give from their charitable acts. It was
perhaps a way in which women, then deprived of political power, could
nonetheless feel powerful: "I like them to come to me when they are in
difficulties and ask for what they need," said one of the London "ladies
bountiful" of the 1890s.[26] She could grant or deny any request, but if, instead, relief is expected or considered a right, the benefactor has no such
power.[27] Josephine Shaw Lowell, an American lady bountiful, made the argument clearly:

> Charity must be exercised toward a person in inferior circumstances to those
> of his benefactor. We cannot be charitable to our equals.[28]

Anyone in need is, by definition, inferior. Mary, an Appalachian mother
of three, put it this way when asked how her interactions with welfare bureaucrats made her feel:

> Dependent. You have to watch every step like you are in prison. All the time
> you are on welfare, yeah, you are in prison. Someone is watching like a guard.
> Someone is watching over you and you are hoping every day that you won't go
> up the creek, so to speak, and [that you will] get out alive in any way, shape, or
> form.[29]

Historian John Alexander, writing about the late eighteenth century, reveals how enduring Mary's bind has been:

> Lack of economic power dictated more than how poor people dressed and
> where they lived. It also gave them little choice but to treat some of the pros-

perous citizens with at least pretended respect, civility, and deference. The poor had to behave this way because, throughout the period 1760–1800 and especially after independence, it was essential to be able to obtain a recommendation from a "respectable" person . . .

That is, if one wanted to receive aid, gain employment, be granted a license for a trade, or even receive care in the hospital. Reported one:

We must bear with those that are above us . . . it is the punishment of dependence.[30]

Or, as Ruby Duncan, Nevada welfare recipient turned activist, said:

When I would stand there in the Vegas sun waiting for our bags of food, I kept thinking: This still costs more than it's worth.[31]

She lamented:

Handouts always come at a price.[32]

For few indeed are welfare benefits free. The cost can be so high that some choose, as they have in the past, to forego the relief available to them and opt for the slightly sharper pangs of hunger rather than the pangs associated with a sacrifice to their dignity or independence.

A Last Resort

Charity is power. We see that power exerted in relief programs, both public and private. This is Jack Conroy in *The Disinherited*, a Depression-era tale of a boy whose father was killed on the job by an explosion:

One day a group of church workers came to see us. They sat decorously in the front room, their inquisitive eyes ferreting into every crevice.

"We have come," announced a lady with a heroic bust, "to make some arrangement for the adoption of the children and for your support and welfare. We know you are having a hard time, and we wouldn't be Christians if we didn't help you. We have been told that the children haven't enough to eat and wear, and we have talked the whole thing over. Mr. Reyerson" (indicating an angular old fellow with mutton-chop whiskers) "will take the boy, and I'll take the girl. It'll be several years before she's big enough to earn her salt, but the boy is big enough now to work in the fields. Jethro Haines' wife has been bedfast for several years, and we have found a place for you there, doing the housework and taking care of her."

Mother's face clouded. She nervously laced and unlaced her fingers.

"You folks are mighty kind," she said, "but I don't like to break up my home. I'm going to try to raise the children the best I can. If I can't do it, then I'll have to make other plans."

The committee members made it plain that they considered themselves bitten by that keenest tooth—ingratitude. They arose collectively and stiffly, and visibly washed their hands of us, saying they were sorry that we would not allow them to help us.

Mother took my face between her hands and looked at me so earnestly I felt uncomfortable. I turned my head away.[33]

It's a familiar tale. Michael Gold related his version of this experience:

The neighbors tried to help us, but they themselves were poor. Some well-meaning neighbor secretly mailed a post card to the Charity society, telling of our plight. One day a stranger called. He was a slim fair-haired, young Christian with a brisk hurry-up manner and a stylish collar and necktie. He placed his umbrella against the wall, and shuffled through a bunch of index cards. . . . This was evidently one of the brusque young men who came from the Board of Health, or the Public School, or the Christian missions, or the settlement houses. They asked many questions, and one must answer them or go to jail. . . .

"And so your husband is out of work? Is he kind to you? Does he drink? What salary does he receive while working? Does he smoke? Has he tried to find a job recently? Does he ever beat you? How much of his salary does he give you when he is working? What rent do you pay? How much do your groceries cost per week?"

My mother . . . resented this brisk stranger who came into her home and asked personal questions with such an air of authority. But he was an official. She cleared her throat, and was about to give him his answers, when my father stalked in. He had been resting in the bedroom, and was half-undressed. His face was pale, he trembled with rage. He glared at the young blond question-asker, and shouted: "'Get out of this house, mister! You have no business here. It is true we are poor, but that does not give you the right to insult us."

"I am not insulting you," said the young investigator, blowing his nose and shuffling his index cards nervously, "I ask these questions in about fifty homes a day. It is just the regular form." My father drew himself up proudly. "I spit on your regular form," he said. "We don't want any charity; we can live without it, mister." . . . What he reported on his cards we never knew, but we were spared the indignity of any further visits by Organized Charity. Every one on the East Side hated and feared that cruel machine that helped no one without first systematically degrading him and robbing him of all human status. One's neighbors were kinder. Tammany Hall was kinder. Starvation was kinder. There were thousands of families like ours that would rather have died than be bullied, shamed and finger-printed like criminals by the callous policemen of Organized Charity.[34]

Some citizens of Maine, Lorena Hickok reported to Harry Hopkins, "would almost starve rather than ask for help":

They still believe in Maine that "there must be something wrong with a fellow if he can't get a job." They really believe it, even as they tell you how desperate their plight is and how hopeless the employment situation looks for the future!

She continues:

You hear so much in Maine about "deserving cases." And to be a "deserving case" in Maine, a family has got to measure up to the most rigid Nineteenth Century standards of cleanliness, physical and moral. They just haven't any patience with people who don't. As a result, a woman who isn't a good housekeeper is apt to have a pretty tough time of it. And Heaven help the family in which there is any "moral problem!"

In one "frightful town in dire need," the mayor even boasted to Hickok of having refused to apply for any state or federal aid.[35] One Rhode Island doctor said to her:

Most of the people we see are not on relief, but are starving. Many of these are white collar people and people in the skilled labor class who avoid relief, whose pride remains stronger than hunger.[36]

As Hopkins himself wrote:

Letters came, delegations arrived, protesting against the indignity of public charity. Men who had never in their lives asked for, or accepted, a cent of alms refused to believe that the situation had gone into permanent reverse. It made no difference to them in what pretty words the unattractive fact of their dependency was dressed. It was charity and they didn't like it. They were accustomed to making a return for their livelihood. It was a habit they liked, and from which they chiefly drew their self-respect. The family of a man working on a Works Progress Administration project looks down its nose at neighbors who take their relief straight. We can talk all we want to about some coming civilization in which work will be outmoded, and in which we shall enjoy a state of being rather than one of action, but contemporary sentiment is still against "a man who gets something for nothing." Those who voluntarily take something for nothing are put in jail. Those who are forced to accept charity, no matter how unwillingly, are first pitied, then disdained.[37]

Lenny Del Genio looked back on the period:

Relief then was a disgrace. I think there was one check that we got when I was seventeen or so. My mother cashed the check. My father wouldn't do it 'cause he was so humiliated.[38]

Many decades later, seventy-six-year-old Brenda Jackson offered a simple explanation to Mark Robert Rank about why she was not receiving Medicaid:

They wanted to know too much of my business and I told 'em forget it.[39]

North Philadelphia's Michelle Manley said this in 1980 about welfare and her refusal to apply, despite her mother's urgings:

They are so nosy. They want to know all your business for that little bit of money.[40]

Renata, in 1990:

You go to welfare when you got no place else, it's the worst, the last stop.[41]

Only rarely have those who control relief been concerned about finding ways to make it more acceptable. Hickok to Hopkins from Washington, D.C., in August 1933:

I met a supervisor . . . who has spent days and nights trying to figure out how to get relief to people who need it and won't ask for it. She is giving cash, out of a fund from a private agency, to some of her exceptionally high class people—a lawyer and his family, for instance . . . to spare them the humiliation of presenting food orders at the grocery, and she has gone to the greatest amount of trouble imaginable to keep secret the fact that they are getting relief.[42]

Throughout her travels, Hickok would make similar approving observations about the importance of protecting "high-class people" from the degradation of charity. Her reports make clear the degree of discrimination in places throughout the nation, and the care that was taken to establish discrete programs for the middling classes. In a letter from Alabama in April 1934, she reports the creation of "A Placement Bureau for Professional People," a separate agency (not in the relief office) without home visiting (until some supposed fraud was detected): "This method of introducing white collar people to relief is about as painless as any could be, I guess," she observes. She wrote to Hopkins of a plan in New Orleans to allow "the white collar people" to "come in by appointment. That spares them the ordeal of having to sit around the intake for hours." In the same letter she noted, "If we were not carrying so many Negroes [on the rolls], I wonder if perhaps we couldn't solve the white collar problem to some extent by giving more adequate relief." From Texas she passed along the suggestion that "the white collar people" might be allowed to apply for relief by mail, to spare them the indignity of the intake process.[43]

Around the same time, social worker Lillian Brandt lamented over the "experience of being dependent" for the newly poor:

Acute shame, embarrassment, reluctance, sullen defiance, or assumed nonchalance; gratitude; matter-of-fact acceptance, dissatisfaction with the aid given; demands for more, resentment when it was discontinued—such is the gamut of attitudes observed. Most of them really wanted work.[44]

Of course, this could have been said of most of those who had been poor before the Depression, and those who would be poor after it, too. Hunger is physical, and fleeting. But the scorn we heap upon relief applicants may linger and touch them more deeply and more cruelly. Elizabeth Cameron, who was herself once a caseworker, noted:

> Yes, I've been hungry at times but the worst thing is the treatment by the welfare office.[45]

Even during the Depression, when the widespread nature of distress supposedly reduced the impulse of charity workers to fault the individual and their moral failings for their poverty, many visitors and nurses were still reluctant to give cash assistance, calling it "terrible," "not especially constructive," and "probably the worst form of relief possible."[46] If anything, it was worse in subsequent years. Juanita Simpson, 1965:

> It is no honor to have to be on relief or aid to dependent children. It's no disgrace, but it's not no honor. It does something to you, something that I can't explain very deep. It makes you feel like you've lost all your rights. You have no right to vote, you feel that way. You feel that you have nothing to look forward to. You are walking around dead in mind, you can't even think straight. The category they put you in, you don't feel human any more. After they get through talking to you you feel just so low like you're smaller than a little animal. . . . It keeps the kids in a bad frame of mind when they aren't living under nice conditions. They don't allow you to have a television. If you got a television, you got to sell it. If you got a new radio or anything in the house new, maybe it doesn't cost over ten or fifteen dollars, they want to know how did you buy it. . . . And many times you know people you would like to invite to your house but you don't want to invite them because you figure, well, our house doesn't look as good as theirs, or probably the social service might come in and want to know, "Well, who are these people visiting you?" . . . They take away all your decency. . . . And the majority of the youngsters it makes almost criminals out of em because the conditions they are living under. Most of the majority of people that are on relief, aid to dependent children, their

children, they don't have the privileges that other people's children have because most of the time they don't have necessary food and without necessary
food, without eating proper, children cannot sit in the classroom in the school
and study properly. . . . People on relief, they eat a lot of starches.[47]

Alissa, speaking to Joe Soss a generation later:

It's a big system. "Stand in this line." You feel like cattle or something being
prodded. That's how I felt. You go all the way through this line to do this, and
then this line to do that. It's like a cattle prod. It's like you're in a big mill. I
felt like a number or like I was in a prison system. . . . It feels like you're in a
cattle prod. They're the cowboys, and you're a cow. I feel like a cowboy would
have more respect for the animals because he knows that the cattle are his
livelihood. But these people are like, "I'm helping you. This is something I'm
doing for you. So just be quiet and follow your line."[48]

Complaining about charity investigators, one woman remarked:

Soon they'll look into my teeth or pump my stomach to find out what foods
I've been eating.[49]

Said Bernice:

When you are on public aid, you are in a state of total submission. You are
dominated by the caseworkers. Your child's teachers put you down. This is all
a form of suppression, to keep you quiet, not to have a life, not to have an
opinion.[50]

Lonnie, one of forty-seven Florida women sociologist Karen Seccombe
and her team interviewed in the late 1990s, described the experience of using food stamps:

When you get ready to buy your groceries, people have made nasty little re-
marks about the groceries you're buying. They'll go, "We're paying for that."
Once there was some university students and I guess they felt like that. They
had a small amount in their buggy, and I had large amounts. He started talking, so his girlfriend kept trying to get him to be quiet. And he kept talking

and talking. And then he said, "That's why the president is trying to cut off welfare because of people like that!" I turned to him and I say, I say, "Well, you know something? I have worked in my time too. And I will work again. It's not like I'm asking you for anything. And I hope you don't come and ask me for anything 'cause with me and my five kids I couldn't give you none anyway!" And he stomped out of there when I told him that. But I was being honest with him. I have worked. I felt real bad that day, I really did.[51]

It's a tale told over and again by poor women. The manner in which the entire citizenry, it sometimes seems, is enlisted in their surveillance. Boxcar Bertha records one woman as saying:

In the big places they send you to the charity officers. And they want your whole life's story. . . . They searched our car and found two quarts of whiskey. They had us arrested, and they said we wasn't fit to take care of the child. They took our baby away from us, kept her in an orphan asylum for awhile, and then sent her back to Indiana. Anybody that's got any sense won't never go to no charity organization or to the police. They don't like the poor, and they never do them no good. I'd rather steal or beg on the street.[52]

Here's Susan, a homeless woman, talking to Gwendolyn Dordick in the 1990s:

I don't get welfare. I just can't fuckin' do it. I hate those people in there. They make you fuckin' sit and sit and ask you questions that don't make any sense. It's none of their fuckin' business anyway. Either you're gonna give me the welfare or you're not. What is the point of all these fuckin' questions? You're homeless but you have to have an address. What kind of shit is that? Give me a break. They want you to get so fuckin' upset that you do get up and walk out. They test you. And if you do get up and walk out, that means you really don't want it.[53]

But it's not just the stigma of public aid that people have resisted; pride can suffer just as much by seeming to be dependent upon the private charity of others, too. This is Jim Sheridan, during the Bonus March:

We had reached a place in Virginia. It was a very hot day. In this jungle, there was a man, a very tall man. He had his wife with him and several small children. We invited them over to have something to eat with us, and they refused. Then I brought something over to them in an old pie plate. They still refused. It was the husband who told me that he didn't care for anything to eat. But see, the baby was crying from hunger. Finally, me and some others went down to bum the center of town. I remember going into a drugstore and bumming a baby bottle with a nipple. Now, can you imagine a guy bumming a baby bottle with a nipple? It took me a few guts to work it up. I explained the circumstances. Then I went and bummed the milk. When I got back to the jungle camp, it was kinda dark. I first reported in to Captain Webb and then he kidded me about the baby bottle. "Christ," I said, "that baby there's gotta eat." And he said, "This afternoon you got pretty much of a rebuff." "Well," I said, "I'm gonna try again." So I went over and addressed myself to his wife. And I told her: here is the baby bottle. We had even warmed up the milk. But she looked at her husband, and her husband said he didn't want it. What could I do about it, but just feel blue? I didn't look upon it as charity. It seemed to me that here was a fella's pride getting the best of him.[54]

Tony, homeless, living in San Francisco in the 1980s, also shunned aid and preferred to redeem recyclable cans and bottles—what he identifies as his work:

The reason I do just about anything for work is I don't believe in the food lines. I know where all of 'em are at, and I can go down there, but I don't depend on 'em. I believe in at least being able to cover my own so I can keep myself fed, keep myself clothed and washed up. . . . I'm not on SSI, GA, or nothing. I work.[55]

In fact, as Dordick notes, few homeless people receive public aid. Steven VanderStaay says that nationwide 70 percent of those who are homeless receive none at all.[56] We don't have reliable data that tell us precisely why that may be, if the estimates are accurate, but the reactions of Susan and Tony are common.

In the many letters written by children to Eleanor Roosevelt during the 1930s, it is striking how frequently they report that they and their family are trying to avoid the relief rolls—despite the dire need they describe—and therefore ask assistance of the first lady herself. "We are trying to keep off relief this winter," one young correspondent reported in 1934 from

Texas, as if that determination, perhaps, would make the request for aid seem more worthy. Wrote another:

I wonder if you would help me just a little . . . [but] Please, Mrs. Roosevelt, dont try to put us on relief for we don't like that.[57]

As one man later told Studs Terkel, thinking back to his threadbare childhood:

We could have gone on relief. But my father refused. Foolish pride. . . . He wouldn't even accept medical relief—stubborn Dutchman![58]

But when pressed with dire need, many will, as Barbara Moss did, quash their pride and proceed through the rituals of supplication. Social worker Eileen Barth, during the Great Depression, as reported by Terkel:

I'll never forget one of the first families I visited. The father was a railroad man who had lost his job. I was told by my supervisor that I really had to *see* the poverty. If the family needed clothing, I was to investigate how much clothing they had at hand. So I looked into this man's closet—(pauses, it becomes difficult)—he was a tall, gray-haired man, though not terribly old. He let me look in the closet—he was so insulted. (She weeps angrily.) He said, "Why are you doing this?" I can remember his feeling of humiliation . . . this terrible humiliation. (She can't continue. After a pause, she resumes.) He said, "I really haven't anything to hide, but if you really must look into it. . . ." I could see he was very proud. He was so deeply humiliated. And I was, too.[59]

Others will muster what resistance they can without losing aid altogether. Malcolm X wrote this in his *Autobiography*:

My mother was, above everything else, a proud woman, and it took its toll on her that she was accepting charity. And her feelings were communicated to us. She would speak sharply to the man at the grocery store for padding the bill, telling him that she wasn't ignorant and he didn't like that. She would talk back sharply to the state Welfare people, telling them that she was a grown woman, able to raise her children, that it wasn't necessary for them to keep coming around so much, meddling in our lives. And they didn't like that. But the monthly Welfare check was their pass. They acted as if they owned us, as if we were their private property. As much as my mother would have liked to, she couldn't keep them out. She would get particularly incensed when they began insisting upon drawing us older children aside, one at a time, out on the porch or somewhere, and asking us questions, or telling us things—against our mother and against each other. We couldn't understand why, if the state was willing to give us packages of meat, sacks of potatoes and fruit, and cans of all kinds of things, our mother obviously hated to accept. We really couldn't understand. I later understood that my mother was making a desperate effort to preserve her pride—and ours.[60]

So great is the stigma that some on relief deny that they are. Here's Etta Dawson, in Chicago in 1965, reflecting on her childhood in Rome, Georgia:

Daddy worked and we got what they call commodities. That wasn't getting a check, you know, it was just goin up and getting food. You get canned meat and go oncet a month and pick up groceries, that's what it is. . . . We was never on welfare down there.[61]

Denial about being on "the dole" is commonly reported to Hopkins. As Hickok wrote:

Never once in West Virginia did I hear the complaint so frequent in Pennsylvania—"You're making paupers out of us." People on relief never talk about being on relief. They call it "working for the R.F.C." and the kicks are always that some other fellow is getting more "R.F.C. work" than the complainant. I asked a miner up in Monogalia county how long he had been on relief, and he didn't know what I meant![62]

Janie, another woman interviewed by Seccombe's researchers, had been on AFDC for two years when she told them:

I'm not on welfare. I don't even know exactly what welfare is. I'm just receiving AFDC, and that might be considered welfare. I'm not sure. As it stands, most of them get on it because they don't want to work; they don't want to take care of their kids.[63]

When Ann Withorn reminded her mother that she had grown up on welfare, her mother slapped her face:

Don't you *ever* say that again. My family did *not* grow up on welfare. Your grandfather was ill, in the hospital, and received veterans benefits. We earned what we received from the government because he fought in the war. We were *never* on welfare.[64]

As Scott Briar noted in his examination of California welfare recipients, "[our] respondents almost never (and most respondents never) referred to welfare recipients as 'we' but as 'they.'" Commenting on Briar's study, Piven and Cloward observed: "Having set themselves apart from and condemned those on the same boat, recipients tend to identify with their oppressors."[65] It's a powerful stereotype. Sheri, a Florida woman who had been receiving welfare for herself and her three children for seven years, put it this way:

I think a lot of them are on it just to be on it. Lazy. Don't want to do nothing. Lot of them on it 'cause a lot of them are on drugs. Keep having kids to get more money, more food stamps. Now that's abusing the system. And a lot of women are abusing the system.[66]

Kate, another Florida welfare recipient, and an African American mother of two, concurred:

I think that some lawmakers think that women on AFDC have more children. . . . Just to get more AFDC. I believe that too. I really believe that too. *But not me.* No. Some women are just breeders. . . . They like to have babies. If they don't get themselves stopped, they'll just keep having them. If it were me, I wouldn't have no more babies just to get more AFDC. No.[67]

As with most of the women Seccombe and her associates interviewed, what ethnographers have usually found is that recipients refer to women on welfare as "they," not "we," and associate with "them" the stereotypical behaviors and attitudes—almost always pointing out the ways in which they (and sometimes their friends) are the exception. As Seccombe observes, "several women acknowledged that they had never personally met anyone who had a baby for the extra money. But they were convinced that it happens, nonetheless."[68] Some do, however, count themselves among the welfare queens. Conservative pundit and former welfare recipient Star Parker professed:

> To me, welfare was still an entitlement and discarding it would be like parting with one of my civil liberties.[69]

But what makes Parker's assertion striking is that it is unusual: one of the most consistent findings among researchers is women's unwillingness to assert a right to welfare and their disdain for public relief and relief recipients. Curiously, opinion about welfare tends to differ little depending upon whether one has needed it—poor women have attributed the same pathologies to welfare recipients that others have, even when this public image conflicted with their own experience. Such is the power of myth, culture, and conventional wisdom.[70] One woman makes this clear in this conflicted statement:

> Knowing welfare doesn't reimburse root canals, [the dentist] offered to save my tooth for only forty dollars. He said it was good for the character of people like me to grow accustomed to buying services. He doesn't seem to know that most of us would buy more if we could earn more. I wanted to bellow, hand on hip and attitude in my voice, in admiring imitation of certain ladies, *Sir, you've been brainwashed by stories about people hopping into Cadillacs after cashing government checks. Most of the people on welfare I know can't drive and react to a ride as if it's a grand vacation.* But I didn't want him to withdraw his offer of a reduced rate, and in a darkened corridor of my conscience I knew what he was referring to.[71]

The stereotype has even found its way into song. This is "Welfare Cadillac," by country and western singer Guy Drake:

> I've never worked much, In fact
> I've been poor all my life
> I guess all I really own
> Is ten kids and a wife

This house I live in is mine
But it's really a shack
But I've always managed to somehow
drive me a brand new Cadillac.

. . . .

I know the place ain't much
But I sure don't pay no rent
I get a check the first of every month
From this here Federal Government

Every Wednesday I get commodities
Sometimes four or five sacks
Pick 'em up down at the Welfare Office
Driving that new Cadillac.

. . . .

Now the way that I see it
These other folk are the fools
They're working and paying taxes
Just to send my young'uns through school

The Salvation Army cuts their hair and
Gives them clothes to wear on their backs
So we can dress up and ride around
And show off this new Cadillac.[72]

But to say that attitudes about welfare differ little between recipients and nonrecipients is not to say that they do not differ at all. One analysis found that eligible women enrolled in TANF were moderately less likely to agree that "being on welfare would make me lazy" or that "women on welfare don't take good care of their kids." They also find that fear of stigma reduced enrollment in both TANF and Medicaid among eligible women.[73] Another investigation found that welfare recipients were significantly less likely to agree that "welfare encourages young women to have babies before marriage" or that marriage was necessary to raise children well.[74] But both studies found that recipients and nonrecipients alike agreed that welfare made people less likely to work—and that women with young children should not work outside the home. Women on relief, it would appear, are as conflicted about welfare as the rest of the population. That's not to dismiss Parker's claim, nor to deny that there are indeed examples, as there have always been, of the welfare queen. They are the exception, not the rule, but they are essential to those, like Parker herself, who are engaged in an ideological campaign that has little respect for what the evidence shows.

7

Escape:
Black and Blue

Teacher:	*Now children, you don't think white people are any better than you because*
	they have straight hair and white faces?
Students:	*No, sir.*
Teacher:	*No, they are no better, but they are different, they possess great power, they*
	formed this great government, they control this vast country. . . . Now what
	makes them different from you?
Students:	*MONEY. (Unanimous shout)*
Teacher:	*Yes, but what enabled them to obtain it? How* did *they get money?*
Students:	*Got it off us, stole it off we all!*

—Catechism from a freedman's school,

Louisville, Kentucky, late 1860s

Attention vagrants: convicton means hard labor on gang.

—Georgia road sign, circa 1936

The history of the American welfare state has been a white history. In most books charting the birth and development of social welfare in the United States, African Americans don't make their first appearance until the Progressive Era, and then they are merely a sidebar to the story of American urban industrialization. They are largely absent again until discussion of the Social Security Act of 1935 (SSA), when the focus turns to how and why congressional Democrats excluded agricultural and domestic workers from the SSA, workers who were disproportionately black and located in the South. Not until discussion about AFDC and then the "welfare back-lash" of the 1980s and 1990s do we again find African Americans incorporated in any substantive way into the narrative, and then it is largely as objects of white and elite animus.[1]

To use one crude measure, in the index of Michael Katz's *In the Shadow of the Poorhouse*, which is among the most widely admired histories of American poverty and welfare (and rightly so), the first entry for "blacks" is on page 181, where they appear in a two-page discussion about housing, school segregation, and race riots (there is no listing for African Americans). The only other entries reference a handful of pages on blacks and the New Deal, the war on poverty, and AFDC—altogether, 7 pages in a text with 334, or 2 percent of the total.[2] Walter Trattner's *From Poor Law to Welfare State* does better, offering references to minister George Whitfield's early efforts to bring slaves into his fold with free education programs (or, less charitably put, with efforts at indoctrination); discrimination against blacks in the early years of the antituberculosis campaigns; black infant mortality; African Americans and the formative juvenile justice system; and then to the New Deal, urban riots in the 1960s, and the civil rights movement, giving us indexed references to a total of 29 out of 395 pages of text, 7 percent of the total. Bruce Jansson's *The Reluctant Welfare State* incorporates references to African Americans and colonial poor relief, black codes, lynching, discrimination in education and in the courts, Head Start, AIDS in cities, and more, for 34 of 454 pages, also 7 percent. Given the centrality of race to American political and social policy history, the African American experience has been underrepresented.[3]

This may be an unfair complaint, I'll admit, since such histories must inevitably pass lightly over many events and issues, each of which might merit its own book-length treatment, and we could hunt through the index of any book (including this one) and object to the relative emphasis on one topic over another. However, even in analyses specifically focused on the history of race and welfare,[4] the narrative rarely begins before the New Deal, and it is *exclusion* that is the focus: African Americans are characters in someone else's story, bit players in a subplot, not protagonists. Yet their experience is more than merely different from whites', and it cannot be understood only in reference to discrimination and their exclusion from "mainstream" welfare programs. Just as feminist critics of comparative welfare state scholarship have urged analysts to attend more carefully to gender and find ways of "making women visible in welfare states,"[5] so too in American welfare state histories do we need to make African Americans more visible and not subsume them within "universal" analyses. By focusing upon the African American experience, the conventional wisdom about the genesis and evolution of the American welfare state might be overturned, and a new story might emerge. We'll begin with something that is perhaps overdue in these pages—a definition of the welfare state.

Redefining the Scope of Welfare State Analysis

A welfare state (WFS) has historically been understood to be the collection of government programs that provide citizens with money, food, shelter, health care, and education,[6] which have typically been evaluated by calculating each nation's total WFS expenditures as a percentage of its gross domestic product (so, for example, Denmark and Sweden each spend about 30 percent of their GDP on welfare, twice the amount of the United States). More recently, thanks to the work of Danish sociologist Gøsta Esping-Andersen, we have undertaken a cross-national analysis of welfare state effort by comparing the degree to which they *decommodify* labor—the extent to which they make it possible for citizens to survive outside of the labor market. Subsequent feminist analyses have added the idea of *defamilialization* to our repertoire—the extent to which the WFS permits one to exist outside of dependence upon a (male) breadwinner, or its effect upon one's "capacity to form autonomous households."[7] These now-standard typologies thus gauge, in part, the manner in which the state impacts an individual's ability to refuse work or marriage and her ability to allocate for herself her relative dependence upon the state, the labor market, or the family.

Using these approaches, it is clear why the availability and generosity of such things as unemployment and disability insurance, cash relief, food stamps, old-age pensions, and health care have commanded our attention. They have clear palliative functions, and their generosity correlates directly with individual power to refuse work. But it is less clear why we have excluded other institutions. Most scholarship has proceeded from the assumption that welfare state institutions are benevolent, that at their core they are efforts to help those in need. But, as the history of AFDC and TANF clearly shows, American relief has also functioned to regulate the sexual, reproductive, and labor market behavior of vulnerable populations. (In fact, Frances Fox Piven and Richard Cloward have long argued that the *principal* functions of relief are to regulate the low-wage labor supply and to placate disruptive poor and unemployed people.)[8] Given this, we should consider programs that serve to commodify labor (those that reduce choice), and not just those that decommodify it (those that increase choice), when evaluating the reach of the welfare state. Slavery, its successors (sharecropping, tenancy, convict labor), and the prison have been as important throughout American history in the lives of (poor) African Americans as have, say, Social Security, homeless shelters, or Medicaid. By excluding them because they are malign in intent, we make all but inevitable a distorted view of the history of the American welfare state.[9] And given that these more repressive institutions have disproportionately impacted black Americans, there may be cause to distinguish between a white welfare state—the benevolent if incomplete one that has predominated in our analyses—and an African American welfare state, one that has been dominated by institutions of repression and control.

Slavery and the Welfare State

American welfare state histories have not included slavery, and from the perspective of white America, this makes sense. But from the perspective of most African Americans, until its abolition, slavery defined their encounters with state power, fundamentally affecting their ability to secure food, shelter, health care, and work for themselves and their families. The denial of the right to work must surely be seen as just as important a state activity as programs (like child care, disability insurance, occupational health and safety laws, job training programs, or tax subsidies) that enable or encourage it. This is the first argument in favor of treating slavery as a WFS institution. What other government-sponsored program so affected the well-being of so many Americans?

I am not the first to suggest that there is a relationship between involuntary servitude and the welfare state. It was slavery, claimed one of its fiercest proponents, George Fitzhugh, that obviated the need for any more pernicious (in his view) program of public welfare. Slavery was welfare program enough, he asserted, and it worked so well for "Negroes" that it could and should solve the subsistence problems of poor whites as well. Fitzhugh went so far as to argue:

> Our Southern slavery has become a benign and protective institution, and our negroes are confessedly better off than any free laboring population in the world.[10]

In this view, slavery was a benevolent and efficient program of public relief, one which merely required work in exchange for aid. That's a criterion that antiwelfare advocates continue to argue should govern assistance, it is worth noting. There is a consistency here, for American WFS programs have always, to varying degrees, concerned themselves with labor market effects.[11] Social Security provided cash to retirees, of course, but in doing so encouraged older, presumably less productive workers to leave the labor market, making room for younger, more productive (and perhaps more compliant) ones. Regulations that forbade the presence of males in the homes of female AFDC recipients functioned, at least in part, to ensure that poor men did not have access to welfare benefits, and were therefore forced to turn to the low-wage labor market.

It should be uncontroversial to assert that the Southern systems of state-sponsored indentured servitude had material effects on those subject to its rule. More controversially, we might further observe that some slaves fared better than some poor whites struggling to survive outside the system: they ate more calories, worked fewer hours, and had better, newer clothes than did their poor white brethren.[12] This is not to suggest that there might be a positive side to slavery. As Harriet Jacobs, a slave who eventually escaped, said:

> I would ten thousand times rather that my children should be the half-starved paupers of Ireland than to be the most pampered among the slaves of America.[13]

Amartya Sen more recently put it this way:

> Even though African American slaves in the pre–Civil War South may have had pecuniary incomes as large as (or even larger) than those of wage laborers elsewhere and may even have lived longer than the urban workers in the

North, there was still a fundamental deprivation in the fact of slavery itself (no matter what incomes or utilities it might or might not have generated). The loss of freedom in the absence of employment choice and in the tyrannical form of work can itself be a major deprivation.[14]

With the notable exception of a growing body of work by Elna Green,[15] we have generally paid little attention to the history of welfare in the American South. While there is more to this neglected history than just slavery, what makes poor relief in the South distinct from relief elsewhere was what made most everything in the South different—slavery. And that system was inextricably linked not only to the immiseration of blacks but also to white poverty, and to Southern programs of white welfare. If we are to evaluate the extent of and possibilities for decommodification or defamilialization in the antebellum American South, we have little choice but to examine slavery.

White poverty in the South was in some measure a consequence of slavery, as blacks provided abundant, cheap labor, skilled and unskilled; in this way, the end of slavery was a boon to poor whites as well as to enslaved blacks.[16] One journalist, visiting Virginia, voiced a common observation that poor whites were "certainly as debased and degraded as the poor negroes."[17] Whatever comfort might have been offered to the "deserving" poor, the rest were expected to work for whatever wages were available, under any conditions, no matter how grueling, gruesome, and exploitative. Poor whites were understood by the white aristocracy to be superior to all blacks, even freedmen (by 1846 the public whipping of white criminals was forbidden, lest the association with slaves be too great to stomach), but they were nonetheless deemed to be incompetent and dangerous. This became even more true when immigrants (especially the Irish) began arriving in large numbers, feared and hated because they were replacing the "submissive, acclimated, non-voting Negro":[18]

The institution of slavery complicated the question of public relief in the southern states. What little public provision existed was generally denied to blacks; slaves were the responsibility of their masters and were prohibited from receiving aid in most states. Free blacks, too, were usually denied public assistance and were forced to develop their own informal self-help mechanisms, setting in motion a trend that would last until the twentieth century. Black churches began assuming the responsibility for supporting indigent members by establishing "poor saints funds" or other methods of caring for their own. Mutual assistance associations, which would become one of the cornerstones of black civic life later in the nineteenth century, provided the equivalent of death benefits, burial policies, and even unemployment insurance for those whom the state refused to assist.[19]

Further, the history of American servitude itself includes poor whites and not only African slaves. In the seventeenth century white indentured servants comprised as much as 75 to 85 percent of all immigrants who went to the colonies south of New York; and while charges of widespread kidnapping from Britain and Ireland may have been overstated, many of these men and women were coerced by recruiting agents, incarcerated and chained, then packed into ships in large numbers for transport. It was sometimes a way of ridding towns of beggars and drunkards; healthy children were stolen away from their homes (the word "kidnapping" comes from the practice: kid-nabbing). For some of the most ill-used and deceived, their experience was little better, if better at all, than that of the African slaves who were also being sent to do the work of building a new colony. That said, for other poor white Britains, as it is today for many groups of immigrants to the United States, a voyage to the colonies was voluntary and seen as their best chance of escaping hard conditions. Others were escaping debts or fleeing crimes, deserting their masters or running out on spouses. The relief could be immediate: upon signing a contract, the servant-to-be was usually given food, clothing, and shelter. For most, after arrival in the colonies, their life expectancy was lower than it had been prior to emigration, despite a relative abundance of food. Working conditions and housing were poor. Perhaps as many as 80 percent "died before they obtained their freedom or became propertyless day laborers, vagrants, or denizens of the local almshouse after completing their indentures," reports Lois Green Carr. In the late eighteenth and early nineteenth century, nearly three-fourths of indentured servants "ended up on the public dole at some point in their life."[20]

Merely to distinguish between slaves and nonslaves oversimplifies, however; even among black slaves, there were distinctions. The black overseers were often to be found at the top of the caste (until they were replaced by white overseers, perhaps in response to Nat Turner's rebellion). Carpenters, blacksmiths, and other highly skilled slaves joined the overseers at the top. Domestics came next, followed by the less skilled workers (gardeners, coach drivers, etc.), and then the unskilled nonagricultural workers. Last were the field workers (none of this includes the free blacks in the South, who were more than 5 percent of the black population in 1860). Those at the top had mortality rates that were half the rates of those at the very bottom.[21] A child on a South Carolina rice plantation was twice as likely to die in infancy as slaves elsewhere in the South.[22] Still, notes Theodore Hershberg:

> The antebellum black community was extremely poor. The total wealth—that is, the combined value of real and personal property holdings—for three out of every five households in both 1838 and 1847 amounted to $60 or less.[23]

The point is that we can identify differences in what we would today call poverty rates depending upon the particular form that slavery took from locale to locale—this state-sanctioned and state-supported means of regulation and control, which included, of necessity, the provision of food, housing, and health care, was a key factor in explaining variations in well-being among African Americans and an important factor in explaining the poverty of Southern whites, too.

A dark, violence-laden confession made in 1860 by murderer Edward Isham reveals, in extreme form, something of the life of a poor white man in the South in the 1840s and 1850s. Among the striking, but not unusual, features of Isham's life is the constant search for work and the variety of occupations held: Isham was variously a gold miner, a rail splitter, a tenant farmer, a fireman, a railroad worker, a livestock driver, a ditch digger, and a logger; he even spent time working for a free black farmer, and, more generally, maintained cordial relations with free blacks as well as with whites, winning him the enmity of those Southern whites who feared just such relations. Like many of the tramps of the later century, Isham's mobility and instability was born of some necessity (though explaining the violence he caused wherever he went is harder to do). As Charles C. Bolton writes:

> Slavery both stunted the growth of industrial wage positions and limited the need for white workers, as well as the wages paid to them, in the region . . . in order to take advantage of what were essentially short-term work opportunities, poor white laborers had to possess a wide range of marketable skills, and

they had to be willing to relocate regularly. In short, they had to be extremely flexible.[24]

Further limiting their opportunities, white workers were less easy to control than blacks, making them less desirable. The condition of poor white women in the South was also exacerbated by slavery, for not only were their wages driven lower by the similar work done by even worse-off women in poorhouses, workhouses, and asylums, but they competed as well with the forced, flexible labor provided by the sorority of slaves:

> There is ample evidence that at one time of pique or another, many plantation wives compared their lot to that of slaves, but only after knowing the fates of a woman alone can one actually imagine that connection between race and gender. A poor woman, like a slave, owned nothing—not her time, not her property, sometimes not her children. And also like a slave, she knew that hard work did not pay.[25]

During the war, Union commanders provided food and cash relief to poor Southern whites, in part in an effort to sway them to their cause, sometimes raising funds through a tax on the richer inhabitants. As Stephen Ash reports, one Union soldier wrote from Alabama in 1862:

> We are getting a good many recruits from this country. All poor people, in fact that is the only kind that pretend to any Unionism here.

A soldier in Virginia similarly noted:

> There are two classes of white people in this country—the poor class and the wealthy aristocratic class. The poor ones are very bitter against the others; [they] charge them with bringing on the war, and are always willing to show where the rich ones have hid their grain, fodder, horses, &c.

Whites in the South were not all of the same mind, of course. Racial hatred, and the knowledge, perhaps only dimly felt, that a class of slaves was the only thing keeping them from being the lowest caste, overcame economic self-interest for many. And life for poor Southern whites during the war could be hard: some Union officers report starvation in the winter of 1864, and many were to be found tramping throughout the South looking for food or, in vain, for work. They gathered at Union outposts in hopes of gaining sustenance or rooted through abandoned campsites. Just as black "contrabands" joined up with the North (see below), so too did large numbers of poor whites, seeing the war as an opportunity for them to better their condition; in fact, the majority of white contrabands were poor. One union soldier observed:

> The poor, wretched refugees that come here. . . . Old men and women, children of all ages, young women without clothing enough even for decency, come here daily for food.

Some went so far as to seize land near Union lines for their own. Many were emboldened in other ways. As one woman in Union-occupied Georgia wrote:

> The white women would come in Mother's yard in the broad daytime and steal peaches and apples, and she did not dare say anything to them for fear that they would tell the Yankees some great story on her. The poor people generally were "hand in glove" with the Yankees.

Such events occurred throughout the South, sometimes culminating in mass looting, near riots, or taking over homes. In general, poor whites were ignored by Union forces, many of whom thought them dirty, uncultured, uneducated, uncivilized—barely one step above their black brothers and sisters.[26]

The argument is not that poor whites had it as bad as slaves or that we have exaggerated the brutality and inhumanity of slavery; it is instead to say that, absent an examination of the architecture of the slavery system, the early poverty of American blacks and whites alike cannot be understood. This is the other face of the American welfare state, and among its first manifestations: a national program of regulation and "relief" that long predates the New Deal. While it was designed to control African Americans, it affected the health and well-being of all marginal populations in the South. This is a poverty created and fostered by government itself, in league with dominant economic interests. It would not be the last such institution.

A Brief Reprieve

There is a more benevolent institution that has also, nonetheless, been given too little attention in welfare state histories. If slavery might be the first national American welfare state program, the Freedman's Bureau can make a claim to being the second. It may be the most neglected of our welfare state institutions, perhaps because it targeted itself so narrowly to former slaves. But its reach, for a time, was notable, and its establishment marks the entry of the national government into cash relief, public education, and more direct subsidies, especially for homesteading.[27] Yet, to return to the measures employed earlier, in the index to Katz's *In the Shadow of the Poorhouse*, there is no entry for the Freedmen's Bureau (nor one under its formal title—The Bureau of Refugees, Freedmen, and Abandoned Land, housed in what was then still called the Department of War).[28] Jansson and Trattner do better: Trattner in fact credits the agency with being the "nation's first federal welfare agency" and devotes some five paragraphs to a discussion of it, while Jansson offers two paragraphs, albeit within the context of a larger discussion of Reconstruction-era issues facing former slaves. But surely there must be more to say if the bureau has a claim to being the first national-level relief program, predating the programs of the New Deal by more than half a century.

During the Civil War, many slaves escaped and sought out the protection of the Union army, often volunteering to fight with it. These were the contrabands. In 1861, General John Wool implemented a policy whereby contrabands within his ranks in Virginia were given food and wages, although most of the wages earned were never received, since they were funneled into an account to reimburse the government for expenses incurred in supporting other former slaves—especially the women, children, old, and disabled who could not work. Some, when "hired," were promised that their families would be fed too, a promise not always kept.[29] In 1862 a Massachusetts clergyman wrote to his senator to protest the forced labor extracted by the military from escaped slaves, a practice that suggests an early form of federal workfare:

> Most of the slaves are compelled to work for government for a miserable pittance. Up to two months ago they had worked for nothing but quarters and

rations. Since that time they have been partially supplied with clothing—costing on an average $4 per man. And in many instances they have received one or two dollars a month cash for the past two months. Some—an engineer Corps, at work on the rail-road, who were promised the pay of freemen by Genl Wool, and whose labor, according to the estimate of the Assistant Engineer, Mr Goddard, was valued at from one to two dollars a day, have received but one dollar cash for five & six months' work & but little clothing. Genl Wool told me that from the earnings of these slaves a surplus fund of $7000 has been accumulated.[30]

In all, about one in five black men of age—180,000 or so—served the Union during the Civil War (36,000 died, although for over 90 percent it was from disease, not battle). They were often treated poorly, paid less than whites, disproportionately called upon to perform manual labor and dirty work, and served in segregated units, but nonetheless emerged as a special class, honored by many and proud of their service. Many even found that the military bureaucracy and hierarchy offered some protection against discriminatory or arbitrary treatment; some were bold enough to demanded equal status during the war, like this corporal, who asked in a letter to Lincoln:

> Are we *Soldiers* or are we *labourers* . . . all we lack, is a paler hue, and a better acquaintance with the Alphabet. Now Your Excellency, We have done a Soldier's Duty. Why cant we have a Soldiers pay? . . . We appeal to You, Sir: as the Executive of the Nation, to have us Justly Dealt with . . . Black men You may well know, are poor.[31]

In the immediate wake of the war, almost all poor relief was still provided by private, voluntary associations and individuals; but soon, the need being so great, states did begin to step in. As early as 1862 Virginia was spending some $400,000 per year on medical care and relief; later, state pension funds were established to provide for Confederate veterans and their families. Mississippi spent fully 20 percent of its total revenue just on artificial limbs for veterans in 1866. The Confederate government even distributed food in the wake of bread riots in Mobile and Richmond. Many Southern states used their own resources to create programs for veterans of the war and their families—pensions, supported housing, funding for medical care, public schools, and other programs designed to serve only whites, leaving former slaves and many of the poorest nonveteran whites to the federal efforts of the Freedman's Bureau (as late as 1908, Florida and Georgia still spent $900,000 on Confederate veterans' pensions, and by 1937 Georgia had spent almost $50 million in total). While Georgia opened its asylum to blacks in 1865, segregated institutions were nonetheless the rule, and African Americans were more likely to be found in jail than in any eleemosynary facility. Partly as a result, Southern relief efforts and expenditures likely lagged behind the rest of the nation at least until the New Deal. By 1923, Alabama could boast the lowest per-pauper spending in its poorhouses, and only one-fourth of Florida's counties had any public relief at all. Four of the five states that did not offer some public program of unemployment relief by 1935 were in the South.[32]

The federal government finally stepped in through the Freedman's Bureau, although in its first three years white Southerners received more than one-quarter of the rations distributed; they also benefited from its hospitals and, to a lesser extent (because they refused to attend, not because they were excluded), from the bureau's schools.[33]

Sherman and others had interviewed black ministers in Savannah in 1865, who told the Union of how they thought government could best help:

> The way we can best take care of ourselves is to have land, and turn it and till it by our own labor . . . and we can soon maintain ourselves and have something to spare. . . . We want to be placed on land until we are able to buy it and make it our own.

Sherman's response was Special Field Order 15, granting each family "forty acres of tillable ground . . . in the possession of which land the military authorities will afford them protection, until such time as they can protect themselves."[34] The 1865 law that created the bureau was vague, did not articulate specific programs, and left much discretion to the commissioner. The famous "forty acres" provision, which contemplated a significant if not massive redistribution of wealth, was repealed within six months of the act's passage; the bureau was continued by Congress in 1866, over President Johnson's veto, who feared it would cause dependence and pauperization. Before it was dissolved in 1872, the bureau had done some good:

in March 1898 alone, it supported the provision of over 18 million meals, mostly to blacks; in its best year, 1869, the bureau supported 149,589 students in over 2,500 schools and paid the salaries of over 3,500 teachers; at one time, it operated 42 hospitals and employed 100 doctors and 350 nurses. Its impact was notable, for a few—less than 1 percent of all freedman actually benefited from its food programs at its peak, and in its best year, less than 4 percent were enrolled in the bureau. (Still, some estimates show black literacy rising to 40 percent by the 1890s; it's hard to know how much to credit bureau schools.) What it did succeed in doing, argues social work professor Ira Colby, was establish an entirely separate public welfare system for African Americans, ultimately limiting their ability to benefit from the broader programs of the welfare state then in existence and from those yet to come.[35] This might be its most enduring legacy.[36]

Jim Crow and the Black New Deal

The end to legal slavery did not end the state-sanctioned and systematic exploitation and abuse of African Americans, and while such practices were part of no formal, national institution, it might nonetheless be productive to think of Jim Crow as a welfare state nonsystem, one that continued to regulate and control African Americans and affect their ability, in Sen's terms, to "lead the kind of lives they value, and have reason to value" (see Epilogue). As historian C. Vann Woodward observed, throughout the ex-slave narratives collected during the Great Depression one can find what seems like genuine nostalgia for slavery—for, as one interviewee put it, the "good ole days." As Woodward notes, some of this may be accounted for by noting the historical moment in which these personal histories were collected; during the Depression, one might fondly remember a time when life, if less free, was more stable and predictable, and when food was more plentiful. And the narratives collectively portray a diverse world of experience:

> A paradise and a hell on earth, food in plenty and daily starvation, no punishment at all and brutal beatings for no reason at all, tender care and gruesome tortures, loving family ties and forced breedings, gentle masters and sadistic monsters.[37]

Still, we should not overestimate the impact that the abolition of slavery had upon the daily lives of many African Americans. From "A Negro Nurse," appearing in 1912 in the *Independent*:

> The condition of this vast host of poor colored people is just as bad as, if not worse than, it was during the days of slavery. Tho today we are enjoying nominal freedom, we are literally slaves.

She described her daily routine, her compulsory residence at the home of her employer, his unwanted sexual advances, being permitted to visit her children once weekly (but not allowed to stay overnight), forced to work at whatever household or caregiving task was demanded of her, all for $10 a month:

> You might as well say that I'm on duty all the time—from sunrise to sunrise, every day in the week. I am the slave, body and soul, of this family.

She complains about the lack of unions, and laments that if there were walkouts, there would be no shortage of others ready to step in and take their places:

> The truth is, we have to work for little or nothing or become vagrants! And that, of course, in this State would mean that we would be arrested, tried, and dispatched to the "State Farm," where we would surely have to work for nothing or be beaten with many stripes![38]

For many children, too, the conditions that governed their lives changed little after slavery had been abolished. In Mississippi, laws were enacted that allowed the state to bound out black orphans and the children of paupers, in some cases explicitly giving preference for their placement with their former masters.[39]

Many former slaves even remained on the same land, now as tenant farmers. Tenants could be divided roughly into two categories: share-renters owned their own equipment and paid 25 or 30 percent of their gain to the landlord; sharecroppers owned little or nothing and paid the landlord one-half of their crop, or more. Croppers were more common than renters and more vulnerable, since they were at the mercy of their landlords; they were forced to pay whatever price he set for equipment and often forced to purchase their food and other supplies from his store. Many tenants, at the end of each year, would find themselves in debt to their landlord for food, equipment, and medical care; one investigation showed that 75 percent of all croppers' debt was for medical expenses.[40] Tenants were described by their white landlords in terms similar to the language of slavery—as "childlike," improvident, inherently lazy, unable to vote wisely, and inferior. As one man told Arthur Raper:

> The Negro should have justice as a human being, but in the light of the kind of human being he is.[41]

The Great Depression and then the Agriculture Adjustment Act (AAA), which was designed to increase the value of crops by destroying some and reducing their production, drove many tenants off the land. Then their conditions grew even worse, as reported here in the travel journals of Erskine Caldwell, famous in his time as the author of *God's Little Acre* and *Tobacco Road*:

> These are the unknown people of today, the tenant farmer of the South. These are the people who hide their nakedness behind trees when a stranger wanders off the main-traveled roads. Here are the deformed, starved, and diseased children born since 1929. Here are the men who strip leaves off trees, dig roots out of the earth, and snare whatever wild animals they can. These are the people who were forced off the fertile land when sharecropping came to an end. These are the men, women, and children that many urban residents deny exist. There is hunger in their eyes as well as their bellies. They grasp for a word of hope. They plead for a word of advice. They have no friend or leader to help them. The government relief agencies in many Southern counties are inadequate to help them. Sometimes neither has ever heard of the other. . . . The Federal Government says that nobody starves, but the Federal Government does not know what its left hand does.[42]

As bad as the period was in general, blacks were three to four times as likely to lose their jobs in the early years of the Depression.[43] By the 1930s, average annual income in the South ($314 in 1937) was half that in the North. For many, it was worse: $73 for the average tenant farmer, and from

$38 to $87 for sharecroppers. Twice as many Southern children worked.[44] It is in this context that the New Deal came to the South. But the tragedy is, as Elna Green observes, that instead of the New Deal tearing down the apartheid regime and bringing a more egalitarian provision of public aid, because of the South's control over the Democratic Party and Congress itself, it shaped New Deal programs to serve white planters' interests.[45]

Despite the growing alphabet soup of new government relief programs, in the early New Deal, African Americans had little to be grateful for. The National Recovery Act (NRA) excluded domestics and unskilled laborers from its provisions, which included minimum wages. In order to avoid raising the wages of those black men and women who were covered by the NRA, some firms simply fired the black workers they had and replaced them with whites. The NRA was, as a result, derided as the Negro Run Around, Negroes Ruined Again, and Negroes Rarely Allowed. Blacks were barred from Tennessee Valley Authority (TVA) jobs, too, and were less likely to have landlords who were willing to electrify their buildings. Few Civilian Conservation Corps (CCC) jobs went to black youths.[46] In the early 1930s, the Red Cross tried to provide food and clothing, but even this was resisted by the planters, just as they later resisted federal aid, until many came to realize that they could use relief as an excuse to lower the wages they were paying.[47] To accommodate plantation owners, the Works Progress Administration (WPA) and other projects were often suspended at harvest time, to ensure an ample supply of cheap labor. When the Federal Emergency Relief Administration (FERA) did reach the South, whites were more likely to receive cash, and blacks were more likely to receive only food. Yet many programs achieved successes in distributing benefits to the neediest cases. This angered planters, since, as one said, "by helping the worst, it puts a premium on improvidence and idleness." Besides, said another, "most any nigger who wants to work can get something to do."[48]

Here's an anonymous letter sent to FDR in September 1935:

Dear Sir I am ritening you a few Lines to Let you no how they are treating we colored people on this releaf I went up to our home Vister and re[ap]plied for some Thing to do an Some Thing to eat and She told me that she had nothing for me at all and to they give all the worke to White people and give us nothing an Sir I wont you to no how we are treated here. So please help us if you can.[49]

But by the end of the decade, things had changed. African Americans doubled their share of CCC jobs, were able to receive more federal farm security loans, gained access to one-third of Public Works Administration (PWA) housing units, secured some five thousand supervisory jobs in the WPA education programs, and gained access to relief. As Joe Trotter writes, "Some even suggested that God 'will lead me' but relief 'will feed me.'"[50] Even by mid-decade, the chance for an African American to have been on relief was over two and a half times that of a white man; while blacks were some 8 percent of the population, they constituted 24 percent of those on relief. This varied greatly by region; blacks in the North were much more likely to receive aid than blacks in the South. Part of the explanation may be simple racism: these were joint federal-state programs, and the important decisions were made at the local level, almost always by whites. So, blacks were denied relief more readily by local administrators in the South. Or, as one New Orleans case worker in 1934 would have it:

> These huge Negro case loads may be due largely to the Negro psychology. . . . They are children, really. If anything is being given away, they want some, too. We encounter that over and over in our intake. They are accustomed to having things handed out to them by white people. And that's the way they look at relief. Why work, if they can get support from the Government?[51]

Another part of the answer for why blacks in the South received less than those in the North may be because they retained their near monopoly on unskilled and low-skilled jobs, causing whites there to be in greater relative need and to have had fewer resources.[52] Regardless, African Americans continued to depend upon their own institutions of self-help. During the Depression, reports historian Joe William Trotter Jr.:

> African-American families took in boarders, cared for each other's children, and creatively manipulated their resources. In rural areas, they maintained gardens, canned fruits and vegetables, fished, hunted, and gathered wild nuts and berries. A Georgia relief official understood these creative responses to poverty: "There is no dearth of resourcefulness. In their efforts to maintain existence, these people are catching and selling fish, reselling vegetables, sewing in exchange for old clothes, letting out sleeping place, and doing odd

jobs. They understand how to help each other. Stoves are used in common, wash boilers go their rounds, and garden crops are exchanged and shared."[53]

By the early twentieth century, the National Association of Colored Women could report that its member organizations throughout the nation had established training schools for kindergarten teachers, day nurseries, vocational schools, old-age homes, reading rooms, prisoner programs, settlement houses, orphanages, Sunday schools, temperance work, and self-help meetings for young mothers.[54]

Poverty, Labor, and the Prison

There is an argument to be made that the institution of the state that poor Americans (and especially poor black men) have been most likely to encounter is the police force, and we might therefore incorporate the criminal justice system generally, and the prison more specifically, into our thinking about the welfare state. According to recent data, some 2 million families receive TANF benefits, six hundred thousand people inhabit a homeless shelter on any given night, some one hundred thousand annually reside in mental hospitals, 6 million receive SSI, and perhaps six hundred thousand children live within the foster-care system. Most will concede that these are institutions and programs legitimately within the purview of welfare state analysts.

At the same time, according to the U.S. Department of Justice, some 2.1 million are confined in American jails and prisons, and another 4.8 million remain under the surveillance of the state on probation or parole. These men (and, in growing numbers, women) are disproportionately black and Hispanic, less educated, drug- or alcohol-addicted, and poor and unemployed at the time of their arrest. Felons and ex-offenders inhabit their own sphere in the welfare state, and they are typically denied eligibility for public housing, food stamps, or, in some states, licenses to be bus drivers or hairdressers. As I've suggested, to comprehend the political economy of the ghetto we must consider the manner in which the mass incarceration of black men has removed potential fathers, partners, and wage earners from their community. Urban poverty cannot be understood without incorporating the prison. This was as true in our past as it is now, when the punishment for poverty—codified in an array of antivagrancy and anti-tramping laws in the North as well as the black codes of the South—was debtor's prison, the work farm, or indentured servitude, just as jail or expulsion from the city is today punishment for loitering, begging, sleeping in public places, or other public displays of need.[55]

It is useful to remember that the Thirteenth Amendment did not abolish slavery: it explicitly retained involuntary servitude "as a punishment for crime whereof the party shall have been duly convicted." African Americans suffered disproportionately from this loophole, and continue to suffer because of their overrepresentation in American prisons. Throughout our history, most executions have taken place in the South, and one is more likely to be executed for murder if the victim is white.[56] Further, it was not merely the Thirteenth Amendment that was evaded, but the Fifteenth too. Massive fraud, the threat of violence, and actual violence was required to keep emancipated slaves from voting. Said one Democrat:

> We were *forced* to a choice between the evils of negro rule and the evils of the questionable practice to overthrow it. We chose what we thought was the lesser evil, and it is now not to be regretted.[57]

That legacy remains: many states continue to deny felons or ex-felons the right to vote; as a result, 13 percent of black men are disenfranchised. If current trends continue, one in three can expect to spend some portion of his life in prison or jail, and many more will be denied the right to vote.[58] Little wonder that some today adopt the language of abolitionism to describe prison reform movements.[59]

One Mississippi state official said after the end of the Civil War that "emancipation . . . will require a system of prisons."[60] One former slave:

> In slavery times . . . jails was all built for the white folks. There warn't never nobody of my color put in none of them. No time . . . to stay in jail; they had to work; when they done wrong they was whipped and let go.[61]

In what may be nothing more than a curious coincidence, New York State emancipated its slaves and created its first state prison on the same day in 1796.[62] As early as the 1720s, there were more jails in the colonies than there were hospitals or public schools.[63]

It is only recently that we have *not* thought of the prison as a welfare state institution. In 1922, for example, in an article about public welfare in the American South, one observer noted "four age-old institutions" of public welfare: the asylum for the insane; relief for the dependent; the prison for criminals; and the courts, "for dispensing of justice," which often meant allocating people to the appropriate welfare institution.[64] Until 1956 the main national organization of welfare was the National Conference on Charities and Corrections, while many states developed Bureaus of Charities and Corrections to coordinate punishment and relief activity. At least until the late 1800s, poorhouses, almshouses, workhouses, poor farms, and asylums were more prison than refuge: what they had in common was containment, rules and regulations, and the demand for deference. In the late 1700s in Philadelphia, blacks were some 15 percent of almshouse inmates and about one-quarter of paupers in prison; about one in ten of those on the "vagrancy dockets" were ill-behaved servants, black or white, being punished on behalf of their masters.[65]

Throughout much of our history, to be poor was a crime. Should you have found yourself in debt in colonial Philadelphia, you would have been jailed and then required to pay for your own food and heat. If you were among the fortunate, you would have been granted a trial, but even if acquitted you would have been obligated to pay court costs; if unable to pay, you would have been incarcerated and would be obliged to bear the cost of your keep. Thus, even to be accused of poverty meant the denial of your most basic liberty, and to be driven deeper into need by your punishment. Conditions in debtor's prisons were typically dreadful—foul and foul-smelling, crowded, and raw and cold in winter. Most were incarcerated for small sums; some were prostitutes who owed money to their brothels; others were sailors guilty of nothing, accused by their captains and incarcerated only to ensure that when he next needed them to set sail they would be available.[66] Historian Laurel Ulrich notes that we can identify another function of debtor's prison:

> In the abstract, imprisonment for debt seems a barbaric practice, something on the order of branding thieves or cutting off the ears of rioters. In reality, it

put as much pressure on a man's connections as on the man himself. A form of coercion rather than punishment, it was a way of forcing a man to reveal hidden property or liquidate capital—social as well as financial.[67]

Indeed, while welfare state histories have focused on public poor relief and pensions, the more typical encounter with government has not been through welfare programs, but through the police and the prison. Because relief and reform institutions were so often used to control, punish, and indoctrinate those marked as poor, we have a compelling reason to include the prison within the purview of the welfare state. Its functions are perhaps easiest to discern in the late nineteenth century.

One Georgia boy was left an orphan after the end of the Civil War. His uncle hired him out to a sea captain. By twenty-one, technically free to leave, he signed on for another year, and another, and another, eventually taking a ten-year contract with the captain's son, a Georgia senator. More striking were the other "workers" who soon appeared on the senator's plantation, black convicts leased from the state for some $200 per year:

> When I saw these men in shackles, and the guards with their guns, I was scared nearly to death. I felt like running away, but didn't know where to go. . . . We free laborers held a meeting. We all wanted to quit. We sent a man to tell the Senator about it. Word came back that we were all under contract for ten years and that the Senator would hold us to the letter of the contract, or put us in chains and lock us up—the same as the other prisoners. . . . We had sold ourselves into slavery—and what could we do about it? The white folks had all the courts, all the guns, all the hounds, all the railroads, all the telegraph wires, all the newspapers, all the money, and nearly all the land—and we had only our ignorance, our poverty, and our empty hands. . . . most of us worked side by side with those convicts during the remainder of ten years.

After the ten years, most of the convicts were informed that they each owed the senator $100 or more for debts supposedly incurred at the "commissary" from which they were required to buy their food and supplies. And "no one of us would have dared to dispute a white man's word—oh no; not in those days." For the next three years, this man lived as a "peon." His nine-year-old son was "given away to a negro family across the river in South Carolina, and I never saw or heard of him after that." This, note, was in the early years of the twentieth century. Such practices were widespread, especially in Georgia, both the forced indentured "contract" servitude and the abundant use of prison labor to take the place of what slavery had previously provided. Many had been charged with public order offenses or with adultery. The state made sure that there were plenty of such prisoners:

> A number of negro lewd women were employed by certain white men to entice negro men into their houses; and then, on certain nights, at a given signal, when all was in readiness, raids would be made by the officers upon these houses, and the men would be arrested. . . . Nine out of ten of these men, so arrested and so charged, would find their way ultimately to some convict camp, and, as I said, many of them found their way every year to the Senator's camp while I was there.[68]

One of the virtues of convict labor was that the worker could never become a tramp—he had no power and could never, finding wages or conditions intolerable, set out for a better deal. Oregon, California, Missouri, and Massachusetts each had some experience with convict leasing, but these were modest, limited experiments. Leasing was a feature of the South, and in the post–Civil War years, the Confederate states often relied upon such labor for plantations, mines, and mills.[69] But while predominantly a Southern phenomenon, it was, until the 1930s, sanctioned and subsidized by the U.S. government, thanks to federal subsidies that encouraged the use of prison labor to build or improve public roads.[70]

Convict leasing masks itself as an alternative institution of the criminal justice system, but, like slavery, it is also an institution of labor market control; as historian Matthew Mancini put it, "the criminal justice apparatus was systematically geared for the collection of labor." It was those industries that had most to gain from the practice that pushed for the creation of new vagrancy laws or the stepped-up enforcement of laws already on the books. In 1907, one Florida turpentine operator, in desperate need of labor, presented the sheriff with a list of some eighty black men he thought might be good workers and offered to pay $5 a head for them; all eighty were then arrested—for vagrancy, gambling, or disorderly conduct—within the span of three weeks. In 1876, Mississippi passed the Pig Law, which made the theft of a farm animal or property valued at $10 or more punishable by up to five years in prison; a few weeks later, the legislature passed a law permitting the leasing of convict labor. Subsequently, we find black men like Rause Echols getting three years for stealing a suit of clothes; Robert Hamber, five years for stealing a horse; Lewis Luckett, two years for a hog. Walter Blake was fined $50 and $132 in court fees for illegal gambling—and, like all large fines levied against poor men, it would have to be served in hard labor. It is no accident that African Americans constituted typically as much as 90 percent of convict laborers, and no accident that the institution still bore an uncanny resemblance to the slave system recently deposed. Mancini says evidence is mixed as to whether leasing depressed wages generally, but it clearly did so in particular industries.[71]

Housing for convict laborers was in "great rolling cages," small railroad cars with as many as thirty or more men in each, often chained together at the ankle, sharing one fetid bucket for waste, wearing clothes that were often—quite literally—never washed; they were replaced once worn out. Conditions, though awful everywhere, were likely the worst in Arkansas, Mississippi, and Louisiana. They were beaten, whipped, and tortured. In some camps, men were made to fight one another for the entertainment of their overseers. Because the pay for guards was so low, in some camps black men also served as guards. A constant of labor camps has been the poor, often unsanitary accommodations; terrible food; and low wages—and because throughout most of our past there were no state-level laws governing their operation, usually only those within city limits were regulated. In most camps, reports Mancini, "perhaps the only statistic in excess of mortality rate would be escape rate." And the mortality rate was high indeed: 11 percent died from 1880 to 1885 in Mississippi, 14 percent died in 1881 in Louisiana, and 16 percent died in 1887 in Mississippi. Between 1877 and 1888, the death rate was 45 percent for convicts tasked to the Greenville and Augusta Railroad in South Carolina. In 1888, one-third of Alabama's prisoners were estimated to have "chronic, incurable diseases." In Mississippi, perhaps one in four convicts was a child or an adolescent—one six-year-old girl, Mary Gay, got thirty days and a fine for stealing a hat. Young Will Evans served two years for taking the change off a grocery store counter.[72]

For some employers leasing was an improvement over slavery: slave masters had to bear the costs of sustaining the entire slave community, including those who could not work—the very young, the old, and the sick. With a lessee, by contrast, he was concerned only with the laborer himself, and many were none too concerned with his well-being. As one planter said, in the title of Mancini's book, if "one dies, get another." Convict labor was probably less productive than "free" labor, but its extraordinary cheapness made the bargain well worth it, at least until the rise of chain gangs and states' increasing determination to use their convicts for their own purposes.[73]

But this is not just a feature of the American past: there are now some 750,000 people employed in American prisons; this would make the prison industry the second-largest employer in the nation if it were counted among the Fortune 500. Because our prison population is disproportionately black and Hispanic, so too are convict laborers, just as they historically have been. They are paid as little as 20 cents an hour, making some of them cheaper than sweatshop labor in Mexico or Indonesia. An enormous range of American companies have used prison labor, including Lexus, Boeing, Honda, Konica, Microsoft, TWA, Toys 'R' Us, IBM, Dell, AT&T, Starbucks, Nintendo, and Victoria's Secret.[74]

Vulnerable American workers have faced similar kinds of conditions, exploited in ways that echo the plantation or the prison. Louise Mitchell writes this in the May 5, 1940, *Daily Worker*:

> Every morning, rain or shine, groups of women with brown paper bags or cheap suitcases stand on street corners in the Bronx and Brooklyn waiting for a chance to get some work. Sometimes there are 15, sometimes 30, some are old, many are young and most of them are Negro women waiting for employers to come to the street corner auction blocks to bargain for their labor. . . . If they are lucky, they get about 30 cents an hour scrubbing, cleaning, laundering, washing windows, waxing floors and woodwork all day long. . . . Once hired on the "slave market," the women often find after a day's backbreaking toil, that they worked longer than was arranged, got less than was promised, were forced to accept clothing instead of cash and were exploited beyond human endurance. . . . Throughout the country more than two million women are engaged in domestic work. . . . About half are Negro women. . . . Though many Negro women work for as little as two dollars a week and as long as 80 hours a week . . . they have no social security, no workmen's compensation, no old age security.[75]

By 2005, most day laborers were immigrant and Latino men—by one estimate there were over 117,000 every day who gathered in open-air markets, waiting to be hired by contractors, movers, landscapers, or home-owners in need of a cheap worker for the yard or the house.[76] Low wages, irregular employment, no benefits—they were, like black women of the recent past, vulnerable, readily exploited, and willing to be because they were in such dire need of work. Here's Albert in Roanoke, Virginia, in the late 1980s:

> This guy comes through to get workers to pick peaches in South Carolina. This is in May. So I get on the migrant bus and I come up to South Carolina with them. I got caught up there for six months. Picking peaches, potatoes, cropin' tobacco, picking cucumbers, picking squash. I was working for like 30 cents an hour because, well, let's put it this way: they paid you 30 cents a bag for peaches. You pick 80 bags a day, and 30 times 80 is $24. And some days I would only pick 50 or 60 bags—so let's say on average I make $20 a day. At the end of the week your room and board was $35. And they had this place, where they served beer and wine, and crack cocaine. The crack cocaine was $35 a hit. The beer was a dollar and a half a can, the wine was $3 a pint. The moonshine was $6 a pint. The first night I was there they passed out the cocaine, said, "Do you smoke?" I said, "No." The guy said, "Here, take this anyway." And then at the end of the week he said, "Remember that little package I gave you? That package cost $30." And you're so intimidated—'cause there's two guys standin' there with pistols sticking out of their pants—you don't say nothin'. Then he holds his hand open and says, "You want another one?" And clearly these guys want you to take it—and you've been high anyway—so you snatch it. Pretty soon I'm gettin' me a rock every night. I'm gettin' me a can of beer every night. I'm gettin' me a bottle of wine and a bottle of moonshine, inviting everyone over to my cabin . . . we'd party up, get up the next morning and go to work. So at the end of the week, instead of me drawing a paycheck, I have a balance due of a hundred dollars. I owed them a hundred dollars.[77]

In June 2005, Ronald Robert Evans was arrested for having drawn mostly black, homeless men into indentured servitude on his cabbage and potato farm in Florida. According to a number of news reports,[78] Evans promised jobs, along with room and board. After each day's work, they were offered alcohol, cigarettes, and crack cocaine on credit—the last at about four times the street cost.[79] And, as in the past, many found themselves with debt instead of income. It was workers at the camp, surrounded by fence and barbed wire, who brought it to the attention of the law. Some of the eighty or so men found there, upon their emancipation, were arrested on outstanding warrants. And thanks to private company contractors like Halliburton and others, in the wake of 2005's Hurricane Katrina, hundreds of Mexican men were lured with the promise of jobs paying $8 per hour with room and board. Instead, they were packed as many as nineteen into a trailer, fed sometimes only once a day (and rather thin fare at that), and told they would be deported if they left the military bases where many of the contractors were located. Many were summarily dismissed after weeks of work without having been paid—left homeless and entirely without resources in a foreign country.[80]

While I have drawn a line here from American slavery through convict leasing and the American prison, it's worth remembering political scientist Marie Gottschalk's warning that we not "flatten out" variation across institutions and over time. As she writes:

> Today's incarceration rate of nearly 7,000 per 100,000 African-American males dwarfs the number of blacks imprisoned in the South under convict leasing.[81]

Though she offers this caution to make a different point, I'll use it as a reminder that progress does not necessarily follow merely from the passage of time, and the American welfare state, rarely a force for good for African Americans, still inclines more toward punishment and control than relief and aid. We should also note a curious irony. African Americans have historically been more likely to be castigated for their dependence on welfare, despite their relative independence from it through exclusion. As I've noted, we could instead claim that it has been whites who have been dependent upon blacks: for cheap labor on the plantation, on the farm, in the factory, and in the prison; for child-rearing and housekeeping; as cannon fodder; and as politically indispensable scapegoats.

8

Surrender:
A Culture of Poverty?

I have no mercy or compassion in me for a society that will crush people, and then penalize them for not being able to stand up under the weight.

—Malcolm X, 1965

Throughout our history, poverty has usually been understood to be rooted in personal, moral failure: weakness of character, the absence of a work ethic, and disdain for the norms of society at large spread like a disease from person to person, from family to family, and produce entire communities beset with vice and despair. Some even suggest that poor Americans inhabit an entirely separate culture, a "culture of poverty," one that manifests itself, according to anthropologist Oscar Lewis, in seventy-five distinct traits. Among them, we find a hatred and fear of the police; the absence of participation in mainstream institutions (and a distrust of them); low marriage rates; a "present-time" and fatalistic orientation; territoriality; early sexual activity; female-centered families; a lack of impulse control; a "tolerance for pathology"; and feelings of marginality, helplessness, dependence, and inferiority.[1] It is the urban poor, others have argued, who are especially distinct, and their inability or unwillingness to alter these "pathologies" is the chief cause of their poverty. As Jacob Riis professed long before Lewis:

> The thief is infinitely easier to deal with than the pauper, because the very fact of his being a thief presupposes some bottom to the man.[2]

It is the supposed passivity among the very poor that often draws the attention of politicians, reformers, and critics of welfare. But it has been prominent even among more liberal voices. American socialist Michael Harrington wrote this in *The Other America*, a book credited with bringing the Kennedy administration's attention to poverty:

> The other America does not contain the adventurous seeking a new life and land. It is populated by the failures, by those driven from the land and bewildered by the city, by old people suddenly confronted with the torments of loneliness and poverty, and by minorities facing a wall of prejudice . . . the other America is becoming increasingly populated by those who do not belong to anybody or anything. They are no longer participants in an ethnic culture from the old country; they are less and less religious; they do not belong to unions or clubs. They are not seen, and because of that they themselves cannot see. Their horizon has become more and more restricted, they see one another, and that means that they see little reason to hope.[3]

Harrington is not quite blaming poor people for their state, but he seems to suggest that there is little that can be done in the face of such deeply ingrained norms. Others have concluded that trying to relieve poverty is therefore futile, or even counterproductive. If people are poor, it is their own fault. In a land of such opportunity, after all, how else could we explain it?

No City on a Hill

It is in many ways our oldest and most enduring national myth, one that has taken many forms: the streets are paved with gold. With hard work, any American can achieve anything. Any boy (or girl, we now add) can grow up to be president. We're a beacon to the world, a land of freedom and opportunity. Even before leaving the *Mayflower* and stepping on our shore, William Bradford proclaimed in 1630:

> We must consider that we shall be as a City upon a Hill, the eyes of all people are upon us.[4]

In 1699, Governor Bellomont of New York boasted, "I believe there is not a richer populace anywhere in the King's dominions," and, when the creation of a workhouse was first suggested, he reported that the Assembly "smiled at [the proposal] because there is no such thing as a beggar in this town or county."[5] Years later, novelist Herman Melville continued the myth:

> Such a being as a beggar is almost unknown; and to be a born American citizen seems a guarantee against pauperism.[6]

America's most famous French visitor, Alexis de Tocqueville, famously remarked upon it in *Democracy in America*:

> No novelty in the United States struck me more vividly during my stay there than the equality of conditions. It was easy to see the influence of this basic fact on the whole course of society. . . . Men there are nearer equality in wealth and mental endowments, or, in other words, more nearly equally powerful, than in any other country of the world or in any other age of recorded history.[7]

Benjamin Franklin, thanks to his rags-to-riches *Autobiography*, must also take part of the blame for this enduring trope, but even Gordon Wood, an eminent historian of our founding era, finds this Shining City evident from our earliest stirrings of resistance to Britain:

> The social conditions that generically are supposed to lie behind all revolutions—poverty and economic deprivation—were not present in colonial America . . . the white American colonists were not an oppressed people; they had no crushing imperial chains to throw off.[8]

We should give Wood credit, and note his caveat (*white* American colonists), but even so, his assertion is unfounded. Recent research by historians of the colonial era shows that claims of a relatively free and equal society, one without dire need, are without much merit, and that it was "a poor man's country for many of its citizens."[9] The number of those needing and receiving aid rose throughout the eighteenth century. Mobility even then was limited, especially in the cities, and poverty was a constant presence throughout people's life spans. Many had to rely upon assistance from churches, private aid societies, friends, neighbors, and family, and by the time of the American Revolution, local officials spent perhaps as much effort in "warning out" (or expelling) the nonresident poor as they did in caring for residents in need.[10] By the end of the eighteenth century all large cities had discovered the need for almshouses and workhouses. Women, then as now, were disproportionately poor and reliant upon public aid, a condition that grew worse, not better, over the course of the eighteenth century. And during that period, while the number of landholders rose, so too did the number who were born and died without property. Infant mortality rates in the colonies were no lower than in England, and as Gary Nash writes, "among the mass of those who sought opportunity in the British American colonies, it is the story of relentless labor and ultimate failure that stands out."[11] John Alexander notes that in the late 1700s Philadelphia "had far more social distance between classes and far more class conflict than is often supposed . . . thus questioning the claim that the late colonial and revolutionary periods were marked by a high degree of social unity, harmony, and simple humanitarianism."[12] Wood himself admits that "wealth was more unequally distributed after the Revolution than before."[13]

Simple narratives of abundance and opportunity, of progress and prosperity, will no longer do. Poverty and inequality have been a constant presence in this country, and the causes have been constant, too: disruption and dislocation brought by war and large-scale economic change; sickness, death, fire, and natural disaster; seasonal fluctuations in the demand for labor; discrimination based on race, ethnicity, and gender; the power conferred by inherited wealth and status; and a political system that inhibits the ability of majorities to exert their will over elite minorities. Yet we have been unwilling to acknowledge this, and instead of relieving poverty we blame poor Americans for their condition, rationalizing our neglect with disdain for their supposed lack of aspiration, their poor work ethic, their despair.

A Rational Surrender

Oscar Lewis is often misread and misused; even if we can identify behaviors and attitudes particular to those who live in concentrated poverty (and I am ambivalent on the question), that is not a condemnation of them. He wrote of the culture of poverty that "there is nothing in the concept that puts the onus of poverty on the character of the poor," for it is the effects of poverty that he has documented, not the causes. The diminished expectations, the refusal to participate in mainstream institutions, the cynicism and other characteristics we might indeed find among very poor people—these are not marks of moral failure, he insists, but complicated (if unconscious) strategies used by those with little discernible power and little cause for hope to protect themselves from disappointment. It first developed centuries ago, Lewis argued, as a reaction to the tumultuous transition from feudalism to capitalism. We've now seen enough into the lives of poor Americans to understand how diminished expectations, or even utter hopelessness, might, alas, be prudent, given the formidable obstacles to their survival, let alone success. If one expects nothing, after all, it is more difficult to be disappointed. Elliot Liebow observed it in the men he chronicled in *Tally's Corner*:

> Convinced of their inadequacies, not only do they not seek out those few better-paying jobs which test their resources, but they actively avoid them, gravitating in a mass to the menial, routine jobs which offer no challenge—and therefore pose no threat—to the already diminished images they have of themselves.[14]

Sugar Turner suggests that for some, it's conscious:

> Welfare mothers dream just like everybody else. . . . But they don't dream that big. A dream is a new dress, not a $100,000 home. . . . Your dream can be realized on the first of the month. Your dream can be realized by screwin' the right nigger. Your dream can be realized by borrowing $10 from your mom.[15]

Thomas Coolidge put it this way in the early 1960s, talking about his home, the Pruitt-Igoe housing project in St. Louis:

> This place is just like a jungle but you can't get away from it, so you must submit yourself.[16]

Another welfare recipient, Emily:

> What do I want to be? Gosh, I don't allow myself the luxury to think of these things. It's a luxury to think of things about myself in any other way than I am now. What I have to do is survive. I can't think about what I want to be.[17]

Angela idealized weakness:

You know, some people believe that only the strong will survive. Can you imagine going through life believing something like that?[18]

Some children give up young. In April 1935, one girl told Martha Gellhorn:

I generally go to bed around seven at night, because that way you get the day over with quicker.

While Edward Devine reported this in 1904:

A dentist who had a considerable practice in a large institution was struck by the comparative docility of these children and their ready submission to whatever pain his operations made necessary, and this he attributed to their drill in accepting quietly whatever experiences came to them and the sense of futility of resistance which had been implanted.[19]

Others don't give up until they are older:

Home is the natural destination of any homeless person. But nothing can be done in a day, in a week, in a year to get nearer that destination. No perceptible progress can be made. In the absence of progress, time is nearly meaningless. Some days are more comfortable than others. And that is all the difference. A homeless life has no storyline. It is a pointless circular rambling about the stage that can be brought to happy conclusion only by a deus ex machina.[20]

Perhaps they give up because they learn to. In July 1891, F.T. Thompson wrote to the Albany orphan asylum director:

I hope the little ones ar enjoying them selves as god nows thare is no comfort for poor popele aftre thay gro up.[21]

A coal miner's daughter, from Roanoke, Virginia, in the late 1980s:

As years went by I went on my own. Just like most everybody, I wanted somethin' better out of life—and found it wasn't any better. There wasn't anything better out of life, though people think there is.[22]

Some surrender out of fear. As one man told Matthew Josephson in 1933:

Most of the men who have been taken in out of the streets seem to grow numbed and submissive in these lodging houses. They have no fight in them. They say: "We don't dare complain. We're afraid of being fired out." They would rather not take part in radical demonstrations, hunger marches and such things; they have a pretty clear notion that the authorities might find out and show displeasure with them.[23]

Mental illness is widely understood to be a cause of homelessness. But "homeless people tend to disagree," writes VanderStaay: it's homelessness and hopelessness that cause mental illness. Cyril, a homeless Philadelphia man:

If you don't have decent clothing, or you're dirty and have no money, you're looked down upon. People turn their heads, say, "Get away from me, scum!" So you don't fit in. Society rejects you, doesn't care for you, and you begin to lose hope. When that happens you just sit alone, thinking about your problems. Dejected. And with no human contact you just totally block everything out. The outer world gets canceled out. You get up off the grate, look this way and that. Self-absorbed.[24]

Mary Childers's memoir might shed some light on why, among some minority students, aspiration may be mocked or derided as "acting white":[25]

To get by, [Mom] breaks the law by working off the books for people who act like they're doing her a favor but pay less than minimum wage. Living in fear of getting caught for necessary lies while knowing she can't get ahead have made her bitter and furtive. As naturally as a child learns language, I've absorbed that bitterness and fear of being taken advantage of even though I make more than she does and have more chances. I stint on baby-sitting and even schoolwork to avoid the humiliation of getting caught believing anything other than the facts of life: Disappointment is the most likely outcome of commitment and the poor stay poor while the rich get richer.[26]

And the lack of political participation among poor Americans makes some sense as well. As reporter Leon Dash observed of Rosa Lee:

Her bedroom television is on, as usual. It is Inauguration Day. On the screen, crowds are gathering at the Capitol to see Bill Clinton take the oath of office. Rosa Lee pays no attention. She has no interest in politics or government. She has never voted. "It's not going to make one bit of difference in my life," she once told me. "White people are going to treat us like they want to anyway." In her mind, white people have all the power, and they don't care about blacks. "I wouldn't go *two* blocks to vote," she says. "I have seen too much and hasn't nothing changed. The only thing that's changed is that we don't have to ride in the back of the bus."[27]

Many blame themselves, as with this homeless teenager:

If I'm not too stoned, I'm sometimes looking at other people lately, people I'm passing on the street. People going to work or coming from work, people going home to wherever they live. I wonder what it's like to be them. And how did they manage to do it, to just be so right and ordinary and safe? Probably they're thinking I'm dirt, Probably they're thinking I'm shit, just a piece of garbage. That makes me want to sink even lower, get so far down no one can see me anymore. To where I have nothing left to lose. Or maybe to where I just plain stop existing. Because I know as long as I continue to exist there's a choice I'm making: staying like this, or getting better. But I don't want to do either one. It hurts too much.[28]

Some blame others:

Being overexposed to other street people can also be a serious problem. Because, let's face it, some of them are flaming assholes. They batter against you like the rain, leaving your soul just a little more damp and soggy from the experience of them.[29]

Others blame some god:

O golden, dyspeptic God of America, you were in a bad mood that winter. We were poor, and you punished us harshly for this worst of sins.[30]

Liebow also sheds light on notions of a supposed "cycle of poverty":

Many similarities between the lower-class Negro father and son (or mother and daughter) do not result from "cultural transmission" but from the fact that the son goes out and independently experiences the same failures, in the same areas, and for much the same reasons, as his father. What appears as a dynamic, self-sustaining cultural process is, in part at least, a relatively simple piece of social machinery which turns out, in rather mechanical fashion, independently produced look-alikes.[31]

Much of the disapprobation directed at those in the poorest communities, then and now, revolves around drug and alcohol use, another perceived mark of cultural decay. I don't want to understate the manner in which substance abuse and addiction do harm to individuals, their families, and their communities, but I suspect that if I were living in a Five Points tenement or one of the worst of our modern public housing projects, I might escape, as best I could, with liquor or drugs: this behavior might also be a rational response. As one early New York tenement dweller lectured a disapproving health inspector, "If you lived in this place you [too] would ask for whisky instead of milk."[32] Perhaps the best response comes from David Simon and Edward Burns in *The Corner*, their searing glimpse into a Baltimore neighborhood at the center of the drug trade in the 1980s:

> Thirty years gone and now the drug corner is the center of its own culture. . . . In the end, we'll blame them. We always do. And why the hell not? . . . If it was us, if it was our lonesome ass shuffling past the corner of Monroe and Fayette every day, we'd get out, wouldn't we? We'd endure. Succeed. Thrive. No matter what, no matter how, we'd find the fucking exit.
>
> If it was our fathers firing dope and our mothers smoking coke, we'd pull ourselves past it. We'd raise ourselves, discipline ourselves, teach ourselves the essentials of self-denial and delayed gratification that no one in our universe ever demonstrated. And if home was the rear room of some rancid, three-story shooting gallery, we'd rise above that, too. We'd shuffle up the stairs past nodding fiends and sullen dealers, shut the bedroom door, turn off the television, and do our schoolwork. Algebra amid the stench of burning rock; American history between police raids. And if there was no food on the table, we're certain we could deal with that. We'd lie about our age to cut taters and spill grease and sling fries at the sub shop for five-and-change-an-hour, walk-

ing every day past the corner where friends are making our daily wage in ten minutes.

No matter. We'd persevere, wouldn't we? We'd work that job by night and go to class by day, by some miracle squeezing a quality education from the disaster that is the Baltimore school system. We'd do all the work, we'd pay whatever the price. . . . Come payday, we wouldn't blow that minimum-wage check on Nikes, or Fila sweat suits, or Friday night movies at Harbor Park with the neighborhood girls. No fucking way, brother, because we pulled self-esteem out of a dark hole somewhere and damned if our every desire isn't absolutely in check. We don't need to buy any status; no, we can save every last dollar, or invest it, maybe. And in the end, we know, we'll head off to our college years shining like a new dime, swearing never to set foot on West Fayette Street again.

That's the myth of it, the required lie that allows us to render our judgments. Parasites, criminals, dope fiends, dope peddlers, whores—when we can ride past them at Fayette and Monroe, car doors locked, our field of vision cautiously restricted to the road ahead, then the long journey to darkness is underway. Pale-skinned hillbillies and hard-faced yos, toothless white trash and gold-front gangsters—when we can glide on and feel only fear, we're well on the way. And if, after a time, we can glimpse the spectacle of the corner and manage nothing beyond loathing and contempt, then we've arrived at last at that naked place where a man finally sees the sense in stretching razor wire and building barracks and directing cattle cars into the compound.[33]

9

Resist:
Bread or Blood

I learned early that crying out in protest could accomplish things. My older brothers and sister had started to school when, sometimes, they would come in and ask for a buttered biscuit or something and my mother, impatiently, would tell them no. But I would cry out and make a fuss until I got what I wanted. I remember well how my mother asked me why I couldn't be a nice boy like Wilfred; but I would think to myself that Wilfred, for being so nice and quiet, often stayed hungry. So early in life, I had learned that if you want something, you had better make some noise.

—Malcolm X, 1964

My God, if they ever realized that they were in the same boat, if they ever quit tearing at each other's throats, if the little shopkeeper ever got it into his head that his friend, his only friend was the poor farmer, not the rich banker, where in hell would the system be then?

—Josephine Herbst, 1934

Why choose to police instead of assist? If the government hurts us we must resist!
—Wisconsin Welfare Warriors chant, 1990s

In addition to the ways in which a poverty culture could serve a protective and defensive function, Oscar Lewis suggested that there is an active side to it as well: the culture of poverty, he observed, can be a revolutionary force, for it contains within it a "high potential for protest and for being used in political movements aimed against the social order." On one side there is pessimism and hopelessness, a defensive lowering of expectations, as we saw in the previous chapter; but the other side is resistance and rebellion. Trapped in poverty, some get depressed and give up, while some get angry and rebel. But rebellion can take many forms.

Poor relief often demands passivity, supplication, and theatrical displays of dependence. JD, from Philadelphia, described it this way:

> See, it takes a lot to go up with a plate and say, "Put something in it." You understand what I mean? This is any human being. If nothing else a man wants to feed himself. But if you in no position to feed yourself you gotta humble yourself and say, "Give me something to eat." But these people who run these shelters, they use that. Everybody does, but these people especially. They'll wave that sandwich in front of you, taunt you with it.[1]

Laura Walker:

> I was called a "good welfare recipient." To this day, I still can't figure out what that means, but I guess it was because I was totally intimidated and always expressed my gratitude for the too little the welfare worker did for us.[2]

When met with something other than deference and gratitude, the "reformer" is taken aback. Jacob Riis tells this tale, circa 1890:

> On one of my visits to "the Bend" I came across a particularly ragged and disreputable tramp, who sat smoking his pipe on the rung of a ladder with such evident philosophic contentment in the busy labor of a score of rag-pickers all about him, that I bade him sit for a picture, offering him ten cents for the job. He accepted the offer with hardly a nod, and sat patiently watching me from his perch until I got ready for work. Then he took the pipe out of his mouth and put it in his pocket, calmly declaring that it was not included in the contract, and that it was worth a quarter to have it go in the picture. The pipe, by the way, was of clay, and of the two-for-a-cent kind. But I had to give in. The man, scarce ten seconds employed at honest labor, even at sitting down, at which he was an undoubted expert, had gone on strike. He knew his rights and the value of "work," and was not to be cheated out of either.[3]

A few years later, Robert D. M'Gonnigle, a charity reformer from Pittsburg, sniffed:

> Every time an applicant receives relief, the bolder and more impudent he becomes. He begins to think that he has a right to it, and that there is no disgrace attached to receiving it, and that any examination on the part of the poor law officials is impudence.[4]

Here's Lorena Hickok in April 1934, appalled by a visit to labor organizers in Alabama:

> Their attitude toward me, for instance, is apt to be one of ordering. "I want you to do this and see that." . . . My assumption is that they are NOT running the Federal Government—at least not YET—and I have a hard time to keep from getting a bit hot under the collar at their attitude.[5]

Stephen Gleich, who worked in a number of mental hospitals in the early 1970s, interpreted it this way:

> When a patient breaks the rules, his or her privileges may be cut back. The interpretation made by staff of such behavior is that the patient is "asking to be pulled in" or "asking for controls." This is nothing less than staff projecting its values onto the patient, without knowing why he or she broke the rules. Simple resentment or anger at restrictions and confinement is never enough, in the staff's eyes, to justify rebellious acts. This is probably a class phenomenon. Most psychiatrists and nurses and aides don't know oppression directly, don't know the rage it generates, and can't see rebellion for what it is: the only way left to survive. Most psychiatric workers view rebellion as pathological behavior, motivated by some deep-seated, unresolved psychological conflict. But most mental patients will tell you about the oppression they experience in the hospital. They will tell you they feel like they're in prison.[6]

Of particular disdain to the early Philadelphia almshouse was Daniel Boyd, sick, probably alcoholic, and "as idle and impudent as possible," who regularly sought the refuge of the almshouse come winter, demanding "every accommodation of Cloathing &c. (with insolence) *as a matter of right.*" Perhaps Boyd so incensed the overseers because he made no pretense of deference and did not play the part of the supplicant.[7] Even the most fragile poor, most in need of shelter and care, were sometimes defiant or "insolent," in the words of the overseers. But these can be phrases not of scorn, but of admiration and celebration, in which indignity is rightly met with rebellion, resistance, insolence, and indignation.

Passive Resistance

Rebellion, as I've said, can take many forms. Its active side is familiar—protests, riots, sit-ins, and other forms of individual and collective defiance. We'll turn to them shortly. But resistance has a passive side, too, in which ostensibly powerless people employ what James C. Scott calls the "weapons of the weak." These are the uncoordinated, small acts of individual resistance to oppression, acts in Scott's words of "foot dragging, dissimulation, desertion, false compliance, pilfering, feigned ignorance, slander, arson, sabotage." They are "everyday forms of resistance." Through the "vast aggregation of petty acts" like these, change is made, and even revolutions are born.[8] This is the form that resistance by American slaves often took: because the penalty for outright revolt was so high (torture and death), many rebelled by working slowly, destroying property, lying, playing dumb, or stealing food, masking their opposition and their contempt with a ritualized and superficial compliance. Industrial workers have resisted by sabotaging machines or slowing down the assembly line.

These kinds of passive resistance to poverty, to the welfare bureaucrat and the caseworker, to the scornful public, have been another constant in our history. Cynthia Cekala, who was in a mental hospital from 1969 to 1970, found a way to rebel even by complying:

> The shrink told me that if I didn't give up being a hippie and wear skirts I could not be considered to be cured. . . . I wore skirts with a wrathful submission.[9]

Indeed, clothing can have a power of its own: many years ago one donor to the Charleston orphanage wanted to provide "little calico dresses" so that the girls might have something for church and special occasions. For three years the board debated whether to accept this gift; they even had to establish a special Committee on Calico Dresses. Some feared that such frippery would undermine their wards' passivity, and perhaps lead them to think that they were just like other little girls; others worried that it would weaken the salutary effects of their very obvious dependence.[10] So, we can see meaning in why Ruby Lee reported getting especially well dressed to go to the welfare office,[11] just as nineteen-year-old food stamp recipient Jill Nelson dresses for the supermarket:

> I feel like I have to be dressed really nice and look nice to use 'em. I don't want to look all dumpy and look like I fit it [the image of a welfare recipient].[12]

Sugar Turner also dressed up for the relief office:

> When I used to come here, I set myself apart. It's like I would go to the food-stamp office at a certain hour 'cause I didn't want to stand up in the line with all those welfare people lookin' hungry. I wouldn't *dare* to go to the food-stamp office lookin' hungry. I don't want to be that needy. I don't want to be that dependent. I don't want anybody to think that I'm not gonna eat if I don't get food stamps.[13]

H. Marie Brown reported in her memoir that she would go to the relief office "in my most dignified clothing" and that she "didn't act like the 'normal' recipient."[14] Riis would have presumably placed these women among the deserving poor: "The true line to be drawn between pauperism and honest poverty is the clothes-line. With it begins the effort to be clean that is the first and the best evidence of a desire to be honest."[15] Nicholas Lemann described welfare-reliant Mary Manley as having kept her house "defiantly clean."[16] This effort at maintaining dignity and taking some control over the public identity they project is a very small resistance of the possible.

Deceit, deception, and "working the system to their minimum disadvantage"[17] are other weapons of the weak. Nels Anderson reporting on nineteenth-century tramps:

> There are men who make a specialty of "working" the charity organizations. Some of them are so adept that they know beforehand what they will be asked and have a stereotyped response for every stereotyped question. These

men know a surprising amount about the inside workings of the charitable agencies and they generously hand on their information to their successor. They usually know, for example, what material aid may be had from each organization.[18]

Inmates of poorhouses and asylums have fought back, too. They have, in the words of Gary Nash, "avoided the workhouse whenever they could, disobeyed rules, did as little labor as possible when they were committed to these institutions, and in general resisted poor relief measures that offended their sense of what was just."[19] If most have historically avoided outright confrontation, it is a measure of their practicality more than their passivity. Inmates have sought opportunities to exert some modicum of control, as when in 1797 in one New York facility, after complaining about the quality of the water in the poorhouse and receiving permission to leave the premises to secure better water, they were found in the local pubs—not drinking water.[20]

Indignation manifests itself in yet other forms, famously here in a 1931 song by E.Y. "Yip" Harburg:

They used to tell me I was building a dream, and so I followed the mob,
When there was earth to plow, or guns to bear, I was always there right on
    the job.
They used to tell me I was building a dream, with peace and glory ahead,
Why should I be standing in line, just waiting for bread?

Once I built a railroad, I made it run, made it race against time.
Once I built a railroad; now it's done. Brother, can you spare a dime?
Once I built a tower, up to the sun, brick, and rivet, and lime;
Once I built a tower, now it's done. Brother, can you spare a dime?

Harburg explained the song to Studs Terkel:

In the song the man is really saying: I made an investment in this country. Where the hell are my dividends? Is it a dividend to say: "Can you spare a dime?" What the hell is wrong? Let's examine this thing. It's more than just a bit of pathos. It doesn't reduce him to a beggar. It makes him a dignified human being, asking questions—and a bit outraged, too, as he should be.[21]

While we might think of begging as a quintessentially passive act, it need not be understood that way. Whether it's accounts of nineteenth-century tramps or more recent studies of homeless men, they often describe begging as "work." Moreover, begging for change may obscure a conscious, strategic effort, an "improvisational performance," as Stephen Lankenau called it in his study of Washington, D.C., panhandlers. The men soliciting assistance on the streets were well aware of the attitudes passers-by held of them, and they adjusted their routines for maximum effectiveness.[22] The strategy may be effective: another study showed that being at the receiving end of a panhandler made people more sympathetic to homeless people, not less so.[23] Note this poem, *Subway Beggar*, by Leo Grachow, published in his high school literary magazine, *The Magpie*, in 1931:

Clink . . . clink . . .
Here comes a subway beggar,
A shuffling, hobbling, one-legged, half-blind,
Dirty, shaveless, shameless, silent,
Callous, unconscious,
World-beaten subway beggar.

He's no use to this world!
The sight of him makes all of us feel his misery;
We all become blind beggars,
Holding tin cups in trembling hands,
Waiting for the clinks of pennies, nickels, dimes;
Dirty, shaveless, shameless, silent,
World-beaten subway beggars!

Damn him!
He makes us think.[24]

Similarly, "begging letters" were a common feature of relief-seeking in the nineteenth century. Poor women, carefully creating "worthy" identities, wrote appeals to churches, newspapers, and wealthy people; their first targets were often their employers or former employers. As Dawn Greeley wrote:

The working class actively and systematically solicited and at times demanded charity. The wealthy did not give spontaneously, but rather in response to these requests. Once received, clients turned charity to their own uses which were often quite distinct from its intended purposes. Charity was thus not freely bestowed, but rather contested for. The meaning and intentions that givers attached to their "gift" were not internalized by recipients, but were redefined. What donors saw as benevolence, clients often saw as obligations.[25]

That is, the letter writers lied to get what they wanted, and thought themselves fully justified in doing so. The practice continues in its own way. Since 1962, through a program called Operation Santa, New Yorkers can pour through the letters written to Santa Claus, which are otherwise destined for the dead-letter box, and select one or two for a personal response. Age-old rituals of judgment and supplication are reenacted. Would-be philanthropists search for letters that "sing" to them—ones that comport to their notion of appropriate behavior from the needy poor. They then send a package or a gift certificate, being careful not to include an address or phone number lest the once-a-year encounter with distant benevolence turn into something more, something perhaps a shade too real. But the letter writers play their parts too, working to maximize their chances by recycling form letters that have been passed around through the neighborhood, trying to ask for as much as possible without asking for so much that they appear greedy, seeking the right tone and just the right plea to evoke sympathy and, in the case of two young Bronx brothers who handwrote fifty identical letters, to maximize their chances of being picked from the pile of over 250,000 requests.[26] This, too, is a form of power, however modest and passive it may seem.

Active Resistance

But those who are supposedly weak, powerless, lazy, and irresponsible have resisted in much more active ways as well, taking what they could not gain through supplication or deceit and threatening order when the need arose, even if it meant risking what little they had.

Between just 1775 and 1779 there were at least three dozen food riots in the American colonies, fully one-third of them led by women. Other riots were avoided by the mere threat of violence. Crowds gathered at one merchant's shop, expressed their displeasure at his prices, suggested more reasonable ones, and gave him the choice: deal with them fairly or suffer the consequences. Such rebellions were understood by many not to be a violation of the law but, quite the contrary, an affirmation of it: they were not the outlaws—the rich merchants who sought to exploit them were. These early riots were often affairs not just of the lowest economic and social classes (although they dominated), but of some of the middling ones as well, who found their tenuous hold on a modest existence under threat and in need of some defense. Many Revolutionary era rioters claimed that theirs, too, was a fight for liberty, as they seized flour, salt, tea, coffee, bread, and sugar.[27] They are almost always treated as either criminals or fools. From the Boston *Independent Chronicle*, January 7, 1808:

> A procession of from 80 to 100 sailors, carrying a flag, marched with martial music to the Governor's house, and demanded *employment* or *bread*. The governor, as soon as he could be heard, addressed them with a presence of mind which became his exalted character, suggesting the impropriety of their manner of seeking relief.[28]

As early as 1809, there were demands by the public for a national welfare program.[29] Food riots during the depressions of 1837 and 1854 forced cities to distribute food, although, as I have emphasized, the most common demand was for work. Said one German immigrant at an 1854 meeting of the unemployed:

> It is said that the stomach does not ask if its food is paid for, but I shall not drink the soup given by the rich as if it were given to dogs. I repeat it—I want work, not charity!

One complaint read: "We don't want temperance! We don't want politics! We want bread." Or as a sign at a November 1857 demonstration promised, "Bread or Blood."[30] Disruption and the threat of violence have historically been among the few powers that poor people have had at their disposal.[31]

During the next great crisis, in 1873, a "short-lived but quite vocal 'movement' demanding public aid for the unemployed spread through many large urban centers" and "struck terror into the hearts of the many" wrote the *Workingman's Advocate*.[32] But again, most demanded work instead of "the crumbs that fall from the tables of the rich in the form of charity" so as to not have to be "obliged to beg what . . . honest labor entitles," as New York trade unions told the local papers. Said a mason in Newark:

> Workers don't want charity but work. No man will lay down and starve. Hunger will go through a stone wall. I don't advocate force, but before I will see my family hungry I will help myself.

Petitions were widely circulated in many cities, and throughout the nation there were marches, protests, and riots. Labor exchanges were set up by the unemployed; some stormed restaurants and demanded food; others organized lobbying trips to their state legislatures. Marchers in Chicago carried signs that read "War Against Idleness" and "We Want Labor and Not Beggary."[33] They pleaded for a program of public works. There were successes here and there, usually when the city felt so threatened that it believed itself to have no choice but to give in. We shouldn't judge these failures too harshly, however. As Piven and Cloward have written about another era, "what was won must be judged by what was possible."[34]

What is possible is often dependent upon making a credible threat. This is General Kelley, arriving in the small town of Red Rock with his band of protesters, according to Jack London:

> You see, gentlemen, the situation. My men have eaten nothing in forty-eight hours. If I turn them loose upon your town, I'll not be responsible for what happens. They are desperate. I offered to buy food for them, but you refused to sell. I now withdraw my offer. Instead, I shall demand. I give you five minutes to decide. Either kill me six steers and give me four thousand rations, or I turn the men loose. Five minutes, gentlemen."[35]

They responded very quickly indeed. In a "Resolution of the Boston Unemployed," a 1914 march affirmed "The Right to Steal":

> Here on historic Boston Common we enact a new morality. We declare that every one has an absolute and inalienable right to work; that if he is deprived

of this he is robbed of the means of life and therefore of life itself; that this is not only robbery but the committal of constructive murder against him by society; that in thus casting him out from all social care and protection society excludes him from the operation of its laws and absolves him from all duty of obedience to them. . . . We consequently advise then unemployed everywhere to steal food and whatever else they need to maintain their health and welfare, and we affirm that it is stealing only in name and not in fact.[36]

One sign at a 1930 march of the unemployed that paraded before the White House, and which ended in a "free-for-all," according to the Associated Press, read "Fight or Starve." The first National Hunger March, in 1931, helped persuade U.S. Senators LaFollette and Costigan to propose massive relief expenditures.[37] Dorothy Day wrote this of the marches:

Drama was what the Communist leaders of the march wanted, and drama, even melodrama, was what they got. They weren't presenting their petitions to Congress with any hope of obtaining cash bonuses and unemployment relief. They were presenting pictorially the plight of the workers of America, not only to the countless small towns and large cities through which they passed, not only to the Senate and the House of Representatives, but through the press to the entire world. And in addition they were demonstrating, to the proletariat, the power of the proletariat. They were saying, "Come, submit yourselves to our discipline,—place yourselves in our hands, you union workers, you seamen, you unemployed, and we will show you how a scant 3,000 of you, unarmed, can terrorize authorities and make them submit to at least some of your demands!" It does not matter that the victory won was only that of marching to the Capitol. To those unarmed marchers who for two days and two cold nights lived and slept on an asphalt street with no water, no fires, no sanitary facilities, with the scantiest of food, surrounded by hysteria in the shape of machine guns, gas guns, tear and nauseous gas bombs, in the hands of a worn and fretted police force, egged on by a bunch of ghouls in the shape of newspaper men and photographers,—to these marchers, the victory was a real one. They had achieved their purpose. They had dramatized for the workers themselves their plight, and they had given them a taste of power. They might be booed by police, sneered at by the Vice President, they might be hungry, unshaven, shivering and exhausted, but they felt a sense of power when they saw a whole capital, the center of their country, mobilized against them. . . .

On Sunday, with the Hunger Marchers approaching Washington, the city, according to the papers, was in a state bordering on hysteria. There were riot drills of the marines at Quantico; guards at the White House, Capitol, Treasury, plants of the electric and gas companies, arsenals of the National Guard and the Sixth Marine Reserve. The police force, the National Guard, the American Legion, countless volunteers, supplemented by 370 firemen, all were armed with machine guns, tear gas, nauseating gas, revolvers, sawed-off shot guns, night sticks, lengths of rubber hose. . . . The papers did their best to make a riot out of it and failed. They merely presented the Communist leaders in the eyes of the discontented unemployed of America as powerful leaders who could carry through successfully a planned and disciplined demonstration. And the Washingtonians who lined the streets by the thousands to watch the procession, laughed tolerantly at the songs and slogans, and said admiringly, "They sure have got gumption, standing up against the police that way."[38]

Quoting the head of the relief agency in Middlesborough, Kentucky, after having raced there in 1933 to witness what was rumored to be a march and possible food riot and finding that the small, "listless" crowd had already disbanded, Lorena Hickok reported, "Why, those people couldn't put on a riot! They were so starved that they didn't have the physical energy."[39] Later, in 1935, Martha Gellhorn wrote ominously to Hopkins from Rhode Island:

Again I can only report that there are no organized protest groups: there is only decay. Each family in its own miserable home going to pieces. But I wonder if some day, crazed and despairing, they won't revolt without organization. It seems incredible to think that they will go on like this, patiently waiting for nothing.

But by 1932 there had already been widespread food riots throughout the country, for example, in the particularly hard hit areas of Kentucky. One official reported:

The crowds have become so aggressive at Hazard at the Red Cross warehouse during the past three weeks that they could not be controlled by the police and they simply had to let them come in to the warehouse and help themselves until the food was all gone. They have adopted the policy now of taking the food to the camps to prevent the gathering of such large crowds.[40]

John Gambs in 1934:

Last January, when the Colorado legislature met to consider the desperate relief situation, the galleries were packed with members of the unemployed league. They sang while the assembly was trying to deliberate; whenever a legislator rose and started to leave the chamber—and legislators usually do—the crowd shouted, "Sit down." He sat down. One senator was so exasperated at the tactics of the unemployed [that] he said: "If this is the kind of people relief agencies are feeding, let them starve."[41]

The anger could be palpable. One man, representing five hundred families, to a relief worker in Pittsburgh:

Damn you! You don't care what happened to the unemployed. God! How I hate you. I could tear your foul body to shreds, cut it up into strips—you don't know what it means to be evicted. You live in a steam-heated apartment. I hate you. I could break every bone in your dirty carcass.[42]

From Oriana Atkinson's *Manhattan and Me*:

[A private welfare] commission [in New York] was attempting to place each so-called "D.P." [displaced person] to the best advantage, not always with the cooperation of the D.P. One man in particular was well suited for farm work, but he would not leave New York. "The trouble with you people," said the chairman angrily, "is that you all insist on staying here. If you would scatter out into the less densely populated parts of the country, you would all have a better chance." The man who was being scolded looked out of an open window thoughtfully. He saw smoky air, smelled the gassy fumes, saw the harried thousands charging through the narrow streets. He turned to the chairman and smiled amiably. "*You* scatter," he said. "I'll stay here."[43]

Circa 1950:

Threats of exposure [for violating man-in-the-house rules] to the authorities came only from the occasional outsider, like the precinct captain who canvassed for Mayor Daley door-to-door one year. He arrived at the front door one afternoon to recruit my mother's vote, issuing a barely concealed threat that a vote for the opposition, a Republican named Benjamin Adamowski, would cause her welfare benefits to mysteriously disappear. . . . I only saw my mother from the back, but I saw the face of that unfortunate man, who began to back away from the door as my mother declared, "If you don't get your ass off this porch I'll cut you from asshole to elbow." The retreating precinct captain must have heard our shrieks of astonished laughter for blocks.[44]

One woman's indignation took physical form. Peggy Dolan reports:

Mrs. Finnegan was on home relief, and she used to work, anything to feed the kids, any kind of job. But one day this welfare lady comes and she says to Mrs. Finnegan, "Ooh, I see you got new sheets on the beds. Well, you're off relief today."

"Oh," she says, "bejeezus, is that right?"

"Yes, that's right."

"Well, by God, you're gonna be off for quite a few weeks."

And, bingo! She knocked her down a whole flight of steps. And she was out of action for quite a while, for three or four months after that.[45]

In some cities, groups formed to conduct their own type of investigations—of relief officers, caseworkers, and public officials in charge of relief.[46] Others took different action. Stretch Johnson:

We saw people starving, people raggedy. We saw people being evicted for nonpayment of rent, put out on the street. We also saw groups like the Communists and other militants putting furniture back after the city marshal would evict people. . . . The Communists were more active than any other group. It seemed to me they meant business when they put furniture back and led demonstrations around the relief bureaus. . . . As far as I was concerned, it was the only game in town.[47]

A Detroit auto worker, janitor, and union organizer:

What we want here is a revolutionary movement geared into the peculiar needs of American workers, and I'll say quite frankly that if it isn't the Communist party, I don't see any other elements in the country who will supply it. The Communists have done a lot—they've practically stopped evictions. When there's an eviction about to take place, the people notify the Unemployed Council and the Communists go around and wait till the sheriff has gone and then move all the furniture back into the house. Then the landlord has to notify the authorities again, and the sheriff has to get a new warrant, and the result is that they usually never get around to evicting the people again. They've got the landlords so buffaloed that the other day a woman called up the Unemployed Council and asked whether she could put tenants out yet. The Unemployed Council said no.[48]

Here's Harold Gates:

I was just beginning to realize that the goddamn system was against the people. Fact is, you're conditioned to think of the system as good—American. But then you find out it wasn't like that. There were really riots for food and everything. You see families sleepin' in the subways, hundreds of 'em. And you see lines from one wall to the middle of the street to get a cup of coffee, and riots at the Home Relief office and no jobs. People were beginnin' to get reckless. You'd see the furniture out on the street, and the people would bring it back in.[49]

In the minds of many today, Tammany Hall was corrupt and the Communist Party was dangerous.[50] But to many poor New Yorkers, Tammany *was* the safety net and the Communist Party was a powerful ally, helping people avoid homelessness and find food, jobs, and relief; perhaps that's one reason they were deemed to be such a threat by anticommunist hysterics. Refusing to honor evictions became common and celebrated events, as did meetings of other "radicals." Horace Cayton:

I was eating lunch on the South Side. I saw a group of Negroes marching by, marching by twos together, and silent. Not loud and boisterous. These people had a destination, had a purpose. These people were on a mission. They were going someplace. You felt the tension. . . . I said to the chap next to me, "Where are we going?" He said, "We just gonna put some people back in the building. They were evicted." It was a ramshackle building. A shanty, really. A solid crowd of black had formed and they were talking great . . . [it was] an "indignation meeting." They used to have these indignation meetings down South, where Negroes just let off steam because they couldn't contain themselves, from some injustice that had been done. They'd lock the doors and have an indignation meeting and curse out white people. Here was action.[51]

That's indignation turned to action. At around the same time, a movement was begun to demand a generous national old-age pension, led by physician Francis Townsend. According to the legend likely created and propagated by the Townsendites themselves, Townsend's activism was spurred on by having seen some old women looking through a garbage can to find food. Townsend would later report:

> A torrent of invectives tore out of me, the big blast of all the bitterness that had been building in me for years. I swore and I ranted, and I let my voice bellow with wild hatred I had for things as they were. My wife came a-running. "Doctor! Doctor!" She always called me doctor, ". . . oh, you mustn't shout like that. All the neighbors will hear you!"
>
> "I want all the neighbors to hear me!" I roared defiantly. "I want God almighty to hear me! I'm going to shout till the whole country hears."[52]

The truth of this tale aside, it captures the passion the Townsend Plan advocates felt for their cause. It's angry and defiant and outraged, couched in a story about seeking justice and moral right. But they did succeed—not in passing the Townsend Plan, which by near universal accord was economically unfeasible, but because the pressure exerted by Townsend and his allies was so great, many historians give the movement at least some credit for the ultimate success of the Social Security Act.[53] It was not long before poor Americans would make their presence felt sharply again.

Welfare Rights

We might place the birth of the national welfare rights movement on June 30, 1966, when some five thousand to six thousand people participated in a Walk for Adequate Welfare, marching from Cleveland to Columbus. There were simultaneous demonstrations and protests in two dozen other cities. Not since the food riots and boycotts of the Great Depression had poor women protested in such numbers.[54] But the movement was a force to be reckoned with long before the National Welfare Rights Organization was founded, and since at least the mid-1950s, local groups of recipient-activists had formed throughout the nation. Over the next years, untold thousands took over relief offices, asking no more than that they follow their own rules and dispense the grants that women qualified for. There were sit-ins, sleep-ins, marches, rent strikes, demonstrations, and rallies, as well as boisterous takeovers of state legislatures, and even some acts of vandalism and arrests, all designed to put pressure on relief offices and rally public attention, if not support. Troubled welfare officials worried: "It can't go on, it can't go on, but it does."[55]

At its founding convention in Chicago, the NWRO issued a Welfare Bill of Rights:

1. The right to be a member of a welfare rights organization
2. The right to fair and equal treatment, free from discrimination based on race and color
3. The right to apply for any welfare program and to have that application in writing
4. The right to have the welfare department make a decision promptly after application for aid
5. The right to be told in writing the specific reason for denial of aid
6. The right to appeal a decision thought to be wrong, including denials and reductions of assistance, and to be given a fair hearing before an impartial referee
7. The right to get welfare payments without being forced to spend the money as the welfare department wants
8. The right to be treated with respect
9. The right to be treated in a way that does not invade your privacy
10. The right to receive welfare aid without having the welfare department ask you questions about who your social friends are, such as who you are going with
11. The right to have the same constitutional protections all other citizens have
12. The right to be told and informed by the welfare department of all your rights, including the ways you can make sure that you can get your welfare money

13. The right to have, to get, and to give advice during all contacts with the welfare department, including when applying, when being investigated, and during fair hearings[56]

Ruby Duncan's entry into the welfare rights movement came from her desire for work, not for relief. In the early 1960s, as a cook at the Sahara in Las Vegas, Duncan was a valued and beloved employee; after suffering a serious on-the-job injury that left her in permanent, chronic pain, she nonetheless wanted to continue to work. She sought out a less taxing job—but even that, she discovered, was impossible. As historian Annelise Orleck tells the story:

> While the union and the hotel battled over giving her disability payments, Duncan was left with no way to support her children. A social worker came into her hospital room one day with an application for public assistance. Duncan was depressed at the thought of going on welfare, she says. She had tried it briefly and hated it. But she was flat on her back, and had no choice. Duncan grabbed a pencil and filled out the form, vowing that her stint on welfare would be short-lived.

It was only after she was told by the welfare office that, because of her injury, they would be unable to offer her job training or find suitable employment for her that she spoke to a reporter for the *Las Vegas Sun*, which resulted in an articled entitled "Welfare Mother Wants to Work." Within a few days, the welfare office was calling her with offers of training. No job came of it, but it was Duncan's epiphany of the power of the press.[57] She went on to become a major force in Nevada welfare activism and policy-making, helped pressure the state to finally join all the rest and operate a food-stamp program, and created a neighborhood health clinic (and one of the very first women-run community development corporations) that was among the most successful in the nation, hailed as a model by Caspar Weinberger, Gerald Ford's secretary of health, education and welfare. She became such a force, and such a thorn in the side of Nevada casino owners—thanks to marches that shut down the Las Vegas strip, sit-ins that shut down casinos, and "eat-ins" in which welfare mothers and their children ate in casino restaurants and refused to pay—that some casino investors considered having her killed.[58]

After one sit-in in a welfare office, Duncan said:

> It was so much fun to demand. To know that we were demanding from this big
> entity, this institution, the state. Knowing how ruthless they were to poor
> people. And especially a group of us so-called uneducated. I think they were
> caught by surprise as much as we were.[59]

Such successes were replicated across the United States. As Piven and
Cloward reported:

> The mood of applicants in welfare waiting rooms had changed. They were no
> longer as humble, as self-effacing, as pleading; they were more indignant, an-
> grier, more demanding. As a consequence, welfare officials . . . employed
> their discretion more permissively.[60]

Though largely defunct by the early 1970s, the NWRO helped expand
the food-stamp program, forced tens of millions of dollars of relief money
to be put into the hands of poor women and men, helped successfully
bring landmark welfare rights cases before the U.S. Supreme Court,
helped mobilize opposition to Nixon's version of welfare reform, the Family Assistance Plan ("Zap FAP!" was the slogan), and, for a time, helped
bring poor women into politics as a force to be reckoned with.[61] The simple act of wearing an NWRO button, the Washington, D.C., United Welfare
Rights Organization claimed, resulted in more efficient and more courte-
ous service, probably because of a combination of caseworkers being afraid
that the NWRO could and would make trouble if they denied aid capri-
ciously and its wearer being more confident, more insistent, and less willing to tolerate disrespect or discrimination.[62] For this was, as much as
anything, a fight for respect. One observer in 1965:

> During the mass meetings [of welfare recipients] held on the Lower East Side
> it was noticeable that more applause was given to the suggestion that clients
> be treated with dignity than for the suggestion that there be a 25 percent in-
> crease in the welfare budget.[63]

A movement supporter:

There are no revolutionaries among the welfare mothers I know. Their values are solidly middle-class American values. They want what you and I want: food and shelter and a good education for their kids and a chance to learn or use a skill themselves in useful work outside the home.[64]

But an assertion of rights, or anything but passive supplication and deference, have historically been considered prima facie evidence of unworthiness. Here's part of a 1967 letter to the Senate Finance Committee in response to NWRO testimony; it's all too familiar and predictable:

I am a working woman and can't afford a trip to Washington, but taxes are withheld from my salary—much of it going for this and other welfare handouts to many loafers, demanding undesirables, and just plain trash. The trash being those who have illegitimate children every year by different men. And to think that they are now organized is the last straw! Such organization means one thing—more and greater demands. . . . Believe me, everyone I know feels as strongly as I do.[65]

Senator Russell Long called NWRO advocates "brood mares." Johnnie Tillmon, the first chair of the NWRO, later organized angry protests she called "Brood Mare Stampedes."[66] Here's an extended portion of Tillmon's most famous statement, "Welfare Is a Women's Issue":

I'm a woman. I'm a black woman. I'm a poor woman. I'm a fat woman. I'm a middle-aged woman. And I'm on welfare.

In this country, if you're any one of those things you count less as a human being. If you're all those things, you don't count at all. Except as a statistic.

I am 45 years old. I have raised six children. There are millions of statistics like me. Some on welfare. Some not. And some, really poor, who don't even know they're entitled to welfare. Not all of them are black. Not at all. In fact, the majority—about two-thirds—of all the poor families in the country are white.

Welfare's like a traffic accident. It can happen to anybody, but especially it happens to women.

And that's why welfare is a women's issue. For a lot of middle-class women in this country, Women's Liberation is a matter of concern. For women on welfare it's a matter of survival.

Survival. That's why we had to go on welfare. And that's why we can't get off welfare now. Not us women. Not until we do something about liberating poor women in this country.

Because up until now we've been raised to expect to work, all our lives, for nothing. Because we are the worst-educated, the least-skilled, and the lowest-paid people there are. Because we have to be almost totally responsible for our children. Because we are regarded by everybody as dependents. That's why we are on welfare. And that's why we stay on it.

Welfare is the most prejudiced institution in this country, even more than marriage, which it tries to imitate. Let me explain that a little.

Ninety-nine percent of welfare families are headed by women. There is no man around. In half the states there can't be men around because A.F.D.C. (Aid to Families with Dependent Children) says if there is an "able-bodied" man around, then you can't be on welfare. If the kids are going to eat, and the man can't get a job, then he's got to go.

Welfare is like a super-sexist marriage. You trade in a man for the man. But you can't divorce him if he treats you bad. He can divorce you, of course, cut you off anytime he wants. But in that case, he keeps the kids, not you. The man runs everything. In ordinary marriage, sex is supposed to be for your husband. On A.F.D.C., you're not supposed to have any sex at all. You give up control of your own body. It's a condition of aid. You may even have to agree to get your tubes tied so you can never have more children just to avoid being cut off welfare.

The man, the welfare system, controls your money. He tells you what to buy, what not to buy, where to buy it, and how much things cost. If things—rent, for instance—really cost more than he says they do, it's just too bad for you. He's always right.

That's why Governor [Ronald] Reagan can get away with slandering welfare recipients, calling them "lazy parasites," "pigs at the trough," and such. We've been trained to believe that the only reason people are on welfare is because there's something wrong with their character. If people have "motivation," if people only want to work, they can, and they will be able to support themselves and their kids in decency.

The truth is a job doesn't necessarily mean an adequate income. There are some ten million jobs that now pay less than the minimum wage, and if you're a woman, you've got the best chance of getting one. Why would a 45-year-old woman work all day in a laundry ironing shirts at 90-some cents an hour? Because she knows there's some place lower she could be. She could be on welfare. Society needs women on welfare as "examples" to let every woman, factory workers and housewife workers alike, know what will happen if she lets up, if she's laid off, if she tries to go it alone without a man. So these ladies stay on their feet or on their knees all their lives instead of asking why they're only getting 90-some cents an hour, instead of daring to fight and complain.

Maybe we poor welfare women will really liberate women in this country. . . .

As far as I'm concerned, the ladies of N.W.R.O. are the front-line troops of women's freedom. Both because we have so few illusions and because our issues are so important to all women—the right to a living wage for women's work, the right to life itself.[67]

The welfare rights movement is long gone, of course. But since then, many men and women have taken to the streets to decry injustice and inhumanity, as they have since the founding. From 1980 to 1990, for example, in just seventeen cities there were 516 protests by and for homeless people, whose numbers have continued to rise.[68] Many continue to criticize those who protest or riot, who threaten public safety or order unless their demands are met. But what other power do poor and unemployed people have?[69] It is true that poorer and less educated Americans are those least likely to vote, and that could be one way for them to effect change, but here again instead of reflexively assuming that they are lazy or apathetic, we might consider that they are acting rationally.

First, we should note the barriers that have been erected to prevent or discourage people from voting, especially poor people and people of color: there are devices no longer formally sanctioned like literacy tests, poll taxes, and outright violence, along with the continued use of arcane registration rules and procedures; inconvenient and limited times for voting; the lack of voter mobilization by the major parties; a feeling that because American elections are so corrupted by our fundraising practices participation does not matter or is not possible; and a belief that neither party is responsive to their needs.[70] Government itself may discourage participation in other ways. As works by both Joe Soss and Staffan Kumlin have shown, people's experience with state bureaucracy can affect their political ideology, their trust in government, and their willingness to participate as citizens.[71] Soss showed that welfare (AFDC) recipients were less than half as likely to vote as disability (SSDI) recipients or others of similar demog-

raphy, in part because their worse experience with the welfare bureaucracy
had spillover effects. As one AFDC recipient told Soss:

> When they start talking about voting, I turn the TV [off]. I do. It's no guar-
> antee. This person can make all these promises, but that don't mean they're
> going to do it. The rest of the government works like the AFDC office. I mean,
> I don't deal with the government when I can.

Just like Rosa Lee. While I'm not necessarily arguing that welfare bureaucracies are designed to demean and discourage citizens (in ways that
bureaucracies targeted at the middle class do not do with such consistency)
as Soss suggests, this may form part of the explanation for why the poorest
Americans are also the least engaged in politics and public political life—
because the overwhelming majority of their experiences with government
have soured them to it. If others have negative experiences with the U.S.
Post Office or the DMV, to take two maligned government agencies, they
do not have the same effects: welfare agencies are central to recipients'
very ability to survive. Kumlin argues that we will be more satisfied with our
bureaucratic encounter the less discretion the agency has, the more we
feel it has listened to us, and the less dependent we are upon it. That may
translate into positive opinions about the state and trust in government.
Thus, how programs treat citizens will have broader and potentially significant consequences. One of Soss's most striking findings was that 60 percent of the SSDI clients he interviewed reported that they thought that
government officials listened to them, but only 8 percent for the AFDC recipients felt this was so.

Throughout the post-1970 history of AFDC, after the U.S. Supreme
Court granted recipients the right to a "fair hearing" if their benefits were
terminated, and during the short history of its successor, TANF, few recipients bother to lodge a formal complaint, even if they feel that they were il-
legitimately punished (New York City has a fairly high appeal rate, which is
just under 7 percent of sanctioned cases); and of those who do, as many
as two in five fail to show up for the proceeding itself. The reasons vary:
the ambivalence (or outright hostility) of caseworkers to the process, the
daunting bureaucratic hurdles, clients' ignorance about their rights, concern that appearing to "cause trouble" might make their situation even
worse, and their resignation that no good would come of it. However, of

those who do petition to hear their grievances redressed, the majority win: success rates in New York City are over 80 percent.[72] Soss also found that AFDC recipients tended to have higher estimations of their own ability to deal with public bureaucracies and of their own knowledge. As Austin Sarat wrote:

> The welfare poor subscribe to neither an allegedly hegemonic "myth of rights" nor to a picture of law as autonomous, apolitical, objective, neutral and disinterested. They are not the passive recipients of an ideology coded in doctrine which is allegedly taken seriously among legal elites. . . . Because welfare recipients are trapped or "caught," because they are involved in an ongoing series of transactions with officials . . . [they] have access to inside knowledge . . . [which] means . . . that they have few illusions about what the law is and what it can do. They are, as a result, able, when the need arises, to respond strategically, to maneuver and to resist the "they say(s)" and "supposed to(s)" of the welfare bureaucracy.

Sarat concludes:

> Resistance exists side by side with power and domination.[73]

Indeed it does.

Embracing Indignation

The Constitution's most fundamental goal is to control political power, since authority held in the hands of the few will almost never work to the advantage of the many. We do not, as a rule, find this proposition objectionable. It is fitting and proper that government intervene, through the structure of its institutions and the allocation of its various resources, to ensure that no political tyranny may grow. Yet economic power, surely as potentially destructive and divisive as political power, has been deemed outside the sphere of state obligation or state interference. This seeming contradiction is in evidence among many of our contemporary antigovernment and antiwelfare ideologues. On the one hand, they say they seek to remand power from the federal government to the states, where it is said to belong; and to minimize government interference by reducing taxation and lifting regulations on private business enterprises, and by scaling back the reach of the welfare state. On the other hand, many of these same people seek to advance the state's role in private family enterprise, whether by encouraging the formation of certain types of families through the tax code, overseeing the reproductive behavior of women, refusing to recognize nontraditional family forms, or stripping away privacy and human rights in the name of national security. This is a muddied notion of the state indeed, in which the greater the personal liberty at issue the more willing they are to intervene; and in which the greater the political and economic power at stake, the bolder the assertion that government is most just when most neutral or inactive. This should be viewed for what it is— sophistry.

If we believe that there truly is equality of opportunity in the United States, then inequality of outcomes becomes a problem of individual weakness. Poverty is thus a moral failure and an illegitimate arena for social action. But by listening to the men, women, and children who have struggled with poverty throughout our long history, we see that such claims are unfounded, blind to the reality of the lives that people actually lead and the battles they have waged to get through the day. We can no longer allow so many with power to make policy based on "but the vaguest notion" of poverty.

But let the response not be sorrow or despair. Take a page from Willie Baptist, the education director for the Kensington Welfare Rights Union:

> The fight, as we see it, is not a fight for pity, it's necessarily a fight for power. You cannot accomplish and sustain anything in a big country like this from a standpoint of getting people to feel sorry for you. We've learned in our experience that with people who kiss your ass, if you do anything wrong, start kicking your ass. If you develop any kind of paternalistic relationship, that flips. The relationship has to be working with each other, in partnership with each other, and not paternalistically in an unequal relationship. That relationship, of working with each other, is a relationship for power, not for pity. Unless we can generate the necessary kind of strength, through organization and building a movement, there's nothing in the history of this country that suggests that we can rearrange the priorities of this nation. Every time, every instance that we can see in history where changes were indeed made, those changes

were made on the basis of a relationship with, a relationship for power, and not a relationship and an organization just for pity. This country is full of pity, it has enjoyed a tremendous development in terms of pity; it is the richest country in the world. The notion of philanthropy, the notion of helping people, the notion of volunteerism is something that abounds in the American psyche. Although it has often been based in a very sincere concern for people, that notion has been a source and means of control.[74]

That's the battle—for power, for dignity, for collective action in the name of real justice. As columnist Molly Ivins admonished:

Keep fightin' for freedom and justice, beloveds, but don't you forget to have fun doin' it. Lord, let your laughter ring forth. Be outrageous, ridicule the fraidy-cats, rejoice in all the oddities that freedom can produce. And when you get through kickin' ass and celebratin' the sheer joy of a good fight, be sure to tell those who come after how much fun it was.[75]

There's work to be done, for bread, to be sure, but also for roses; and as Ivins urges, it should be fought for in celebration. And with raucous, righteous, rebellious indignation.

EPILOGUE
Poor Math

Poverty is but the worst form of violence.

—Mahatma Gandhi

It's heavy, this life, you know?

—Marcello Perez, 1963

As we've now seen, the reality of poverty in the United States comports little to the myth. Even today, it is not a problem confined to a small minority; it will be experienced at some point by a majority of Americans, and there are greater opportunities for escaping poverty in other nations. Nor is welfare the province of the few: over the course of their lives, most Americans will receive some form of means-tested assistance. But how we think about poverty—how we evaluate its severity, its causes and effects, the progress we have made (or not made) over time—has much to do with how we measure it. And we measure it poorly. Given that there is consensus on that, it seems useful to conclude by examining just what it is we mean when we talk about poverty.

Official Poverty

According to the U.S. Department of Health and Human Services, a family of three was poor in 2005 if its annual income was below $16,090; it was not poor if it had income above that. For a single person, the number was $9,570; for a family of five, $22,610. So, by official Census Bureau measures, which use that standard, 37 million Americans were poor in that year, almost 13 percent of the population—the equivalent of the combined populations of California, Alaska, and Wyoming.[1] The official rates were substantially higher for African Americans (one in four), Hispanics (one in five), and children under eighteen, 13 million of whom (almost 18 percent) were poor by government measures. Perhaps 40 percent of the children of illegal immigrants were poor.[2] Those over age sixty-five, by contrast, had a poverty rate of just over 10 percent. Rates vary by geography, too: fully one-third of all Detroit residents are poor, as are a quarter or more of people living in Philadelphia, Buffalo, Milwaukee, Long Beach, Atlanta, Newark, Miami, and El Paso. According to the Community Service Society of New York, in 2005 "the number of poor people in the five boroughs would form the fifth-largest city in the United States."[3] At the time of Hurricane Katrina, which devastated the Gulf Coast in 2005, almost 40 percent of all New Orleans children lived in poverty, in a state with the second-highest rate of deep poverty among children. Over 40 percent of black children live in poor families in Louisiana, Mississippi, and Alabama,[4] while poor white Americans are concentrated disproportionately in the Mississippi Delta, New Mexico, and Appalachia.[5]

The method of calculating this "poverty line" has remained largely unchanged since it was devised in the 1960s by the Social Security Administration's Molly Orshansky (who died in 2007 at ninety-one years old). Even then she warned that her calculation was a "research tool" that would inevitably understate poverty, and that it was "not designed to be applied directly to an individual family with a specific problem."[6] That's nonetheless how we use it now. She took the Department of Agriculture's estimate for the cost of a survival-level food budget (which was designed for short-term use in an emergency), adjusted it for family size, and multiplied it by three, since it was then estimated that food represented one-third of a family's total expenses. That's the poverty line. Critics of the left and right find legitimate fault with this measure. The former argue that it understates the problem of poverty: its design presumed that this would be a minimal budget only practicable for short-term emergencies; food now typically represents less of a family's budget, while housing costs are often 40 percent or more, and in some locales transportation alone is 20 percent of household expenditures.[7] It doesn't take into account unavoidable out-of-pocket expenditures (especially for medical care) that can substantially reduce a family's income, and therefore make it impossible for them to provide for basic needs even if their income is above the threshold. And the index doesn't vary by region, so the poverty line is the same dollar amount in New York and San Francisco as it is for rural Mississippi, despite large differences in the relative cost of living in those places. Other critics, by contrast, argue that, because income calculations do not include the value of "in-kind" benefits like Medicaid, housing subsidies, or food stamps, the measure overstates poverty.

One in a series of alternative measures developed by the Census Bureau in response to studies done by the National Academy of Sciences, which adds in most in-kind benefits and the Earned Income Tax Credit and deducts expenses for health care and payroll taxes, raised the official 1999 rate by 3.2 percentage points, and it's likely more today, making American poverty rates closer to 16 or 17 percent of the population.[8] Given just how badly the official measures capture what's needed to support a household, some double the threshold (some public aid programs use 200 percent of poverty as their maximum eligibility level); one effort to create a typology of four hundred separate family budgets found that the median family need was about twice the official rate.[9] Official rates also don't account for just how poor poor Americans are; in 2004, while almost 13 percent were poor, 5.4 percent were *very* poor, with incomes at or below one-half the poverty line. By 2005, deep poverty had reached a thirty-two-year high.[10] And, as with any absolute measure with an essentially arbitrary cutoff, official poverty lines cannot account for the fact that families just above the line may experience the same hardships as those just below. But a binary poor, not-poor definition identifies one as a social and political problem, but not the other.

Finally, whatever the flaws in the Orshansky measure, it was not adopted until 1965—therefore, estimates of poverty prior to that, however accurate or inaccurate we may judge them to be, are not directly comparable, although many have much in common with the Orshansky approach. Perhaps the first effort at establishing an absolute poverty line was by the Massachusetts Bureau of Statistics and Labor in 1870. W.E.B. Du Bois designed a line in 1899 specifically for blacks in Philadelphia; five years later Robert Hunter attempted to do the same for the nation as a whole, setting the line at $460 in the North and $300 in the South (which would today be about 40 percent of Orshansky's line, adjusted for inflation). At around the same time, New York charity administrator Edward Devine said the figure in New York should be closer to $600 a year, since a reasonable standard of living would have to include, he thought, burial (this was often a huge portion of a family's expenses), food, shelter, furniture, clothing, clean water, education, religion, justice in courts, electoral participation (i.e., poll taxes), medical care, and rest and recreation. He anticipated Amartya Sen's thinking about poverty in many ways (see below). Devine argued, and this sets him apart from most of his predecessors and successors, that it would be better to risk overstating poverty with a high threshold than understating it:

> Those who are aided as part of a general and systematic scheme of relief should be aided to live at the normal standard of living, and should not be tempted or required to live below it. . . . There is in each community a definite standard of living, and that charitable relief is concerned, not with raising or lowering it, but rather with eliminating the obstacles which particular individuals have in realizing the standard, and in securing the withdrawal from the industrial class of those who are unfit for a place in it.

The WPA set its own line in 1937, as did a Joint Congressional Committee in 1949. CIO president Walter Reuther proposed a line of $3,000 in 1953, the amount coincidentally adopted a dozen years later by Lyndon Johnson to help measure the success of his war on poverty. In the same year, Rose Friedman of the conservative American Enterprise Institute argued for an alternative measure, one that would have been about 30 percent lower.[11] Whether it's Hull House's efforts in the late 1800s and early 1900s (inspired, like Hunter, by Britain's Charles Booth and Joseph Rowntree), or more recent attempts by economic historians to measure poverty in Revolutionary-era New England or the post–Civil War South, all efforts to establish an absolute poverty line should be viewed with suspicion, taken on their own terms, and judged to be, at best, reasoned estimates—a healthy skepticism we should also apply to our more recent, and supposedly more "scientific," efforts. Official data will not get us far in evaluating or understanding the lived experience of poor Americans, which is why I have chosen not to privilege these measures in this book.

Poverty over the Life Course

There is another problem with most poverty data. Official rates are snap-shots: they seek to count how many people are poor at any one point in time. But Americans move in and out of poverty over the course of their lives—the line between working, working poor, and poor can be very thin indeed. Many families are poor one year, not poor (at least officially so) the next, and then poor again the following year. One harsh winter, a fire, an epidemic or illness (cholera, smallpox, and yellow fever swept through the ghettoes in the past; today poor households face AIDS, diabetes, asthma, tuberculosis, or gun violence), divorce, the death or incarceration of the main breadwinner, an injury or disability, or the sudden loss of a job— these can push a family from just getting by into dire crisis.[12]

Thus, it would seem useful also to ask how many Americans are *ever* poor. Mark Robert Rank and Thomas A. Hirschl have sought to do just that, and their findings strike at the heart of the claim that poverty is a state confined to a minority of Americans.[13] By the time they reach age seventy-five, Rank and Hirschl find, 58.5 percent of Americans will have been officially poor at least once, with income at or below 100 percent of the Orshansky poverty line. The numbers are even more striking if we take seriously the extent to which the official line understates poverty: some 68 percent of Americans will survive on 125 percent of the official standard, and fully three-quarters will have incomes below 150 percent of the poverty line. Worse, by age seventy-five, almost one-third of Americans will be very poor, with incomes at only half the official poverty line. And, lest we conclude that these are isolated incidents of one-time hardship, some 30 percent of those who are poor at least once are poor for five years or more. This is not some measure of a very brief episode these data magnify beyond reason. For a majority, it's an event, and for nearly a third, it's a durable condition.[14]

Still, we misdiagnose the problem, for these are data about the entire pop-ulation, and it's worse for particular groups of Americans. By the time they reach age seventy-five, for example, over 90 percent of African Americans can expect to have experienced poverty; for people with less than a high school education, it is over 75 percent. By age seventy-five, some 52.6 per-cent of whites can expect to have had a spell of poverty; but African Ameri-cans have reached that percentage by the time they are twenty-eight years old. And if you are black and female, expect to be among the 98.8 percent of your peers who will be poor at least once. Some 34 percent of all Americans will be poor once before they reach the age of seventeen; said another way, we can expect one-third of our children to live in poverty at some point. But if they are black, the number is 69.5 percent (compared to 25.9 percent for white children). If they are raised by a single mom with less than a high school diploma, 99.4 percent will be poor. And while we make much, and rightly so, of the advances that Social Security has brought us, between age sixty and ninety, over 40 percent will still be poor at least once.

As noted in Chapter 2, one study in the early 1990s sought similarly to identify life-course incidences of homelessness, and suggested that 14 percent of all Americans are homeless at least once in their lives (including living doubled up with friends or relatives), with more than half absolutely homeless, sleeping outdoors or in a shelter. About half of all spells of homelessness lasted from one month to one year, with 13 percent for more than a year.[15] Between 1987 and 1995, one in twenty New Yorkers used a homeless shelter at least once; between 1987 and 1992, it was one in ten for African American children.[16] Mental illness is also more widespread than point-in-time measures might suggest: almost half of all Americans will experience an officially recognized (DSM-IV) anxiety, mood, impulse control, or substance use disorder, usually for the first time as children or adolescents.[17]

Hardships are part of our national experience, and poverty is not the exception, but the rule; it is not an anomaly confined to some marginal and marginalized population. In America, poverty is endemic.

Relative Poverty

Some will insist, however, that poverty isn't what it used to be. For instance, according to Robert Rector and his colleagues at the Heritage Foundation, by the late 1990s, 41 percent of all poor households owned their own homes, almost 70 percent owned a car or a truck (and 27 percent owned two or more), 60 percent had a washing machine, 48 percent had a clothes dryer, 66 percent had air conditioning, almost all had a refrigerator, 87 percent had a telephone, and more than half had a stereo, color television, VCR, or microwave. For these reasons, and more, "we have triumphed over poverty," he claims.[18] There's much that's wrong with this style of argumentation.

First, people do not compare themselves to their ancestors, but to their neighbors. To suggest that because poor families today have televisions and microwaves they are therefore less poor than their nineteenth-century cousins is a nonsensical comparison. And as Timothy Smeeding notes, "lower-income Americans are no better off and often worse off than low-income persons in other nations."[19] That is, looking not to the past, but to other nations in the present, living standards for many are better elsewhere. Second, few of these indicators shed light on the quality of life of the family under investigation—a car, for example, is now a necessity in most parts of America if one is to work (a lesson that poor and welfare-reliant families have tried to tell us over and again, as their ability to hold down a job is hampered by transportation expenses and car problems). Moreover, having a car is at best a double-edged sword, for with it comes a monthly payment, mandated insurance expenses and licensing fees, the cost of gasoline, and maintenance expenses. Does commuting in a car indicate a better quality of life than taking a streetcar to the factory or walking to the mill? Similarly, home ownership should not be read as meaning too much, since it too can be as much burden as opportunity, and we should be careful about what we mean by ownership—for most Americans what we really mean is that they possess not a home but an enormous mortgage, which, if they can make payments regularly for three decades, will result in home ownership. It's an important distinction if we are going to suggest that ownership rates should be used to argue that poverty today is of a different kind than in the past.

Such efforts like Rector's to minimize the reality of poverty are not new. In 1800, for example, the Society for the Relief of Poor Widows proclaimed, "Almost every class of mechanics live not only plentifully but luxuriously; an evil too general to be cured."[20] Set aside whatever dour Calvinism might make these moralists opposed to living plentifully; there is little evidence that mechanics at the turn of the century lived well, and scarcity was a common feature of life. But such complaints are echoed throughout our history, as reformers complain about how easy poor people really have it, in an effort, conscious or not, to rationalize inaction. In three editorials in 2002 and 2003, the *Wall Street Journal* used the phrase "lucky duckies," without irony, to describe those who are so poor that they do not pay income taxes.[21]

Nonetheless, it seems right to suggest that the nature of material poverty has changed, and it is not hard to understand, even while disagreeing, how the Heritage Foundation could elsewhere say:

> To the average man on the street, to say someone is poor implies that he is malnourished, poorly clothed, and lives in filthy, dilapidated and overcrowded housing. In reality, there is little material poverty in the U.S. in the sense generally understood by the public.[22]

In the 1300s, by contrast, up to one-third of the population of western Europe was killed by plague, while well into the 1500s and beyond peasants lived in constant fear of hunger; famine, though usually localized, was common and expected.[23] We face many grave public-health threats today, gun violence and exploding AIDS caseloads in low-income communities being perhaps the most dramatic, but nowhere near a third of our population will die of sudden disease. That's an extreme example, but it is a reminder of how far we have, in fact, progressed. In 1772 in Philadelphia, perhaps 25 percent of all free men (whom one would presume to be the richest of residents) were what we might call poor or near-poor. Jacob Riis reported that in 1889 in New York, "in a population of a million and a half, very nearly, if not quite, half a million persons were driven, or chose, to beg for food," and "many a mother has told me at her child's death bed, 'I cannot afford to lose it. It costs too much to bury it.'" By 1900, fully 40 percent of all Americans were still poor, and even by 1950 the American poverty rate was likely 30 percent. Only very recently has any sustained reduction below this level occurred in official measures. By the mid-1950s, U.S. poverty had declined to 25 percent, the official rate was at 17 percent in 1965, and by the early 1970s, it hit 11 percent. While that rate has now climbed again, the official estimate is nonetheless some 300 percent lower than its equivalent at the beginning of the century.[24]

One might plausibly argue that never before in human history has so much real progress been made, and made so quickly. Compared to feudal societies, early industrial economies, or even the United States at the beginning of the last century, we no longer have widespread incidence of abject poverty, as the Heritage Foundation claims. But we don't live in a feudal or early industrial era. We don't live at the turn of the century. We live here, now. While historical comparisons of official poverty rates may reveal general trends (though they may not, given the historical variation in methods used to count poor persons), such measures are, at best, of limited practical use if our goal is to evaluate the degree of want that Americans face. And again, it does not "reckon with the tendency of men to compare themselves with their contemporaries rather than their ancestors," in the words of historian Robert Bremner.[25] Victoria Byerly, in the 1980s, reflecting upon her childhood:

> We used outhouses instead of indoor toilets; we lived on beans and potatoes; we wore different clothes; and when the heels came off our shoes we hammered the nails down and went on wearing the shoes. In the mill village, where everyone lived this way, I had never thought anything about it. I didn't even know we were poor. But when we moved, I felt surrounded by people who seemed incredibly wealthy and who made me feel terribly inferior because of the clothes I wore, the way I talked, and the food I ate.[26]

Moreover, living standards may be subject to what Richard Layard calls the "hedonic treadmill." As he puts it, it's "like alcohol or drugs. Once you have a certain new experience, you need to keep on having more of it if you want to sustain your happiness."[27] People adapt and adjust to their surroundings and to their living standards, and we know that people feel a loss more acutely than an equivalent gain.[28] As Amartya Sen observes, "in a generally opulent country, more income is needed to buy enough commodities to achieve the *same social functioning*."[29]

This is why many seek definitions of poverty that move beyond mere brute calculations of money income.[30] One relative measure, and the one often used in international comparisons of poverty, is half the median income. By this way of counting, poverty in the United States was 17 percent in 2000 (almost 6 percentage points higher than the official measure, or some 16 million more people who would be counted as poor).[31] For much of its life, the Orshansky measure equaled about one-half the median income; it's about one-third now, however, and if current trends continue, it will soon be one-fourth the median income—it's yet another indication that our official measure understates poverty.[32]

The 1986 National Conference of Catholic Bishops report titled "Economic Justice for All" defined poverty not in terms of absolute money income but as the "denial of full participation in the economic, social and political life of society and an inability to influence decisions that affect one's life."[33] John Kenneth Galbraith said similarly:

> People are poverty-stricken when their income, even if adequate for survival, falls markedly behind that of the community. Then they cannot have what the larger community regards as the minimum necessary for decency, and they cannot wholly escape, therefore, the judgment of the larger community that they are indecent. They are degraded for, in the literal sense, they live outside the grades or categories which the community regards as acceptable.[34]

Dwight Macdonald, in a *New Yorker* review of Galbraith's *The Affluent Society* and Harrington's *The Other America*, said it more succinctly: "Not to be able to afford a movie or a glass of beer is a kind of starvation—if everybody else can."[35] Nineteenth-century novelist William Dean Howells suggested that "poverty is not the lack of things, it is the fear and the dread of want."[36] "Poverty consists in feeling poor," wrote Ralph Waldo Emerson.[37] Even Adam Smith concedes the utility of such an approach: "Every man is rich or poor according to the degree to which he can afford to enjoy the necessaries, conveniences, and amusements of human life."[38] He elaborates later in *Wealth of Nations*:

> By necessaries I understand, not only the commodities which are indispensably necessary for the support of life, but whatever the custom of the country renders it indecent for creditable people, even of the lowest order to be without. A linen shirt is, strictly speaking, not a necessary of life. The Greeks and Romans lived, I suppose, very comfortably, though they had no linen. But in the present times, through the greater part of Europe, a creditable day-labourer would be ashamed to appear in public without a linen shirt, the want of which would be supposed to denote that disgraceful degree of poverty, which, it is presumed, no body can well fall into without extreme bad conduct.

Smith won't go as far as Macdonald, and explicitly excluded beer, ale, and wine from the list, since "nature does not render them necessary for the support of life, and custom nowhere renders it indecent to live without them," but he did have a notion of poverty that would make him something of a wild-eyed radical today, given the value he placed upon "the ability to appear in public without shame."

Such ideas of a relative poverty—a poverty defined by one's relation to others and one's freedom to act as others do—are not widely accepted in the United States today. Charles Murray has argued that "welfare is not a right but a largesse,"[39] and for decades people are revealed in opinion polls to believe that welfare spending is greater than it actually is, sometimes by orders of magnitude; in 1990, 90 percent of Americans surveyed thought a "lack of effort" was "very or somewhat" important as a cause of poverty, while only 17 percent of Europeans thought so.[40] Similar attitudes are evident every time someone in a grocery store judges a purchase made with food stamps and thinks "she shouldn't be buying that; that's a luxury." It's apparent when people express outrage when a mother on public assistance spends $150 on sneakers for her teenage son. That is to say, we don't apply middle-class standards of living to poor relief, and certainly we don't expect our relief programs to attempt such a radical egalitarianism. Quite the opposite. Most relief programs are designed and implemented to provide minimal benefits to as few as possible.

Most Americans nonetheless aspire to more than mere subsistence. Yet in a culture in which advertising businesses earn some $63 billion in annual revenue, it is absurd to expect those messages to inspire nonpoor households to purchase goods they don't strictly need and simultaneously expect poor people to resist those same come-ons.[41] One may well be walking into dangerous territory by presuming to know what constitutes "necessities" for a poor black woman in New York if you are a rich white man in Washington, D.C. And vice versa, for that matter. Poverty can't be assigned an absolute measure, for what we think of as poverty not only varies over time, it is relative among people at any point in time. As has been said of power, perhaps poverty is a relationship, not a thing unto itself.

This excerpt from Abraham Cahan's 1917 novel, *The Rise of David Levinsky*, suggests that we might understand poverty along at least three dimensions: as the experience of those living it, as it compares to others nearby, and as it compares to the individual's past experience:

> I went wandering over the Ghetto. Instead of stumbling upon nuggets of gold,
> I found signs of poverty. In one place I came upon a poor family who—as I
> learned upon inquiry—had been dispossessed for non-payment of rent. A

mother and her two little boys were watching their pile of furniture and other household goods on the sidewalk, while the passers-by were dropping coins into a saucer placed on one of the chairs to enable the family to move into new quarters. What puzzled me was the nature of the furniture. For in my birthplace chairs and a couch like those I now saw on the sidewalk would be a sign of prosperity. But then anything was to be expected of a country where the poorest devil wore a hat and a starched collar. I walked on.[42]

Inequality

If poverty is best thought of as a relative measure, it is inevitable that, if some have great wealth while many have little or none, those with little will perceive themselves to be more poor than they would if everyone were in the same boat: inequality exacerbates poverty. And income inequality is higher in the United States than in any other advanced nation—and has been increasing for the past forty years, after a brief period in the midtwentieth century when it was in decline.[43] While official poverty has declined modestly over the past forty years (from 17.3 percent in 1965 to 12.6 percent in 2005), inequality is much worse, at levels not seen since the Gilded Age or the eve of the Great Depression.

But perhaps, as economist Charles Peguy said, inequality in and of itself is not necessarily of great concern: "When all men are provided with the necessities . . . what do we care about the distribution of luxury?"[44] George Gilder even argued in 1981 that inequality was the means toward equality:

> To lift the incomes of the poor, it will be necessary to increase the rates of investment, which in turn will tend to enlarge the wealth, if not the consumption, of the rich. The poor, as they move into the workforce and acquire promotions, will raise their income by a greater percentage than the rich, but the upper classes will gain by greater absolute amounts, and the gap between the rich and the poor may grow.[45]

He predicted accurately, in part. From 1947 to 1973, incomes of all Americans rose, with those of the poorest rising the most, but since 1973 income gains have been concentrated among the top wage earners, with incomes stagnant or declining for the rest of the population.[46] From 1989 to 1995, only those in the upper 20 percent saw real growth in wages. By 1997, 10 percent of families with the highest income owned 66 percent of all stock; the bottom 75 percent owned less than 20 percent. The richest 1 percent of our population owned more private wealth than the bottom 90 percent *combined*. While the total wealth held by the richest Americans has remained relatively steady since World War II, from 1983 to 1989 the richest 1 percent *gained* more wealth than the total held by the bottom 60 percent. By 1992, the share of total wealth held by the top 10 percent was almost 72 percent.[47] By 2004, it was over 80 percent, trends that were accelerated early in the twenty-first century as regressive changes to tax policy further concentrated American income and wealth in fewer and fewer hands.[48] So-called trickle-down policies certainly started off in the right place—at the top. But the wealth didn't go anywhere. This was not lost on the public: a late 2004 poll by the Maxwell School at Syracuse University found that more than two-thirds of those surveyed agreed that "we are becoming a society of the haves and have-nots," and half thought that government should do more to reduce inequality. Less than one-third thought that "everyone in American society has an opportunity to succeed."[49]

The causes of growing inequality are likely complex and varied—some combination of the declining value of the minimum wage, declining rates of unionization, regressive changes in tax policy, the declining value of welfare benefits, the effects of international trade and immigration, and changes in the labor market wrought by deindustrialization.[50] One analysis even found a connection between whether states have lotteries and their levels of income inequality, perhaps not quite so surprising as it might at first appear, given how often lotteries are described by policy analysts as the most regressive tax.[51]

The effects of inequality are pernicious: as British sociologist T.H. Marshall asked, "How can equality of citizenship coexist with capitalism, a system based on social class inequality?"[52] One recent study of 129 countries even found that inequality increases corruption (the use of public power used for private gain)—it both legitimizes it and makes it easier to achieve—and that corruption, in turn, exacerbates inequality. This dynamic is especially true in democratic societies and makes clear that without economic equality, political equality is in jeopardy.[53] Similarly, as economists Samuel Bowles and Herbert Gintis write:

Economic inequality—particularly when overlaid with racial, ethnic, language, and other differences—increases social distance, which in turn undermines the motivational basis for reaching out to those in need. Indeed, surveys consistently reveal that the support for those in need is stronger in societies whose before-tax and -transfer incomes are more equal.[54]

This may also help explain why lower-income Americans give a greater share of their income to charity, and why conventional wisdom among tramps and panhandlers was to seek aid in poor and working-class neighborhoods, never in the wealthier ones, as we have seen.

The American Political Science Association convened a task force on inequality and American democracy in the fall of 2002. Their report, published in December 2004, was a measured, cautious affair, yet they concluded:

> We find disturbing inequalities in the political voice expressed through elections and other avenues of participation. We find that our governing institutions are much more responsive to the privileged than to other Americans. And we find that the policies fashioned by our government today may be doing less than celebrated programs of the past to promote equal opportunity and participation. Indeed, trends in all three areas—citizen voice, government decision making, and public policy—may together be amplifying the influence of the few and promoting government unresponsiveness to the values and needs of the many.[55]

In short, inequality matters.

Mobility

Another way in which we might think about the well-being of Americans is to examine economic mobility—the extent to which citizens who are born into the lower classes are able to rise over the course of their lives. This has become another key element of the myth of American political culture, the classless society in which hard work is all that is required for anyone to advance. But the reality is different, just as it has been throughout most of

American history: the single best predictor of a child's future success is his or her parents' income and wealth.[56] In fact, as noted, Americans born poor are much more likely to remain trapped in poverty than people born poor in other Western, industrialized nations. If you are born to parents in the bottom 10 percent in the United States, you are twenty-four times more likely to remain there than to rise to the top 10 percent; odds are worse if you are black.[57]

The inequality described above may bear some of the blame for poor prospects at upward mobility.[58] Take education. As *The Economist* reported in 2005:

> Three-quarters of the students at the country's top 146 colleges come from the richest socio-economic fourth, compared with just 3% who come from the poorest fourth (the median family income at Harvard, for example, is $150,000). This means that, at an elite university, you are 25 times as likely to run into a rich student as a poor one.[59]

This, too, matters, if some groups of Americans, through the accident of their birth, have fewer meaningful opportunities to live the kinds of lives they would like to lead.

Poverty as Lack of Freedom

In an effort to take seriously the bottom-up approach of this volume—to shift analysis from policy per se to the lived experience of those who are poor and otherwise marginalized—we should pay some attention to economist Amartya Sen's redefinition of poverty as *lack of freedom*, or *capability deprivation*, in which freedom is the "capacity of people to live the kinds of lives they value—and have reason to value."[60] This would focus our attention upon how well Americans have managed to survive and thrive, and how that has differed for different groups, in different places, at various times throughout our history. For Sen:

> Development requires the removal of major sources of unfreedom: poverty as well as tyranny, poor economic opportunities as well as systematic social dep-

rivation, neglect of public facilities as well as intolerance or overactivity of repressive states.

Thus, the United Nation's Millennium Development goals include reducing poverty and hunger, as we might expect, but also encompass forty-eight distinct measures focused upon such things as child and maternal health, combating diseases (especially HIV/AIDS), environmental sustainability, improving education (especially for women), forging ties between rich and poor nations, all within a larger commitment to expanding civil and political liberty.[61] Poverty matters, but is insufficient alone if we truly seek to improve people's freedom in the way Sen understands it. One way in which the World Bank has thought of this is through the ostensibly simple move from "ill-being" to "well-being," or from what they call powerlessness, bad social relations, insecurity, material poverty, and physical weakness to freedom of choice and action, good social relations, security, having resources enough for a good life, and physical well-being.[62]

The U.S. Agency for International Development and the Population Reference Bureau have evaluated the well-being of women throughout the world along such dimensions as lifetime birth rates per woman; contraception use; percent of births attended by trained medical personnel; maternal deaths per one hundred thousand live births; AIDS/HIV, literacy, and school enrollment rates; percentage of women in the labor force; their percentage in national legislatures; and more.[63] These, too, give us a richer sense of capabilities, of freedom, than mere poverty data can. Looking just at the United States, Heather Boushey and her colleagues broaden the traditional poverty measure by evaluating instances of *critical* hardships (missing meals, eviction, disconnected utilities, or not receiving essential medical care) and *serious* hardships (lack of child care, worries about access to food and stable shelter, missing utility payments, disconnected phone).[64]

The Annie E. Casey Foundation has tracked children's well-being since 1990 for all fifty American states along seventy-five measures, and has created an index of ten key indicators: infant mortality, low birth rate, child death rate, teen death rate, teen birth rate, high school dropout rate, parents' employment, number in two-parent households, number not in school, number employed or in the military, and the child poverty rate.[65] Similar national-level efforts have been undertaken by the Federal Interagency Forum on Child and Family Statistics (since 1997) and the U.S. Department of Health and Human Services (since 1996), among others, all in the belief that aggregate measures of poverty, whether absolute or relative, convey too little information.[66] Whether these more complicated approaches enable us to make sense of the world is another matter, of course. The Federal Interagency Forum's 2005 report, for example, showed that since its previous report, the child population was up, births to unmarried women were up, child poverty was up, food security was down, incidences of being overweight were up, immunizations were up, low birth weight and infant mortality were both up, but child mortality, births to adolescents, and drug use were down, although the numbers of young people who were victims or perpetrators of violence were both up.[67]

American organizations are increasingly turning to the Universal Declaration of Human Rights to make claims about well-being in the United States. The National Economic and Social Rights Initiative goes so far as to identify an American "human rights crisis":

> Civil, political, economic, social and cultural rights have all been attacked and undermined in the courts, legislatures, workplaces and the streets. Economic and social rights in particular are virtually unrecognized in the U.S. The United States faces: the highest rate of child poverty among industrialized nations, over 45 million people without health insurance, over 36 million people suffering food insecurity, a shortfall of 5 million affordable housing units and 14% of households with critical housing needs, 20% of the population being functionally illiterate, the longest working hours in the industrialized world, and working families that cannot afford basic needs such as housing and health care.[68]

It's not traditionally the way in which we think about poverty (FDR's failed Economic Bill of Rights notwithstanding), but this broader look at citizens' well-being may be a more useful way to judge the effectiveness of the welfare state. Other organizations throughout the United States have adopted international human rights claims in order to try to change policy, whether it's advocating for increased funding for and easier access to food stamps by citing Article 25 of the Universal Declaration ("everyone has the right to a standard of living adequate for the health and well-being of himself and of his family, including food, clothing, housing and medical care"), or by seeking reform of domestic violence and child custody laws in the language of both the Universal Declaration ("no one shall be subject to torture or cruel, inhuman or degrading treatment") or the UN Convention on the Rights of the Child (which requires that governments "protect the child from all forms of physical or mental violence, injury or abuse, neglect or negligent treatment"). Others focus on the rights of immigrants and indigenous peoples, gender and race-based discrimination, environmental justice issues, or the rights of workers or prisoners.[69] These are the conceptions of poverty I have had most in mind throughout these pages, ones which take seriously the "practical strain" of poverty and allow that it will differ for each of us.

Notes

Introduction: The Indignant Poor
and the Constants of Relief

1. The story is told in M.H. Dunlop, *Gilded City: Scandal and Sensation in Turn-of-the-Century New York* (New York: HarperCollins/Perennial, 2000), 18–19, drawing upon articles in the *New York Herald*, December 24, 29, and 31, 1893. For a more recent case, see "Street Kids Raid Poverty Summit," BBC News, January 24, 2007.

2. John Spargo, *The Bitter Cry of the Children* (Chicago: Quadrangle Books, 1906 [1968]), chap. 5.

3. Alexander Irvine, *From the Bottom Up: The Life Story of Alexander Irvine* (New York: Grosset & Dunlap, 1909 [1910]), 150–51.

4. Edith Wharton, *The House of Mirth* (New York: Vintage, 1905 [1990]), 80.

5. Beverly Stadum, *Poor Women and Their Families: Hard Working Charity Cases, 1900–1930* (Albany: SUNY Press, 1992), 31.

6. James Oppenheim and Caroline Kolsaat, "Bread and Roses" (1911).

7. Conversation with author, May 7, 2007.

8. Michael B. Katz, *In the Shadow of the Poorhouse: A Social History of Welfare in America* (New York: Basic, 1986 [1996]).

9. John K. Alexander, *Render Them Submissive: Responses to Poverty in Philadelphia, 1760–1800* (Amherst: University of Massachusetts Press, 1980), 137–39 and fn 61.

10. E.S. Savas, ed., *Managing Welfare Reform in New York City* (Lanham, MD: Rowman and Littlefield, 2005), 359.

11. Premilla Nadasen, *Welfare Warriors: The Welfare Rights Movement in the United States* (New York: Routledge, 2005), 50.

12. Gwendolyn Mink and Rickie Solinger, eds., *Welfare: A Documentary History of U.S. Policy and Politics* (New York: NYU Press, 2003), chap. 70.

13. Ibid., chap. 98.

14. John Kenneth Galbraith, *The Affluent Society* (Boston: Houghton Mifflin, 1958), 330.

15. Stephen E. Lankenau, "Stronger than Dirt: Public Humiliation and Status Enhancement Among Panhandlers," *Journal of Contemporary Ethnography* 28, no. 3 (June 1999): 288–318.

16. Dwight Macdonald, "Our Invisible Poor," *New Yorker*, January 19, 1963.

17. I adopt the use of "constants" here from Stephen T. Ziliak, "Some Tendencies of Social Welfare and the Problem of Interpretation," *Cato Journal* 21, no. 3 (winter 2002): 499–513. For a more comprehensive analysis of conventional welfare histories, their failings, and why this kind of bottom-up approach matters, see Sanford Schram, *Words of Welfare: The Poverty of Social Science and the Social Science of Poverty* (Minneapolis: University of Minnesota Press, 1995); Stephen Pimpare, "Toward a New Welfare History," *Journal of Policy History* 19, no. 2 (2007): 234–52.

18. Jacob Riis: "Long ago it was said that 'one half of the world does not know how the other half lives.'" Historian Billy G. Smith found a 1767 letter in the *Pennsylvania Gazette* in which the author wrote, "no Observation is more common, and at the same time more true, than that one half of the world are ignorant [of] how the other half lives." Billy G. Smith, *The Lower Sort: Philadelphia's Laboring People: 1750–1800* (Ithaca, NY: Cornell University Press, 1990), xi.

19. Eva Feder Kittay, "Welfare, Dependency and a Public Ethic of Care," *Social Justice* 25, no. 1 (spring 1998); see also Eva Feder Kittay, *Love's Labor: Essays on Women, Equality, and Dependency* (New York: Routledge, 1998).

20. Thomas Paine, "Agrarian Justice," in *The Thomas Paine Reader*, ed. Michael Foot and Isaac Kramnick (New York: Viking Penguin, 1795 [1987]), 403; see also the notion of "strong reciprocity" in Samuel Bowles and Herbert Gintis, "Is Equality Passe? Homo Reciprocans and the Future of Egalitarian Politics," *Boston Review*, December 1998/January 1999.

21. Timothy M. Smeeding, Lee Rainwater, and Gary Burtless, "U.S. Poverty in a Cross-national Context," chap. 5 in *Understanding Poverty*, ed. Sheldon H. Danziger and Robert H. Haveman (New York and Cambridge, MA: Russell Sage Foundation and Harvard University Press, 2001); "US and the World," *State of Working America 2004–05*, www.epinet.org; Timothy M. Smeeding, "Public Policy, Economic Inequality, and Poverty: The United States in Comparative Perspective," *Social Science Quarterly* 86, no. 5 (December 2005), 955–83.

22. Sweden, Denmark, Finland, Austria, Germany, the Netherlands, Norway, Canada, Australia, and the United Kingdom. The worst were Eritrea, Cambodia, Nepal, Mauritania, Congo, Yemen, Chad, Ethiopia, and, tied for last place, Mali and Burkina Faso. See "A Mother's Day Report Card: The Best—and Worst—Countries to Be a Mother and Child," May 3, 2005, www.savethechildren.org/news/releases/release_042205.asp. They compared ten indicators of well-being, in-

cluding maternal and infant mortality, access to safe drinking water, childhood malnutrition, women's literacy rates, and participation in national government.

23. Kevin Watkins, "Human Development Report 2005," United Nations Development Programme.

24. Amartya Sen, *Development as Freedom* (New York: Anchor, 1999), 23. African American women in the United States have mortality rates three times greater than white women (ibid., 97). See also Colin McCord and Harold P. Freeman, "Excess Mortality in Harlem," *New England Journal of Medicine* 322, no. 3 (January 18): 173–77. Moreover, African Americans are more likely to live in neighborhoods with dangerous levels of pollution and near hazardous-waste sites; and they will live shorter lives. During those lives, they are more likely to receive inferior medical care than whites and are less likely to receive life-saving tests, operations, and medications. David Pace, "More Blacks Live with Pollution," Associated Press, December 2005; American Sociological Association, "Race, Ethnicity, and the Health of Americans," July 2005; David R. Williams and Chiquita Collins, "US Socioeconomic and Racial Differences in Health: Patterns and Explanations," *Annual Review of Sociology* 21 (1995): 349–86; Peter B. Bach et al., "Primary Care Physicians Who Treat Blacks and Whites," *New England Journal of Medicine* 351, no. 6 (August 5, 2004); Institute of Medicine, "Unequal Treatment: What Healthcare Providers Need to Know About Racial and Ethnic Disparities in Healthcare," March 2002; "Race Gap Persists in Health Care," *Washington Post*, August 18, 2005; Harvard School of Public Health, "New Study Shows African American Seniors Receive Fewer Life-Saving Surgeries than Whites," press release, August 17, 2005.

25. David Wagner, *What's Love Got to Do with It? Beyond the Altruistic Myths of American Charity* (New York: The New Press, 2000).

26. Bronislaw Geremek, *Poverty: A History* (Oxford, UK: Blackwell, 1994), 29; Joel Schwartz, *Fighting Poverty with Virtue: Moral Reform and America's Urban Poor, 1825–2000* (Bloomington: Indiana University Press, 2001), xiv.

27. Charles Murray, *In Our Hands: A Plan to Replace the Welfare State* (Washington, DC: AEI Press, 2006), 52.

28. See Martin Gilens, *Why Americans Hate Welfare: Race, Media and the Politics of Antipoverty Strategy* (Chicago: University of Chicago Press, 1999).

29. William Rhinelander Stewart, ed., *The Philanthropic Work of Josephine Shaw Lowell* (New York: Macmillan, 1911), 129–30.

30. Jeff Place reports: "This song describes life on welfare from a participant's perspective—the Friesens had to rely on welfare support for some years after they were blacklisted in the 1950s, and, as Mike Millius recalled, 'Gordon would sit and talk to us for hours and we'd drink his Schaefer Beer with him while Sis bustled around the apartment keeping the place going. The idea for the welfare song came from Gordon. We were talking about government (he was still a dyed-in-the-wool communist) and Gordon said, 'You can't fight city hall. All you can do is burn it

down.' He then told me that the Rev. F.D. Kirkpatrick was organizing a rally to protest Governor Rockefeller's cutback on welfare budgets. Gordon said, 'You know what they say about welfare, don't you? That it's not enough to live on but a little too much to die. And that was the title of the song.'" Smithsonian Folkways Recordings, *The Best of Broadside 1962–1988*.

31. In Alan Bloom, "A Failed Experiment: The Poorhouse of Cook County (Chicago), Illinois, 1835–1871," paper presented at the Policy History Conference, Institute for Political History/*Journal of Policy History*, St. Louis, May 20–23, 2004. I am indebted to Bloom for drawing my attention to this phrase.

32. Perhaps biologist Stephen Jay Gould's claim holds here too: "stasis is the norm for complex systems; change, when provoked at all, is usually rapid and episodic." Gould, "The Panda's Thumb of Technology," chap. 4 in *Bully for Brontosaurus: Reflections in Natural History* (New York: W.W. Norton, 1992).

33. We might identify yet another welfare state: one for wealthy individuals and corporate interests. As one in a series of 1996 reports in the *Boston Globe* put it then: "Every year, an estimated $150 billion—in the form of direct federal subsidies and tax breaks that specifically benefit businesses—is funneled to American companies. Critics call it 'corporate welfare.' The $150 billion for corporate subsidies and tax benefits eclipses the annual budget deficit of $130 billion. It's more than the $145 billion paid out annually for the core programs of the social welfare state: Aid to Families with Dependent Children (AFDC), student aid, housing, food and nutrition, and all direct public assistance (excluding Social Security and medical care)." See Charles M. Sennott, "The $150 Billion 'Welfare' Recipients: U.S. Corporations" and "Helping Companies Grab All They Can Get," *Boston Globe*, July 7, 1996; Aaron Zitner, "Tax Code Gives Companies a Lift," *Boston Globe*, July 8, 1996; Charles M. Sennott and Aaron Zitner, "Business' Clout Keeps the Government Breaks Coming," *Boston Globe*, July 9, 1996.

34. Frederic Almy, "Public or Private Outdoor Relief," *Proceedings of the National Conference on Charities and Corrections* (1900), 137.

35. Smeeding, Rainwater, and Burtless, "U.S. Poverty in a Cross-national Context."

36. Herbert J. Gans, "The Uses of Poverty," *Social Policy* 2, no. 2 (July/August 1971); Claus Offe, *Contradictions of the Welfare State*, ed. John Keane (Boston: MIT Press, 1993); Katz, *In the Shadow of the Poorhouse*.

37. Eliana Garces, Duncan Thomas, and Janet Currie, "Longer Term Effects of Head Start," RAND reprint, December 2000; Joe Soss, Sanford F. Schram, Thomas P. Vartanian, and Erin O'Brien, "Setting the Terms of Relief: Explaining State Policy Choices in the Devolution Revolution," *American Journal of Political Science* 24, no. 2 (April 2001); Katherine Beckett and Bruce Western, "Governing Social Marginality: Welfare, Incarceration, and the Transformation of State Policy," *Punishment & Society* 3, no. 1 (2001): 43–59; Joshua A. Guetzkow, "The Carrot and the Stick: An Inquiry into the Relationship Between Welfare and Criminal Justice" (PhD diss., Princeton University, 2004).

38. Peter H. Lindert, *Growing Public: Social Spending and Economic Growth Since the Eighteenth Century* (Cambridge, UK: Cambridge University Press, 2004).

39. In Nadasen, *Welfare Warriors*, 199.

40. A.J. Liebling, "Horsefeathers Swathed in Mink," in Mink and Solinger, *Welfare*, chap. 37.

41. David Zuccino, *The Myth of the Welfare Queen* (New York: Simon & Schuster, 1997), 65; *New York Times*, February 15 and 29, 1976.

42. Peter Nabokov, *Native American Testimony*, rev. ed. (New York: Penguin, 1978 [1999]), 432.

43. Jacob Hacker, "Bringing the Welfare State Back In: The Promise (and Perils) of the New Social Welfare History," *Journal of Policy History* 17, no. 1 (2005). As Hacker wrote in the same article: "At root, most analyses of U.S. social policy are interested in power. Who set the agenda? Who decided which alternatives to consider? Who won out in debate over these alternatives? Who benefited or lost under the policies finally chosen, or not chosen? These are the classic questions of social welfare history." These are good questions; they are not the questions here.

44. For other efforts to legitimize these forms of policy expertise, see Michal Krumer-Nevo, "Listening to 'Life Knowledge': A New Research Direction in Poverty Studies," *International Journal of Social Welfare* 14 (2005): 99–106. We must simultaneously be aware that speech is a performance in which the speaker or writer creates, recreates, shapes, and distorts memory, belief, and opinion in response, among other things, to the effect he or she intends to have on the audience (the reader, interviewer, caseworker, charity agent, etc.). Not all of those included in these pages should necessarily be taken at their word, no more than elite interpreters should automatically be taken at their word. See Judith Butler, *Gender Trouble: Feminism and the Subversion of Identity* (New York: Routledge, 1990); Patricia Hill Collins, *Black Feminist Thought: Knowledge, Consciousness, and the Politics of Empowerment* (New York: Routledge, 2000). For a caution against "ethnography as voyeurism," see Schram, *Words of Welfare*, chap. 3.

45. Howard Zinn, *A People's History of the United States: 1492–Present*, twentieth-anniversary ed. (New York: HarperCollins, 2002); see also Schram, *Words of Welfare*.

46. See especially Walter I. Trattner, *From Poor Law to Welfare State: A Social History of Welfare in America*, 6th ed. (New York: Free Press, 1998); Bruce S. Jansson, *The Reluctant Welfare State*, 4th ed. (Belmont, CA: Wadsworth, 2001); Katz, *In the Shadow of the Poorhouse*.

1. Survive: My Brother's Keeper

1. Andrew Carroll, ed., *Letters of a Nation* (New York: Kodansha International, 1997), 345–47.

2. Louis Wirth in Loïc Wacquant, "The New 'Peculiar Institution': On the

Prison as Surrogate Ghetto," in *Race, Crime, and Justice: A Reader*, ed. Shaun L. Gabbison and Helen Taylor Greene (New York: Routledge, 2005).

3. U.S. Census Bureau; Alan Berube and Elizabeth Kneebone, "Two Steps Back: City and Suburban Poverty Trends, 1999–2005," Brookings Institution, December 2006; John Iceland, *Poverty in America: A Handbook* (Berkeley: University of California Press, 2003), table 4.3; Mary Jo Bane and David T. Ellwood, *Welfare Realities: From Rhetoric to Reform*, cited in Harold L. Wilensky, *Rich Democracies: Political Economy, Public Policy, and Performance* (Berkeley: University of California Press, 2002), chap. 8.

4. For the urban bias of poverty and welfare studies—and this book is culpable, too—see Lisa R. Pruitt, "Toward a Feminist Theory of the Rural," *Utah Law Review* (2007): 421–88; Debra Lyn Bassett, "Distancing Rural Poverty," *Georgetown Journal on Poverty Law & Policy* 13 (2006). See also the Rural Poverty Research Center at www.rprconline.org.

5. Lee Rainwater and William L. Yancey, *The Moynihan Report and the Politics of Controversy* (Boston: MIT Press, 1967); *Report of the National Advisory Commission on Civil Disorders* (Washington, DC: U.S. Government Printing Office, 1968).

6. In Billy G. Smith, ed., *Down and Out in Early America* (University Park: Pennsylvania State University Press, 2004), 12 and 33, fn 49. It may be that growing poverty in evidence from the 1760s contributed to the radical forces that gave life to the Revolution itself. See Raymond A Mohl, *Poverty in New York, 1783–1825* (New York: Oxford University Press, 1971), 46–47.

7. John K. Alexander, *Render Them Submissive: Responses to Poverty in Philadelphia, 1760–1800* (Amherst: University of Massachusetts Press, 1980), 21.

8. Mohl, *Poverty in New York*, 21.

9. James D. McCabe Jr., *Lights and Shadows of New York Life or Sights and Sensations of the Great City* (New York: Farrar, Straus and Giroux, 1872 [fac. ed. 2000]), 398.

10. Tyler Anbinder, *Five Points: The 19th-Century New York City Neighborhood That Invented Tap Dance, Stole Elections, and Became the World's Most Notorious Slum* (New York: Plume, 2002), 359.

11. Michael Gold, *Jews Without Money* (New York: Carroll & Graf, 1930 [2004]), 71–72. If not memoir, we could call Gold's book an autobiographical novel or a fictionalized autobiography.

12. James Baldwin, *Nobody Knows My Name*, cited in Terry M. Williams and William Kornblum, *Growing Up Poor: A Literary Anthology* (Lexington, MA: Lexington Books, 1985), 73.

13. Quoted in Steven Durlauf, "Groups, Social Influences, and Inequality," chap. 6 in *Poverty Traps*, ed. Samuel Bowles, Steven N. Durlauf, and Karla Hoff (Princeton, NJ, and New York: Princeton University Press and Russell Sage Foundation, 2006). Emphasis in original.

14. LeAlan Jones and Lloyd Newman with David Isay, *Our America: Life and Death on the South Side of Chicago* (New York: Pocket Books, 1997), 33–36.

15. Agence France Presse, April 4, 2005.

16. Alan Berube and Bruce Katz, "Katrina's Window: Confronting Concentrated Poverty Across America," Brookings Institution, October 2005.

17. In 1855, some 22 percent of New York men were unskilled laborers; when we glance at the residents of the Five Points, the number rises to 40 percent. Anbinder, *Five Points.* The same pattern holds today.

18. Anne R. Pebley, "Neighborhoods, Poverty and Children's Well-being: A Review," Russell Sage Foundation, February 2003; GAO, "Poverty in America: Consequences for Individuals and the Economy," January 24, 2007; Mary Corcoran, "Mobility, Persistence, and the Consequences of Poverty for Children," in *Understanding Poverty*, ed. Sheldon H. Danziger and Robert H. Haveman (New York and Cambridge, MA: Russell Sage Foundation and Harvard University Press, 2001), chap. 4; Steven H. Woolf, Robert E. Johnson, and H. Jack Geiger, "The Rising Prevalence of Severe Poverty in America: A Growing Threat to Public Health," *American Journal of Preventive Medicine* 21, no. 4 (October 2006): 332–41.

19. In the colonial era, "those most heavily involved in poor relief, however, were those who took in the poor as lodgers, daily providing food, shelter, and heat and making the poor person a part of the household. From the wealthiest squire to the poorest laborer, nearly every inhabitant could and did participate in poor relief." Ruth Wallis Herndon, "'Who Died an Expence to This Town': Poor Relief in Eighteenth-Century Rhode Island," in *Down and Out in Early America* (see note 6), 142.

20. William Julius Wilson, *The Truly Disadvantaged: The Inner City, the Underclass, and Public Policy* (Chicago: University of Chicago Press, 1987); see also Paul A. Jargowsky, *Poverty and Place: Ghettos, Barrios, and the American City* (New York: Russell Sage Foundation, 1997).

21. Rick Shenkman, "Interview with Elliot Jaspin: Racial Cleansing in America," History News Network, April 2, 2007, hnn.us/articles/35900.html; James W. Loewen, *Sundown Towns: A Hidden Dimension of American Racism* (New York: The New Press, 2005).

22. Even accounting for higher risks in cities, it is race that explains the patterns, not other nonracial factors. Gregory D. Squires, "Racial Profiling, Insurance Style: Insurance Redlining and the Uneven Development of Metropolitan Areas," *Journal of Urban Affairs* 25, no. 4 (2003): 391–410.

23. Robert J. Sampson and Jeffrey D. Morenoff, "Durable Inequality: Spatial Dynamics, Social Processes, and the Persistence of Poverty in Chicago Neighborhoods," chap. 7 in *Poverty Traps*, ed. Samuel Bowles, Steven N. Durlauf, and Karla Hoff (Princeton, NJ, and New York: Princeton University Press and Russell Sage Foundation, 2006).

24. McCabe, *Lights and Shadows of New York Life*, 50.

25. Anbinder, *Five Points*, 21.

26. Luc Sante, *Low Life: Lures and Snares of Old New York* (New York: Farrar, Straus and Giroux, 1991), 39.

27. Ibid., 35

28. Anbinder, *Five Points*, 433–34.

29. Arthur Simon, *Faces of Poverty* (New York: Macmillan, 1966 [1968]), 94. See also Robert Caro, *The Power Broker: Robert Moses and the Fall of New York* (New York: Vintage, 1975). The relocation and dispersal of Japanese Americans during World War II also broke up thriving communities, some of it an intentional effort to force them to spread out throughout the country and to accelerate their assimilation. David A. Neiwert, *Strawberry Days: How Internment Destroyed a Japanese American Community* (New York: Palgrave Macmillan, 2005). Ironically, the War Relocation Authority camps' commitment to providing health care to its internees meant that not only did most of the Japanese prisoners enjoy the best access to health care they had ever had, but also a privileged position over noninterred Americans, receiving care comparable in reach (if not in quality) to that received by members of the armed forces. Susan L. Smith, "Women Health Workers and the Color Line in the Japanese American 'Relocation Centers' of World War II," *Bulletin of the History of Medicine* 73, no. 4 (1995): 585–601.

30. Simon, *Faces of Poverty*, 97–98.

31. Jeff Kisseloff, *You Must Remember This: An Oral History of Manhattan from the 1890s to World War II* (New York: Schocken, 1989), 420. Poor people can be racist too, of course; they may even be more so, given the well-established correlation between education levels and tolerance for all kinds of difference and the correlation between lower levels of education and poverty. Reducing poverty might, therefore, increase social and political equality. See Michael X. Delli Carpini and Scott Keeter, *What Americans Know About Politics and Why It Matters* (New Haven, CT: Yale University Press, 1996), chap. 6; and Task Force on Inequality and American Democracy, "American Democracy in an Age of Rising Inequality," American Political Association, www.apsanet.org/section_256.cfm.

32. Anu Yadav, *Capers*, unpublished play (2006; first produced in 2004 at the District of Columbia Arts Center).

33. Susan J. Popkin, Bruce Katz, Mary K. Cunningham, et al., *A Decade of Hope VI: Research Findings and Policy Challenges* (Washington, DC: Urban Institute, 2004).

34. For an extended account of community formation and dissolution within the Robert Taylor projects in Chicago, see Sudhir Alladi Venkatesh, *American Project: The Rise and Fall of a Modern Ghetto* (Cambridge, MA: Harvard University Press, 2000).

35. Quoted in Andrew Karmen, "Poverty, Crime, and Criminal Justice," in *From Social Justice to Criminal Justice: Poverty and the Administration of Criminal Law*, ed. William C. Heffernan and John Kleinig (New York: Oxford University Press, 2000), 28.

36. See Bonnie Yochelson and Daniel Czitrom, *Rediscovering Jacob Riis: Exposure Journalism and Photography in Turn-of-the-Century New York* (New York: The New Press, 2007).

37. Sante, *Low Life*, 294–96; "Buy Your Harlem Spiritual Tour Vouchers," nycvp.com/TicketOrder-HS.htm (accessed December 8, 2007).

38. Anbinder, *Five Points*, 2. We can trace similar kinds of practices to an earlier

time. In the decade after the erection of the first mental hospital in Philadelphia in 1751, "it was customary, particularly on Sundays and holidays, for idlers and thrill-seekers to gather about the cell windows of the insane which stood at ground level and to take turns at 'teasing them crazy people,' with the aim of rousing them into raving fury." In later years, to control the numbers of the curious, a fee was charged for the privilege. Not until perhaps the 1820s was the practice finally discontinued. Albert Deutsch, *The Mentally Ill in America: A History of their Care and Treatment from Colonial Times* (New York: Columbia University Press, 1937 [1949]), 64–65.

39. Jones and Newman, *Our America*, 177.

40. Jacob Riis, *How the Other Half Lives: Studies Among the Tenements of New York* (New York: Hill & Wang, 1890 [1933]), 121.

41. Ace Backwords, *Surviving on the Streets: How to Go Down Without Going Out* (Port Townsend, WA: Loompanics, 2001), 189.

42. Gold, *Jews Without Money*, 13–14.

43. Crockett's memoir was cowritten with or ghostwritten by Congressman William Clark. Cited in Anbinder, *Five Points*, 26.

44. Ibid., 36–37. "The race mixing in New York slums of the period tended to fascinate European witnesses, while the Americans found it unutterably loathsome and avoided going into too many details. It is striking how seldom black people are ever mentioned in journalistic accounts of New York in the nineteenth century, unless they had the misfortune to get themselves publicly lynched." Sante, *Low Life*, 294–95.

45. Charles Dickens, *American Notes for General Circulation* (New York: Penguin, 1842 [2000]).

46. Anbinder, *Five Points*, 88.

47. Katherine S. Newman, *No Shame in My Game: The Working Poor in the Inner City* (New York: Vintage, 1999), 194.

48. Jane Addams, "The Subtle Problems of Charity," *Atlantic Monthly* 83 (1899): 163–78.

49. Gold, *Jews Without Money*, 241–42.

50. Edward T. Devine, *The Principles of Relief*, repr. ed. (New York: Arno, 1904 [1971]), 314.

51. Mohl, *Poverty in New York*, 154–57.

52. Some 140 years later, New York's Holy Apostles soup kitchen, the largest in the city (although one among many hundreds, now) would also serve over a thousand meals per day.

53. Anbinder, *Five Points*, 254ff.

54. Welfare states are often identified as the onset of broad, national social insurance programs, a product of industrialization, as distinct from the long tradition (since at least the late middle ages) of relief programs targeted narrowly to the very poor. But if our focus is on the poor, and not the middling classes that have reaped much of the benefits of welfare states, then this is not a useful distinction or an

appropriate definition. Which highlights part of the story here: the experience of the poorest has not changed significantly, although it has for others.

55. Steven J. Ross, "'Objects of Charity': Poor Relief, Poverty, and the Rise of the Almshouse in Early Eighteenth-Century New York City," in *Authority and Resistance in Early New York*, ed. William Pencak and Conrad Edick Wrights (New York: New York Historical Society, 1988); Robert E. Cray Jr., *Paupers and Poor Relief in New York City and Its Rural Environs, 1700–1830* (Philadelphia: Temple University Press, 1988), 58–62.

56. Anbinder, *Five Points*, 77.

57. The median age was nine. Douglas Lamar Jones, "The Strolling Poor: Transiency in Eighteenth-Century Massachusetts," in *Walking to Work: Tramps in America, 1790–1935*, ed. Eric H. Monkkonen (Lincoln: University of Nebraska Press, 1984).

58. Reprinted at poorhousestory.com.

59. Mary L. Eysenbach, "Caring for the Poor: Thetford and the Baker Family, 1792–1817," *Vermont History* 72 (winter/spring 2004): 55–62.

60. Kisseloff, *You Must Remember This*, 516.

61. Ibid., 73.

62. Ibid., 496.

63. Mark Jonathan Harris, Franklin Mitchell, and Steven Schechter, *The Homefront: America During World War II* (New York: Putnam, 1984), 152.

64. Studs Terkel, *Hard Times: An Oral History of the Great Depression* (New York: The New Press, 1970 [2000]), 112.

65. Kisseloff, *You Must Remember This*, 465–66.

66. Terkel, *Hard Times*, 380.

67. Suzanne Wasserman, "'Our Alien Neighbors': Coping with the Depression on the Lower East Side," *American Jewish History* 88, no. 2 (June 2000): 209–32.

68. Lillian Brandt, *An Impressionistic View of the Winter of 1930–31 in New York City* (New York: Welfare Council of New York City, 1932), 23, 7.

69. Kisseloff, *You Must Remember This*, 514.

70. Robert Cohen, ed., *Dear Mrs. Roosevelt: Letters from Children of the Great Depression* (Chapel Hill: University of North Carolina Press, 2002), 92.

71. Terkel, *Hard Times*, 47.

72. David Caplovitz, *The Poor Pay More* (New York: Free Press, 1963 [1967]).

73. *Proceedings of the National Conference on Charities and Corrections* (1912), 119.

74. Gwendolyn Mink and Rickie Solinger, eds., *Welfare: A Documentary History of U.S. Policy and Politics* (New York: NYU Press, 2003), chap. 63.

75. Gold, *Jews Without Money*, 255.

76. Noah Sawyer and Kenneth Temkin, "Analysis of Alternative Financial Service Providers," Fannie Mae Foundation and the Urban Institute, February 19, 2004, www.urban.org/url.cfm?ID=410935; John P. Caskey, "Fringe Banking and the Rise of Payday Lending," chap. 2 in *Credit Markets for the Poor*, ed. Patrick Bolton and Howard Rosenthal (New York: Russell Sage Foundation, 2005).

77. Matt Fellows, "From Poverty, Opportunity: Putting the Market to Work for Lower Income Families," Brookings Institution, Metropolitan Policy Program, July 2006; Matt Fellows, testimony before the House Committee on Financial Services, Subcommittee on Housing and Community Opportunity, March 8, 2008.

78. Carol Stack, *All Our Kin* (New York: Basic, 1974 [1997]), 32.

79. Ibid., 32.

80. Philippe Bourgois, *In Search of Respect: Selling Crack in El Barrio* (New York: Cambridge University Press, 2003 [1996]), 2.

81. Venkatesh, *American Project*, 91; for an extended examination of the topic, see Sudhir Alladi Venkatesh, *Off the Books: The Underground Economy of the Urban Poor* (Cambridge, MA: Harvard University Press, 2006).

82. Timothy J. Gilfoyle, *City of Eros: New York City, Prostitution, and the Commercialization of Sex, 1790–1920* (New York: W.W. Norton, 1992), 59; Christine Stansell, *City of Women: Sex and Class in New York 1789–1860* (Urbana: University of Illinois Press, 1982 [1987]); Jody Raphael, *Listening to Olivia: Violence, Poverty, and Prostitution* (Boston: Northeastern University Press, 2004), 26–28. Archeological digs in the former Five Points area of New York suggest that the material lives of prostitutes in brothels were likely little or no better than that of their sisters in the tenements, and that these working women's contact with the upper classes did not necessarily mean that they benefitted from it—merely that they surrounded themselves with the trappings of a middle-class life (like fancy tea sets) in order to appear more acceptable to certain of their clientele, while they ate the same cuts of meat, ate off the same cheap dishes, and smoked the same poor tobacco as their compatriots in the neighborhood. If we are to go by William Sanger's 1858 study, almost half of New York's prostitutes admitted to having syphilis, and the high infant mortality rates of the period were as much as four times higher for the children of prostitutes. Rebecca Yamin, "Wealthy, Free, and Female: Prostitution in Nineteenth-Century New York," *Historical Archaeology* 39, no. 1 (2005): 4–18; Thomas A. Crist, "Babies in the Privy: Prostitution, Infanticide, and Abortion in New York City's Five Points District," *Historical Archaeology* 39, no 1 (2005): 19–46.

83. Stack, *All Our Kin*, 68–69.

84. Karen Seccombe, *So You Think I Drive a Cadillac? Welfare Recipients' Perspectives on the System and Its Reform* (Boston: Allyn & Bacon, 1999), 133; see also Lisa Dodson, *Don't Call Us Out of Name: The Untold Lives of Women and Girls in Poor America* (Boston: Beacon, 1998 [1999]).

85. Mark Robert Rank, *Living on the Edge: The Realities of Welfare in America* (New York: Columbia University Press, 1994), 71.

86. Ruth Wallis Herndon, *Unwelcome Americans: Living on the Margin in Early New England* (Philadelphia: University of Pennsylvania Press, 2001), 18.

87. William L. Parish, Lingxin Hao, and Dennis P. Hogan, "Family Support Networks, Welfare, and Work Among Young Mothers," *Journal of Marriage and the Family* 53 (February 1991): 203–15; see also Dodson, *Don't Call Us Out of Name*; and

Kathryn Edin and Laura Lein, *Making Ends Meet: How Single Mothers Survive Welfare and Low-Wage Work* (New York: Russell Sage Foundation, 1997).

88. Beverly Stadum, *Poor Women and Their Families: Hard Working Charity Cases, 1900–1930* (Albany: SUNY Press, 1992). Mary Richmond also finds that these relief recipients received income from relatives, churches, mutual aid societies, their husband's former employer or family, other charities, and public coffers. Mary E. Richmond and Fred S. Hall, "A Study of Nine Hundred and Eighty-Five Widows Known to Certain Charity Organization Societies in 1910," Russell Sage Foundation, 1913.

89. Marvin B. Sussman, "The Help Pattern in the Middle Class Family," *American Sociological Review* 18, no. 1 (February 1953): 22–28.

90. Wacquant cited in Venkatesh, *American Project*, 235.

91. For contemporary data, see U.S. Census Bureau, *Statistical Abstract of the United States: 2004–2005*, table 561; and Newtithing Group, "The Demographics of Charitable Giving," December 2005, newtithing.org. Further, one 2007 study showed that while over 40 percent of the charitable giving of households with annual income under $100,000 was "focused on the needs of the poor," it was only just under 15 percent for households with incomes over $1 million. And in absolute dollars, the amounts contributed by the under $100,000 group was more than for those over $1 million, and nearly as much as that contributed by all households with income over $200,000 per year. See the Center on Philanthropy at Indiana University, "Patterns of Household Charitable Giving by Income Group, 2005," summer 2005.

92. In Franklin Folsom, *Impatient Armies of the Poor: The Story of Collective Action of the Unemployed, 1808–1942* (Niwot: University Press of Colorado, 1991), 51.

93. Benjamin Franklin, *The Autobiography of Benjamin Franklin* (Mineola, NY: Dover, 1996), 19.

94. Southern Regional Council magazine, November 1965, in *Black Women in White America: A Documentary History*, ed. Gerda Lerner (New York: Vintage, 1972 [1992]), 311–13.

2. Sleep: A Place to Call Home

1. William K. Bunis, Angela Yancik, and David A. Snow, "The Cultural Patterning of Sympathy Toward the Homeless and Other Victims of Misfortune," *Social Problems* 43, no. 4 (November 1996): 387–402.

2. This is a principle derived from English Poor Law and known as "less eligibility": relief should always be less desirable (less eligible) than work.

3. Gary B. Nash, for instance, highlights the growth in inequality in the "conservative era" of the 1790s and the reassessment of poor relief practices that came with it, a pattern we see again in the Gilded Age and the late twentieth century. Efforts to control and marginalize the poor and working-class majority seem to be neces-

sary concomitants to an upward redistribution of wealth. Nash, "Poverty and Politics in Early American History," in *Down and Out in Early America*, ed. Billy G. Smith (University Park: Pennsylvania State University Press, 2004), 36–37, fn 107; Stephen Pimpare, *The New Victorians: Poverty, Politics, and Propaganda in Two Gilded Ages* (New York: The New Press, 2004). See also Naomi Klein, *The Shock Doctrine: The Rise of Disaster Capitalism* (New York: Metropolitan Books, 2007).

4. Robert E. Cray Jr., *Paupers and Poor Relief in New York City and Its Rural Environs, 1700–1830* (Philadelphia: Temple University Press, 1988), 78.

5. Although states in the Midwest had pension and other relief programs for the blind in the late nineteenth century, and by 1919 fourteen states had some such provision (the first was in 1866 in the city of New York), by 1920 Colorado was the best place to be if you were blind, since the greatest number of its blind residents received some form of state relief. Of course, you were perhaps more likely to be blind in the first place if you had worked in Colorado, since it was not an uncommon occurrence in the mines. If you lived in Alabama, Indiana, Minnesota, Nebraska, Ohio or Rhode Island and were blind you were exempt from anti-begging laws; elsewhere you did not have to pay property or poll taxes and could sell goods or play music in public without a license. Charity workers, predictably, had opposed almost all "blind pensions" and "blind relief laws," fearful of their potential for pauperizing the recipients. They were perhaps also fearful of losing their (local) control over relief-giving to these (state) programs. They made an enormous difference. Coloradoan Evelyn Tozer received $300 a year under the blind benefit program, almost double the average annual benefit for female relief recipients; William Henderson's benefits went from $69.05 in county relief to $270 in 1920 from the state's Blind Benefit Commission. And thanks to widespread resistance by an active and engaged blind community to the efforts of the bureaucrats and social workers of Board of Charities, there was—for a time—virtually nothing by way of investigation into their lives or monitoring of their behavior; the law in Colorado required only that they meet criteria for age, income, residency, and, of course, eyesight. That's the freedom of an entitlement—a little less infantilization and a little more privacy and dignity for the recipient. Almost all qualified applicants received the maximum monthly benefit. Thomas A. Krainz, *Delivering Aid: Implementing Progressive Era Welfare in the American West* (Albuquerque: University of New Mexico Press, 2005), 161.

6. Adapted from Stephen Pimpare, "The Poorhouse," in *Poverty in the United States*, ed. Gwendolyn Mink and Alice O'Connor (Santa Barbara: ABC-CLIO, 2004). See also Michael B. Katz, *In the Shadow of the Poorhouse: A Social History of Welfare in America* (New York: Basic, 1986 [1996]).

7. See David U. Himmelstein, Elizabeth Warren, Deborah Thorne, and Steffie Woolhandler, "Market Watch: Illness and Injury as Contributors to Bankruptcy," *Health Affairs*, February 2, 2005.

8. Albert Deutsch, "The Sick Poor in Colonial Times," *American Historical Review* 46, no. 3 (April 1941): 560–79.

9. Raymond A. Mohl, *Poverty in New York, 1783–1825* (New York: Oxford University Press, 1971), 93–96; Deutsch, "The Sick Poor in Colonial Times," 560–79.

10. From "Report and Memorial of the County Supervisors of the Poor of [New York] on Lunacy and Its Relation to Pauperism, and for Relief of the Insane Poor" (1856), in Gerald N. Grob, "Deinstitutionalization: The Illusion of Policy," *Journal of Policy History* 9, no. 1 (1997): 48–73.

11. Lars Eighner, *Travels with Lizbeth* (New York: St. Martin's, 1993), 149.

12. Nellie Bly, "Ten Days in a Mad-House" (1888), digital.library.upenn.edu/women/bly. These stories of meager or indifferent care, of cruelty and abuse, of filthy, degrading institutions for the poorest and sickest among us are not remnants of a distant past. Paul von Zielbauer more recently reported of the Limestone Correctional Facility, an Alabama facility for HIV positive prisoners: "the court monitor described an H.I.V. unit riddled with rats, where broken windows had been replaced with plastic sheeting that itself was falling apart. Thousands of doses of prescribed medications had never been given." It was overcrowded; patient-inmates were barely attended by too few nurses, who ignored doctors' orders and prescribed drugs as they saw fit; there were no quarantine procedures for infected patients (in a facility in which everyone had a compromised immune system); they falsified charts and records; patients died waiting days to be seen by doctors, while others were forced to get up at three in the morning to stand in line for medications, sometimes outdoors and in the rain; and so on (*New York Times*, August 1, 2005).

13. Elizabeth Parsons Ware Packard, *Modern Persecution, or Insane Asylums Unveiled*, 2 vols., repr. ed. (New York: Arno, 1873 [1973]). For more on Packard, see Chapter 9.

14. Clyde E. Buckingham, "Early American Orphanages: Ebenezer and Bethesda," *Social Forces* 26, no. 3 (March 1948): 311–21.

15. See also David Wagner, *The Poorhouse: America's Forgotten Institution* (Lanham, MD: Rowman & Littlefield, 2005), chap. 2.

16. John K. Alexander, *Render Them Submissive: Responses to Poverty in Philadelphia, 1760–1800* (Amherst: University of Massachusetts Press, 1980), 94–99, 116–17.

17. Monique Bourque, "Poor Relief 'Without Violating the Rights of Humanity': Almshouse Administration in the Philadelphia Region, 1790–1860," in *Down and Out in Early America* (see note 3), 197.

18. Mary Roberts Smith, "Almshouse Women: A Study of Two Hundred and Twenty-Eight Women in the City and County Almshouse of San Francisco," *Publications of the American Statistical Association* 4, no. 31 (September 1895): 219–62.

19. Ben Reitman, *Sisters of the Road: The Autobiography of Boxcar Bertha* (Edinburgh: AK Press/Nabat, 1937 [2002]), 95–96.

20. Edmund Wilson, *The American Earthquake: A Chronicle of the Roaring Twenties, the Great Depression, and the Dawn of the New Deal* (New York: Da Capo, 1958 [1996]), 461–62.

21. Jonathan Kozol, *Rachel and Her Children: Homeless Families in America* (New York: Fawcett Columbine, 1988), 27–30.

22. Steven VanderStaay, *Street Lives: An Oral History of Homeless Americans* (Philadelphia: New Society Publishers, 1992), 14.

23. Elliot Liebow, *Tell Them Who I Am: The Lives of Homeless Women* (New York: Penguin, 1993 [1995]), 121, fn 7.

24. Gwendolyn A. Dordick, *Something Left to Lose: Personal Relations and Survival Among New York's Homeless* (Philadelphia: Temple University Press, 1997), 162.

25. Ibid., chap. 4.

26. Liebow, *Tell Them Who I Am*, 123.

27. Ibid., 127.

28. "Flophouses," said one wag, are a "cheap hotel or relief station where the homeless sleep poorly and the bedbugs live well." Minehan, in Joan M. Crouse, *The Homeless Transient in the Great Depression: New York State, 1929–1941* (Albany: SUNY Press, 1986), 99.

29. Matthew Josephson, "The Other Nation," *New Republic*, May 17, 1933, 14–16.

30. Alexander Irvine, *From the Bottom Up: The Life Story of Alexander Irvine* (New York: Grosset & Dunlap, 1909 [1910]), 95.

31. Wilson, *American Earthquake*, 457–58.

32. In Frank Tobias Higbie, *Indispensable Outcasts: Hobo Workers and Community in the American Midwest, 1880–1930* (Urbana: University of Illinois Press, 2003), 190.

33. M. Alfredo Gonzalez, "Sexuality and Love in the Lives of Homeless Men in New York City" (PhD diss., City University of New York, 2004), 126–27.

34. Although some of these, too, insisted that residents leave during the day and search for work; see above, Josephson, "The Other Nation."

35. Chip Ward, "What They Didn't Teach Us in Library School: The Public Library as an Asylum for the Homeless," TomDispatch.com, April 1, 2007.

36. Wagner, *The Poorhouse*, 77.

37. New York City Coalition for the Homeless, "Homelessness in New York City," February 2003, coalitionforthehomeless.org.

38. Ana Maria Arumi and Andrew L. Yarrow with Amber Ott and Jonathan Rochkind, *Compassion, Concern and Conflicted Feelings: New Yorkers on Homelessness and Housing* (New York: Public Agenda, 2007).

39. Andrew White, Kim Nauer, Sharon Lerner, and Beth Glenn, *Spanning the Neighborhood: The Bridge Between Housing and Supports for Families* (New York: Center for New York City Affairs, New School, 2005).

40. Ian Urbina, "Gay Youths Find Place to Call Home in Specialty Shelters," *New York Times*, May 17, 2007. Poverty among gays and lesbians remains an area ripe for investigation and analysis. For an overview of some relevant issues, see M.V. Lee Badgett, *Money, Myths, and Change: The Economic Lives of Lesbians and Gay Men* (Chicago: University of Chicago Press, 2001).

41. VanderStaay, *Street Lives*.

42. Jackie Spinks, "Poverty or at Home in a Car," *Z Magazine*, February 1996.

43. Timothy E. Donohue, *In the Open: Diary of a Homeless Alcoholic* (Chicago: University of Chicago Press, 1996), 162.

44. Noel Rae, ed., *Witnessing America: The Library of Congress Book of Firsthand Accounts of Life in America, 1600–1900* (New York: Stonesong, 1996), 235–36.

45. Irving Bernstein, *A Caring Society: The New Deal, the Worker, and the Great Depression* (New York: Houghton Mifflin, 1985), 19.

46. Lars Eighner, *Travels with Lizbeth* (New York: St. Martin's, 1993), 128. Eighner is likely referring to something written by French novelist Anatole France in 1894: "They [the poor] have to labour in the face of the majestic equality of the law, which forbids the rich as well as the poor to sleep under bridges, to beg in the streets, and to steal bread." Anatole France, *The Red Lily* (1894), chap. 7, in *The Oxford Dictionary of Modern Quotations*, ed. Tony Augarde (New York: Oxford University Press, 1991).

47. VanderStaay, *Street Lives*, 24.

48. Priscilla Ferguson Clement, "The Transformation of the Wandering Poor in Nineteenth-Century Philadelphia," in *Walking to Work: Tramps in America, 1790–1935*, ed. Eric H. Monkkonen (Lincoln: University of Nebraska Press, 1984).

49. Associated Press, "U.S. Says Terrorists May Pose As Vagrants," August 22, 2005.

50. Ace Backwords, *Surviving on the Streets: How to Go Down Without Going Out* (Port Townsend, WA: Loompanics, 2001), 62.

51. Author's calculations based on "Homeless Counts in Major US Cities and Counties," Institute for the Study of Homelessness and Poverty, Weingart Center, December 2005. For a review of the challenges involved in creating accurate homeless counts, see Anne B. Shlay and Peter H. Rossi, "Social Science Research and Contemporary Studies of Homelessness," *Annual Review of Sociology* 18 (1992): 129–60.

52. National Coalition for the Homeless, NCH Fact Sheet No. 2, February 1999, www.nationalhomeless.org.

53. Bruce G. Link, Ezra Susser, Ann Stueve, et al., "Lifetime and Five-Year Prevalence of Homelessness in the United States," *American Journal of Public Health* 84, no. 12 (December 1994): 1907–12.

54. Jennifer Toth, *The Mole People: Life in the Tunnels Beneath New York City* (Chicago: Chicago Review Press, 1993). See also *Dark Days*, dir. Marc Singer (New York: Wide Angle Pictures, 2000).

55. Backwords, *Surviving on the Streets*, 111–26.

56. United States Conference of Mayors, "Hunger and Homelessness Survey: A Status Report on Hunger and Homelessness in America's Cities: A 27-City Survey," December 2004; for challenges to these data, see Shlay and Rossi, "Social Science Research," 129–60.

57. Shlay and Rossi, "Social Science Research," 129–60.

58. "Homelessness in Los Angeles," Institute for the Study of Homelessness and Poverty/Weingart Center, 2005.

59. National Coalition for the Homeless, "Hate, Violence, and Death on Main Street USA: A Report on Hate Crimes and Violence Against People Experiencing Homelessness 2004," 2005.

60. Associated Press, August 18, 2005; local6.com/wkmg-tv, December 16, 2005.

61. William K. Bunis, Angela Yancik, and David A. Snow, "The Cultural Patterning of Sympathy Toward the Homeless and Other Victims of Misfortune," *Social Problems* 43, no. 4 (November 1996): 387–402.

62. U.S. Department of Veteran's Affairs, www.va.gov; Libby Perl, "Veterans and Homelessness," Congressional Research Service, May 31, 2007; Erin McClam, "New Generation of Homeless Vets Emerges," Associated Press, January 20, 2008.

63. United Press International, December 7, 2004; *Stars and Stripes*, June 2, 2005; U.S. Department of Defense Task Force on Mental Health, "An Achievable Vision: Report of the Department of Defense Task Force on Mental Health," June 2007.

64. Michael Davis, "Forced to Tramp: The Perspective of the Labor Press, 1870–1900," in *Walking to Work* (see note 48).

65. John Marriott, "Sweep Them Off the Streets," *History Today* 50, no. 8 (August 2000): 26–28.

66. William P. Quigley, "The Earliest Years of Federal Social Welfare Legislation: Federal Poor Relief Prior to the Civil War," *University of Detroit Mercy Law Review* 79, no. 157 (2002): 157–88.

67. Laura Jensen, *Patriots, Settlers, and the Origins of American Social Policy* (New York: Cambridge University Press, 2003), 87.

68. John P. Resch, "Federal Welfare for Revolutionary War Veterans," *Social Service Review* (June 1982): 171–95.

69. Jensen, *Patriots, Settlers.* Even federal disaster relief—for earthquakes, fires, and damages suffered at the hands of Native Americans—can be traced back at least as far as the early 1800s. Since the late 1700s, land grants for the establishment of primary, secondary, and postsecondary schools were common, and, slightly less common, land given for the erection of educational institutions for the deaf, blind, and mute. We have given pride of place in our traditional welfare state narratives to Pierce's veto, but that act was the anomaly, for the federal government had been involved in much of what we might call relief or welfare state activity long before its expansion in the mid-1930s and beyond. William Quigley writes that even before the Civil War, "federal assistance was provided to disabled veterans, widows and orphans of veterans, the poor in the District of Columbia, subjugated Indians, those needing education, merchant marines, and to victims of disasters and calamity." While it is true that, as part of treaty negotiation efforts, federal monies were allocated for providing gifts, food, animals, tools, and cash to Native Americans, and that annual federal payments were often part of the terms of treaties, I'm not convinced that this is within the scope of federal poor relief (although I am best de-

scribed as ambivalent on the question). And while it is also true that Congress created a broad array of relief institutions in the District of Columbia for poor children, lunatics, the sick and disabled, and more, because of its peculiar legal status Congress was in truth acting as local government, not as a federal body. This ambivalence aside, the other programs Quigley points to are more easily read as evidence that, for some individuals and for some groups, there has been an American welfare state since the founding. Perhaps we might instead argue that we have had a municipal welfare state since the 1600s, a county and state welfare state since the 1800s, and a national welfare state since the 1930s. But even that seems to understate the national role. Quigley, "The Earliest Years of Federal Social Welfare Legislation."

70. Theda Skocpol, *Protecting Soldiers and Mothers: The Political Origins of Social Policy in the United States* (Cambridge, MA: Belknap, 1992).

71. K. Walter Hickel, "War, Region, and Social Welfare: Federal Aid to Servicemen's Dependents in the South, 1917–1921," *Journal of American History*, March 2001.

72. Suzanne Mettler, "The Creation of the G.I. Bill of Rights of 1944: Melding Social and Participatory Citizenship Ideals," *Journal of Policy History* 17, no. 4 (2005): 345–74. For the extended case that the reach and generosity of the GI Bill is a significant part of the explanation for this generation's civic-mindedness, see Suzanne Mettler, *Soldiers to Citizens: The G.I. Bill and the Making of the Greatest Generation* (New York: Oxford University Press, 2005).

73. Brian Gifford, "The Camouflaged Safety Net: The U.S. Armed Forces as Welfare State Institution," *Social Politics* 13, no. 3 (August 2006): 372–99; Kyle L. Pehrson and William G. Black Jr., "The United States of America," special issue on veteran's policy, *Journal of International and Comparative Social Welfare* 10 (1994): 58–75; U.S. Census Bureau.

74. Adapted from Stephen Pimpare, "Tramps," in *Encyclopedia of the Gilded Age and Progressive Era*, ed. John D. Buenker and Joseph D. Buenker (New York: M.E. Sharpe, 2005). See also Pimpare, *New Victorians*, chap. 6.

75. Nels Anderson, *The Hobo: The Sociology of the Homeless Man* (Chicago: University of Chicago Press, 1923 [1961]), xvii. Similarly, Frederick Law Olmstead reported that Dr. Samuel Cartwright "believes that slaves are subject to a peculiar form of mental disease, termed by him *Drapetomania*, which, like a malady that cats are liable to, manifests itself by an irrestrainable propensity to *run away*; and in a work on the diseases of negroes . . . he advises planters of the proper preventive and curative measures to be taken for it." Most prominent among them, whipping. Rae, *Witnessing America*, 466–67.

76. *Walking to Work* (see note 48).

77. Anderson, *The Hobo*, 100–103.

78. Ibid., 87.

79. Cited in Tim Cresswell, *The Tramp in America* (London: Reaktion, 2001), 57.

80. For all London quotes, see Jack London, *Jack London on the Road: The Tramp Diary and Other Writings* (Miami, FL: Synergy International of the Americas, 1894 [2002]), 70–75, 89.

81. Jim Tully, *Beggars of Life: A Hobo Autobiography* (Edinburgh: AK Press/Nabat, 1924 [2004]), 168–69.

82. Anderson, *The Hobo*, xiv.

83. Ibid., 14, 19, 150.

84. *Walking to Work* (see note 48).

85. Ira Berlin, Barbara J. Fields, Steven F. Miller, Joseph P. Reidy, and Leslie S. Rowland, eds., *Free at Last: A Documentary History of Slavery, Freedom, and the Civil War* (New York: The New Press, 1992), 209, 214.

86. Roger A. Bruns, *Knights of the Road: A Hobo History* (New York: Methuen, 1980), 43.

87. Ibid.

88. Quoted in ibid., 9.

89. Frank Tobias Higbie, *Indispensable Outcasts: Hobo Workers and Community in the American Midwest, 1880–1930* (Urbana: University of Illinois Press, 2003), 30–31.

90. Patricia Cooper, "The 'Traveling Fraternity': Union Cigar Makers and Geographic Mobility, 1900–1919," in *Walking to Work* (see note 48). As a machinist said to efficiency expert Frederick Winslow Taylor in 1914: "We don't want to work as fast as we are able to. We want to work as fast as we think it's comfortable for us to work. We haven't come into existence for the purpose of seeing how great a task we can perform through a lifetime. We are trying to regulate our work so as to make it an auxiliary to our lives." Daniel T. Rodgers, *The Work Ethic in Industrial America, 1850–1920* (Chicago: University of Chicago Press, 1974 [1979]), 168.

91. Ann Banks, ed., *First Person America* (New York: Vintage, 1980 [1981]), 79.

92. Tully, *Beggars of Life*, 142.

93. See Jules Tygiel, "Tramping Artisans: Carpenters in Industrial America, 1880–1990," and Cooper, "The 'Traveling Fraternity,'" in *Walking to Work* (see note 48).

94. James D. McCabe Jr., *New York by Gaslight*, repr. ed. (New York: Greenwich House, 1882 [1984]), 654–55.

95. Lescohier in Anderson, *The Hobo*, 119.

96. Davis, "Forced to Tramp."

97. Tygiel, "Tramping Artisans."

98. Thus "Bertha" is, I would argue, *authentic* even if she is not *real.*

99. Cresswell, *Tramp in America*, 93.

100. In Lynn Weiner, "Sisters of the Road: Women Transients and Tramps," in *Walking to Work* (see note 48).

101. In Harvey Swados, ed., *The American Writer and the Great Depression* (Indianapolis: Bobbs-Merrill, 1966), 187–88.

102. Tom Kromer, *Waiting for Nothing and Other Writings* (Athens: University of Georgia Press, 1935 [1986]), 65–66.

103. It does not account for why Le Sueur does not find women on the breadlines or in the shelters.

104. Crouse, *Homeless Transient in the Great Depression*, 84.

105. Reitman, *Sisters of the Road*, 50, 13.

106. Becky Dennison, Anisa Mendizabal, and Pete White, "Many Struggles, Few Options: Findings & Recommendations from the 2004 Downtown Women's Needs Assessment," Downtown Women's Action Coalition, January 2005. The median age for women on skid row was forty-five, and the median duration of their stay was two years, with nearly one-third having been there for four or more years; more than 60 percent were African American, 11 percent Latina, and almost 14 percent white; over 92 percent were native-born; almost 40 percent had children under eighteen years old, although not quite half of them had custody, and of those, over 70 percent had their children with them. Eighty-four percent were receiving some form of public aid, most typically food stamps, general relief, or SSI, for a median income of $221 per month, and an average of $401. Only just over 8 percent reported any income from employment within the past year (and as the report points out, this is so low as to be anomalous—typically half or more homeless people have employment income). Sixteen percent reported no income or benefits at all.

107. Crouse, *Homeless Transient in the Great Depression*.

108. Latah County Historical Society, historymatters.gmu.edu/d/30.

109. Terkel, *Hard Times*, 40.

110. In Franklin Folsom, *Impatient Armies of the Poor: The Story of Collective Action of the Unemployed, 1808–1942* (Niwot: University Press of Colorado, 1991), 156.

111. Alexander Keyssar, *Out of Work: The First Century of Unemployment in Massachusetts* (New York: Cambridge University Press, 1986), 165.

112. Bruns, *Knights of the Road*, 86–87.

113. Terkel, *Hard Times*, 44.

114. Harry L. Hopkins, *Spending to Save: The Complete Story of Relief* (Seattle: University of Washington Press, 1936 [1972]), 111.

115. Kisseloff, *You Must Remember This*, 207.

116. See their Web site, www.outofthedoorways.org.

3. Eat: Dumpster Diving

1. Mark Nord, Margaret Andrews, and Steven Carlson, "Household Food Security in the United States, 2005," USDA Economic Research Report ER-29, November 2006; "Hunger in America 2006," America's Second Harvest, www .hungerinamerica.org; U.S. Conference of Mayors, "Hunger and Homelessness Survey," various years, www.usmayors.org/uscm/home.asp; Bryan Hall, Brandeis University, Center on Hunger and Poverty Bulletin, October 2005; Food Research

and Action Center, "Food Stamp Access in Urban America: A City-by-City Snapshot," September 2005, www.frac.org.

2. Yvonne M. Vissing, *Out of Sight, Out of Mind: Homeless Children and Families in Small-Town America* (Lexington: University Press of Kentucky, 1996), 59.

3. Franklin Folsom, *Impatient Armies of the Poor: The Story of Collective Action of the Unemployed, 1808–1942* (Niwot: University Press of Colorado, 1991), 239.

4. Thomas A. Krainz, *Delivering Aid: Implementing Progressive Era Welfare in the American West* (Albuquerque: University of New Mexico Press, 2005), 73.

5. And just as in late-twentieth-century New York City the greatest funding for emergency food went to community districts with the lowest need, one 1938 study revealed that "the funds available for health and welfare work, including relief, are least in those cities where need is greatest." Sharryn Kasmir, "Thirty Million Meals a Year: Emergency Food Programs in New York City," Food & Hunger Hotline, 1995; Ellery F. Reed, "Welfare Expenditures and Relief Rolls Compared with Community Need," *Social Forces* 19, no. 2 (December 1940): 219–27.

6. Mark R. Rank and Thomas A. Hirschl, "Estimating the Probabilities and Patterns of Food Stamp Use Across the Life Course," USDA and Joint Center for Poverty Research, October 2004.

7. "WIC in the States," Food Research and Action Center, 2005.

8. Linda D. Kozaryn, "Family Size Big Factor in Food Stamp Use," American Forces Press Services, January 1997, www.defenselink.mil/news/Jan1997/n01171997_9701173.html.

9. He has engaged in similar exercises upon release of hunger data from the USDA. See, for examples, Robert Rector, "Hunger Hysteria: Examining Food Security and Obesity in America," Heritage Foundation WebMemo No. 1701, November 13, 2007; and "Mayors' Claims of Growing Hunger Are Once Again Exaggerated," Heritage Foundation Backgrounder No. 1813, December 16, 2004. The USDA went one step further in 2006, eliminating the word "hunger" from its annual report on access to food. See Elizabeth Williamson, "Some Americans Lack Food, but USDA Won't Call Them Hungry," *Washington Post*, November 16, 2006.

10. Complained one man on a New Deal work project in Wyoming: "It's a funny thing. If our kids get run down because they don't get enough to eat, they start this nutrition business, or send 'em away to camps to feed 'em. Wouldn't it be better to give us enough to live on right, so we can feed our kids ourselves?" In Richard Lowitt and Maurine Beasley, eds., *One Third of a Nation: Lorena Hickok Reports on the Great Depression* (Urbana: University of Illinois Press, 1981 [2000]), 331.

11. USDA, "Obesity, Poverty, and Participation in Nutrition Assistance Programs," February 2005.

12. From "DB's Medical Rants: Explorations of Medicine and the Healthcare System," Medrants.com; see Anderson's post, medrants.com/index.php/archives/864 (accessed April 21, 2006).

13. The average monthly food stamp benefit in 2003 was $195, with much variation; the average was $80 for a single-person household. USDA, "Characteristics of Food Stamps Households 2003."

14. Arthur Simon, *Faces of Poverty* (New York: Macmillan, 1966 [1968]), 30–31.

15. Harvey Swados, ed., *The American Writer and the Great Depression* (Indianapolis: Bobbs-Merrill, 1966), 186.

16. Karen M. Jetter and Diana L. Cassady, "The Availability and Cost of Healthier Food Items," University of California Agricultural Issues Center, AIC Issues Brief No. 29, March 2005; Food Research Action Center, "Obesity, Food Insecurity and the Federal Child Nutrition Programs: Understanding the Linkages," October 2005; Food Research Action Center, "The Paradox of Hunger and Obesity in America," n.d., www.frac.org; P.E. Wilde and J.N. Peterman, "Individual Weight Change Is Associated with Household Food Security Status," *Journal of Nutrition* 136, no. 5 (May 2006): 1395–400; Alex Cohen, Patricia R. Houck, Katalin Szanto, Mary Amanda Dew, Stephen E. Gilman, and Charles F. Reynolds III, "Social Inequalities in Response to Antidepressant Treatment in Older Adults," *Archives of General Psychiatry* 63 (January 2006): 50–56.

17. Gwendolyn Mink and Rickie Solinger, eds., *Welfare: A Documentary History of U.S. Policy and Politics* (New York: NYU Press, 2003), chap. 61. We'll set aside how it is that "lazy loafers" manage to muster the significant energy required to riot.

18. Vivyan C. Adair, "Disciplined and Punished," in *Reclaiming Class: Women, Poverty, and the Promise of Higher Education in America*, ed. Vivyan C. Adair and Sandra L. Dahlberg (Philadelphia: Temple University Press, 2003), 32–33. Adair here also describes what have been called "poverty traps" in the literature on international development and global poverty. See Stephen C. Smith, *Ending Global Poverty: A Guide to What Works* (New York: Palgrave Macmillan, 2005).

19. Ezra Stiles Ely, *Visits of Mercy* (Philadelphia: Samuel P. Bradford, 1812 [1829]), 69. As Bellows writes, "Only the lissome and elusive street waif could hope to escape the well-meaning who prowled the alleys and paths of the most disreputable sections of the town seeking new faces to scrub and uncorrupted hearts to inculcate with the lessons of the Sunday school." Barbara L. Bellows, *Benevolence Among Slaveholders: Assisting the Poor in Charleston, 1670–1860* (Baton Rouge: Louisiana State University Press, 1993), 33.

20. Ace Backwords, *Surviving on the Streets: How to Go Down Without Going Out* (Port Townsend, WA: Loompanics, 2001), 83.

21. *IWW Songs: To Fan the Flames of Discontent* (Chicago: Charles H. Kerr, 1923 [1989]).

22. Nels Anderson, *The Hobo: The Sociology of the Homeless Man* (Chicago: University of Chicago Press, 1923 [1961]), 46.

23. Ben Reitman, *Sisters of the Road: The Autobiography of Boxcar Bertha* (Edinburgh: AK Press/Nabat, 1937 [2002]), 50–51.

24. Vissing, *Out of Sight, Out of Mind*, 148.

25. Alexander Irvine, *From the Bottom Up: The Life Story of Alexander Irvine* (New York: Grosset & Dunlap, 1909 [1910]), 158–59.

26. Bellows, *Benevolence Among Slaveholders*, 40.

27. Robert M. Solow et al., *Work and Welfare* (Princeton, NJ: Princeton University Press, 1998), 88.

28. Mariner J. Kent, "The Making of a Tramp," *The Independent*, March 19, 1903, 667–70.

29. Harry L. Hopkins, *Spending to Save: The Complete Story of Relief* (Seattle: University of Washington Press, 1936 [1972]), 108.

30. In Janet Poppendieck, *Breadlines Knee-Deep in Wheat: Food Assistance in the Great Depression* (New Brunswick, NJ: Rutgers University Press, 1986), 27.

31. Edmund Wilson, *The American Earthquake: A Chronicle of the Roaring Twenties, the Great Depression, and the Dawn of the New Deal* (New York: Da Capo, 1958 [1996]), 462–63.

32. Backwords, *Surviving on the Streets*, 84.

33. Ibid., 96.

34. Lars Eighner, *Travels with Lizbeth* (New York: St. Martin's, 1993), 117–18. The seminal text on Dumpster diving may be John Hoffman, *The Art and Science of Dumpster Diving* (Port Townsend, WA: Loompanics, 1992). Hoffman claims it is, at any rate. See also John Hoffman, *Dumpster Diving: The Advanced Course* (Boulder, CO: Paladin Press, 2002).

35. Eighner, *Travels with Lizbeth*, 13.

36. From *Somebody in Boots* by Nelson Algren, with WPA Writers' Project, in Swados, *The American Writer*, 323.

37. In Folsom, *Impatient Armies of the Poor*, 126.

38. Jennifer Toth, *The Mole People: Life in the Tunnels Beneath New York City* (Chicago: Chicago Review Press, 1993); Eighner, *Travels with Lizbeth*; Backwords, *Surviving on the Streets*; Eric H. Monkkonen, ed., *Walking to Work: Tramps in America, 1790–1935* (Lincoln: University of Nebraska Press, 1984).

39. Jeannette Walls, *The Glass Castle: A Memoir* (New York: Scribner, 2005), 173.

40. David Zucchino, *Myth of the Welfare Queen* (New York: Touchstone, 1997 [1999]), 21.

41. Timothy E. Donohue, *In the Open: Diary of a Homeless Alcoholic* (Chicago: University of Chicago Press, 1996), 124.

42. Walls, *Glass Castle*, 5.

43. David M. Katzman and William M. Tuttle, eds., *Plain Folk: The Life Stories of Undistinguished Americans* (Urbana: University of Illinois Press, 1982), 176–85.

44. Harriet Jacobs, *Incidents in the Life of a Slave Girl* (Mineola, NY: Dover, 1861 [2001]), 14. See a discussion of other such practices of "passive resistance" in Chapter 8.

4. Work: (In)Dependence

1. Anthony Ramirez, "A Job Prospect Lures, Then Frustrates, Thousands," *New York Times*, November 4, 2006.

2. Franklin Folsom, *Impatient Armies of the Poor: The Story of Collective Action of the Unemployed, 1808–1942* (Niwot: University Press of Colorado, 1991), 51.

3. Jack London, "The Tramp," in *Jack London on the Road: The Tramp Diary and Other Writings* (Miami, FL: Synergy International of the Americas, 1894 [2002]), 124.

4. Proceedings of the National Conference on Charities and Corrections (1896), 261.

5. Leah Hannah Feder, *Unemployment Relief in Periods of Depression* (New York: Russell Sage Foundation, 1936), 227.

6. Beverly Stadum, *Poor Women and Their Families: Hard Working Charity Cases, 1900–1930* (Albany: SUNY Press, 1992), 65–66.

7. Nels Anderson, *The Hobo: The Sociology of the Homeless Man* (Chicago: University of Chicago Press, 1923 [1961]), 114–15.

8. Richard Lowitt and Maurine Beasley, eds., *One Third of a Nation: Lorena Hickok Reports on the Great Depression* (Urbana: University of Illinois Press, 1981 [2000]), 126.

9. Ibid., 113.

10. Yvonne M. Vissing, *Out of Sight, Out of Mind: Homeless Children and Families in Small-Town America* (Lexington: University Press of Kentucky, 1996), 15.

11. Katherine S. Newman, *No Shame in My Game: The Working Poor in the Inner City* (New York: Vintage, 1999), 62.

12. See www.njfac.org.

13. John K. Alexander, *Render Them Submissive: Responses to Poverty in Philadelphia, 1760–1800* (Amherst: University of Massachusetts Press, 1980), 14–15.

14. Lowitt and Beasley, *One Third of a Nation*, 10.

15. Todd Gitlin and Nanci Hollander, *Uptown: Poor Whites in Chicago* (New York: Harper & Row, 1970), 168.

16. Sondra Youdelman with Paul Getsos, "The Revolving Door: Research Findings on NYC's Employment Services Placement System and its Effectiveness in Moving People from Welfare to Work" (New York: Community Voices Heard, 2005), 4.

17. Shanta Pandey, Eddie F. Brown, Leslie Scheuler-Whitaker, and Shannon Collier-Tenison, "Welfare Reform on American Indian Reservations: Initial Experience of Service Providers and Recipients on Reservations in Arizona," *Social Policy Journal* 1, no. 1 (2002): 83.

18. Mimi Abramovitz, "Challenging the Myths of Welfare Reform from a Woman's Perspective," *Social Justice* 21, no. 1 (spring 1994): 17–21.

19. Jodi-Levin Epstein, "Welfare, Women, and Health: The Role of Temporary Assistance for Needy Families," Henry J. Kaiser Family Foundation, 2003.

20. Richard M. Tolman and Jody Raphael, "A Review of Research on Welfare and Domestic Violence," *Journal of Social Issues* 56, no. 4 (2000): 655–82.

21. Devah Pager, *Marked: Race, Crime, and Finding Work in an Era of Mass Incarceration* (Chicago: University of Chicago Press, 2007).

22. For an examination of these issues in the wake of 1996's welfare reform, see Sharon Hays, *Flat Broke with Children: Women in the Age of Welfare Reform* (New York: Oxford University Press, 2004).

23. Virginia E. Schein, *Working from the Margins: Voices of Mothers in Poverty* (Ithaca, NY: ILR/Cornell University Press, 1995), 88–89.

24. In Kathryn Edin and Laura Lein, *Making Ends Meet: How Single Mothers Survive Welfare and Low-Wage Work* (New York: Russell Sage, 1997), 75–76.

25. Lisa Featherstone, "Down and Out in Discount America," *The Nation*, January 3, 2005.

26. Jill Duerr Berrick, *Faces of Poverty: Portraits of Women and Children on Welfare* (New York: Oxford University Press, 1995 [1997]), 83.

27. Kathleen Mullan Harris, "Work and Welfare Among Single Mothers in Poverty," *American Journal of Sociology* 99, no. 2 (September 1993): 317–52.

28. Mary E. Richmond and Fred S. Hall, "A Study of Nine Hundred and Eighty-five Widows Known to Certain Charity Organization Societies in 1910," Russell Sage Foundation, 1913. More than two-thirds needed help within a year of their husband's death, while only fifty had been able to delay their application for five years or more. Over 40 percent were dependent upon children's income, too, while one-third had children in an institution at some point during their "treatment" by the COS.

29. Lisa Dodson, *Don't Call Us Out of Name: The Untold Lives of Women and Girls in Poor America* (Boston: Beacon, 1998 [1999]), 141.

30. Ibid., 140.

31. Karen Seccombe, Kimberly Battle Walters, and Delores James, "'Welfare Mothers' Welcome Reform, Urge Compassion," *Family Relations* 48, no. 2 (April 1999): 148–49.

32. John Gilliom, *Overseers of the Poor: Surveillance, Resistance, and the Limits of Privacy* (Chicago: University of Chicago Press, 2001), 54, 63.

33. Arthur Simon, *Faces of Poverty* (New York: Macmillan, 1966 [1968]), 31.

34. Lowitt and Beasley, *One Third of a Nation*, 360. Hopkins sent sixteen people throughout the country to report to him on the Depression. In these pages we hear from Lorena Hickok, Ernestine Ball, Martha Bruere, Louisa Wilson, Robert Washburn, Henry Francis, Wayne Parrish, and Martha Gellhorn.

35. Jeff Kisseloff, *You Must Remember This: An Oral History of Manhattan from the 1890s to World War II* (New York: Schocken, 1989), 73.

36. Newman, *No Shame in My Game*, 52–53.

37. Raymond A. Mohl, *Poverty in New York, 1783–1825* (New York: Oxford University Press, 1971), 222–23.

38. Emily K. Abel, "Valuing Care: Turn-of-the-Century Conflicts between Charity Workers and Women Clients," *Journal of Women's History* 10, no. 3 (autumn 1998): 32–52.

39. Gerda Lerner, ed., *Black Women in White America: A Documentary History* (New York: Vintage, 1972 [1992]), 21.

40. This is in part why black women reformers of the Progressive Era devoted much more energy to creating programs of child care than did their white sisters. Linda Gordon, "Black and White Visions of Welfare: Women's Welfare Activism, 1890–1945," *Journal of American History* 78, no. 2 (September 1991): 559–90.

41. Victoria Byerly, *Hard Times Cotton Mill Girls: Personal Histories of Womanhood and Poverty in the South* (Ithaca, NY: ILR Press, 1986), 125.

42. John Spargo, *The Bitter Cry of the Children* (Chicago: Quadrangle Books, 1906 [1968]), 36–37.

43. Ibid.

44. Eva Feder Kittay, "Welfare, Dependency and a Public Ethic of Care," *Social Justice* 25, no. 1 (spring 1998).

45. See Joan Tronto, *Moral Boundaries: A Political Argument for an Ethic of Care* (New York: Routledge, 1993); Julie A. White and Joan C. Tronto, "Political Practices of Care: Needs and Rights," *Ratio Juris* 17, no. 4 (December 2004): 425–52; Lynne Haney and Robin Rogers-Dillon, "Welfare Reform and the Reconfiguration of Social Assistance," in *Blackwell Companion to Social Inequalities*, ed. Mary Romero and Eric Margolis (New York: Blackwell, 2005). See also Nancy Fraser and Linda Gordon, "A Genealogy of Dependency: Tracing a Keyword of the U.S. Welfare State," *Signs: Journal of Women in Culture and Society* 19, no. 2 (1994).

46. Edward T. Devine, *The Principles of Relief*, repr. ed. (New York: Arno, 1904 [1971]), 44.

47. Ibid., 92.

48. Jane Addams, *Twenty Years at Hull-House* (New York: Signet Classics, 1910 [1961]), 115.

49. S. Humphreys Gurteen, *A Handbook of Charity Organization* (Buffalo: Courier Company, 1882), 82.

50. Judith Berck, *No Place to Be: Voices of Homeless Children* (Boston: Houghton Mifflin, 1992), 19.

51. Berrick, *Faces of Poverty*, 136.

52. Priscilla Ferguson Clement, "Nineteenth-Century Welfare Policy, Programs, and Poor Women: Philadelphia as a Case Study," *Feminist Studies* 18, no. 1 (spring 1992): 35–58, 48–49.

53. Simon Newman, "Dead Bodies: Poverty and Death in Early National Philadelphia," in *Down and Out in Early America*, ed. Billy G. Smith (University Park: Pennsylvania State University Press, 2004), 42.

54. One 2006 study placed the value of women's unpaid domestic labor at over $130,000. See Ellen Wulfhorst, "US Mothers Deserve $134,121 in Salary," Reuters, May 3, 2006.

55. Heather Koball, Ayana Douglas-Hall, and Michelle Chau, "Children in Urban Areas Are Increasingly Low Income," National Center for Children in Poverty, November 2005.

56. Dependence now has an official government definition—for the U.S. Department of Health and Human Service's reporting purposes, a person is dependent if he or she receives more than half of their total income from TANF, SSI, and/or food stamps. See their Annual Reports to Congress, "Indicators of Welfare Dependence." The antiwelfare Heritage Foundation has constructed its own version: see William W. Beach, "The 2005 Index of Dependency," Heritage Foundation Center for Data Analysis, May 13, 2005.

57. S.J. Kleinberg, *Widows and Orphans First: The Family Economy and Social Welfare Policy, 1880–1939* (Urbana: University of Illinois Press, 2006), 32.

58. Fraser and Gordon, "A Genealogy of Dependency," 309–37.

59. Jane E. Schultz, "Seldom Thanked, Never Praised, and Scarcely Recognized: Gender and Racism in Civil War Hospitals," *Civil War History* 48, no. 3 (2002): 220–36.

60. Edith Abbott, "A Study of the Early History of Child Labor in America," *American Journal of Sociology* 14, no. 1 (July 1908): 15–37. By the mid-1700s, entire factories were constructed to serve as training grounds for child workers—some offering apprenticeships in a useful trade, most offering mere habituation to routine and long hours of monotonous experience to boys and girls as young as five or six years old, at lower wages than the adults performing the same or comparable work. One 1816 report shows 25 percent of cotton mill labor was performed by boys under seventeen, and another two-thirds by "women and girls." Even in those states that passed maximum hour and other child-labor laws in the mid-1800s, little changed since such laws were rarely enforced.

61. Spargo, *Bitter Cry of the Children*, 172–73.

62. S.J. Kleinberg, "Children's and Mothers' Wage Labor in Three Eastern U.S. Cities, 1880–1920," *Social Science History* 29, no. 1 (spring 2005): 45–76.

63. Kleinberg, *Widows and Orphans First*, 60.

64. Annelise Orleck, *Storming Caesar's Palace: How Black Mothers Fought Their Own War on Poverty* (Boston: Beacon, 2005), 11.

65. Dodson, *Don't Call Us Out of Name.*

5. Love: Women and Children First

1. Mark Robert Rank, *One Nation, Underprivileged: Why American Poverty Affects Us All* (New York: Oxford University Press, 2004); Mark R. Rank and Thomas A.

Hirschl, "Welfare Use as a Life Course Event," *Social Work* 47, no. 3 (July 2002). When government jobs are included, one estimate suggests that half of all Americans in 2004 alone had some direct dependence on government aid. See Mark Trumbull, "As U.S. Tax Rates Drop, Government's Reach Grows," *Christian Science Monitor*, April 16, 2007.

2. Sugar Turner and Tracy Bachrach Ehlers, *Sugar's Life in the Hood: The Story of a Former Welfare Mother* (Austin: University of Texas Press, 2002), 96.

3. Beverly Stadum, *Poor Women and Their Families: Hard Working Charity Cases, 1900–1930* (Albany: SUNY Press, 1992), 146.

4. Jill Duerr Berrick, *Faces of Poverty: Portraits of Women and Children on Welfare* (New York: Oxford University Press, 1995 [1997]), 106–7.

5. Sharon Hays, *Flat Broke with Children: Women in the Age of Welfare Reform* (New York: Oxford University Press, 2003), 102.

6. In Robin L. Jarrett, "Welfare Stigma Among Low-Income, African American Single Mothers," *Family Relations* 45, no. 4 (October 1996): 368–74.

7. Karen Seccombe, Kimberly Battle Walters, and Delores James, "'Welfare Mothers' Welcome Reform, Urge Compassion," *Family Relations* 48, no. 2 (April 1999): 202.

8. "Welfare Made a Difference," Queers for Economic Justice, www.queersforeconomicjustice.org.

9. Diane Dujon, "Out of the Frying Pan," in *For Crying Out Loud: Women's Poverty in the United States*, ed. Diane Dujon and Ann Withorn (Boston: South End, 1996), 11.

10. Rosemary L. Bray, *Unafraid of the Dark: A Memoir* (New York: Anchor, 1998), 277.

11. Turner and Ehlers, *Sugar's Life in the Hood*, 83, 87.

12. Leon Dash, *Rosa Lee: A Mother and Her Family in Urban America* (New York: Basic, 1996).

13. Elijah Anderson, *Code of the Street: Decency, Violence, and the Moral Life of the Inner City* (New York: W.W. Norton, 1999), 162.

14. Berrick, *Faces of Poverty*, 63.

15. Marieka Klawitter, Robert D. Plotnick, and Mark Evan Edwards, "Determinants of Initial Entry onto Welfare by Young Women," *Journal of Policy Analysis and Management* 19, no. 4 (2000): 527–46.

16. Steven VanderStaay, *Street Lives: An Oral History of Homeless Americans* (Philadelphia: New Society Publishers, 1992), 170.

17. Joe Soss, *Unwanted Claims: The Politics of Participation in the U.S. Welfare System* (Ann Arbor: University of Michigan Press, 2002), 45.

18. Katherine S. Newman, *No Shame in My Game: The Working Poor in the Inner City* (New York: Vintage, 1999), 219.

19. Jane Jacobs, *The Death and Life of Great American Cities* (New York: Vintage, 1961).

20. Nicholas Lemann, "Bad Choices: A Welfare Soap Opera," *Washington Post,* October 5–8, 1980 (four-part series).

21. Note also Mexican American field laborer Grace Palacio Arceneaux, interviewed in 1977, about growing up in California and the stinginess of relief: "Man, they never gave us anything, but they watched us like a hawk. We'd go sometimes to the garbage cans and take good cans and wash them out, dry them, leave the label on . . . and put them so that our cupboard always had a lot of food. It was a little rinky-dink house, but all our cupboards had little curtains, cloth curtains. You just pulled them open. That wasn't what we were really eating. We were eating beans or weeds, the greens from the fields." Meri Knaster, interview with Grace Arceneaux (UC Santa Cruz Regional History Project, 1977), library.ucsc.edu/reg-hist/arceneaux.html.

22. Gerda Lerner, ed., *Black Women in White America: A Documentary History* (New York: Vintage, 1972 [1992]), 102.

23. Kathryn Edin and Maria Kefalas, *Promises I Can Keep: Why Poor Women Put Motherhood Before Marriage* (Berkeley: University of California Press, 2005), 178.

24. Newman, *No Shame in My Game,* 196.

25. See Robert Rector, Kirk A. Johnson, and Sarah E. Youssef, "The Extent of Material Hardship in the United States," Heritage Foundation WebMemo No. 187, 1999.

26. Bray, *Unafraid of the Dark,* 22.

27. Lerner, *Black Women in White America,* 314–15.

28. Edin and Kefalas, *Promises I Can Keep.* See also Ellen K. Scott, Andrew S. London, and Glenda Gross, "'I Try Not to Depend on Anyone but Me': Welfare-Reliant Women's Perspectives on Self-Sufficiency, Work, and Marriage," *Sociological Inquiry* 77, no. 4 (November 2007): 601–25.

29. Barbara Ehrenreich, "Two, Three, Many Husbands," in *The Worst Years of Our Lives: Irreverent Notes from a Decade of Greed* (New York: HarperPerennial, 1990).

30. See also Carol Stack, *All Our Kin* (New York: Basic, 1974 [1997]); Patricia K. Jennings, "What Mothers Want: Welfare Reform and Maternal Desire," *Journal of Sociology and Social Welfare* 31, no. 3 (September 2004); Susan D. Holloway, Bruce Fuller, Marylee F. Rambaud, and Constanza Eggers-Pierola, *Through My Own Eyes: Single Mothers and the Cultures of Poverty* (Cambridge, MA: Harvard University Press, 1997); Lisa Dodson, *Don't Call Us Out of Name: The Untold Lives of Women and Girls in Poor America* (Boston: Beacon, 1998 [1999]).

31. Edin and Kefalas, *Promises I Can Keep,* 175.

32. Ibid., 184–85.

33. See also Dodson, *Don't Call Us Out of Name*; Angelia M. Paschal, *Voices of African-American Teen Fathers* (New York: Haworth Press, 2006), chap. 3.

34. Mary Childers, *Welfare Brat: A Memoir* (New York: Bloomsbury, 2005), 59.

35. Thomas A. Crist, "Babies in the Privy: Prostitution, Infanticide, and Abortion in New York City's Five Points District," *Historical Archaeology* 39, no 1 (2005):

19–46; Paul A. Gilje, "Infant Abandonment in Early Nineteenth-Century New York City: Three Cases," in *Growing Up in America: Children in Historical Perspective*, ed. N. Ray Hiner and Joseph M. Hawes (Urbana: University of Illinois Press, 1985).

36. Tyler Anbinder, *Five Points: The 19th-Century New York City Neighborhood That Invented Tap Dance, Stole Elections, and Became the World's Most Notorious Slum* (New York: Plume, 2002), 224.

37. Crist, "Babies in the Privy."

38. Sharon Parrott and Robert Greenstein, "Welfare, Out-of-Wedlock Childbearing, and Poverty: What Is the Connection?" Center on Budget and Policy Priorities, January 1995, esp. 15–18.

39. Due in part to a decline in extended multigenerational families living under the same roof and sharing resources, the number of poor people concentrated in female-headed households began to rise as early as 1939. So, while some blame the feminization of poverty on public welfare programs and childbearing and marriage trends of the 1960s, it's a more complicated dilemma with deeper roots. Although an American child was as likely to grow up in a single-parent household in 1870 as she was in 1970, the cause in the first instance was more likely to be the death of a parent, and in the latter, divorce. And while there is much consternation today about children born to unmarried women, in Hallowell, Maine, we learn from midwife Martha Ballard's diary that from 1785 to 1812, 38 percent of the births she aided in were out-of-wedlock *conceptions*. The difference is that the mores of the time required marriage, so that only 8 percent wound up as out-of-wedlock *births*. As Laurel Ulrich reports, "Premarital pregnancy was common throughout New England." And misinformation, misconception, and hysteria notwithstanding, teen birthrates have been declining in the United States steadily since the late 1950s, from 96 births per 1,000 among fifteen- to nineteen-year-old-women in 1957 to 49 in 2000; the single blip is a rise from 1988–1991, before the decline then continued. This is a result of reduced pregnancy rates, not increased abortions, thanks to higher contraception use and the use of more effective contraception. Still, American teen birth rates remain higher than in most of the rest of the developed world (four times as high as France or Sweden); across all countries, however, pregnancy and birth rates are higher among poorer teens, and since the United States has a much higher poverty rate than most other advanced industrial nations, this too accounts in part for our higher rates of teen pregnancy and childbirth. At the same time, the proportion of teen births to unmarried young women has grown from 13 percent in 1950 to 79 percent in 2000, in large part the result of reduced pressure to marry at all costs. George Masnick and Mary Jo Bane, *The Nation's Families, 1960–1990* (Boston: Auburn House, 1980); Laurel Thatcher Ulrich, *A Midwife's Tale: The Life of Martha Ballard, Based on Her Diary, 1785–1812* (New York: Knopf, 1990); Heather Boonstra, "Teen Pregnancy: Trends and Lessons Learned," Alan Guttmacher Institute Issues in Brief Series, no. 1, 2002; Linda Barrington and Cecilia A. Conrad, "At What Cost a Room of Her Own? Factors Contributing to the Feminization of

Poverty Among Prime-Age Women, 1939–1959," *Journal of Economic History* 54, no. 2 (June 1994): 342–57.

40. David Zucchino, *Myth of the Welfare Queen* (New York: Touchstone, 1997 [1999]), 221.

41. Turner and Ehlers, *Sugar's Life in the Hood,* 79–80.

42. Tonya Mitchell, "If I Survive, It Will Be Despite Welfare Reform," in *Reclaiming Class: Women, Poverty, and the Promise of Higher Education in America,* ed. Vivyan C. Adair and Sandra L. Dahlberg (Philadelphia: Temple University Press, 2003).

43. See www.sentencingproject.org.

44. David Simon and Edward Burns, *The Corner: A Year in the Life of an Inner-City Neighborhood* (New York: Broadway, 1997 [1998]), 225, 233.

45. Ibid., 236.

46. Edin and Kefalas, *Promises I Can Keep,* 85.

47. Black women, like their Native American sisters, have been especially subject to sexual violence. It was endemic in the slavery system—white men raped their black female slaves with what appears to be frequency and impunity. In the wake of an 1865 riot by a white mob in Memphis, Tennessee, in addition to the forty-six African Americans killed (no whites were killed, and only one injured), the U.S. House of Representatives gathered testimony from women who reported similar accounts of groups of men coming to their homes, demanding to be fed, stealing what money or valuables were present, and then taking turns beating and raping the women and girls of the household. Some policemen participated. "They drew their pistols and said they would shoot us and fire the house if we did not let them have their way with us." . . . "I bled from what the first man had done to me. The [next] man said, 'Oh, she is so near dead I won't have anything to do with her.'" They then, in some instances, burned down the houses. They continue to suffer disproportionately from sexual violence from men. Lerner, *Black Women in White America,* 172–79.

48. Jody Raphael, *Saving Bernice: Battered Women, Welfare, and Poverty* (Boston: Northeastern University Press, 2000), 85.

49. Ibid.

50. "Homelessness in New York City," New York City Coalition for the Homeless, February 2003, www.coalitionforthehomeless.org.

51. Cris M. Sullivan, Rebecca Campbell, Holly Angelique, Kimberly K. Eby, and William S. Davidson, "An Advocacy Intervention Program for Women with Abusive Partners: Six-Month Follow-up," *American Journal of Community Psychology* 22, no. 1 (1994), cited in *For Crying Out Loud* (see note 9), 65.

52. Virginia E. Schein, *Working from the Margins: Voices of Mothers in Poverty* (Ithaca, NY: ILR/Cornell University Press, 1995), 32.

53. Barbara Ehrenreich, "Profile of a Welfare Cheat," in *The Worst Years of Our Lives* (see note 29).

54. Raphael, *Saving Bernice,* 113.

55. In one study, about one in five welfare recipients reported having used drugs in the prior year; although only about 20 percent would qualify as addicted. Still, drug dependence (it's mostly marijuana, by perhaps three to one) is about twice as likely among TANF recipients than among others, and longer-term recipients, those not working, and, importantly, those with psychiatric disorders are more likely to be counted among the drug dependent (perhaps half of all drug-dependent welfare recipients suffered a DSM-III-R disorder). Welfare reform in 1996 also allowed states to drug test TANF applicants and to bar those with felony drug convictions from receipt of benefits (although by 2002 some twenty-eight states had passed legislation setting aside this provision). During the same session of Congress, alcoholism and drug addiction were formally revoked as eligible categories for SSI and SSDI, knocking a hundred thousand off the rolls in 1997. Harold A. Pollack, Sheldon Danziger, Kristin S. Seefeldt, and Rukmalie Jayakody, "Substance Abuse Among Welfare Recipients: Trends and Policy Responses," *Social Service Review* 76, no. 2 (June 2002): 256–74.

56. Raphael, *Saving Bernice*, 32

57. Ibid., 66.

58. Jeff Kunerth in ibid., 36.

59. Raphael, *Saving Bernice*, 34.

60. Ibid., 105.

61. Stadum, *Poor Women and Their Families*, see esp. 116, table 14.

62. Raphael, *Saving Bernice*.

63. Margaret Somers and Fred Block, "From Poverty to Perversity: Ideas, Markets, and Institutions over 200 Years of Welfare Debate," *American Sociological Review* 70, no. 2 (April 2005): 260–87.

64. Josephine Shaw Lowell, *Public Relief and Private Charity* (New York: Arno, 1971 [1884]).

65. See Stephen Pimpare, *The New Victorians: Poverty, Politics, and Propaganda in Two Gilded Ages* (New York: The New Press, 2004); Richard J. Herrnstein and Charles Murray, *The Bell Curve: Intelligence and Class Structure in American Life* (New York: Free Press, 1996). For critiques of Herrnstein and Murray, see Stephen Jay Gould, *The Mismeasure of Man* (New York: Norton, 1996); and Orley Ashenfelter and Cecilia Rouse, "Schooling, Intelligence, and Income in America: Cracks in the Bell Curve," November 1998, www.irs.princeton.edu/pubs/pdfs/407.pdf. Jacqueline Jones called *The Bell Curve* "hate literature with footnotes." Jones cited in Steve Macek, *Urban Nightmares: The Media, the Right, and the Moral Panic over the City* (Minneapolis: University of Minnesota Press, 2006).

66. Robert Rector, "Welfare: Broadening the Reform," in *Issues 2000: The Candidate's Briefing Book*, ed. Stuart M. Butler and Kim R. Holmes (Washington, DC: Heritage Foundation, 2000).

67. James C. Cobb, "'Somebody Done Nailed Us on the Cross': Federal Farm

and Welfare Policy and the Civil Rights Movement in the Mississippi Delta," *Journal of American History* 77, no. 3 (December 1990): 912–36.

68. John K. Alexander, *Render Them Submissive: Responses to Poverty in Philadelphia, 1760–1800* (Amherst: University of Massachusetts Press, 1980), 128; Cobb, "'Somebody Done Nailed Us on the Cross,'" 932.

69. Almost two-thirds were in the South. See Ellen Reese, *Backlash Against Welfare Mothers: Past and Present* (Berkeley: University of California Press, 2005), appendix I.

70. What the law requires and what occurs in practice can be very different, naturally. See Michael Lipsky, *Street-Level Bureaucracy* (New York: Russell Sage Foundation, 1983).

71. New Deal Network's Document Library, newdeal.feri.org.

72. "Judge Gives Views on Sterilization," *New York Times*, May 25, 1966; "Sterilization-or-Jail Order Is Reversed on Coast," *New York Times*, June 9, 1966.

73. Myla Vicenti Carpio, "The Lost Generation: American Indian Women and Sterilization Abuse," *Social Justice* 31, no. 4 (2004): 40–53. Now the Government Accountability Office, the GAO is the federal government's nonpartisan research and program evaluation agency.

74. Jane Lawrence, "The Indian Health Service and the Sterilization of Native American Women," *American Indian Quarterly* 24, no. 3 (summer 2001): 400–419.

75. David Sink, "Making the Indian Child Welfare Act Work: Missing Social and Governmental Linkages," *Phylon* 43, no. 4 (1992): 360–67.

76. Gwendolyn Mink and Rickie Solinger, eds., *Welfare: A Documentary History of U.S. Policy and Politics* (New York: NYU Press, 2003), chaps. 94–95.

77. Cobb, "'Somebody Done Nailed Us on the Cross,'" 912–36.

78. Annelise Orleck, *Storming Caesar's Palace: How Black Mothers Fought Their Own War on Poverty* (Boston: Beacon, 2005), 30.

79. Ibid., 77.

80. Lerner, *Black Women in White America*, 602–7.

81. Mary E. Odem, *Delinquent Daughters: Protecting and Policing Adolescent Female Sexuality in the United States, 1885–1920* (Chapel Hill: University of North Carolina Press, 1995), 96; ACLU in "Suit Seeks to Void Sterilization Law," *New York Times*, July 13, 1973.

82. Special Collections Library, Duke University, scriptorium.lib.duke.edu/wlm/poor/.

83. Barbara L. Bellows, *Benevolence Among Slaveholders: Assisting the Poor in Charleston, 1670–1860* (Baton Rouge: Louisiana State University Press, 1993), 81.

84. Judith A. Dulberger, *"Mother Donit fore the Best": Correspondence of a Nineteenth-Century Orphan Asylum* (Syracuse, NY: Syracuse University Press, 1996), 57–58.

85. Mark Jonathan Harris, Franklin Mitchell, and Steven Schechter, *The Homefront: America During World War II* (New York: Putnam, 1984), 193–94.

86. Bellows, *Benevolence Among Slaveholders*, 69.

87. Thomas A. Krainz, *Delivering Aid: Implementing Progressive Era Welfare in the American West* (Albuquerque: University of New Mexico Press, 2005).

88. Dulberger, *"Mother Donit fore the Best"*.

89. Ibid.

90. Marian J. Morton, "Institutionalizing Inequalities: Black Children and Child Welfare in Cleveland, 1859–1998," *Journal of Social History* 34, no. 1 (2000): 141–62; S.J. Kleinberg, *Widows and Orphans First: The Family Economy and Social Welfare Policy, 1880–1939* (Urbana: University of Illinois Press, 2006), 64.

91. Dulberger, *"Mother Donit fore the Best"*.

92. Ibid., 125–26.

93. William Loren Katz and Laurie R. Lehman, eds., *The Cruel Years: American Voices at the Dawn of the Twentieth Century* (Boston: Beacon, 2001), 70; see also David M. Katzman and William M. Tuttle, eds., *Plain Folk: The Life Stories of Undistinguished Americans* (Urbana: University of Illinois Press, 1982).

94. Christine Stansell, *City of Women: Sex and Class in New York, 1789–1860* (Urbana: University of Illinois Press, 1982 [1987]), 53.

95. Stephen O'Connor, *Orphan Trains: The Story of Charles Loring Brace and the Children He Saved and Failed* (Boston: Houghton Mifflin. 2001).

96. Charles Loring Brace, "The 'Placing Out' Plan for Homeless and Vagrant Children," *Proceedings of the National Conference on Charities and Corrections* (1876), 139.

97. Clay Gish, "Rescuing the 'Waifs and Strays' of the City: The Western Emigration Program of the Children's Aid Society," *Journal of Social History* 33, no. 1 (1999): 121–41.

6. Respect: The Price of Relief

1. Center on Budget and Policy Priorities, "What Does the Safety Net Accomplish?" July 2005; Food Research and Action Center, "WIC in the States," 2005.

2. Lawrence Mishel, Jared Bernstein, and John Schmitt, *The State of Working America 1996–1997* (New York: Economic Policy Institute/M.E. Sharpe, 1997), 403.

3. Richard B. Freeman, ed., *Working Under Different Rules* (New York: Russell Sage Foundation, 1994).

4. Gøsta Esping-Andersen with Duncan Gallie, Anton Hemerijk, and John Myers, *Why We Need a New Welfare State* (New York: Oxford University Press, 2002), table 2.9.

5. Although there may not be, or may be very little. See Peter H. Lindert, *Growing Public: Social Spending and Economic Growth Since the Eighteenth Century* (New York: Cambridge University Press, 2004).

6. Freeman, *Working Under Different Rules*.

7. Timothy M. Smeeding, "Public Policy, Economic Inequality, and Poverty: The United States in Comparative Perspective," *Social Science Quarterly* 86, no. 5 (December 2005): 955–83.

8. Charles R. Lee, "Public Poor Relief and the Massachusetts Community, 1620–1715," *New England Quarterly* 55, no. 4 (December 1982): 564–85.

9. Robert Hunter, *Poverty* (New York: Grosset & Dunlap, 1904), 337.

10. S.J. Kleinberg, *Widows and Orphans First: The Family Economy and Social Welfare Policy, 1880–1939* (Urbana: University of Illinois Press, 2006), 105.

11. Irving Bernstein, *A Caring Society: The New Deal, the Worker, and the Great Depression* (New York: Houghton Mifflin, 1985).

12. Lee G. Burchinal and Hilda Siff, "Rural Poverty," *Journal of Marriage and the Family* 26, no. 4 (November 1964): 399–405.

13. Gertrude Schaffner Goldberg and Marguerite G. Rosenthal, eds., *Diminishing Welfare: A Cross-National Study of Social Provision* (Westport, CT: Auburn House, 2002), 53; www.epinet.org.

14. SSI participation rates, by contrast, were much higher—70 percent, although still down from their peak of 76 percent in 2000. Anne B. Shlay and Peter H. Rossi, "Social Science Research and Contemporary Studies of Homelessness," *Annual Review of Sociology* 18 (1992): 129–60.

15. Traci McMillan, "The New Safety Net?" *City Limits*, November/December 2005.

16. U.S. Department of Health and Human Services, "Indicators of Welfare Dependence," Annual Report to Congress (2005).

17. Stephen T. Ziliak, "Some Tendencies of Social Welfare and the Problem of Interpretation," *Cato Journal* 21, no. 3 (winter 2002): 499–513.

18. "William Graham Sumner Elaborates the Principles of Social Darwinism, 1885," in *Major Problems in the Gilded Age and Progressive Era, Documents and Essays*, 2nd ed., ed. Leon Fink (Boston: Houghton Mifflin, 2001), 230.

19. Andrew Carroll, ed., *Letters of a Nation* (New York: Kodansha International, 1997), 196–99; also at us.history.wisc.edu/hist102/pdocs/depression_letters.pdf.

20. See Stephen Pimpare, *The New Victorians: Poverty, Politics, and Propaganda in Two Gilded Ages* (New York: The New Press, 2004).

21. Barbara Robinette Moss, *Change Me into Zeus's Daughter: A Memoir* (New York: Touchstone, 1999 [2000]), 190; see also Barbara Robinette Moss, *Fierce: A Memoir* (New York: Scribner, 2004), 190.

22. Moss, *Change Me into Zeus's Daughter*, 229.

23. Moss, *Fierce*, 97–100.

24. Robert E. Cray Jr., *Paupers and Poor Relief in New York City and Its Rural Environs, 1700–1830* (Philadelphia: Temple University Press, 1988), 41; John K. Alexander, *Render Them Submissive: Responses to Poverty in Philadelphia, 1760–1800* (Amherst: University of Massachusetts Press, 1980), 17; see also Steven J. Ross, "'Objects of Charity': Poor Relief, Poverty, and the Rise of the Almshouse in Early Eighteenth-Century New York City," in *Authority and Resistance in Early New York*, ed. William Pencak and Conrad Edick Wrights (New York: New York Historical Society, 1988).

25. See Michael B. Katz, *In the Shadow of the Poorhouse: A Social History of Welfare in*

America (New York: Basic, 1986 [1996]); Andrew J. Polsky, *The Therapeutic State* (Princeton, NJ: Princeton University Press, 1991); John H. Ehrenreich, *The Altruistic Imagination* (Ithaca, NY: Cornell University Press, 1985); David Wagner, *What's Love Got to Do with It? Beyond the Altruistic Myths of American Charity* (New York: The New Press, 2000). Piven and Cloward call this "the ritual degradation of a pariah class." Frances Fox Piven and Richard A. Cloward, *Regulating the Poor: The Functions of Public Welfare* (New York: Vintage, 1971 [1993]).

26. In Gertrude Himmelfarb, *Poverty and Compassion: The Moral Imagination of the Late Victorians* (New York: Vintage, 1992), 198.

27. Individual giving is motivated by many factors and serves many functions. Some give out of moral obligation. For others, it's a social obligation: especially among the wealthy, charity functions as a means to reinforce status and to comport to class expectations. Charity can be merely business: balls and benefits serve as networking opportunities. For some, it's a function of ego: they want others to note their generosity or see their name on a plaque or building. For others, giving is self-interested altruism: they help in part because they want others to help them when they are in need. Perhaps this forms part of the explanation for why, although the wealthy give more in total, poor people give more as a percentage of their income, as we have seen. For many, it's done out of religious obligation, "tithing" in some traditions: 60 percent of contributions in the United States are to religious organizations. Some give because they want a tangible benefit—the tote bag, the Girl Scout cookies, or the tax break. Some seek an intangible benefit—to feel good, noble (or less generously, to relieve guilt and obviate the need to do more). Charity has even been a form of punishment: one mideighteenth-century Pennsylvania law required that, if found guilty of blasphemy, in addition to three months at hard labor, the criminal was to donate 10 pounds to the poor (just as "community service" remains a means of restitution for those convicted of certain crimes). U.S. Census Bureau, *Statistical Abstract of the United States: 2004–2005*, table 561; "The Demographics of Charitable Giving," Newtithing Group, December 2005, newtithing.org; "Giving USA," in Rob Reich, "A Failure of Philanthropy," *Stanford Social Innovation Review*, winter 2005; Noel Rae, ed., *Witnessing America: The Library of Congress Book of Firsthand Accounts of Life in America, 1600–1900* (New York: Stonesong, 1996), 419.

28. Josephine Shaw Lowell, *Public Relief and Private Charity* (New York: Arno, 1884 [1971]), 89.

29. John Gilliom, *Overseers of the Poor: Surveillance, Resistance, and the Limits of Privacy* (Chicago: University of Chicago Press, 2001), 51.

30. Alexander, *Render Them Submissive*, 22–23.

31. Annelise Orleck, *Storming Caesar's Palace: How Black Mothers Fought Their Own War on Poverty* (Boston: Beacon, 2005), 88.

32. Ibid., 13.

33. Conroy in *The American Writer and the Great Depression*, ed. Harvey Swados (Indianapolis: Bobbs-Merrill, 1966), 21–22.

34. Michael Gold, *Jews Without Money* (New York: Carroll & Graf, 1930 [2004]), 291–94.

35. Richard Lowitt and Maurine Beasley, eds., *One Third of a Nation: Lorena Hickok Reports on the Great Depression* (Urbana: University of Illinois Press, 1981 [2000]), 36.

36. Ibid., 358–59.

37. Harry L. Hopkins, *Spending to Save: The Complete Story of Relief* (Seattle: University of Washington Press, 1936 [1972]), 109.

38. Jeff Kisseloff, *You Must Remember This: An Oral History of Manhattan from the 1890s to World War II* (New York: Schocken, 1989), 362.

39. Mark Robert Rank, *Living on the Edge: The Realities of Welfare in America* (New York: Columbia University Press, 1994), 101.

40. Nicholas Lemann, "Bad Choices: A Welfare Soap Opera," *Washington Post*, October 5–8, 1980 (four-part series).

41. Lisa Dodson, *Don't Call Us Out of Name: The Untold Lives of Women and Girls in Poor America* (Boston: Beacon, 1998 [1999]), 114.

42. Lowitt and Beasley, *One Third of a Nation*, 4.

43. Ibid. It is not unreasonable to suggest that "white collar" here means "white." Discrimination was common and often government-sanctioned. In a 1941 letter to FDR, Mrs. Henry Weddington, whose husband was regularly passed over for work in favor of white men, makes a simple plea: "We want to live, not merely exist from day to day, but to live as you or *any* human being desires to do." Like so many letters FDR and Eleanor received during the worst years of the Great Depression, it is a demand for dignity. Gerda Lerner, ed., *Black Women in White America: A Documentary History* (New York: Vintage, 1972 [1992]), 301.

44. Lillian Brandt, *An Impressionistic View of the Winter of 1930–31 in New York City* (New York: Welfare Council of New York City, 1932), 23.

45. Ruth Sidel, *Women and Children Last: The Plight of Poor Women in Affluent America*, rev. and updated ed. (New York: Penguin, 1992), 91.

46. Brandt, *Impressionistic View*, 193, 37.

47. Todd Gitlin and Nanci Hollander, *Uptown: Poor Whites in Chicago* (New York: Harper & Row, 1970), 336–39.

48. Joe Soss, *Unwanted Claims: The Politics of Participation in the U.S. Welfare System* (Ann Arbor: University of Michigan Press, 2002), 99.

49. Suzanne Wasserman, "'Our Alien Neighbors': Coping with the Depression on the Lower East Side," *American Jewish History* 88, no. 2 (June 2000): 209–32.

50. Jody Raphael, *Saving Bernice: Battered Women, Welfare, and Poverty* (Boston: Northeastern University Press, 2000), 117.

51. Karen Seccombe, *So You Think I Drive a Cadillac? Welfare Recipients' Perspectives on the System and Its Reform* (Boston: Allyn & Bacon, 1999), 57.

52. Ben Reitman, *Sisters of the Road: The Autobiography of Boxcar Bertha* (Edinburgh: AK Press/Nabat, 1937 [2002]), 62.

53. Gwendolyn A. Dordick, *Something Left to Lose: Personal Relations and Survival Among New York's Homeless* (Phildelphia: Temple University Press, 1997), 58.

54. Studs Terkel, *Hard Times: An Oral History of the Great Depression* (New York: The New Press, 1970 [2000]), 14–15.

55. Steven VanderStaay, *Street Lives: An Oral History of Homeless Americans* (Philadelphia: New Society Publishers, 1992), 38–39.

56. Ibid., 4.

57. Robert Cohen, ed., *Dear Mrs. Roosevelt: Letters from Children of the Great Depression* (Chapel Hill: University of North Carolina Press, 2002), 63.

58. Terkel, *Hard Times*, 114. There are a total of some 15 million letters from Americans to FDR or Eleanor in the Roosevelt Library. What's apparent from the letters McElvaine and Cohen sampled is that so many wanted to remain anonymous—ashamed to be writing and asking for help; often, in letters from children, we encounter the fear of being discovered by their parents. As McElvaine points out, when African Americans asked for anonymity, it was often out of fear of reprisals from local relief officials, who sometimes were the substance of the letter writer's complaint, more than it was concern about social disapprobation. As one Georgia resident wrote in October 1935: "I can't sign my name Mr President they will beat me up and run me away from here and this is my home." Of all letter writers, almost one-fifth wanted money, 15 percent wanted a job, one in ten wanted a loan to save their homes, and 7 percent sought loans to save the family farm. Robert S. McElvaine, ed., *Down & Out in the Great Depression: Letters from the Forgotten Man* (Chapel Hill: University of North Carolina Press, 1983); Cohen, *Dear Mrs. Roosevelt*.

59. Terkel, *Hard Times*, 420.

60. Alex Haley and Malcolm X, *The Autobiography of Malcolm X*, quoted in *America's Other Youth: Growing up Poor*, ed. David Gottlieb and Anne Lienhard Heinsohn (Englewood Cliffs, NJ: Prentice-Hall, 1971), 169–70.

61. Gitlin and Hollander, *Uptown*, 69.

62. Lowitt and Beasley, *One Third of a Nation*, 18. The RFC was the Reconstruction Finance Corporation, which funded local work relief programs.

63. Karen Seccombe, Delores James, and Kimberly Battle Walters, "'They Think You Ain't Much of Nothing': The Social Construction of the Welfare Mother," *Journal of Marriage and the Family* 60 (November 1998): 849–65.

64. Diane Dujon and Ann Withorn, eds., *For Crying Out Loud: Women's Poverty in the United States* (Boston: South End, 1996), 14.

65. Scott Briar, "Welfare from Below: Recipients' Views of the Public Welfare System," *California Law Review* 54 (1966): 370–85; Piven and Cloward, *Regulating the Poor*, 172.

66. Seccombe, *So You Think I Drive a Cadillac?*, 63.

67. Karen Seccombe, Kimberly Battle Walters, and Delores James, "'Welfare Mothers' Welcome Reform, Urge Compassion," *Family Relations* 48, no. 2 (April 1999): 203. Emphasis added.

68. Ibid.

69. Star Parker with Lorenzo Benet, *Pimps, Whores and Welfare Brats: From Welfare Cheat to Conservative Messenger, the Autobiography of Star Parker* (New York: Pocket Books, 1997).

70. Gilliom, *Overseers of the Poor*; Joe Soss, "Lessons of Welfare: Policy Design, Political Learning, and Political Action," *American Political Science Review* 93, no. 2 (June 1999): 363–80; Soss, *Unwanted Claims*; Briar, "Welfare from Below," 370–85; Seccombe, James, and Walters, "'They Think You Ain't Much of Nothing,'" 849–65; Seccombe, Walters, and James, "'Welfare Mothers' Welcome Reform," 197–206; Seccombe, *So You Think I Drive a Cadillac?*; Patricia K. Jennings, "What Mothers Want: Welfare Reform and Maternal Desire," *Journal of Sociology and Social Welfare* 31, no. 3 (September 2004); Dodson, *Don't Call Us Out of Name*; Sharon Hays, *Flat Broke with Children: Women in the Age of Welfare Reform* (New York: Oxford University Press, 2003).

71. Mary Childers, *Welfare Brat: A Memoir* (New York: Bloomsbury, 2005), 146.

72. Guy Drake, "Welfare Cadillac" (1970); Orleck (*Storming Caesar's Palace*) reports that Richard Nixon asked Johnny Cash to sing the song at the White House. Cash declined. Instead, he played "The Man in Black," whose lyrics include: "And why does my appearance seem to have a somber tone / Well, there's a reason for the things that I have on/I wear the black for the poor and the beaten down / Livin' in the hopeless, hungry side of town." My thanks to Paul Adam for bringing this to my attention.

73. Jennifer Stuber and Karl Kronebusch, "Stigma and Other Determinants of Participation in TANF and Medicaid," *Journal of Policy Analysis and Management* 23, no. 3 (2004): 509–30.

74. Richard Wertheimer, Melissa Long, and Sharon Vandivere, "Welfare Recipients' Attitudes Toward Welfare, Nonmarital Childbearing, and Work: Implications for Reform?" Urban Institute, *New Federalism*, Series B, No. B-37 (June 2001).

7. Escape: Black and Blue

1. This chapter is based in part upon Stephen Pimpare, "An African American Welfare State," *New Political Science* 29, no. 3 (2007).

2. And Katz is sensitive to and interested in matters of race. See Michael B. Katz, ed., *The "Underclass" Debate: Views from History* (Princeton, NJ: Princeton University Press, 1993); Michael B. Katz, Mark J. Stern, and Jamie J. Fader, "The New African American Inequality," *Journal of American History* (June 2005): 75–108.

3. This is indicative of a problem evident in scholarship more generally: in over a hundred years of publishing in the two oldest political science journals, 27 of 6,157 articles "address[ed] the experience of African Americans." That's roughly 2 percent of the total. See Dorian T. Warren, "Will the Real Perestroikniks Please

Stand Up? Race and Methodological Reform in the Study of Politics," chap. 15 in *Perestroika! The Raucous Rebellion in Political Science*, ed. Kristen Renwick Monroe (New Haven, CT: Yale University Press, 2005), 219.

4. Jill Quadagno, *The Color of Welfare: How Racism Undermined the War on Poverty* (New York: Oxford University Press, 1994); Michael K. Brown, *Race, Money, and the American Welfare State* (Ithaca, NY: Cornell University Press, 1999); Martin Gilens, *Why Americans Hate Welfare: Race, Media and the Politics of Antipoverty Strategy* (Chicago: University of Chicago Press, 1999); Robert C. Lieberman, *Shifting the Color Line: Race and the American Welfare State* (Cambridge, MA: Harvard University Press, 2001); Robert C. Lieberman, *Shaping Race Policy: The United States in Comparative Perspective* (Princeton, NJ: Princeton University Press, 2005); Kenneth J. Neubeck and Noel A. Cazenave, *Welfare Racism: Playing the Race Card Against America's Poor* (New York: Routledge, 2001); see also Jeff Manza, "Race and the Underdevelopment of the American Welfare State," *Theory and Society* 29, no. 6 (December 2000): 819–32.

5. Julia S. O'Connor, "Gender, Citizenship and Welfare State Regimes," in *A Handbook of Comparative Social Policy*, ed. Patricia Kennett (Cheltenham, UK: Edward Elgar, 2004), 189.

6. Or as Wilensky defined it: "The essence of the welfare state is government-protected minimum standards of income, nutrition, health and safety, education, and housing assured to every citizen as a social right, not as charity." Harold L. Wilensky, *Rich Democracies: Political Economy, Public Policy, and Performance* (Berkeley: University of California Press, 2002), 211.

7. Gøsta Esping-Andersen, *The Three Worlds of Welfare Capitalism* (Princeton, NJ: Princeton University Press, 1990); Diane Sainsbury, *Gender, Equality and Welfare States* (Cambridge, UK: Cambridge University Press, 1996); Julia S. O'Connor, Ann Shola Orloff, and Sheila Shaver, *States, Markets, Families* (Cambridge, UK: Cambridge University Press, 1999); Helga Maria Hernes, *Welfare State and Woman Power: Essays in State Feminism* (Oslo: Norwegian University Press, 1987).

8. Frances Fox Piven and Richard A. Cloward, *Regulating the Poor: The Functions of Public Welfare* (New York: Vintage, 1971 [1993]); Katz, *In the Shadow of the Poorhouse*; Mimi Abramovitz, *Regulating the Lives of Women: Social Welfare Policy from Colonial Times to the Present* (Boston: South End Press, 1988 [1996]). See also Herbert J. Gans, "The Uses of Poverty: The Poor Pay All," *Social Policy* 2, no. 2 (July/August 1971): 20–24.

9. I am merely arguing over definitions, some might say—the welfare state has been understood as a national-level public response to nineteenth-century industrialization, elaborated upon and expanded in the post–World War II, postindustrial period. Following directly from Esping-Andersen, I am proposing that we now expand our purview to include any institutions that have measurable effects upon one's ability to relocate dependence. If our only concern is understanding policy formation, the "old" definition may be appropriate. But this seems of limited use unless we also undertake an evaluation of the lived experiences of people in need,

and inquire into how their well-being has been affected by government activity over time. Decommodification and defamilialization may be imperfect as dependent variables (given that historically people have not sought to exist apart from dependence upon the labor market or the family), but they offer more analytic leverage and more insight than explanations only of policy change. See also Stephen Pimpare, "Toward a New Welfare History," *Journal of Policy History* 19, no. 2 (2007): 234–52.

10. George Fitzhugh, "Sociology for the South: Or the Failure of Free Society, 1854," in Paul Finkelman, *Defending Slavery: Proslavery Thought in the Old South, A Brief History with Documents* (Boston: Bedford/St. Martin's, 2003); John Hope Franklin, "Public Welfare in the South During the Reconstruction Era, 1865–80," *Social Service Review* 44, no. 4 (December 1970): 379–92.

11. Piven and Cloward, *Regulating the Poor*; Fred Block and Margaret Somers, "In the Shadow of Speenhamland: Social Policy and the Old Poor Law," *Politics & Society* 31, no. (2003): 283–23.

12. Philip D. Morgan, "Slaves and Poverty," in *Down and Out in Early America*, ed. Billy G. Smith (University Park: Pennsylvania State University Press, 2004).

13. Ibid., 122.

14. Amartya Sen, *Development as Freedom* (New York: Anchor, 1999), 113.

15. Elna C. Green, ed., *Before the New Deal: Social Welfare in the South, 1830–1930* (Athens: University of Georgia Press, 1999); Elna C. Green, ed., *The New Deal and Beyond: Social Welfare in the South Since 1930* (Athens: University of Georgia Press, 2003). For examples: Charleston could boast its first orphanage by 1792; a Virginia state hospital for the insane was erected in 1769; there was one for the deaf, dumb, and blind by 1838; and Georgia had its first penitentiary by 1817. Charleston also had one of the largest Jewish communities in the young nation, and its Hebrew Orphan Asylum, in operation since 1801, is "the oldest incorporated Jewish charity in America." Public pensions for poor "idiots" or the "feeble-minded" began as early as 1793 in Kentucky, an amount that would rise to $75 per year by 1870 (until it was abolished in 1918). In Louisville in 1910, 1 in 1,175 residents were on the idiot pension rolls. But not all this money went to those who, by yesterday's standards or by today's, suffered from some intellectual disability—a state auditor's report in 1881 suggests that some funds allocated for idiots pensions were used, in practice, as mother's pensions; the auditor attributes the failure to lack of proper investigation, but it seems just as likely that officials with limited resources used the pauper-idiot fund as a resource to support other of their city and county poor. And, given the history of the administration of American poor relief funds, we might also assume there to have been some out-and-out fraud. See also Barbara L. Bellows, *Benevolence Among Slaveholders: Assisting the Poor in Charleston, 1670–1860* (Baton Rouge: Louisiana State University Press, 1993), 29; Arthur H. Estabrook, "The Pauper Idiot in Kentucky," *Social Forces* 7, no. 1 (September 1928): 68–72.

16. Slaves and poor whites were united, perhaps, by much. "In America, free laborers worked about 280 to 290 days, and slaves between 280 and 310 days," while

"Philadelphia slaves apparently received about 1,800 to 2,400 calories a day at a time when the city workhouse may have provided 2,600." But note that across North America, slaves worked some 2,800 hours per year, compared to, on average, 1,851 hours worked by Americans in 2002. See Morgan, "Slavery and Poverty," 113; Lawrence Mishel, Jared Bernstein, and Sylvia Allegretto, *The State of Working America 2004–05* (Ithaca, NY: ILR/Cornell University Press, 2005), 113, table 2.1.

17. William M. Brewer, "Poor Whites and Negroes in the South Since the Civil War," *Journal of Negro History* 15, no. 1 (January 1930): 26–37; Stephen V. Ash, "Poor Whites in the Occupied South, 1861–1865," *Journal of Southern History* 57, no. 1 (February 1991): 39–62.

18. Bellows, *Benevolence Among Slaveholders*, 163.

19. Green, *Before the New Deal*, xi.

20. Abbot Emerson Smith, "Indentured Servants: New Light on Some of America's 'First' Families," *Journal of Economic History* 2, no. 1 (May 1942): 40–53; Louis Green Carr, "Emigration and the Standard of Living: The Seventeenth Century Chesapeake," *Journal of Economic History* 52, no. 2 (June 1992): 271–91; Louis Green Carr and Russell R. Menard, "Wealth and Welfare in Early Maryland: Evidence from St. Mary's County," *William and Mary Quarterly* 56, no. 1 (January 1999): 95–120; Gary B. Nash, "Poverty and Politics in Early American History," in *Down and Out in Early America* (see note 12), 6–8.

21. Martin Ruef and Ben Fletcher, "Legacies of American Slavery: Status Attainment Among Southern Blacks after Emancipation," *Social Forces* 82, no. 2 (December 2003): 445–80.

22. Morgan, "Slaves and Poverty," 118.

23. Theodore Hershberg, "Free Blacks in Philadelphia," in Allen F. Davis and Mark H. Haller, *The Peoples of Philadelphia: A History of Ethnic Groups and Lower-Class Life, 1790–1940* (Philadelphia: University of Pennsylvania Press, 1973), 114.

24. Charles C. Bolton and Scott P. Culclasure, eds., *The Confession of Edward Isham: A Poor White Life of the Old South* (Athens: University of Georgia Press, 1998 [1860]), 23.

25. Bellows, *Benevolence Among Slaveholders*, 91.

26. Ash, "Poor Whites in the Occupied South," 39–62.

27. I set aside here whether the systems of national veteran's pensions, inaugurated with the Revolutionary War, would better be identified as the first American welfare state institution.

28. It was reorganized and renamed the Department of Defense in 1949.

29. Ira Berlin, Barbara J. Fields, Steven F. Miller, Joseph P. Reidy, and Leslie S. Rowland, eds., *Free at Last: A Documentary History of Slavery, Freedom, and the Civil War* (New York: The New Press, 1992), 168, 228.

30. Ibid., 169.

31. Ibid., 435–36, 477, 461–63.

32. Green, *Before the New Deal*; Green, *New Deal and Beyond.*

33. Franklin, "Public Welfare in the South," 379–92.

34. Berlin et al., *Free at Last*, 314, 318.

35. Ira C. Colby, "The Freedman's Bureau: From Social Welfare to Segregation," *Phylon* 46, no. 3 (1985): 219–30. Lerner reports that the Freedman's Bureau established more than four thousand schools, which had by 1870 educated almost 250,000 black children; these were in many ways precursors to the broader public school system that would be established throughout the United States in the late century. Lerner, *Black Women in White America*, 93.

36. Note this talk given by Yurok Indian Robert Spott in 1926: "There are many Indian women that are almost blind, and they only have one meal a day. . . . Most of these people used to live on fish, which they cannot get, and on acorns, and they are starving. They hardly have any clothing to cover them. Many children up along the Klamath River have passed away with disease. . . . To reach doctors they have to take their children down the Klamath River. . . . It costs us $25.00. Where are the poor Indians to get this money from to get a doctor for their children? They go from place to place to borrow the money. If they cannot get it, the poor child dies without aid. Inside of four or five years there will be hardly any Indians left upon the Klamath River. I came here to notify you that something has to be done. . . . My father was an Indian chief, and we used to own everything there. When the land was allotted they allotted him only ten acres, a little farm of land which is mostly gravel and rock, with little scrubby trees and redwood. My father was not satisfied with the land and he said, 'We owned this land. We ought to pick out what we want.' 'Well,' the surveyor said, 'You cannot do it, because it is already taken up by homesteaders. I will tell you what I will do. I will have furnished to you a plow, also a cow and horse and everything so that you can improve your land.' Then, of course, my father said, 'All right, I am satisfied with that.' Well, we still waiting." Peter Nabokov, *Native American Testimony*, rev. ed. (New York: Penguin, 1978 [1999]), 315. Native Americans are waiting for their cow and horse and plow as some African Americans are still waiting for their forty acres and a mule.

37. "History from Slave Sources" in *The Slave's Narrative*, ed. Charles T. Davis and Henry Louis Gates Jr. (New York: Oxford University Press, 1985).

38. David M. Katzman and William M. Tuttle, eds., *Plain Folk: The Life Stories of Undistinguished Americans* (Urbana: University of Illinois Press, 1982), 176–85; Lerner, *Black Women in White America*, 227–29.

39. Franklin, "Public Welfare in the South," 379–92.

40. Gordon W. Blackwell, "The Displaced Tenant Farm Family in North Carolina," *Social Forces* 13, no. 1 (October 1934/May 1935): 65–73.

41. Arthur F. Raper, *Preface to Peasantry* (New York: Atheneum, 1968), chap. 15.

42. In Harvey Swados, ed., *The American Writer and the Great Depression* (Indianapolis: Bobbs-Merrill, 1966), 133.

43. Robert Cohen, ed., *Dear Mrs. Roosevelt: Letters from Children of the Great Depression* (Chapel Hill: University of North Carolina Press, 2002), 196–98.

44. David L. Carlton and Peter A. Coclanis, eds., *Confronting Southern Poverty in the Great Depression: The Report on Economic Conditions of the South with Related Documents* (Boston: Bedford Books, 1996), 54ff.

45. Introduction and Kathleen Gorman, "Confederate Pensions as Southern Social Welfare," in Green, *Before the New Deal*; introduction in Green, *New Deal and Beyond.*

46. Joe William Trotter Jr., *From a Raw Deal to a New Deal? African Americans, 1929–1945* (New York: Oxford University Press, 1996), chaps. 1 and 2.

47. The EITC may function in this manner, as a subsidy to low-wage employers. See Robert M. Solow et al., *Work and Welfare* (Princeton, NJ: Princeton University Press, 1998); Jamie Peck, *Workfare States* (New York: Guilford Press, 2001).

48. Raper, *Preface to Peasantry*; James C. Cobb, "'Somebody Done Nailed Us on the Cross': Federal Farm and Welfare Policy and the Civil Rights Movement in the Mississippi Delta," *Journal of American History* 77, no. 3 (December 1990): 912–36.

49. Andrew Carroll, ed., *Letters of a Nation* (New York: Kodansha International, 1997), 196.

50. Trotter, *From a Raw Deal to a New Deal?* chaps. 1 and 2.

51. Richard Lowitt and Maurine Beasley, eds., *One Third of a Nation: Lorena Hickok Reports on the Great Depression* (Urbana: University of Illinois Press, 1981 [2000]), 221.

52. John H. Mueller, "Some Social Characteristics of the Urban Relief Population," *Social Forces* 15, no. 1 (October 1936): 64–70.

53. Trotter, *From a Raw Deal to a New Deal?* 64.

54. Lerner, *Black Women in White America*, 450–58.

55. This is not a phenomenon only of the South. During the second great wave of black migration during World War I, Northern cities controlled the influx of African Americans in various ways, often by incarcerating them. In Pittsburgh, for example, the number of blacks arrested went from 1,681 in 1914–1915 to 2,998 in 1916–1917, virtually all of the increase for minor offenses—disorderly conduct, drunkenness, and being "suspicious characters." Harrisburg doubled its black prison population during the same time. Blacks in Cleveland jails went from 13 percent of the total in 1916 to 87 percent in 1917. Their crimes were typically "loafing" and being "suspicious." Those who received aid instead of incarceration depended upon black churches and self-help organizations. Few received public poor relief, although many unable to find shelter were sent to the workhouse. Henderson H. Donald, "Dependents and Delinquents," *Journal of Negro History* 6, no. 4 (October 1921): 458–70; see also Stephen Pimpare, *The New Victorians: Poverty, Politics, and Propaganda in Two Gilded Ages* (New York: The New Press, 2004), chap. 6.

56. Marie Gottschalk, *The Prison and the Gallows: The Politics of Mass Incarceration*

in America (New York: Cambridge University Press, 2006), 199; David Cole, *No Equal Justice: Race and Class in the American Criminal Justice System* (New York: The New Press, 1999).

57. David M. Oshinsky, *"Worse Than Slavery": Parchman Farm and the Ordeal of Jim Crow Justice* (New York: Free Press, 1996), 39.

58. Jeff Manza and Christopher Uggen, "Punishment and Democracy: Disenfranchisement of Nonincarcerated Felons in the United States," *Perspectives on Politics* 2, no. 3 (September 2004): 491–505; Angela Behrens, Christopher Uggen, and Jeff Manza, "Ballot Manipulation and the 'Menace of Negro Domination': Racial Threat and Felon Disenfranchisement in the United States, 1850–2002," *American Journal of Sociology* 109, no. 3 (November 2003): 559–605. Some efforts are underway in a number of states to soften their felony voting rules. See www .sentencingproject.org.

59. See Kim Gimore, "Slavery and Prison: Understanding the Connections," historyisaweapon.org; Joy James, ed., *The New Abolitionists: (Neo)slave Narratives and Contemporary Prison Writings* (Albany: SUNY Press, 2005). See also Loïc Wacquant, "The New 'Peculiar Institution': On the Prison as Surrogate Ghetto," chap. 23 in *Race, Crime and Justice: A Reader*, ed. Shaun L. Gabbidon and Helen Taylor Green (New York: Routledge 2005).

60. Oshinsky, *"Worse Than Slavery"*, 35.

61. Ibid., 35.

62. Scott Christianson, "Our Black Prisons," *Crime & Delinquency* 27, no. 3 (July 1981): 364–75.

63. Gottschalk, *Prison and the Gallows*, 43.

64. Burr Blackburn, "State Programs of Public Welfare in the South," *Journal of Social Forces* 1, no. 1 (November 1922): 6–11.

65. Simon P. Newman, *Embodied History: The Lives of the Poor in Early Philadelphia* (Philadelphia: University of Pennsylvania Press, 2003).

66. Raymond A. Mohl, *Poverty in New York, 1783–1825* (New York: Oxford University Press, 1971), 122–35. Without the benevolence of the Humane Society (founded as the Society for the Relief of Distressed Debtors), many prisoners would have gone without food, clothing, and wood. Some received free legal assistance, which otherwise would have been out of reach (as it was for many until 1963 when the United State Supreme Court in *Gideon v. Wainright* finally required that states provide lawyers to the poor). The society met with success in getting a few poor prisoners released each year. They would go on to found a small health clinic (1790), a free soup house (1802), and delivered food during the yellow fever epidemic of 1803, but their emphasis was on imprisoned debtors, where they counted their successes by the quarts of soup provided (over 9,000 in 1806 to 183 debtors and 21,000 quarts in 1811 to 536—not quite a quart a day to the confined). To quote Mike Millius again, it was "not enough to live on, but a little too much to die." The society only turned its attention away after 1817, when the city abolished im-

prisonment for debts under $25 (they would not entirely eliminate debtor's prison until 1831), thus freeing most of the poor, when it sent its soup more widely into the city, and thereafter broadened its purview to other efforts at reform, from "the liquor problem," to cleaning chimneys, to resuscitating drowning victims.

67. Laurel Thatcher Ulrich, *A Midwife's Tale: The Life of Martha Ballard, Based on Her Diary, 1785–1812* (New York: Knopf, 1990), 267. The usual vagrant prison term in pre–Revolutionary War Philadelphia was about one month. From then until the late nineteenth century, treatment of tramps was less harsh than it was in the last quarter of the century, during the second great mass incarceration of the century (1805–1835 marked the first), when even sick and disabled inmates were forced to undertake hard, manual labor, and violence and threats of violence were used as tools to motivate the poor inmates. There were twice as many foreign-born as natives in the late century, and as many as 43 percent in 1879. Only in the 1820s were there blacks in large numbers—51 percent in 1823, and 53 percent in 1825, five times their representation in the population. From the 1820s until just after the Civil War, when their opportunities for employed substantially improved, women were often half or more of the inmate population of tramps and vagrants. Black women were more common in the prison than were black men from the 1840s to 1860s. Priscilla Ferguson Clement, "The Transformation of the Wandering Poor in Nineteenth-Century Philadelphia," in *Walking to Work: Tramps in America, 1790–1935*, ed. Eric H. Monkkonen (Lincoln: University of Nebraska Press, 1984).

68. William Loren Katz and Laurie R. Lehman, eds., *The Cruel Years: American Voices at the Dawn of the Twentieth Century* (Boston: Beacon, 2001), 170–82; Katzman and Tuttle, *Plain Folk*, 151–63.

69. Matthew J. Mancini, *One Dies, Get Another: Convict Leasing in the American South, 1866–1928* (Columbia: University of South Carolina Press, 1996).

70. Gottschalk, *Prison and the Gallows*, 51.

71. Mancini, *One Dies, Get Another*.

72. Ibid.; Frank Tobias Higbie, *Indispensable Outcasts: Hobo Workers and Community in the American Midwest, 1880–1930* (Urbana: University of Illinois Press, 2003); Oshinsky, *"Worse Than Slavery"*.

73. Mancini, *One Dies, Get Another*; Oshinsky, *"Worse Than Slavery"*.

74. Chris Levister, "A Sweatshop Behind Bars," New America Media (posted on *WireTap*, September 13, 2006, www.wiretapmag.org/stories/41481/); Angela Y. Davis, "Masked Racism: Reflections on the Prison Industrial Complex," *ColorLines*, September 1, 1998; Pimpare, *New Victorians*.

75. Lerner, *Black Women in White America*, 229–30.

76. Abel Valenzuela, Nik Theodore, Edwin Melendez, and Ana Luz Gonzalez, "On the Corner: Day Labor in the United States," UCLA Center for the Study of Urban Poverty, January 2006.

77. Steven VanderStaay, *Street Lives: An Oral History of Homeless Americans* (Philadelphia: New Society Publishers, 1992), 51–52.

78. *New York Times*, June 11, 2005; *Washington Post*, June 11, 2005; CNN.com, June 5, 2005.

79. This is an old practice; drug dealers were often to be found (sometimes at the request of the owners) at migrant labor camps. See David Gottlieb and Anne Lienhard Heinsohn, eds., *America's Other Youth: Growing Up Poor* (Englewood Cliffs, NJ: Prentice-Hall, 1971), 51, for a case from the late 1960s.

80. Roberto Lovato, "Gulf Coast Slaves," *Salon.com*, November 15, 2005.

81. Gottschalk, *Prison and the Gallows*, 15.

8. Surrender: A Culture of Poverty?

1. Oscar Lewis, "The Culture of Poverty," in *The Study of Slum Culture—Backgrounds for La Vida* (New York: Random House, 1968). For more virulent forms, see Edward Banfield, *The Unheavenly City: The Nature and Future of Our Urban Crisis* (Boston: Little, Brown, 1970); and Banfield, *The Unheavenly City Revisited* (Long Grove, IL: Waveland Press, 1974 [1990]).

2. Jacob Riis, *How the Other Half Lives: Studies Among the Tenements of New York* (New York: Hill & Wang, 1890 [1933]), 186.

3. Michael Harrington, *The Other America: Poverty in the United States* (New York: Touchstone, 1962 [1997]), 10–11.

4. John Winthrop, "A Model of Christian Charity" (1630), in *The American Puritans: Their Prose and Poetry*, ed. Perry Miller (Garden City, NY: Doubleday, 1956).

5. Steven J. Ross, "'Objects of Charity': Poor Relief, Poverty, and the Rise of the Almshouse in Early Eighteenth-century New York City," in *Authority and Resistance in Early New York*, ed. William Pencak and Conrad Edick Wrights (New York: New York Historical Society, 1988).

6. Cited in Roger A. Bruns, *Knights of the Road: A Hobo History* (New York: Methuen, 1980), 28.

7. Alexis de Tocqueville, *Democracy in America*, trans. George Lawrence, ed. J.P. Mayer (New York: Perennial, 1988 [1835]).

8. Gordon S. Wood, *The Radicalism of the American Revolution* (New York: Knopf, 1992), 4.

9. Gary B. Nash, "Poverty and Politics in Early American History," in *Down and Out in Early America*, ed. Billy G. Smith (University Park: Pennsylvania State University Press, 2004), 3.

10. Warning out, as with many tools of state control, was sometimes used arbitrarily not to punish poor people for being poor, but to punish people, poor and not poor, for failing to comport to others' ideas of appropriate behavior. Herndon finds people warned out because neighbors complained about their dog barking, keeping a brothel or pub, or in the case of Mary Worsley, for having an "unruly tongue." This was not a tool reserved only for recent entrants; Abigail Carr was

given a month to vacate Providence once she became dependent, despite having been a resident for thirty years. Ruth Wallis Herndon, *Unwelcome Americans: Living on the Margin in Early New England* (Philadelphia: University of Pennsylvania Press, 2001), 166.

11. Nash, "Poverty and Politics"; Susan E. Klepp, "Malthusian Miseries and the Working Poor in Philadelphia, 1780–1830: Gender and Infant Mortality," in *Down and Out in Early America* (see note 9).

12. John K. Alexander, *Render Them Submissive: Responses to Poverty in Philadelphia, 1760–1800* (Amherst: University of Massachusetts Press, 1980), x.

13. Gordon S. Wood, *The American Revolution: A History* (New York: Modern Library, 2002). As Alexander wrote, "the transforming hand of revolution fell rather lightly on the poor of Philadelphia" and "the image of easy mobility for Philadelphians, which is strikingly reminiscent of the booster literature produced in the eighteenth century, simply will not stand close scrutiny. Philadelphia did not, as Jackson Turner Main argued on the basis of very little and questionable evidence, offer the poor a good chance to improve their lot." Alexander, *Render Them Submissive*, 161, 171.

14. Elliot Liebow, *Tally's Corner: A Study of Negro Streetcorner Men* (New York: Little, Brown, 1967), 54.

15. Sugar Turner and Tracy Bachrach Ehlers, *Sugar's Life in the Hood: The Story of a Former Welfare Mother* (Austin: University of Texas Press, 2002), 95.

16. Lee Rainwater, *Behind Ghetto Walls: Black Families in a Federal Slum* (Chicago: Aldine, 1970), 19.

17. Virginia E. Schein, *Working from the Margins: Voices of Mothers in Poverty* (Ithaca, NY: ILR/Cornell University Press, 1995), 117.

18. Elliot Liebow, *Tell Them Who I Am: The Lives of Homeless Women* (New York: Penguin, 1993 [1995]), 198.

19. Edward T. Devine, *The Principles of Relief*, repr. ed. (New York: Arno, 1904 [1971]), 118.

20. Lars Eighner, *Travels with Lizbeth* (New York: St. Martin's, 1993), 97.

21. Judith A. Dulberger, *"Mother Donit fore the Best": Correspondence of a Nineteenth-Century Orphan Asylum* (Syracuse, NY: Syracuse University Press, 1996), 31.

22. Steven VanderStaay, *Street Lives: An Oral History of Homeless Americans* (Philadelphia: New Society Publishers, 1992), 66.

23. Matthew Josephson, "The Other Nation," *New Republic*, May 17, 1933, 14–16.

24. VanderStaay, *Street Lives*, 119.

25. On the actual extent of the phenomenon, see Roland G. Fryer, "'Acting White': The Social Price Paid by the Best and Brightest Students," *Education Next*, winter 2006, 53–59.

26. Mary Childers, *Welfare Brat: A Memoir* (New York: Bloomsbury, 2005), 174.

27. Leon Dash, *Rosa Lee: A Mother and Her Family in Urban America* (New York: Basic, 1996), 223.

28. Tina S. and Jamie Pastor Bolnick, *Living at the Edge of the World: A Teenager's Survival in the Tunnels of Grand Central Station* (New York: St. Martin's, 2000), 8.

29. Ace Backwords, *Surviving on the Streets: How to Go Down Without Going Out* (Port Townsend, WA: Loompanics, 2001), 11.

30. Michael Gold, *Jews Without Money* (New York: Carroll & Graf, 1930 [2004]), 244.

31. Liebow, *Talley's Corner*, 223.

32. Cited in Tyler Anbinder, *Five Points: The 19th-Century New York City Neighborhood That Invented Tap Dance, Stole Elections, and Became the World's Most Notorious Slum* (New York: Plume, 2002), 232.

33. David Simon and Edward Burns, *The Corner: A Year in the Life of an Inner-City Neighborhood* (New York: Broadway, 1997 [1998]), 477–78.

9. Resist: Bread or Blood

1. Steven VanderStaay, *Street Lives: An Oral History of Homeless Americans* (Philadelphia: New Society Publishers, 1992), 12.

2. Diane Dujon and Ann Withorn, eds., *For Crying Out Loud: Women's Poverty in the United States* (Boston: South End, 1996), 23.

3. Jacob Riis, *How the Other Half Lives: Studies Among the Tenements of New York* (New York: Hill & Wang, 1890 [1933]), 57–58.

4. J. Nevin Nill et al., "Arguments Against Public Outdoor Relief," *Proceedings of the National Conference on Charities and Corrections* (1891), 39.

5. Richard Lowitt and Maurine Beasley, eds., *One Third of a Nation: Lorena Hickok Reports on the Great Depression* (Urbana: University of Illinois Press, 1981 [2000]), 213.

6. Michael Glenn, ed., *Voices from the Asylum* (New York: Harper & Row, 1974), chap. 24.

7. Simon P. Newman, *Embodied History: The Lives of the Poor in Early Philadelphia* (Phialdelphia: University of Pennsylvania Press, 2003).

8. James C. Scott, *Weapons of the Weak: Everyday Forms of Peasant Resistance* (New Haven, CT: Yale University Press, 1985).

9. In Glenn, *Voices from the Asylum*, 83.

10. Barbara L. Bellows, *Benevolence Among Slaveholders: Assisting the Poor in Charleston, 1670–1860* (Baton Rouge: Louisiana State University Press, 1993), 137–38.

11. Leon Dash, *Rosa Lee: A Mother and Her Family in Urban America* (New York: Basic, 1996).

12. In Mark Robert Rank, *Living on the Edge: The Realities of Welfare in America* (New York: Columbia University Press, 1994), 139.

13. Sugar Turner and Tracy Bachrach Ehlers, *Sugar's Life in the Hood: The Story of a Former Welfare Mother* (Austin: University of Texas Press, 2002), 73.

14. H. Marie Brown, *When the Compass of My Life Got Stuck on Stupid* (Xlibris, 2003), 147.

15. Riis, *How the Other Half Lives*, 35.

16. Nicholas Lemann, "Bad Choices: A Welfare Soap Opera," *Washington Post*, October 5–8, 1980 (four-part series).

17. Eric Hobsbawm in James C. Scott, *Weapons of the Weak: Everyday Forms of Peasant Resistance* (New Haven, CT: Yale University Press, 1985), 301.

18. Nels Anderson, *The Hobo: The Sociology of the Homeless Man* (Chicago: University of Chicago Press, 1923 [1961]), 48.

19. Gary B. Nash, "Poverty and Politics in Early American History," in *Down and Out in Early America*, ed. Billy G. Smith (University Park: Pennsylvania State University Press, 2004), 21; Monique Bourque, "Poor Relief 'Without Violating the Rights of Humanity': Almshouse Administration in the Philadelphia Region, 1790–1860," in *Down and Out in Early America*.

20. Robert E. Cray Jr., *Paupers and Poor Relief in New York City and Its Rural Environs, 1700–1830* (Philadelphia: Temple University Press, 1988), 80.

21. Studs Terkel, *Hard Times: An Oral History of the Great Depression* (New York: The New Press, 1970 [2000]), 21.

22. Stephen E. Lankenau, "Panhandling Repetoires and Routines for Overcoming the Nonperson Treatment," *Deviant Behavior: An Interdisciplinary Journal* 20 (1999): 183–206.

23. Barrett A. Lee and Chad R. Farrell, "Buddy, Can You Spare a Dime? Homelessness, Panhandling, and the Public," *Urban Affairs Review* 38, no. 3 (January 2003): 299–324.

24. *The Magpie* 32, no. 2 (June 1931), available at the New Deal Network, newdeal.feri.org.

25. Dawn Greeley, "Beyond Benevolence: Gender, Class and the Development of Scientific Charity in New York City, 1882–1935" (PhD diss., State University of New York at Stony Brook, 1995).

26. Debbie Nathan, "Miracle on 33rd Street," *City Limits*, December 2003, 20–27.

27. Barbara Clark Smith, "Food Rioters and the American Revolution," *William and Mary Quarterly* 51, no 1 (January 2004): 3–38; see also Nash, "Poverty and Politics."

28. In Franklin Folsom, *Impatient Armies of the Poor: The Story of Collective Action of the Unemployed, 1808–1942* (Niwot: University Press of Colorado, 1991), 13.

29. Raymond A. Mohl, *Poverty in New York, 1783–1825* (New York: Oxford University Press, 1971), 112.

30. Folsom, *Impatient Armies of the Poor*, 72, 95, 102.

31. See Frances Fox Piven and Richard A. Cloward, *Poor People's Movements: Why They Succeed, How They Fail* (New York: Vintage, 1977 [1979]); Frances Fox Piven, *Challenging Authority: How Ordinary People Change America* (Lanham, MD: Rowman & Littlefield, 2006).

32. Herbert G. Gutman, "The Failure of the Movement by the Unemployed for Public Works in 1873," *Political Science Quarterly* 80, no. 2 (June 1965): 254.

33. Ibid., 254–76; Folsom, *Impatient Armies of the Poor*, 115.

34. Piven and Cloward, *Poor People's Movements*.

35. In Folsom, *Impatient Armies of the Poor*, 166.

36. Ibid., 451.

37. Ibid., 284, 297.

38. Dorothy Day, "Hunger Marchers in Washington," *Commonweal*, December 1932, 227–29.

39. Lowitt and Beasley, *One Third of a Nation*, 28.

40. Harry L. Hopkins, *Spending to Save: The Complete Story of Relief* (Seattle: University of Washington Press, 1936 [1972]), 86–87.

41. John S. Gambs, "United We Eat," *Survey Graphic* 23, no. 8 (August 1934): 357ff.

42. Ibid.

43. B.A. Botkin, ed., *Sidewalks of America: Folklore, Legends, Sagas, Traditions, Customs, Songs, Stories and Sayings of City Folk* (Indianapolis: Bobbs-Merrill, 1954), 65.

44. Rosemary L. Bray, *Unafraid of the Dark: A Memoir* (New York: Anchor, 1998), 59.

45. Jeff Kisseloff, *You Must Remember This: An Oral History of Manhattan from the 1890s to World War II* (New York: Schocken, 1989), 515.

46. Lowitt and Beasley, *One Third of a Nation*, 12.

47. Kisseloff, *You Must Remember This*, 329.

48. Edmund Wilson, *The American Earthquake: A Chronicle of the Roaring Twenties, the Great Depression, and the Dawn of the New Deal* (New York: Da Capo, 1958 [1996]), 229.

49. Kisseloff, *You Must Remember This*, 469.

50. On Tammany, see Jon C. Teaford, *The Unheralded Triumph: City Government in America, 1870–1900* (Baltimore: Johns Hopkins University Press, 1984).

51. Terkel, *Hard Times*, 435.

52. Irving Bernstein, *A Caring Society: The New Deal, the Worker, and the Great Depression* (New York: Houghton Mifflin, 1985), 63.

53. Edwin Amenta, Neal Caren, and Sheera Joy Olasky, "Age for Leisure? Political Mediation and the Impact of the Pension Movement on U.S. Old-Age Policy," *American Sociological Review* 70 (June 2005): 516–38. The Towensendites, still an active force until 1950, continued to place pressure upon states regarding their OAA programs after the SSA's passage, and had significant effect on the size of benefits.

54. Guida West, *The National Welfare Rights Movement: The Social Protest of Poor Women* (New York: Praeger, 1981). West argues that the NWRO never became an organization of poor people, but was an organization of poor black women—few men, few whites, and few of the poor elderly, disabled, or blind were to be found among its membership. The leadership, by contrast, was male, West claims, and the

financial support came largely from middle-class, liberal whites. "While [the NWRO] endorsed the doctrine of maximum feasible participation of the poor in its organizations, in reality it was largely dominated by the nonpoor" (p. xiii). Protestant churches were significant contributors, especially in its early years, while little support came from black churches or from black civil rights organizations— perhaps for fear of being associated with such a pariah class (although the SCLC, Black Panthers, and some others would eventually become modest allies). Synagogues stood idly by (although individual Jews and Jewish foundations lent their support), as did labor unions.

55. Ibid., 296.

56. Ibid., 70, fn 130.

57. Annelise Orleck, *Storming Caesar's Palace: How Black Mothers Fought Their Own War on Poverty* (Boston: Beacon, 2005), 76–77.

58. Ibid., 220, 191.

59. Ibid., 125–26. American history is filled with the successful activism of strong women, of course. Abolitionism was largely a women's movement, for example, and women were at the forefront of the American labor movement. See Meredith Tax, *The Rising of the Women: Feminist Solidarity and Class Conflict, 1880–1917* (New York: Monthly Review Press, 1980). The rebellious Elizabeth Packard, whom we met briefly in Chapter 2, was incarcerated in an asylum by her husband. Her ordeal is unusual mostly in that such a detailed and passionate record of it has survived. Despite her protestations that she tried to bear her incarceration passively, she fought not only against her own unjust treatment, but on behalf of other patients, and could not hold her tongue, issuing "reproofs" to the asylum director and its trustees with catalogues of abuses she witnessed, and claiming that it was the director who was truly insane—"devoid of reason like the beasts"—while she compiled a catalogue of testimonies of abuse and mistreatment, which she wielded as both threat and recrimination. The near frenzy of her outrage, running on for hundreds of pages, might well be read as insanity; or instead as desperation and determination to make a rational case against intolerable acts. As she titled one of her chapters, "My Battle with Despotism—No Surrender." Upon her release, Packard's activism took on new life, and she implored those with power to heed her tales and to bring some measure of dignity and freedom to those still subject to the prison-asylum. Packard can take credit for the Illinois "Personal Liberty Law" and similar statutes in Iowa and Connecticut, which expanded the rights of women and of the "insane," and imposed restraints upon forced commitment to an asylum. One of the happy consequences of her single-mindedness was the removal of her oppressor, asylum director Andrew McFarland, from his post. Reunited even with her children, Elizabeth could not help but gloat (and who, perhaps, can blame her) that Mr. Packard ended up "homeless, penniless, and childless; while I have a home of my own, property, and the children." Elizabeth Parsons Ware Packard, *Modern Persecution, or Insane Asylums Unveiled*, 2 vols., repr. ed. (New York: Arno, 1873 [1973]).

60. Piven and Cloward, *Poor People's Movements*, 275.

61. Nixon, who grew up poor, defended the plan—a modest guaranteed income with work requirements—this way: "I thought that people should have the responsibility for spending carefully and taking care of themselves. I abhorred snoopy, patronizing surveillance by social workers which made children and adults feel stigmatized and separate. The basic premise of the Family Assistance Plan was simple: what the poor need to help them rise out of poverty is money." Edward D. Berkowitz, *America's Welfare State from Roosevelt to Reagan* (Baltimore: Johns Hopkins University Press, 1991), 128.

62. West, *National Welfare Rights Movement*; Piven and Cloward, *Poor People's Movements*; Premilla Nadasen, *Welfare Warriors: The Welfare Rights Movement in the United States* (New York: Routledge, 2005); Orleck, *Storming Caesar's Palace*.

63. In Nadasen, *Welfare Warriors*, 47.

64. In ibid., 75.

65. Gwendolyn Mink and Rickie Solinger, eds., *Welfare: A Documentary History of U.S. Policy and Politics* (New York: NYU Press, 2003), chap. 61.

66. *New York Times*, September 20, 1967; Orleck, *Storming Caesar's Palace*, 114.

67. Johnnie Tillmon, "Welfare Is a Woman's Issue" (1972), excerpted in *Ms.*, "Best of 30 Years," spring 2002, www.msmagazine.com/spring2002/tillmon.asp. For similar and equally powerful statements, see Julia Dinsmore, "My Name Is Not 'Those People,'" depts.loras.edu/scw/poem.html; and Frances Payne Adler's 1995 testimony during Wisconsin Senate hearings on welfare reform in *Speaking Out: Women, Poverty and Public Policy*, ed. Katherine A. Rhoades and Anne Statham, Proceedings of the Twenty-Third Annual Women's Studies Consortium, University of Wisconsin–Madison, October 29–31, 1998.

68. David A. Snow, Sarah A. Soule, and Daniel M. Cress, "Identifying the Precipitants of Homeless Protest Across 17 U.S. Cities, 1980 to 1990," *Social Forces* 83, no. 3 (March 2005): 1183–210.

69. See Piven and Cloward, *Poor People's Movements*; Piven, *Challenging Authority*.

70. Frances Fox Piven and Richard A. Cloward, *Why Americans Still Don't Vote: And Why Politicians Want It That Way* (Boston: Beacon, 2000).

71. Joe Soss, "Lessons of Welfare: Policy Design, Political Learning, and Political Action," *American Political Science Review* 93, no. 2 (June 1999): 363–80; Joe Soss, *Unwanted Claims: The Politics of Participation in the U.S. Welfare System* (Ann Arbor: University of Michigan Press, 2002); Staffan Kumlin, *The Personal and the Political: How Personal Welfare State Experiences Affect Political Ideology* (New York: Palgrave Macmillan, 2004).

72. Vicki Lens and Susan Elizabeth Vorsanger, "Complaining After Claiming: Fair Hearings After Welfare Reform," *Social Service Review* (September 2005): 430–53. This is another example of what Lipsky and Brodkin have called "bureaucratic disentitlement."

73. Austin Sarat, "The Law Is All Over: Power, Resistance and the Legal Con-

sciousness of the Welfare Poor," in Julie A. Nice and Louise G. Trubek, *Cases and Materials on Poverty Law: Theory and Practice* (St. Paul, MN: West Publishing, 1997), 21.

74. Willie Baptist, "On the Poor Organizing the Poor: The Experience of Kensington" (2004), Poor People's Economic Human Rights Campaign, www.universityofthepoor.org/library/kwrumodl.html.

75. In John Nichols, "Remembering Molly Ivins," *The Nation*, January 21, 2007, www.thenation.com/doc/20070219/molly_ivins.

Epilogue: Poor Math

1. Unless otherwise noted, poverty data are from the U.S. Census Bureau; for visual representations see Amy K. Glasmeier, *Poverty in America: One Nation, Pulling Apart, 1960–2003* (New York: Routledge, 2006). Portions of this chapter are adapted from Stephen Pimpare, "The Failures of American Poverty Measures," *Journal of Sociology and Social Welfare* (forthcoming).

2. Pew Hispanic Center, "Unauthorized Migrants: Numbers and Characteristics," June 14, 2005, pewhispanic.org. But there is a fairly large body of scholarship going back several decades now demonstrating that immigrants are, all else equal, less likely than natives to receive public assistance—this despite their higher rates of poverty and lower income; and that the net gain to the government balance sheet, from sales and income taxes, exceeds any service-provision expenses. See Leif Jensen, "Patterns of Immigration and Public Assistance Utilization, 1970–1980," *International Migration Review* 22, no. 1 (spring 1988): 51–83.

3. See Community Service Society, www.cssny.org.

4. National Center for Children in Poverty, September 2005, nccp.org.

5. Native Americans occupy a separate sphere within the American welfare state. They have higher rates of poverty, childhood poverty, fertility, incidences of female-headed families, and unemployment and lower levels of education than other racial and ethnic groups. Poor women on reservations have faced special challenges in the wake of 1996's welfare reform because they have tended to be geographically isolated from work and services (and there are few job opportunities on reservations); have relatively low levels of education and work experience; suffer particular forms of discrimination because of assumptions employers make about Native people and their families; and disproportionately lack basic modern conveniences, like telephones and access to transportation. Native American women have the highest rates of domestic and sexual violence, and one-third will be the victim of sexual assault. Shanta Pandey, Eddie F. Brown, Leslie Scheuler-Whitaker, and Shannon Collier-Tenison, "Welfare Reform on American Indian Reservations: Initial Experience of Service Providers and Recipients on Reservations in Arizona," *Social Policy Journal* 1, no. 1 (2002); Sarah Dee, "Federal Indian

Law and Violent Crime: Native Women and Children at the Mercy of the State," *Social Justice* 31, no. 4 (2004).

6. John Cassidy, "Relatively Deprived," *New Yorker*, April 3, 2006; Orshansky in Michael B. Katz, *The Undeserving Poor: From the War on Poverty to the War on Welfare* (New York: Pantheon, 1989), 116.

7. See Center for Neighborhood Technology, Surface Transportation Policy Project, "Driving to Spend," June 2005.

8. See Economic Policy Institute, *State of Working America 2002–03*. In 2006, the Bush administration's Census Bureau appeared to have abandoned this measure, publishing only an alternative that better calculated income, but took no realistic account of expenses, which would, of course, reduce the poverty *rate* without any of the complicated and expensive measures necessary to reduce poverty itself.

9. Heather Boushey, Chauna Brocht, Bethney Gundersen, and Jared Bernstein, *Hardships in America: The Real Story of Working Families* (Washington, DC: Economic Policy Institute, 2002); see also Hsien-Hen Lu, Julian Palmer, Youngwan Song, et al., "Living at the Edge: America's Low-Income Children and Families," Institute for Social and Economic Research and Policy, Columbia University, 2003.

10. Census data analysis by Tony Pugh, "U.S. Economy Leaving Record Numbers in Severe Poverty," McClatchy, February 22, 2007.

11. Gordon M. Fisher, "From Hunter to Orshansky," U.S. Department of Health and Human Services, March 1994, aspe.os.dhhs.gov/poverty/papers/htrssmiv .htm; Edward T. Devine, *The Principles of Relief*, repr. ed. (New York: Arno, 1904 [1971]); Robert Hunter, *Poverty* (New York: Grosset & Dunlap, 1904); David S. Johnson, John M. Rogers, and Lucilla Tan, "A Century of Family Budgets in the United States," *Monthly Labor Review*, May 2001.

12. For a survey of recent data, see Signe-Mary McKernan and Caroline Ratcliffe, "Events That Trigger Poverty Entries and Exits," Urban Institute, December 2002.

13. Data in this section are principally from Mark Robert Rank, *One Nation, Underprivileged: Why American Poverty Affects Us All* (New York: Oxford University Press, 2004); see also Rank and Thomas A. Hirschl, "The Likelihood of Poverty Across the American Adult Life Span," *Social Work* 44, no. 3 (May 1999); "The Occurrence of Poverty Across the Life Cycle," *Journal of Policy Analysis and Management* 20, no. 4 (2001); and "Rags or Riches?" *Social Science Quarterly* 82, no. 4 (December 2001).

14. For one rebuttal, see Lawrence M. Mead, "Comment on Rank and Hirschl, 'Rags or Riches,'" *Social Science Quarterly* 82, no. 4 (2001): 670–75.

15. Bruce G. Link, Ezra Susser, Ann Stueve, et al., "Lifetime and Five-Year Prevalence of Homelessness in the United States," *American Journal of Public Health* 84, no. 12 (December 1994).

16. New York City Coalition for the Homeless, "Homelessness in New York City," February 2003, coalitionforthehomeless.org.

17. Ronald C. Kessler, Patricia Berglund, Olga Demler, et al., "Lifetime Preva-

lence and Age-of-Onset Distributions of *DSM-IV* Disorders in the National Comorbidity Survey Replication," *Archives of General Psychiatry* 62 (June 2005). For good context for this study, and some cautions about it, see Benedict Carey, "Most Will Be Mentally Ill at Some Point, Study Says" *New York Times*, June 7, 2005; and Carey, "Who's Mentally Ill? Deciding Is Often All in the Mind," *New York Times*, June 12, 2005.

18. Robert Rector, Kirk A. Johnson, and Sarah E. Youssef, "The Extent of Material Hardship in the United States," Heritage Foundation WebMemo No. 187, 1999.

19. Timothy M. Smeeding, "Public Policy, Economic Inequality, and Poverty: The United States in Comparative Perspective," *Social Science Quarterly* 86, no. 5 (December 2005): 955–83.

20. Raymond A. Mohl, *Poverty in New York, 1783–1825* (New York: Oxford University Press, 1971), 164–65.

21. "The Non-Taxpaying Class," *Wall Street Journal*, November 20, 2002; "Lucky Duckies Again," *Wall Street Journal*, January 20, 2003; and "Even Luckier Duckies," *Wall Street Journal*, June 3, 2003.

22. Quoted in Randy Albelda, Nancy Folbre, and the Center for Popular Economics, *The War on the Poor: A Defense Manual* (New York: The New Press, 1996), 12.

23. Bronislaw Geremek, *Poverty: A History* (Oxford: Blackwell, 1994), 78, 53.

24. Walter I. Trattner, *From Poor Law to Welfare State: A Social History of Welfare in America*, 5th ed. (New York: Free Press, 1994); Jacob Riis, *How the Other Half Lives: Studies Among the Tenements of New York* (New York: Hill & Wang, 1890 [1933]); James Patterson, *America's Struggle Against Poverty, 1900–1994* (Cambridge, MA: Harvard University Press, 1994); Bruce S. Jansson, *The Reluctant Welfare State* (Belmont, CA: Wadsworth, 2001); Christopher Jencks, *Rethinking Social Policy* (New York: Harper-Perennial, 1992).

25. Robert H. Bremner, *From the Depths: The Discovery of Poverty in the United States* (New York: NYU Press, 1956 [1972]), 13.

26. Victoria Byerly, *Hard Times Cotton Mill Girls: Personal Histories of Womanhood and Poverty in the South* (Ithaca, NY: ILR Press, 1986), 6.

27. Richard Layard, *Happiness: Lessons from a New Science* (New York: Penguin, 2005), 48.

28. Daniel Kahneman and Amos Tversky, "Prospect Theory: An Analysis of Decision Under Risk," *Econometrica* 47, no. 2 (March 1979): 263–92.

29. Amartya Sen, *Development as Freedom* (New York: Anchor, 1999), 89. Emphasis in original.

30. Still, if 40 percent of all Americans were poor in 1900, that represents some 30,397,830 souls; but a 13.8 percent poverty rate in 1995 means that 36,317,184 people were poor. More Americans were poor in 1995 than in 1900 (population figures from U.S. Department of Commerce, 1997, 8).

31. Luxembourg Income Study (LIS), "LIS Key Figures: Relative Poverty Rates for the Total Population, Children and the Elderly," www.lisproject.org.

32. Howard Glennerster, "United States Poverty Studies and Poverty Measurement: The Past Twenty-Five Years," *Social Service Review* (March 2002): 83–107; *State of Working America 2002–03*, epinet.org.

33. Katz, *Undeserving Poor*, 181.

34. John Kenneth Galbraith, *The Affluent Society* (Boston: Houghton Mifflin, 1958), 323.

35. Dwight Macdonald, "Our Invisible Poor," *New Yorker*, January 19, 1963, 132.

36. In Hunter, *Poverty*, 1.

37. In Adam Smith, *The Wealth of Nations* (New York: Modern Library, 1776 [1994]).

38. Ibid.

39. Charles Murray, "What to Do About Welfare," *Commentary*, December 1994.

40. William Julius Wilson, *When Work Disappears: The World of the New Urban Poor* (New York: Vintage, 1996), 160.

41. U.S. Census Bureau, "Service Annual Survey 2004," April 2006.

42. B.A. Botkin, ed., *Sidewalks of America: Folklore, Legends, Sagas, Traditions, Customs, Songs, Stories and Sayings of City Folk* (Indianapolis: Bobbs-Merrill, 1954), 56.

43. Smeeding, "Public Policy, Economic Inequality, and Poverty," 955–83.

44. Quoted in Macdonald, "Our Invisible Poor," 86.

45. George Gilder, *Wealth and Poverty* (San Francisco: ICS, 1981 [1993]), 78.

46. Smeeding, "Public Policy, Economic Inequality, and Poverty," 955–83.

47. Lawrence Mishel, Jared Bernstein, and John Schmitt, *The State of Working America 1996–1997* (New York: Economic Policy Institute/M.E. Sharpe, 1997).

48. Lawrence Mishel, Jared Bernstein, and Sylvia Allegretto, *The State of Working America 2006/2007* (Ithaca, NY: ILR/Cornell University Press, 2007).

49. "The Maxwell Poll: Civic Engagement and Inequality," April 2005, poll.campbellinstitute.org.

50. Gabriel Lenz, "The Policy-Related Causes and Consequences of Income Inequality," Russell Sage Foundation, January 2003; Benjamin I. Page and James R. Simmons, *What Government Can Do: Dealing with Poverty and Inequality* (Chicago: University of Chicago Press, 2000).

51. Elizabeth A. Freund and Irwin L. Morris, "The Lottery and Income Inequality in the States," *Social Science Quarterly* 86, no. 5 (December 2005): 996–1012.

52. Quoted in Jill Quadagno, "Theories of the Welfare State," *Annual Review of Sociology* 13 (1987): 110.

53. Jong-sung Yoo and Sanjeev Khagram, "A Comparative Study of Inequality and Corruption," *American Sociological Review* 70 (February 2005): 136–57. See also Richard H. McAdams, "Economic Costs of Inequality," University of Chicago Law and Economics, Olin Working Paper No. 370, November 2007, ssrn.com/abstract=1028874.

54. Samuel Bowles and Herbert Gintis, "Is Equality Passé? Homo Reciprocans and the Future of Egalitarian Politics," *Boston Review*, December 1998/January

1999; see also Eric Uslaner and Mitchell Brown, "Inequality, Trust, and Civic Engagement," *American Politics Research* 31 (2003).

55. See "APSA Task Force Report: American Democracy in an Age of Rising Inequality" and Commentaries, *Perspectives on Politics* 2, no. 4 (December 2004); and further responses to the Report in *PS: Political Science & Politics,* January 2006.

56. M. Corcoran, "Rags to Rags: Poverty and Mobility in the United States," *Annual Review of Sociology* 21 (1995): 237–67.

57. See Samuel Bowles, Steven N. Durlauf, and Karla Hoff, eds., *Poverty Traps* (Princeton, NJ, and New York: Princeton University Press and Russell Sage Foundation, 2006); Samuel Bowles, Herbert Gintis, and Melissa Osborne, eds., *Unequal Chances: Family Background and Economic Success* (Princeton, NJ, and New York: Princeton University Press and Russell Sage Foundation, 2005).

58. Research is inconclusive, but suggestive of a link. See Michael Hout, "How Might Inequality Affect Intergenerational Mobility? A Review and an Agenda," UC Berkeley Survey Research Center Working Paper, January 2003.

59. "Meritocracy in America: Ever Higher Society, Ever Harder to Ascend," *The Economist,* December 29, 2004.

60. Sen, *Development as Freedom.*

61. See www.un.org/millenniumgoals/.

62. See Deepa Narayan et al., "Global Consultations with the Poor," Poverty Group, World Bank, September 20, 1999, fig. 1.

63. See www.bridge.ids.ac.uk/index.html.

64. Boushey et al., *Hardships in America.*

65. See www.aecf.org.

66. Laura Lippman, "Indictors and Indices of Child Well-being; A Brief History," Annie E. Casey Foundation, August 2005.

67. See www.childstats.gov/americaschildren.

68. National Economic and Social Rights Initiative, www.nesri.org/about_us/index.html.

69. Mark F. Massoud, "The Influence of International Law on Local Social Movements," *Peace & Change: A Journal of Peace Research* 31, no. 1 (2006): 3–34; see also Kenneth J. Neubeck, *When Welfare Disappears: The Case for Economic Human Rights* (New York: Routledge, 2006); New York City Welfare Reform and Human Rights Documentation Project, "Hunger Is No Accident: New York and Federal Welfare Policies Violate the Human Right to Food," July 2000; Wellesley Centers for Women, "Battered Mothers Speak Out: A Human Rights Report on Domestic Violence and Child Custody in the Massachusetts Family Courts," November 2002; Ford Foundation, "Close to Home: Case Studies of Human Rights Work in the United States," 2004. For potential insufficiencies of a human rights-based approach, see Lucy Williams, ed., *International Poverty Law: An Emerging Discourse* (London: Zed Books, 2006), esp. chaps. 1–3.

Index